The Fulfilling Workplace

Psychological and Behavioral Aspects of Risk Series

Series Editors: Professor Cary L. Cooper and Professor Ronald J. Burke

Risk management is an ongoing concern for modern organizations in terms of their finance, their people, their assets, their projects and their reputation. The majority of the processes and systems adopted are very financially oriented or fundamentally mechanistic; often better suited to codifying and recording risk, rather than understanding and working with it. Risk is fundamentally a human construct; how we perceive and manage it is dictated by our attitude, behavior and the environment or culture within which we work. Organizations that seek to mitigate, manage, transfer or exploit risk need to understand the psychological factors that dictate the response and behaviors of their employees, their high-flyers, their customers and their stakeholders.

This series, edited by two of the most influential writers and researchers on organizational behavior and human psychology explores the psychological and behavioral aspects of risk; the factors that:

- define our attitudes and response to risk;
- are important in understanding and managing "risk managers"; and
- dictate risky behavior in individuals at all levels.

Titles Currently in the Series Include:

Safety Culture
Assessing and Changing the Behaviour of Organisations
John Bernard Taylor

Crime and Corruption in Organizations
Why It Occurs and What To Do About It
Edited by Ronald J. Burke, Edward C. Tomlinson and Cary L. Cooper

New Directions in Organizational Psychology and Behavioral Medicine
Edited by Alexander-Stamatios Antoniou and Cary Cooper

Corporate Reputation
Managing Opportunities and Threats
Edited by Ronald J. Burke, Graeme Martin and Cary L. Cooper

Occupational Health and Safety
Edited by Ronald J. Burke, Sharon Clarke and Cary L. Cooper

The Fulfilling Workplace

The Organization's Role in Achieving Individual and Organizational Health

Edited by

RONALD J. BURKE
and
CARY L. COOPER

Routledge
Taylor & Francis Group

LONDON AND NEW YORK

First published 2013 by Gower Publishing

Published 2016 by Routledge
2 Park Square, Milton Park, Abingdon, Oxfordshire OX14 4RN
711 Third Avenue, New York, NY 10017, USA

First issued in paperback 2016

Routledge is an imprint of the Taylor & Francis Group, an informa business

Gower Applied Business Research
Our programme provides leaders, practitioners, scholars and researchers with thought provoking, cutting edge books that combine conceptual insights, interdisciplinary rigour and practical relevance in key areas of business and management.

British Library Cataloguing in Publication Data
The fulfilling workplace : the organization's role in achieving individual and organizational health.—(Psychological and behavioural aspects of risk series)
    1. Personnel management. 2. Organizational effectiveness. 3. Job stress. 4. Job satisfaction.
    5. Employee motivation.
    I. Series II. Burke, Ronald J. III. Cooper, Cary L.
    658.3—dc23

The Library of Congress has cataloged the printed edition as follows:
Burke, Ronald J.
    The fulfilling workplace : the organization's role in achieving individual and organizational health / by Ronald J. Burke and Cary L. Cooper.
        p. cm.—(Psychological and behavioural aspects of risk)
    Includes bibliographical references and index.
    ISBN 978-1-4094-2776-6 (hardback : alk. paper)
    1. Work environment. 2. Organizational behavior. 3. Psychology, Industrial. 4. Quality of work life. 5. Employees—Attitudes. I. Cooper, Cary L. II. Title.
    HD7261.B95 2012
    658.3'8—dc23

                                                                                    2012029741

ISBN 13: 978-1-138-27146-3 (pbk)
ISBN 13: 978-1-4094-2776-6 (hbk)

Contents

List of Figures

List of Tables

List of Contributors

Arnold B. Bakker is Professor and Chair of the department of Work & Organizational Psychology, Erasmus University Rotterdam, The Netherlands, and Adjunct Professor at the department of Sociology and Social Policy, Lingnan University, Hong Kong. He is also president of the European Association of Work and Organizational Psychology, and fellow of the Association for Psychological Science. Bakker's research interests include positive organizational phenomena such as work engagement, flow, and happiness at work. See also: www.arnoldbakker.com.

Richard E. Boyatzis is Distinguished University Professor, as well as Professor in the Departments of Organizational Behavior, Psychology, and Cognitive Science at Case Western Reserve University and Adjunct Professor at ESADE. He is the author of more than 150 articles and books on leadership, competencies, emotional intelligence, coaching, and change from a complexity perspective, including: *The Competent Manager; Primal Leadership* with Daniel Goleman and Annie McKee, in 28 languages; *Resonant Leadership*, with Annie McKee; and *Transforming Qualitative Information*.

Lieke L. ten Brummelhuis obtained her PhD in organizational sociology at Utrecht University. In her dissertation she studied positive and negative effects of family life on work outcomes. She continued her line of research on the work-home interface as a Postdoc at the Erasmus University Rotterdam. Currently, she is visiting The Wharton School (University of Pennsylvania) and LeBow College of Business (Drexel University) as a postdoctoral fellow. Research topics on which she is working include employee recovery, workaholism, and work-life balance.

Ronald J. Burke is Emeritus Professor of Organization Studies at the Schulich School of Business, York University and is also affiliated with ESADE in Barcelona. His research interests include women in management, women in science, crime and corruption in organizations, human frailties and transgressions, work and health, improving human resource management practices in workplaces, encouraging employee voice, and bringing about organizational changes that foster both individual and organizational health.

Amanda L. Christensen is a PhD student in management at the Arizona State University's W.P. Carey School of Business. Her research interests include leadership and person–environment fit. She has an MBA from Brigham Young University and spent several years working in the manufacturing industry (Department of Management, W.P. Carey School of Business, Arizona State University, P. O. Box 874006, Tempe, AZ 85287-4006, United States. Tel.: +1 480 965 3431; fax: +1 480 965 8314, e-mail: Amanda. Christensen@asu.edu).

Sharon Clarke is Professor of Organizational Psychology at Manchester Business School, University of Manchester. She has research interests in safety culture, safety climate, leadership, and workplace accidents. Her work has been widely published in leading journals and she is co-author of the successful book *Human Safety and Risk Management* (2006). She is currently Associate Editor for the *Journal of Occupational and Organizational Psychology*.

Cary L. Cooper, CBE, is Distinguished Professor of Organizational Psychology and Health, Lancaster University, England. He is Founding Editor of the Journal of Organizational Behavior and Editor in Chief of the medical journal Stress & Health. He is Fellow of the Academy of Management, Honorary Fellow of the British Psychological Society and of the Royal College of Physicians. He is currently Chair of the Academy of Social Sciences. In 2001, Cary was awarded a CBE by the Queen for his contribution to organizational health. He was the lead scientist on the UK Government's Foresight project on Mental Capital and Wellbeing.

Evangelia Demerouti is a full professor at Eindhoven University of Technology, the Netherlands. Her research interests include topics from the field of work and health, including positive organizational behavior, the job demands–resources model, work-family interface, crossover of strain, and recovery.

Lindsay Dhanani is a doctoral student in the Industrial/Organizational psychology program at the University of Central Florida. (UCF). She also obtained her bachelors of science degree in psychology from the UCF. Her research focus is on diversity and discrimination as it applies to the workplace, and she has been involved in several research projects that address these topics.

Robert L. Dipboye is Professor of Psychology at the University of Central Florida. He has conducted research on discrimination in employment and co-edited (with Adrienne Collella) the book, *Psychological and Organizational Bases of Discrimination at Work*. He is a Fellow of the American Psychological Association and the Society for Industrial and Organizational Psychology and served as Associate Editor of the *Journal of Applied Psychology*.

Fritz Drasgow is a Professor of Psychology and of Labor and Employment Relations at the University of Illinois at Urbana-Champaign. His research focuses on psychological measurement, computerized testing, and the antecedents and outcomes of sexual harassment. Drasgow is a member of the editorial review board of eight journals, including *Applied Psychological Measurement, Journal of Applied Psychology*, and the *International Journal of Selection and Assessment*. He is a former President of the Society for Industrial and Organizational Psychology (SIOP) and received the SIOP Distinguished Scientific Contributions Award in 2008.

Paul Fairlie is a Sessional Assistant Professor in the School of Human Resource Management at York University. He received his Ph.D. in psychology from York Univerity. His research interests include the measurement and impact of meaningful work, and the role of personality in the workplace (e.g., perfectionism). He is also an applied consultant in industrial-organizational psychology, specializing in various forms of individual and organizational measurement and research.

Louise F. Fitzgerald is Emeritus Professor of Psychology and Gender & Women's Studies at the University of Illinois at Urbana-Champaign. She is a triple Fellow of APA, an inaugural fellow of APS, and recipient of the American Psychological Association's Life Time Career Award for Distinguished Contributions to Research in Public Policy for her research on sexual harassment in organizations.

Jill Flint-Taylor is a founding Director of Rusando Ltd, a business psychology company based in the UK. A full-time Practitioner Psychologist with an academic background, she specializes in assessment, leadership and psychological well-being at work, and maintains an active involvement in research through collaboration with university departments and business schools. She is also a Board member of the award-winninig international development charity, BasicNeeds. As Client Solutions Director at Robertson Cooper Ltd, she led on the development and delivery of products and services to help boost leadership effectiveness, employee well-being and organizational success. Her recent publications include a chapter on leadership, psychological well-being and organizational outcomes (co-authored with Professor Ivan Robertson) in *The Oxford Handbook on Organisational Well-Being*, published in 2009.

Barbara A. Fritzsche is Associate Professor and Director of the Master's degree program in industrial and organizational psychology at the University of Central Florida. She is on the editorial board of the *Journal of Organizational Behavior* and has published in prestigious journals, such as the *Journal of Personality and Social Psychology*, *Journal of Occupational and Organizational Psychology*, and *Journal of Vocational Behavior*.

Clive J. Fullagar is full Professor of Industrial/Organizational Psychology at Kansas State University in the USA. His main areas of interest are psychological involvement and participation in labor organizations and understanding the situational and dispositional predictors of work "flow" and its impact on psychological and physical well-being.

Adrian Furnham is Professor of Psychology at University College London and Adjunct Professor of Management at the Norwegian School of Management. He has written over 1,000 scientific papers and 70 books. He is a Fellow of the British Psychological Society and on the editorial board of a number of international journals. He has been a consultant to over 30 major international companies, with particular interests in top team development, management change, performance management systems, psychometric testing and leadership derailment.

Amanda Griffiths is Professor of Occupational Health Psychology at the University of Nottingham in the UK, and an Academician of the UK's Academy of Social Sciences. She was a founder member of the European Academy of Occupational Health Psychology. Her main research interests are preventing work-related ill-health and promoting well-being and performance, particularly with regard to the ageing workforce.

Sara Guediri is a doctoral researcher at the University of Manchester. Her PhD focuses on leadership within safety-critical contexts. She holds an MSc in Organisational Psychology with distinction and a First Class BSc in Psychology.

Fikry W. Isaac is Vice President, Global Health Services, Johnson & Johnson. He leads the development of health & wellness strategies, policies, guidelines, and services worldwide (Occupational Medicine, Employee Assistance Program (EAP) and Wellness). He has been with Johnson & Johnson since 1989, and for the past ten years, he has been driving the comprehensive Total Health programs that have reduced the Company's healthcare costs and improved the health of employees. He also serves as the Chief Medical Officer, Wellness & Prevention, Inc., a Johnson & Johnson Company. In this role, he provides Health Management expertise, strategic direction and supports customer acquisition and lead generation. In addition to his MD, he received his degree of Master of Public Health in Occupational Medicine from the Medical College of Wisconsin in May 2001 and is a Fellow of the American College of Occupational and Environmental Medicine where he chairs the Pharmaceutical Section and the Corporate Health Achievement Award. He is the industry Co-chair of the Life Science and Innovation Forum—APEC. He also serves on several boards including the Partnership For Prevention, the Global Health & Benefits Institute and the Health Enhancement Research Organization (HERO).

Alec Knight is a Consultant Psychologist at Work Psychology Group Ltd., and works with diverse client groups across the UK. He gained his Bachelor's degree in Psychology from the University of Warwick, and his Master's degree in Occupational Psychology and his Doctorate at the University of Nottingham in the UK. Alec maintains an active research interest in the psychology of age, ageing and ageism, particularly in organizational contexts.

Roy Lubit MD, PhD is an organizational consultant, executive coach and forensic psychiatrist. He has published on a variety of issues including organizational learning, dealing with difficult managers and employees, substance abuse and narcissism. He works with individual executives and executive teams to improve productivity and avoid burnout. His home base is New York City but he has a national practice.

Vicki J. Magley is an Associate Professor in the Department of Psychology at the University of Connecticut in Storrs, CT. The main focus of her research lies within the domain of occupational health psychology and combines organizational and feminist perspectives in the study of the workplace mistreatment. She is on the editorial boards of Journal of Occupational Health Psychology and Journal of Business and Psychology. She is currently the President of the Society for Occupational Health Psychology (SOHP).

Nor Diana Mohd Mahudin is Assistant Professor at Department of Psychology, International Islamic University in Malaysia. She trained in ergonomics (human factors) at Loughborough University and obtained her doctorate in applied psychology at the University of Nottingham, both in the UK. Diana's current research interests and publications are in the areas of public transport crowding, commuting stress, and travel behavior.

Christina G. L. Nerstad is a Postdoctoral fellow at the Department of Leadership and Organizational Behaviour, BI Norwegian Business School. She recently received her PhD from BI Norwegian Business School. Her research activities are in the areas of Organizational Behavior, Human Resource Management, and Occupational Health Psychology, focusing on the motivational determinants of achievement, health and well-being at work. She has particularly focused on how work climates affect employee motivation, performance and well-being, as well as the antecedents of work climates. She is involved in research collaboration projects with several Norwegian and international organizations. She has also presented her studies at several international conferences, such as the Academy of Management Annual Meeting, and she publishes in peer-reviewed international journals. She also teaches at Master of Science, Bachelor, and Executive programs.

Elinor O'Connor is a Lecturer in Occupational Psychology at Manchester Business School and is a Chartered Psychologist. She has worked in the field of human error and occupational safety, including the investigation of human error in accidents, and her research interests include the effects of workplace stressors on psychological performance and well-being.

Wido G. M. Oerlemans is a post-doctoral researcher at the department of Work & Organizational Psychology, Erasmus University Rotterdam, The Netherlands. Wido is currently conducting an online follow-up study on the topic of happiness. The project aims to identify what kind of lifestyle and life choices are important for an individual's happiness and well-being (see also: www.happinessindicator.com). A second research topic of interest is how acculturation and social identity processes in ethnically diverse teams impact team processes and team performance.

Scott C. Ratzan is Vice President, Global Health, Johnson & Johnson. In his role, he is charged with promoting communication, innovation and programs that focus on health literacy and public health policy. He is a pioneer in the areas of health literacy and health communication, having co-authored the definition that serves as the basis for US health literacy efforts. Additionally, he is Editor-in-Chief of the peer-reviewed *Journal of Health Communication: International Perspectives*, and serves as co-chair of the United Nations Secretary General's Every Woman Every Child Innovation Working Group. He is a member of the US Institute of Medicine (IOM) Roundtable on Health Literacy, the World Economic Forum Global Agenda Council on health and well-being, and is a former Ambassador for global health research selected by Research!America. He advocates for better health in multiple ways. Last year he presented the industry's "Framework for Action for the Prevention and Control of Non-Communicable Diseases" at the UN General Assembly interactive hearing, and recently at the Harvard Kennedy School Women and Public Policy Board on Global Health Diplomacy. He maintains faculty appointments at Tufts University School of Medicine and George Washington University School Medical Center. He earned his MD from the University of Southern California; his MPA from the John F. Kennedy School of Government, Harvard University; and an MA in Communication from Emerson College.

Astrid M. Richardsen is Professor of Organizational Psychology and Head of the Department of Leadership and Organizational Behaviour, BI Norwegian Business School. She is also Associate Dean of MSc in Leadership and Organizational Psychology. Her research activities are in the area of Occupational Health Psychology, focusing on work stress and health, burnout and engagement. Most recently she has been involved in research on work motivation, passion for work, and consequences of incivility in the workplace. She has also done work in the area of women in management and diversity. She has published in journals such as *Human Relations*; *Work and Stress*; *Anxiety, Stress and Coping*; *International Journal of Stress Management*; *Journal of Occupational and Organizational Psychology*; and *International Journal of Human Resource Management*. She teaches Master of Science, Bachelor, and Executive programs in Stress and Stress Management and HRM.

Glyn C. Roberts is Professor Emeritus from both the Norwegian University of Sport Science and the University of Illinois. His research has focused on the motivational determinants of achievement especially of children in the competitive sport experience. He has been on research grants for over 2 million dollars, has over 200 publications, 15 books, and over 70 book chapters published. He has several distinguished scholar awards, including ISSP (1997), AASP (2008), and NASPSPA (1998). He is a Past President of NASPSPA, FEPSAC, Division 12 of IAAP, and AASP. He is a Fellow of AAK, AASP, and IAAP. He is a certified consultant of AASP.

Ivan T. Robertson's main role is as a Director of Robertson Cooper Ltd – a leading provider of well-being services to organizations. He is also Professor of Organisational Psychology at Leeds University Business School and Emeritus Professor at the University of Manchester. He is a Fellow of the British Psychological Society. He has published over 40 books on Work & Organizational Psychology and approaching 200 scholarly articles/ conference papers. He has held visiting posts in the USA, Singapore and Australia. His latest book (co-authored with Professor Cary Cooper), *Well-Being: Happiness and Productivity at Work*, was published in the spring of 2011.

Jan Salisbury is President of Salisbury Consulting. As an executive coach credentialed the International Coaching Federation and consultant for over 25 years, she develops leaders, teams and organizations to create engaging, inclusive work cultures that inspire innovation and results. She has co-authored a book on investigating harassment and discrimination, numerous articles on the prevention and resolution of harassment and has testified in over 25 cases as an expert witness. Her recent publications are focused on coaching and emotional intelligence in the workplace. She teaches classes in leadership and emotional intelligence at Boise State University.

Mark S. Schwartz MBA, JD, PhD, is an Associate Professor at the School of Administrative Studies at York University (Toronto, Canada). He has taught at several other universities including The Wharton School of the University of Pennsylvania, Dalhousie University, and Tel Aviv University. He has published in a number of academic journals including the *Journal of Business Ethics*, *Business & Society*, and *Business Ethics Quarterly*, and is the author of *Corporate Social Responsibility: An Ethical Approach* (2011). He has been quoted in several media outlets including *The New York Times*, the *Financial Times of London*, and the *National Post*, and he has consulted for a number of business firms and governments on business ethics-related matters.

Fred O. Walumbwa is Associate Professor of Management at the Arizona State University's W.P. Carey School of Business. He is also a senior research advisor with the Gallup Organization, Washington, DC. His research interests include leadership, organizational climate and culture, business ethics, justice, and cross-cultural issues in management research (Department of Management, W.P. Carey School of Business, Arizona State University, P. O. Box 874006, Tempe, AZ 85287-4006, United States. Tel.: +1 480 965 3431; fax: +1 480 965 8314, e-mail: Fred.Walumbwa@asu.edu).

Michael J. Zickar received his PhD in industrial-organizational psychology at University of Illinois at Urbana-Champaign. He is a Professor of Psychology at Bowling Green State University where he is also Department Chair. He has published widely on psychometric theory and personality measurement as well as the history of applied psychology. He is a Fellow and Executive Board member of the Society for Industrial-Organizational Psychology and is on the editorial boards of *Journal of Management* and *Journal of Business and Psychology*.

Acknowledgements

Cary Cooper and I continue to have a productive relationship across the pond. Living proof that two heads are almost always better than one.

Gerry Wood at Lancaster did her usual outstanding job of riding herd on me and Cary and our contributors.

Hats off to Martin West and Jonathan Norman and their staff at Gower for their social and administrative support.

Thanks to Carla D'Agostino for the little things that make a big difference.

And to my former doctoral students who shared their journeys with me: Monica Belcourt, Gene Deszca, Cobi Wolpin, Catherine Kirchmeyer, and Jim Lyttle.

Finally, to my family who continue to make life full and joyous. Thanks for making it interesting and keeping me young.

My contributions were supported in part by York University.

Ronald J. Burke
Toronto, Canada

Nature of the Issues

1

The Healthy Organization: Reducing High-risk Individual Behavior and Organizational Toxicity

RONALD J. BURKE

Introduction

Consider these observations about men and women in managerial and professional jobs:

- At least half the occupants of managerial and professional jobs are falling short in their performance (Hogan & Hogan, 2001).
- A growing number of surveys of managers and professionals have found that their levels of work stress has increased, and this has elevated levels of psychological distress and diminished physical health (Barling, Kelloway & Frone, 2005; Schabracq, Winnubst & Cooper, 2003).
- More managers and professionals have reported working more hours in more intense jobs and taking less than their full allotment of vacation time (Burke, 2006; Burke, 2010a; Burke & Cooper, 2008; Hewlett & Luce, 2006).
- Increasing numbers of managers and professionals report work–family and family–work concerns (Drago, 2007; Friedman & Greenhaus, 2000; Hochschild, 1997).
- Concerns have been raised about the character (greed, materialism, corruption) of managers and professionals given the increasing number of corporate scandals worldwide (Baker, 2010a, 2010b; Burke, 2011; Burke & Cooper, 2009; Dillon & Cannon, 2010; Glasbeek, 2002; Henriques, 2011; Lewis, 2010, 1989; Madrick, 2011; McLean & Elkind, 2005; Michaelson, 2009; Naylor, 2011; Rosen & Rosen, 2011; Smith, 2010; Sorkin, 2011). Executives at Goldman Sachs (and elsewhere) apparently walked a fine line between immoral/unethical actions and illegal actions. Big banks and law firms are increasingly being accused of turning a blind eye or failing to stop fraud artists. JPMorgan agreed to pay $153.6 million to settle a probe undertaken by the Securities and Exchange Commission for its role in approving mortgage securities but as almost always happens admitted to no wrongdoing (Moore, 2011). None of the central Wall Street figures have been convicted of any crimes. Issues of character have come to be seen as a significant factor in leadership success (Bakan, 2004; Burke,

2009a, 2009b; Gandz, Crossan & Seijts, 2010; Huffington, 2003; Parker, 2011; Rate & Sternberg, 2007; Schyns & Hansbrough, 2010). Shapiro and Von Glinow (2007) note the financial costs to organizations when senior executives engage is such behaviors and are convicted for their transgressions.

- Managers and professionals, including members of boards of directors, have their reputations compromised by being associated with firms guilty of financial fraud (Cowen & Marcel, 2011; Pozner, 2008). Being associated with a fraud incident indicates that individuals failed to fulfill important professional obligations. For example compromised directors are often dismissed from existing board seats and have difficulty in getting new board appointments.

- The current (July 2011) frenzy about the phone hacking and bribery initiatives undertaken by some employees of News Corporation in the UK reflects many of these elements. Some employees felt a need to engage in unethical and illegal activities to get an edge on the competition, sometimes involving hacking of phone and e-mail messages and the bribery of police officers to obtain scoops; police officers offered inside information in return for monetary benefits, some mangers were aware of these activities and signed off on them, resulting in what some have termed a culture that both encouraged and supported these behaviors. These activities have resulted in criminal charges being filed against some individuals and other individuals convicted and serving jail sentences, the resignation of high-ranking News Corporation executives and high-ranking police officers, the death of one whistle-blower, the loss of reputation to both News Corporation and the media more broadly, and the loss of billions of dollars worth of News Corporation stocks. It is doubtful whether Rupert Murdoch and his son James will be able to retain control of News Corporation. Hackgate, as this crisis has been dubbed in the UK, reflects the four stage of crisis laid out by Jordan-Meier (2011): fact finding, the unfolding drama, finger-pointing, and ultimate resolution and fallout.

- More people worldwide are getting fed up with "bad companies" (Bassi, Frauenheim, McMurrer & Costello, 2011); tired of the greed, pollution, product recalls, tainted food, poor service, and shabby employers. People are longing for "worthy companies"

- We are fed up and we're not going to take it any more—corruption that is. Anna Hazare, a 74-year-old Indian who has stood up for justice throughout his life and career, currently jailed, will be holding a 15-day hunger strike to protest levels of corruption in India. His stance had received the support of millions (Fatah, 2011). In India, a bribe must be paid for almost everything.

- Increasing numbers of women who obtain business education, start their careers in large organizations, and "opt out," reflecting a loss of talent (Barreto, Ryan & Schmitt, 2009; Maineiro & Sullivan, 2006). Women continue to be seriously underrepresented in science, technology, engineering, and mathematics (Burke & Mattis, 2007; Ceci & Williams, 2007) and in the ranks of senior levels of management worldwide (Davidson & Burke, 2011; Wittenberg-Cox & Maitland, 2008) and on corporate boards of directors (Vinnicombe, Singh, Burke, Bilimoria & Huse, 2008). Talents of half the population are underappreciated and underutilized as a result.

- Although the standard of living has increased over the past two decades in developed countries, indicators of satisfaction and happiness have remained flat. Materialism has not increased levels of individual well-being. Something seems to be missing in people's lives (Diener & Seligman, 2004; Kasser, 2002; Roberts, 2011; Whybrow, 2005).

- There has been some writing that addresses issues such as the paradox of success, the failure of success, the costs of success, the dark side of success, and career success and personal failure (Korman & Korman, 1980; O'Neill, 2004). Important writing in the past 20 years has shed light on the costs of success (Albion, 2000; Bogle, 2005, 2009). We have come to understand the mythology of success (success is absolute and final, money is central to the meaning of success, craving more, ambition to achieve success, success will make one free). We have come to better understand antecedents of "career success and personal failure" and possible resolutions (Bronson, 2005; Cloud, 2008; Porras, Emery & Thompson, 2007; Seligman, 2002). We are slowly but surely coming to better understand why leaders fail—and failure rarely results from a lack of intelligence, not working hard enough, or not possessing adequate technical skills (Charan & Colvin, 1999; Dotlich & Cairo, 2003; Finkelstein, 2003; Furnham, 2004).
- These experiences also impact the performance of men and women holding jobs at all levels, particularly managerial and professional jobs where employee discretion and commitment are critical to peak performance. They make it harder to compete in a "war for talent" (Michaels, Handfield-Jones & Axelrod, 2001). They also affect an organization's effectiveness and success.
- Initiatives have been developed for individuals to address many of these concerns. Solutions have been proposed including integrating one's life roles, stepping back and renewing oneself, getting past the fear of letting go, and being satisfied with "enough." Individuals who successfully integrate their important life roles (for example, work, family, community, self) perform better in their jobs and are in better psychological and physical health (Friedman, 2008). But success in these efforts also requires change on the part of workplaces (Rothstein & Burke, 2010).

In *Risky Business: Psychological, Physical and Financial Costs of High Risk Behavior in Organizations* (Burke & Cooper, 2010), we laid out several areas of high-risk individual behavior and organizational values, tasks and processes that had psychological, physical, and financial impact on individuals, families, organizations, and communities. The former included human frailties—individual attitudes and behaviors, and the latter—work and organizational experiences harmful to individual well-being and ultimately to organizational effectiveness. Human frailties included engaging in theft, criminal and fraudulent behaviors, work addiction, alcohol and substance abuse, and engaging in high-risk sexual relationships both inside and outside the workplace (Adebowale & Reed, 2010; Burke, 2011, 2010b, 2010c; Carnes, 2001; Ghodse, 2005; Kingston, 2011; Lefkowitz, 2009; Roman & O'Brien, 2010; Shulman, 2010; Tobutt, 2011; Tomlinson, 2009). Velez-Mitchell and Mohr (2011) believe that addiction is rampant in many countries and they review addiction to consumption, alcohol, drugs, sex, food, celebrity, porn, gambling, pharmaceuticals, and the internet (see also Leonard, 2010; Shaeffer, 1997; Underhill, 2008; Van Cleave, 2010).

It seems today that scandals involving human frailties are as likely to involve money as sex (for example, Bernie Madoff, Raj Rajaratnam, Eliot Spitzer, Bill Clinton, John Edwards, Tiger Woods, Silvio Berlusconi, John Ensign, and Dominque Strauss-Kahn). Most people can relate easily to sex scandals since sex involves desires shared by almost everyone. But why would anyone risk their reputation, career, and family for a few minutes of gratification? Money, on the other hand, lasts much longer.

Toxic organizational environments included those that exhibited acts of employee discrimination (for example, age, gender, race, sexual orientation), instances of sexually intimate and sexually harassing relationships, job demands leading to diminished employee well-being and performance, those that tolerate fraud and corruption, being exposed to unsafe or unhealthy working practices and conditions leading to sickness and sometimes death, abusive bosses, workplace bullying and occasional acts of workplace violence (Albrecht, Sanders, Holland & Albrecht, 2011; Anand, Ellstrand, Rajagopalan & Joshi, 2009; Ashforth, 1997, 1994; Cartwright, 2010; Clarke, 2010; Dipboye, 2010; Einarsen, Aasland & Skogstad, 2010; Glasso, Vie & Hoel, 2010; Kusy & Holloway, 2009; Lubit, 2004; Magley, Bauerle & Walsh, 2010; Zyglidopoulos & Fleming, 2009).

The Royal Canadian Mounted Police (RCMP) has been rocked by a series of sexual harassment clams. The newly appointed head of the RCMP stated that he would be addressing these claims and changing the culture to make it more hospitable to women. Yet a senior RCMP officer was found guilty of abuse of authority, sexual assault, sexual harassment, sexual discrimination and lying to a senior officer but was punished by a reprimand and the loss of ten days of pay when he admitted to having a sexual relationship with a fellow officer (*Toronto Star*, 2012) This "slap on the wrist" does not seem to be an effective way to change their culture.

Bennett and Randolph (2011) reported that there has been a 42 percent increase since 2009 in the filing of disability-discrimination charges with about 30,000 charges filed with the US government in 2011. It is not clear whether this represents an increase in actual disability-discrimination or the inclusion of more mental and physical impairments now, but this figure is worrisome.

This chapter includes the following content: real-life examples of human frailties and organizational toxicity, the key role of leadership, toxic leadership, the toxic triangle, leadership pathologies, "dark side" personality traits, workplace incivility, ethics and values, corporate wellness programs, and organizational initiatives that address both human frailties and levels of organizational toxicity.

The present collection, while looking at individuals, places the spotlight on initiatives that organizations can undertake to support the development of attitudes, values, character and behaviors in employees that will lessen the incidence and consequences of human frailties and particular risky work place experiences and events. Thus it is an antidote to some of the issues raised in *Risky Business*. How can individuals prevent themselves from becoming a casualty of some risky individual choices and behaviors (for example, work addiction, greed, hubris, failings of character, unbridled ambition, materialism)? What can organizations do (for example, improving quality of relationships, increasing equity and fairness, creating a safety culture, supporting ethical behaviors) to better understand and identify human frailties and limit their risks and to become less toxic or not toxic at all (Kusy & Holloway, 2009)?

This volume extends our work deeper into organizations and their role in coming to grips with both human frailties that end up causing damage, and toxic workplaces, again destructive to individual and organizational health. A toxic culture exhibits high levels of mistrust, dishonesty, abuse and lack of fairness and equity.

Connection to Workplace and Organizational Realities

Anyone who reads the business press today will see the relevance of these volumes to workplace realities (BP in the Gulf of Mexico, recent resignation of the CEO of Hewlett Packard, Alan Hurd, for harassment and questions about his expense accounts).

Here are some recent and current examples of human frailties and organizational toxicity that have been reported in various media to give the reader a sense of why and how we see this volume applicable to actual workplace experiences.

- British Petroleum (BP) oil rig explosion in the Gulf of Mexico causing deaths has raised the issue of whether BP put production and profits before worker safety. BP has had other safety violations and fines in their sites.
- Research reported by The Canadian Press (*Toronto Star*, 2011a) indicated that truck drivers hauling explosive or flammable materials have killed or badly injured people after getting drunk or stoned.
- Mining disasters in New Zealand, West Virginia (US), Columbia, Chile and China (several) causing deaths.
- Shooting of dozens of police officers in Mexico killing some and wounding others.
- Abusive bosses and too many assholes at work (Sutton, 2007, 2010).
- Workplace violence and employee rampages against others in their organization (Lester, 2011).
- Fraudulent elections in several counties (Haiti, Afghanistan, Egypt, Iraq, Ivory Coast, Russia, among others).
- A Canadian firm, Niko, was fined $9.5 million for offering bribes to a Bengladeshi government minister (car, travel) to deal with protests for locals following a natural gas explosion (Krugel, 2011).
- Spate of suicides in both France and China (France Telecom, Foxcom) attributed to workplace stress.
- British designer John Galliano was immediately terminated at Dior following accusations he made racial insults and expressed an admiration for Adolf Hitler (National Post, 2011a). He will likely be prosecuted for his remarks and also likely go into rehab. American actor Charlie Sheen was also terminated by ABC from his TV sitcom which paid him well over $1 million an episode for his rant against his producer and a host of other people. Sheen has been in rehab on several previous occasions.
- Germany's defense minister, Karl-Theodor van und zu Guttenberg, an up and coming star in German politics, resigned from his post following information that he likely plagiarized other people work in his PhD thesis (National Post, 2011b). A second German politician, Silvana Koch-Mehrn, was stripped of her doctorate for plagiarism and resigned at least two of her high-profile political positions. Other scientists found guilty of unethical behavior recently include Andrew Wakefield and Joachim Boldt (Globe and Mail, 2011). Philip Baker, Dean of the Medical School at the University of Alberta resigned after it was noted that his commencement speech at the 2011 graduation was lifted from one given by another physician at a graduation ceremony at Stanford University previously (*Toronto Star*, 2011b).
- Kesterton (2012) cites examples of fraud by scientists discussed in Discover magazine. Apparently Isaac Newton fudged some of the numbers in his Principia, thought by

many to be the greatest physics treatise ever written. Marc Hauser, an evolutionary psychologist at Harvard resigned after he was found guilty of fraud. Immunologist

- William Summerlin used a black felt tip pen to color patches of fur on white mice to support his claim that he transplanted tissue from black mice to white mice.
- James Frey, an American author, wrote "a million little pieces" which he claimed was a memoir—thus true—but later acknowledged it was partially fabricated. Before confessing, the book moved to the best-seller list partly due to its selection by Oprah Winfrey as one of her book club selections. Frey knew he was lying but once on the "slippery slope" it became difficult to get off and admit the truth.
- Bullying in the workplace is fairly common worldwide (Langan-Fox & Sankey, 2007, Tepper, 2007, 2000). Namie (2011) found that 72 percent of those demonstrating bullying behavior were bosses.
- Corruption—Afghan minister arrives in Gulf coast country with bags containing millions of dollars. The head of the Italian multi-national, Parmalat, sentenced to 18 years in jail in late 2010. Hardly a day goes by without an article appearing in the business section of major newspapers that describes an incident of individual theft, crime, fraud and corruption or organizational wrong-doing such as paying bribes, price fixing and fraud. Recent events in the Middle East (Egypt, Libya) have highlighted extensive corruption among the country leaders. The wife of Hosni Mubarak, following his removal from the Presidency of Egypt and imprisonment, returned a Cairo villa and US$3.4 million to the state. The first thing that other countries do when a ruler is deposed is to freeze all the assets of this individual and his family. Former Egyptian President, Hosni Mubarak, and members of his family were charged with corruption in July, 2011, and faced trial.
- A recent headline in the *Financial Times* (June 17, 2011) read "Corrupt officials smuggles $124 bn out of China, says Beijing report." About 2 weeks earlier, an Indian Guru, Swami Ramdev, along with his followers, began a hunger strike against "corrupt crooks." Ramdev wants the Indian government to retrieve millions of dollars stashed in overseas accounts, hold trials for alleged corrupt officials and impound the properties of corrupt officials.
- A corruption "Hall of Shame" was created in China (Schiller, 2011). Upon hearing that 3,000 Chinese officials were convicted of corruption in one year, a figure said to be low, Chinese artist Zhang Bingjian began painting pictures of these officials, working along with 20 other artists, now termed the Corruption Hall of Fame. The wall now contains almost 1,200 portraits.
- Timofeyev (2011) suggests that more than 2.5 million officials in Russia—the police, taxation, education, among other occupations—receive US$40–$45 million per year in bribes. He reports that 21 percent of Russians admit to bribing tax inspectors, 16.2 percent to bribing police officers and judges, and 13.9 percent to bribing fire inspectors. The average Russian company pays US$136,000 in bribes annually according to his research.
- Bribery—Federation of International Football Associations (FIFA) accused of being a corrupt organization and having to deny this. A few individuals entrusted with casting votes on the cities hoping to host major world events have been accused of accepting money for their votes. Voters for the Golden Globe awards were been accused by a former employee of selling their votes. Coca Cola, the biggest financial

sponsor of FIFA, was distressed by the FIFA corruption allegations since they tarnish the game of football.

- At least three former teammates of Lance Armstrong, seven time winner of the Tour de France, have indicated that Armstrong used banned substances. A large number of cycling race winners have later had their victories denied them because of their failing drug tests. Cycling has joined other sports (baseball, track and field) in having "drug eras" in which athletes cheated to gain an advantage. The 2011 Tour de France took pride in claiming that they found fewer drug test failures (that is, cheats) in 2011 than in previous years.
- Griffin (2011) describes how at least one official working basketball games in the National Basketball Association betted on the outcomes.
- Jim Tressel, football coach at Ohio State University in Columbus, Ohio, whose teams performed very well, winning the National championship in 2010, was fired from his university coaching job on May 27, 2011 for lying to the university administration about some activities involving a few of his players. An investigation revealed an eight-year pattern of rule violations under Tressel. As often happens, the cover up was worse than the crime. Tressel also wrote a book titled *Life Promises for Success: Promises from God on Achieving Your Best*. Apparently God said to Tressel, "Let your athletes trade in their championship rings for cash and tattoos and ride around in free cars."
- Several prominent individuals from business, politics and sports admitted having sexual relationships while married (for example, John Edwards, Tiger Woods) or engaging in sexually harassing behaviors (Dominique Strauss-Kahn, Arnold Schwarzenegger). They join a longer list including Mark Sanford, John Edwards, Bill Clinton, Larry Craig and Eliot Spitzer, among others. It seems however that we are getting tired of these scandals (Kingston, 2011).
- McKeon and Cain (2011) found a relationship between the personal risk taking of CEOs and more aggressive company policies (for example, business acquisitions and higher financial leverage, but greater volatility of equity returns).
- A sex scandal without the sex. Anthony Weiner, Democratic member of the US congress representing a New York district, resigned his congressional seat after it was revealed that, though recently married, he sent lewd photos of himself to several women. Weiner was also considered to be a New York City mayoral possibility.
- Miller and Shales (2011) wrote a book on the history of ESPN, the Entertainment and Sports Programming Network, documenting a workplace culture that was rampant with sexual harassment—a fraternity boy atmosphere.
- Holbrook (2011) lists several financial settlements US firms have made to settle discrimination suits. These included Coca Cola, $192.5 million, Lockheed, $2.5 million, Sears, $62 million, Warren Properties, $1.25 million, and two dozen entertainment firms (including ABC, CBS, NBC and Fox) paid $70 million. Discrimination costs (Wright & Conley, 2011). A class action suit against Walmart for gender discrimination will now be heard by the US Supreme Court. The Supreme Court decided however that the class action suit was too big, leaving the aggrieved women to pursue other legal avenues against Walmart. Deere & Co, the world's largest maker of agricultural equipment, is facing a lawsuit filed by women claiming that Deere discriminated against women in hiring, placement and promotion (*Financial Post*, 2011). Weimer and Thornton (1997) found long-lasting negative effects of ongoing sexual harassment in Mitsubishi after the problem was acknowledged and addressed.

- A new report on Toronto's law firms that examined 3,500 people in leadership positions found less than 7 percent of high-ranking legal professionals were visible minorities (Friesen, 2011). Significantly more visible minorities were at lower-level positions however.

Risky Business was written in 2009. The first chapter, titled "Human frailties and toxic organizations" (Burke, 2010b), included well-known publicly available examples of both to illustrate the concepts with concrete incidents and events. Each chapter in the collection (13 in total) contained suggestions for addressing human frailties and reducing organizational toxicity. Examples of human frailties and of toxic organizational experiences playing themselves out in the workplace and beyond, that have impacts on individuals, their families, their workplaces and in the wider community, are both common and never ending. While human frailties and organizational dysfunction are evident to organizational employees (insiders) they have been until relatively recently unknown to outsiders. These dysfunctions have traditionally been hidden or ignored.

Our view is consistent with the approach taken by Langan-Fox, Cooper & Klimoski 2007). They suggest two themes: individual barriers to productive work and managing organizational mayhem. Individuals are seen as the cause of organizational dysfunction, and broader issues of dysfunction in teams and organization-wide.

There are both personal challenges (for example, addiction, narcissism, greed) and organizational barriers (for example, bullying, discrimination, conformity) to productive work. Personal barriers (human frailties) can lead to and support system-wide dysfunction (organizational mayhem) (Langan-Fox, Cooper & Klimoski, 2007).

Healthy Individuals and Healthy Workplaces

Our goal is to support the development of healthy individuals and healthy workplaces. What do we mean by a healthy workplace? Sainforth, Kapsh, Broske & Smith (2001) suggest that healthy organizations are both financial successes and have a healthy workforce. Shain and Kramer (2004, p. 643) identify two factors: "what employees bring with them to the workplace in terms of personal resources, health practices, beliefs, attitudes, values and hereditary endowment" (healthy individuals) and "what the workplace does to employees once they are there in terms of organization of work, in both the physical and psychological sense" (a healthy, non-toxic work environment). Organizations therefore need to be proactive in creating work environments supporting positive experiences among their employees.

Addressing Addictions in the Workplace

Ghodse (2005) includes contributions from various authors that lay out what organizations might do to tackle addictions in the workplace and provides case studies of company efforts in this regard. These involve the establishment of drug and alcohol policies, screening and detection, testing of employees, employee assistance programs, the availability of specialist care and addressing psychosocial problems in the workplace. Organizational members often become "willfully blind" (Heffernan, 2011) to such addictive behaviors. Policies and programs at Shell International and British Airways are outlined in some detail.

Wilfully Blind

Heffernan (2011) suggests that individuals, in both their personal and professional work lives, engage in: "wilful blindness" to avoid reality. Individuals deny reality though this denial may have significant personal and organizational costs. She notes that "wilful blindness" is a legal concept in which individuals claim they did not know what was going on though they could have known and should have known. Wilful blindness results from several factors such as cognitive limits, information overload, fatigue, working too hard, desire to please others and be liked by them, working with others who all think the same, overconfidence, being taught to obey authorities, working in large and complex organizations, and a denial of problems. Individuals in marriages do not see signs that their partner is having an affair, is drinking too much, is spending heavily and going into debt, and families do not see that a child that is becoming addicted to painkillers. Investigators failed to see Madoff's Ponzi scheme. Japanese authorities failed to anticipate the risks of building nuclear power stations on major earthquake fault lines. BP failed to see the risks that inadequate safety systems posed to the disaster in the Gulf of Mexico. The Corps of Engineers failed to see the risks that hurricanes posed to New Orleans. The Catholic Church did not see the signs that some of its priests were engaged in sexual abuse of children. Wilful blindness keeps individuals and organizations in the dark, unaware of potential and increasingly dangerous problems, until it is too late to address them when they are just beginning. Interestingly all the actors involved in the examples noted above were "good" people trapped by human and organizational limitations.

Silence in Not Golden

Several organizational researchers (for example, Milliken, Morrison & Newlin, 2003; Morrison & Milliken, 2000; Pinder & Harlos, 2001) have highlighted the costs to individuals and organizations of what they term "organizational silence," the factors supporting and maintaining organizational silence including the belief that speaking up is unwise. Detert & Edmondson (2011) identified taken-for-granted beliefs about when and why speaking up at work is risky or inappropriate (for example, not enough data, negative career consequences, not wanting to embarrass the boss in public). Organizational silence creates stress among employees, increases employees' withdrawal from the organization, and impedes organizational learning and development. Employees remain silent though they are aware of "problems" out of fear, being at a low level in the hierarchy, concern about being labeled negatively and a belief that speaking up will not make a difference. Organizational leaders need to address factors causing "organizational silence" before employees will speak up.

Why do Good People do Bad Things?

The women and men we have described above, with likely a very few exceptions, were not "evil," the vast majority were good people who ended up doing bad or stupid things that caused distress and pain to themselves and others (family, friends, work colleagues).

Why do good people do bad things? Are there ways that these good people can learn and then stop doing unethical self-defeating and self-sabatoging things? Gibbs (2011), Bazerman and Tenbrunsel (2011), Ford (2008), Hollis (2007) and Zimbardo (2007) address these questions.

Gibbs (2011) analyzes recent examples of powerful men behaving badly (Strauss-Kahn, Schwarzeneger) and previous examples (Clinton, Edwards, Woods, among others). She notes that powerful men can be powerfully reckless, likely assess risks differently, believe that ordinary rules do not apply to them and are often surrounded by others that cover up their indiscretions. Powerful men have confidence and opportunity, and with confidence a sense of sexual entitlement. Men having more opportunity are likely to act on these opportunities. Both Strauss-Kahn and Schwarzenegger had history of groping women, and worse, this history did not impede their career progress. Strauss-Kahn issued an apology for an affair with a female staffer at the International Monetary Fund (IMF) in 2008.The goddaughter of Strauss-Kahn's second wife (he is now with his fourth) has recently claimed that she was sexually assaulted by Strauss-Kahn in 2002.

Bazerman and Tenbrunsel (2011) tackle the question of why so many of us fail to do what is right. Most individuals believe they are ethical but they overestimate their ability to act ethically and are unaware of acting unethically without meaning to They identify a number of "blind spots" that contribute to these effects. Ethical blind spots refer to the gaps between the ethical person one would like to be and the ethical person one really is. Ethical blind spots include the following. These are the result of psychological processes that cause "good people" top do "bad things," contrary to their stated values and outcomes. They cite considerable evidence showing that most people will cheat if there is no chance of being caught. Most people lie yet most people see themselves as highly ethical.

- Ethical fadeout or bounded awareness. Ethical issues are eliminated from a decision, instead decisions become business decisions not ethical decisions, with an emphasis on the bottom line being used to reinforce this.
- Shifting ethical standards. Individuals use a different standard when looking at their past behaviors. They believe that they should have behaved ethically and would have behaved ethically so when looking back at their earlier behavior they believe that they in fact did behave ethically.
- Blind to in-group favoritism. Individuals tend to make decisions favoring family, friends, people they like and people like themselves, raising conflicts of interests that they are unaware of.
- Use of a double standard. Individuals see unethical behavior they engage in as less objectionable than the same behavior committed by others.
- Emphasis on the short rather than the long term. Putting a greater weight on the short term will cause potential long-term ethical issues to be downplayed.
- Ignoring unethical behavior of others. Bazerman and Tenbrunsel note several factors supporting the ignoring of unethical behaviors. These include: being busy focusing

on other things such as one's own goals, not being rewarded for noticing unethical behavior of others, motivated blindness—do not see unethical behavior of others when it is not in our best interest to notice these acts, and indirect blindness—do not see unethical behavior when it is done through the behavior of others (for example, done indirectly), the slippery slope of small unethical behaviors escalating into larger ones, placing a higher value on the outcomes achieved rather than on the processes though which this was achieved, not seeing unethical behavior of others if this would end up harming the observer, and work group norms and pressures.

They identify workplace factors also likely to support "blind spots." These include functional boundaries between units that make it harder to spot ethical issues that are involved in another unit, the presence of group think in work teams, and excessive workloads, stress and time pressures which tend to support faster, emotional reactions.

There are sometimes rewards for unethical behavior, and efforts to punish unethical behavior sometimes actually increases levels of unethical behavior.

They correctly conclude that efforts to teach ethics in MBA programs and in executive education offerings, and most efforts by organizations to develop an ethical culture are likely to fall short as a result of these blind spots. For example, an increasing number of MBA programs have developed a code of ethics that they encourage their graduates to sign. Bernie Madoff would have signed the code. Thus changing organizations and "fixing" corrupt organizations is difficult. Many prefer what is known, the stability of things the way they are. Change is hard and there is no guarantee that efforts to increase ethical behavior will work. In addition there is no agreement on the need for change. When one adds living in a materialistic and consumption-driven world with increasing levels of hyper-sexuality, it is not surprising that so many people "fall off" the ethical wagon.

Baserman and Tenbrunsel propose a two-pronged effort for improving ethical behavior—changing individuals and changing organizations.

CHANGING YOURSELF

- Individuals need to align the gap between what they would have done and should have done.
- Engage more planning and more honest reflections of one's behaviors (act slower, logical, more reasoned).
- Examine your own self-interests—your wants.
- Rehearse or practice your response.
- Obtain as much accurate information relevant to your situation as you can.
- Consider a wide range of options.
- Evaluate potential unethical choices carefully.

CHANGING ORGANIZATIONS

- Identify often hidden but strong organizational values supportive of both unethical and ethical behaviors.
- Reduce time pressure and stress.
- Integrate individuals and groups into the organization to reduce functional barriers.

- Minimize a short-term focus in favor of a long-term focus.
- Reduce the amount of uncertainty in the organizational environment.

Boivie, Lange, McDonald and Westphal (2011), in a study of 739 US CEOs, found that those having a smaller identification with their firms (for example, do not take criticisms of the firm personally, use they not we to refer to the firm) were more likely to abuse perks. They received higher levels of compensation, less use of corporate jet for personal use—in essence greater personal enrichment.

Ford (2008) proposes that denied and suppressed emotions that then surface are the causes of self-destructive behavior. Most good people who do bad and self-destructive things rarely know why they do them. Ford believes that the pain caused to an individual from engaging in this bad behavior is usually the impetus for personal change. Dark side emotions such as shame, fear and denial underpin bad behavior (weaknesses, flaws, shortcomings). Ford terms this the "beach-ball effect;" you use lots of energy to keep a beach ball under water but when one stops keeping it under it surfaces. The same occurs when one suppresses something in their psyches; it appears later as bad behavior and self-sabotaging acts. It is important then to express the "beach balls" in one's life. People need safe and healthy ways to express their suppressed emotions and rejected qualities. People need to admit, accept and appreciate their dark sides (for example, greed, lust, stupidity, lies, deceit, betrayal) and identify harmless ways to express them. Acknowledging one's dark side thoughts and impulses and then asking for help with these feelings is one way of understanding and reducing bad behavior.

Killinger (1991) draws a link between workaholism and the loss of integrity often resulting in the loss of both reputation and careers. She notes that addiction to power and control leads to a loss of feelings and a loss of integrity. Such feelings of entitlement and power lead to harassing and promiscuous behaviors as evidenced by Strauss-Kahn and Schwarzenegger. Lammers and Stapel (2011, 2009) conclude that power increases dehumanization, decreases moral behavior and increases hypocrisy (Lammers, Stapel & Galinsky, 2010). Baron-Cohen (2011) also highlights the role of the loss of empathy and similar behaviors. Lammers, Stoker, Jordan, Pollmann and Stapel (2011) reported that power increases infidelity among both men and women.

In this line of research, power has been shown to impede judgment and lower inhibitions. People with power behave differently, standing closer to others, use more touching of others, make more direct eye contact with others, and believe that they are more attractive than they really are, and project a confidence that women may find attractive. In addition, the motivation to seek power may also lead to infidelities and less ethical workplace behaviors. Thus the power of men (and women) may actually be the seeds of their own career and personal life downfalls.

Gino, Schweitzer, Mead and Ariely (2011), in a series of studies, have shown that self-control depletion, often the result of exhaustion and fatigue, increases the prevalence of cheating, which they attribute to a lowering of self-control. Individuals with a weaker sense of moral identity were more likely to demonstrate the negative effects of exhaustion on cheating. Barnes, Schaubroeck, Huth and Ghumman (2011) also found that fatigue was associated with less ethical behavior.

Wiltermuth (2011), in a series of experiments, found that an individual's likelihood to cheat doubled from 21 percent to 43 percent, when the benefits from cheating were shared with another individual. It appears that splitting the gains from cheating makes cheating less unethical.

There are also potential rewards and befits from cheating. Kesterton (2011) reports that teachers in Atlanta, Georgia spent evenings and weekends changing wrong answers on student tests to correct ones, and students were placed next to better students so they could copy their answers so that these schools could raise their test scores. About half of Atlanta's schools allowed this cheating to continue for at least a decade. One hundred and seventy-eight teachers and principals were identified in this investigation.

Finally, some researchers have suggested that genetics, a specific variant in the DRD4 gene, which influenced the functioning of D4 dopamine receptors in one's brain, is associated with increased thrill-seeking behavior such as gambling, drug use, skydiving and promiscuity (Wallace 2011).

Can Bad Habits be Changed?

Most individuals can identify some "habit" that limits their potential at work as well as prove damaging to their careers and personal lives (Immen, 2011a). Yet Patterson, Grenny, Maxfield, McMillan and Switzer (2011) found that few do anything about it. They reported, in an online survey of 493 individuals, that 97 percent said they knew of at least one thing they did regularly that could limit their career yet only one-third had taken serious steps to stop their bad habits. In a separate survey of 479 supervisors and managers of others, they reported that only about 22 percent of their employees made lasting changes to their bad habits. The five most common bad habits were unreliability, unwillingness to take responsibility, procrastination, resistance to change and having negative attitudes. These "liabilities" are tame compared to some of the human frailties mentioned above. Trying to change a bad habit was rarely successful.

Patterson, Grenny, Maxfield, McMillan and Switzer (2011) offer the following advice:

1. Create a motivation statement based on your "default future." What would happen to you if you continue with this bad habit, what costs might you incur?
2. Invest in the development of new skills.
3. Avoid spending time with others that support your bad habit.
4. Get help from a trusted friend or mentor.
5. Control your work and social environment. Avoid going to places that support your bad habits.

Toxic Individuals

Kusy and Holloway (2009) focus on the prevalence and effects of toxic personalities in the workplace. In a survey of 404 managers and professionals, 64 percent said that they were currently working with a toxic personality and 94 percent had worked with a toxic personality at some point in their work lives. Toxic personalities make a workplace toxic and thrive best in a toxic organizational environment. They identified three behaviors among these personalities: shaming behavior, passive-aggressive hostility and work team sabotage. Unfortunately most organizational leaders tolerate toxic personalities.

Leaders rarely use formal strategies to address toxic personalities (for example, termination), but more often use less-effective informal strategies (for example, minimizing the damage caused) or feedback strategies (for example, performance feedback). Toxic individuals damage an organization's culture and promote continuing toxicity.

Toxic Organizations

In *Risky Business*, we identified the following as characteristics of a toxic organization: bad leadership (Einarsen, Aasland & Skogstad, 2010); too many assholes at work (Sutton, 2007); sexual behaviors and sexual harassment; discrimination based on sex, age, sexual orientation, race and religion; job demands and workplace stressors; violence in the workplace, crime, corruption and fraud; catastrophic errors leading to disasters (for example, Bhopal); and jobs that are associated with traumatic events such as police officers, soldiers and emergency first responders.

Bad News Travels Fast

Misery loves company. There is research evidence that once news of individual character flaws and organizational toxicity become public it travels fast (Yu, Sengul & Lester, 2008). In addition, this information not only reflects badly on individual and organizations, it can also reflect badly on entire industrial sectors. Employees and organizations need to realize that today we all live in glass houses.

Leadership in Organizations

Working on earlier volumes in the Gower Series on Risk led to the conclusion that the values, character and courage of all employees, but particularly of those holding leadership positions, is central in understanding human frailties and toxic organizations (Burke, Clarke & Cooper, 2011; Burke Martin & Cooper, 2011; Burke, Tomlinson & Cooper, 2011). Others have come to the same realization (Boyatzis & McKee, 2005; Cameron, Dutton & Quinn, 2003; Csikszentmihalyi, 2003; Freeman, Moriarty & Stewart, 2009; George, 2003).

Leadership plays a critical role in tolerating, addressing and managing human frailties in the workplace as well as changing toxic elements in an organizational environment. Leaders make a difference to the performance of organizations, whether it be in organizational units or total organizations. The majority of early leadership writing emphasized qualities of what were thought to be successful leaders, typically those who had advanced in their careers. There was less writing on effective leaders, those that contributed to higher levels of unit or organizational performance. And it has been only within the last 20 years that writers and researchers have considered the "dark side" of leadership, those individual leadership traits that undermine effective leaders and fail to contribute to unit or organizational performance.

Bitti (2011) quotes Susannah Kelly, executive vice-president of DHR International as saying: "Fifty people caused the stock market to collapse. They had that much power and arrogance and the systems and processes we have in place valued that arrogance and compensated it."

Bitti concludes that one positive learning from the financial meltdown was that leadership matters and the wrong type of leadership was rewarded and cultivated. New types of leaders and organizational cultures that encourage learning, questioning, discussion, disagreement and honesty are needed. One solution is to make human resources (HR) issues a bigger part of corporate board responsibilities beyond CEO compensation, and provide board members with greater knowledge and understanding of the role of HR in business success.

Gandz, Crossan and Seijts (2010) address some critical questions about leadership. What leadership qualities and characteristics contributed to the 2008/2009 financial crisis and the devastation that followed? Did these leadership issues exist in a few organizations at the center of the financial crisis or were they widespread? What can be learned from the organizations and leaders that anticipated the crisis and are now better able to respond to it? And how can we better prepare leaders and organizations to deal with these, and other challenges, in the future? To address these questions, they first prepared a working paper based on their understanding of events and the literature, then conducted focus groups and conferences with knowledgeable CEOs, HR leaders and business students, then presented their findings and conclusions to various stakeholders, culminating in their 2010 report.

They compared those organizations that failed or were badly hurt with those that survived and prospered on five dimensions: competencies, character, commitment, learning and governance.

COMPETENCIES

Organizations that survived and prospered had a basic understanding of economic cycles, complexity and systems thinking, were able to manage their balance sheets, had good organizational designs, and cultures that supported discussion, debate and arguments. Organizations that failed or were badly hurt relied heavily on quantitative models, failed to analyze risk, had limited understanding of complexity and systems, poor organizational designs, and cultures that stifled disagreement.

CHARACTER

Organizations that survived were temperate, prudent, open-minded and socially responsible. Those that failed were arrogant, overly confident, highly competitive, greedy, self-absorbed and exhibited a group think mentality.

COMMITMENT

Organizations that survived were able to control risk throughout their businesses. Those that failed had little contact with parts of their businesses.

LEARNING

Organizations that survived were aware of past events related to economic and financial crises; those that failed seemed to have learned nothing from these historical events.

GOVERNANCE

Organizations that survived had boards of directors that possessed high levels of risk management skills and had developed ways to oversee risk issues. Organizations that failed had boards of directors that did not understand risk issues very well, were not active in their monitoring and discussion of risk concerns.

They propose four leadership competences for success: people, organizational, business and strategic. A competence includes knowledge (facts, figures, concepts, ideas), understanding (relationships among these, the context, what is important), skills (analysis, decision making, communication, getting results, building teams), and intuition (timing, methods and processes, staffing, approaches).

Leadership character is significant and includes values, virtues and personality traits (see Peterson & Seligman, 2004, for a complete taxonomy on character strengths and virtues). Leadership commitment includes a desire to lead, working hard, and motivation beyond self-interest (that is, sacrifice). Individual leader learning is based on character, competence and commitment, leading to learning capability and learning motivation. Group learning is based on group dynamics, identification with the organization and it mission, and motivation. Organizational learning is based on organizational culture, policies and processes, and its importance for organizational actions.

Gandz, Crossan and Seijts (2010) offer some thoughts on the development of good/ better leaders. These include:

- *profile*—a clear articulation of what the organization expects leaders to know, understand, achieve and be (results, competencies, character, commitment);
- *policies*—a statement of goals and principles underlying their leadership development initiatives;
- *pathways*—job assignments given to individuals that provide critical challenges and learning;
- *programs*—programs/sessions that offer knowledge, understanding, skills and judgment related to the organization's leadership expectations and profile;
- *processes*—HR policies and processes that support the development of young talent into seasoned leaders;
- *pool*—the availability of talent to the organization;
- *partnerships*—the relationship of organizational leaders and leadership development experts.

Gandz and his colleagues (2010) also offer some tips for various stakeholders.

- *Management educators*—provide students exposure to economic and social history, a better understanding of complexity and systems thinking, the use of values in decision making, socially responsible leadership as both smart and good leadership, less emphasis on shareholder value as the only bottom line, and being a role model of good leadership.
- *Business leaders*—advocate the anticipation of events and the perils of complacency, challenge the sole use of current business models as the only ways of viewing and understanding one's environment, support the development of organizational leadership profiles, support cultures of debate, disagreement and honesty, support

continuous learning, and use character as a factor in leadership assessment and development.

- *HR and organizational change leaders*—support the development of leadership profiles that include competencies, character and commitment, create effective partnerships with senior organizational executives for the development of leaders, and create the policies, pathways, processes and programs that incorporate and integrate competencies, character and commitment in the development of leaders.
- *Corporate directors*—meet other executives in addition to the CEO. Strengthen understanding of risk and risk management, solicit external assessments of risk, consider executive pay as a risk issue, and be wary of arrogant, controlling, defensive and closed CEOs that attempt to control their boards.
- *Future leaders*—know yourself by engaging in self-assessment of your values, personality and leadership potential and solicit the views of trusted outsiders; take some risks in your career to learn, to make mistakes and to learn from them. Be humble regardless of your success.

It is difficult, perhaps even impossible, to be a superb or perfect leader. All leaders likely have shortcomings (Conger, 1990). Bones (2011) believes that we have placed too much emphasis on individual leaders and their development, creating almost a cult of leadership. He advocates that rather than focusing on developing the leadership talents of a few individuals, it would be better to develop leadership throughout the organization. Leadership would then be organizational rather than individual. This involves developing collaboration across individuals (more use of team goals, team accountability, team rewards) to counteract our misplaced emphasis on the heroic individual leader. The latter leads to hubris, arrogance, narcissism, celebrity, greed and outlandish salaries.

Leadership—the Good, the Bad and the Ugly

In exit interviews, most people who leave an organization say it is to pursue better prospects or to spend more time with their families. Hogwash. The vast majority of those who leave an organization leave because of bad managers and bad management.

There has been relatively little attention paid to leader misbehavior until recently. There are several reasons for this (Shapiro & Von Glinow, 2007) including the leader's status and power and difficulty removing them in any event. The increased research and practical attention devoted to "dark side" personality characteristics has provided a more complete understanding of experience in organizations and their performance (Kellerman, 2004; Lipman-Blumen, 2005; Rayment & Smith, 2010).

Schaubroeck, Walumbwa, Ganster and Kepes (2007), in a study of the effects of supervisor hostility and negative affectivity on organizational commitment, job satisfaction and anxiety, reported modest relationships of supervisor hostility and negative affectivity with various outcomes, and these relationships were strong among employees in "unenriched" jobs.

Harris, Kacmar and Zivnuska (2007), in a sample of employees from an automotive organization, in some cases involving supervisor–subordinate pairs, found that abusive supervision was negatively related to both formal and supervisor ratings of job performance.

Some have proposed that bullying can be a strategic tactic used by supervisors to influence others. Ferris, Zinko, Brouer, Buckley and Harvey (2007), in a conceptual paper, in fact suggest that "strategic bullying behavior" may be a useful influence tactic and can produce positive effects.

Why is Toxic Leadership so Pervasive?

Shapiro and Von Glinow (2007) consider why bad leaders remain in good places. Leaders behave badly (Al Dunlap, Martha Stewart, Ken Lay) but retain their jobs.

But why are bad leaders not penalized? Antecedents of bad behavior include leaders' competence and integrity; outcomes of a leader's bad behavior vary from trivial to serious. A key issue is what is perceived to be responsible for their failure. A leader is seen as bad as a result of their outcomes. And good people sometimes act badly (Ford, 2008; Hollis, 2007; Zimbardo, 2007). Ford (2008) suggests that for most individuals there is an ongoing and never-ending battle between their dark and light sides.

Shapiro and Von Glinow (2007) offer some practical implications of their thinking:

- make more information available on what leaders are doing;
- support the reporting of leaders' misconduct by others;
- look at how leaders' status and power operate to silence discussion;
- look at how leaders use their power and status.

We know the following about leadership in organizations. Over half the individuals in supervisory/leadership positions are falling short in achieving expected results. (Hogan & Hogan, 2001). Organizations believe that they are not doing a good job in developing leadership talent; these organizations note the absence of qualified leaders in their pipelines (Rothstein & Burke, 2010). Too many leaders are arrogant, abusive, self-centered and autocratic; Sutton (2007 has used the term "assholes" to describe leaders, and colleagues, having these qualities. Others have been even more critical (Babiak, 1993; Babiak & Hare, 2006; Furnham, 2004; Hare, 1993). Improving leadership effectiveness then becomes important to reducing organizational toxicity and achieving peak performance.

Immen (2011b) highlights the role played by achieving results in the tolerance of bad managers. Managers that bully, disrespect others and play favorites were found to be a major difficulty for many HR managers. In a survey of almost 800 HR managers, 73 percent indicated spending a considerable amount of time dealing with problems caused by bad managers. Thirty-four percent of respondents said that their organization would tolerate almost any behavior from mangers getting results. Most common issues cited were: inappropriate comments to staff (74 percent), favoritism (70 percent), treating others with disrespect (62 percent), and bullying or intimidation (57 percent). Managers were more likely to exhibit such bad behavior if poorly trained and promoted to jobs beyond their skill, and those with values and attitudes at odds with those of their organization.

Problem mangers were seen to be more common at lower than at higher organizational levels:

- 46 percent—problem managers are a "big" concern;
- 27 percent—problem managers were a "huge" problem;

- 53 percent—have "difficult" communications with a problem manger at least once a month.

Respondents highlighted the importance of early identification of these "bad" apples.

Hogan and Hogan (2001) considered career derailment factors among mangers. They believe that personality, personality assessment and leadership performance are necessarily related. Managers that are incompetent tend to "blow up, show off, or conform under pressure" (Hogan & Hogan, 2001, p. 50). Narcissism, which will be considered in more detail below, emerges as an important leadership flaw. Narcissistic leaders, high on selfishness, operate in ways that damage employee trust. In addition, narcissistic managers have some difficulty learning from their experiences, this being a key factor to leadership performance.

Here are some indicators of destructive leadership. The leader imposes goals on staff without their agreement or concern about their long-term welfare, ignores reality, disregards the views of others, overestimates their personal talents and capabilities, and intimidates others (Kets de Vries, 2006). Negative leader behavior falls on a continuum with one end reflecting ineffective and incompetent individuals and the other end reflecting unethical and evil individuals.

Padilla, Hogan and Kaiser (2007) advance our understanding of destructive leaders in their "toxic triangle" integrating characteristics of destructive leaders, the role of susceptible followers and the influence of conducive environments. These three factors make destructive leaders possible, pervasive and long lasting. There are personally destructive leaders as well as organizationally destructive leaders. Personally destructive leaders may get fired, demoted, career plateaued, acquire blemished reputations, receive reprimands, have criminal records and serve jail time. Organizationally destructive leaders may bring about low employee satisfaction, low quality products and service, workplace accidents, environmental damage (Exxon, Union Carbide) and damaged reputations (BP).

The key feature of destructive/toxic leadership is negative job/organizational outcomes and the process leading to such outcomes (Kaiser & Hogan, 2007).

Destructive leadership has five elements according to Padilla and his colleagues (2007, p. 179). These are: destructive leaders can produce both good and bad outcomes; leadership processes involving dominance, coercion and manipulations instead of influence, persuasion and commitment; leadership processes involving selfishness, meeting the needs of the leader not the work team; leadership effects that lower the quality of life of employees and reduce the organizations' effectiveness; and are dependent not only on destructive leaders, but also willing followers and conducive environments.

They illustrate their toxic triangle by offering examples of factors that fall into each of the three components (2007, p. 180).

1. *Destructive leaders*—charisma, personalized power, narcissism, negative life themes, ideology of hate.
2. *Susceptible followers*—a) conformers—unmet needs, low core self-evaluations, low maturity; b) colluders—ambition, similar world views, bad values.
3. *Conducive environments*—instability, perceived threat, cultural values, lack of checks and balances, and ineffective institutions.

Padilla and his colleagues offer the following practical implications for preventing or reducing the incidence, pervasiveness, tenure and costs of destructive leadership.

1. Improve leader selection and development. Incorporate validated measures of narcissism and dark side personality characteristics. Assess negative behaviors as well as positive behaviors for development.
2. Develop stronger followers (Offerman, 2004). Develop a culture of empowerment. Reward leaders who develop leadership talents of their staff. Encourage candor from staff, discourage telling the manager what he/she wants to hear.
3. Create environmental factors that foster accountability through the monitoring of behaviors by all employees at every level.

Healthy individuals lead to higher levels of individual well-being across the board and healthy workplaces that are more likely to deliver peak performance. Character and courage are necessary for personal and organizational health but both are sorely lacking in many contemporary workplaces. Character, courage and virtue stand in opposition to human frailties and engaging in toxic behavior in the workplace.

Managerial Pathologies

Kyrios, Nedeljkovic, Moulding and Doron (2007) consider obsessive–compulsive personality disorder (OCPD)—excessive rigidity, wanting perfection, high personal and moral standards, need control and order, emotional control, interpersonal reticence and indecisiveness These characteristics affect an individual's work as well as their relationship with others at work. But some qualities of mild OCPD can be seen as strengths in an organization and are encouraged (for example, work devotion, perfectionism). But there is a risk that these might lead to work addiction, to avoidance of tasks, to depression and anger, to a need for control and difficulty delegating tasks to others.

Furnham (2007) builds on the link between personality disorders and derailment at work. Leaders fail for more than incompetence. A leader's personality disorder leads to behaviors associated with a dysfunctional workplace.

There are obviously degrees of pathology. Three personality "types" have been discussed in relation to derailment at work: antisocial personalities (psychopaths), narcissistic personalities and histrionic personalities. These have been lumped into what Paulus and Williams (2006) call the "dark triad of personality." Psychopaths are selfish and callous, superficially charming, lacking in empathy and remorseless. Narcissists are attention seeking, vain, self-focused and exploitative. Machiavellians are deceptive, manipulative, strongly self-interested. There are some benefits of these disorders: charm, self-confidence, emotional openness and clever deceptiveness (see Cangemi & Pfohl, 2009) who conclude that sane men may make poor leaders). Physically attractive, educated, intelligent and the "dark side" personality traits are qualities often used in selection for senior management positions. And there are several well-known examples of successful narcissists (for example, Sutton (2007) lists Scott Rudin, John Bolton, Linda Wachner) and successful psychopaths (for example, Belfort, 2010, 2007). Schlimm (2011) adds Donald Trump, Frank Stronach, Ted Rogers, Bill Paley and Steve Jobs to the list of "difficult and demanding" managers.

It gets complicated. Personality traits, both "dark side" and "bright side" can be shown to have positive and negative outcomes (Judge & LePine, 2007, Judge, LePine & Rich, 2006; Judge, Piccolo & Kosalko, 2009). Their analyses identified some personality traits to be associated with career progress but not necessarily job performance In addition, some personality traits can be an asset to individuals at the start of their careers but not in the long run and even add to the distress of their subordinates. Judge and LePine (2007) advocate the use of selection, select individuals high on bright side traits and low on dark side traits, and then use training to address the "costs" of dark side traits.

Narcissism in Organizations

You ask me if I have a God complex? Let me tell you something, I am God.
                                Line spoken by Alec Baldwin in the 1993 movie *Malice*

The term narcissism derives from the story of Narcissus, a young attractive man, who fell in love with his reflected image. Today, narcissism is viewed as a stable personality trait that includes feelings of grandiosity, arrogance, entitlement, self-absorption, feelings of threatened self-esteem and a quick response with anger. Many organizational leaders possess these traits (Rosenthal & Pittinsky, 2006).

Here are some of the things we now know about narcissists and narcissism:

- Celebrities, not surprisingly, score very high on narcissism (Young & Pinsky, 2006).
- Levels of narcissism have risen over the past 20 years in the general population (Twenge, 2006; Twenge, Konrath, Foster, Campbell & Bushman, 2008).
- Business students in universities score higher on narcissism than do university students in other disciplines or departments (Bergman, Westerman & Daly, 2010).
- Narcissists rate themselves more favorably on various dimensions than do non-narcissists (Twenge & Campbell, 2009; Wallace & Baumeister, 2002). Narcissists make riskier decisions than non-narcissists when both have equal knowledge or skill (Chatterjee & Hambrick, 2007; Campbell, Goodie & Foster, 2004).
- Narcissists are more likely to respond with anger than are non-narcissists to interferences and obstacles. Narcissists are more likely to blame others and external events for their failures than are non-narcissists (Glad, 2002). Narcissism was found to be related to the trait of anger, number of constraints to doing their jobs and higher levels of counterproductive work behaviors (Penney & Spector, 2002).
- Narcissists are less likely to be involved in committed relationships and more likely to be involved in affairs and/or extra-marital relationships (Campbell & Foster, 2002).
- Narcissistic supervisors were more likely to have subordinates that scored high on job tension and depression at work (Thompson, 2010).
- Protégés in mentoring relationships scoring higher on narcissism had shorter duration relationships, less career mentoring support, lower relationship quality, and greater negative mentoring experiences than did protégés with less narcissism (Allen, Johnson, Xu, Bioga, Rodopman & Ottinot, 2009).
- Organizations themselves can take on narcissistic qualities (Chatterjee & Hambrick, 2007; Kets de Vries, 2010).Some have linked narcissism in organizations with their eventual decline, the case of General Motors being prime example (Schwartz, 1991).

Narcissists seem to be good at advancing their careers and obtaining senior-level managerial jobs but less successful at performing well in these jobs once they get them. Writers have indicated both an upside and a downside of narcissistic leaders (Hill & Youney, 1998; Maccoby, 2004, 2000; Kets de Vries, 1993; Lubit, 2002; Rosenthal & Pittinsky, 2006). Productive narcissists exhibit the upside while destructive narcissists exhibit the downside. The upside includes confidence, dominance, the ability to inspire followers, creating an inspiring vision of the future, innovative and transformational. The downside includes self-promotion, self-nomination, greater deception, more intimidation, damaged relationships, and damaged organizational processes and systems.

How might organizations deal with narcissism? Bergman, Westerman and Daly (2010) suggest that business schools can play a role in pointing out the pitfalls and perils of narcissism and providing opportunities for students to get feedback on their own behaviors. Kets de Vries (1993) suggests that narcissistic managers develop a trusted colleague that can temper their downside by pointing it out and offering both feedback and other alternatives. Kets de Vries has also suggested that some narcissists might benefit from therapy. Higgs (2009), in a paper on "bad" leadership, suggests that a more realistic approach to dealing with narcissism in the workplace is to encourage a moving away from the concept of "heroic" leaders to one of "relational" leadership. This obviously is a long-term initiative. In addition, organizations would benefit from using less heroic concepts in their selection and development of leaders, and potential leaders.

Workplace Incivility

Workplace incivility (for example, teasing, sarcasm, rudeness, bullying) seems to have increased over the past 20 years. Such behaviors serve to reduce job performance and organizational commitment as well as having effects on employee psychological health (Pearson & Porath, 2009, 2008; Pearson, Anderson & Wegner, 2001; Porath & Erez, 2007). Pearson and Porath (2009, 2008) estimate the cost of workplace incivility to be several billion dollars annually. Ironically, examples of workplace incivility seem to be more common when the instigator is at higher rank and earning significantly larger salaries (Desai, Brief & George, 2010). Workplace incivility also affects employees' families and partners, who in turn take this stress into their own workplaces (Ferguson, 2011)

Pearson and Porath (2008) report the following in a survey of 800 professionals in the US:

- 80 percent said they had been insulted or bullied at work;
- 78 percent said their commitment to the organization declined as a result;
- 63 percent said they lost time at work to avoid the offender;
- 48 percent decreased work effort after uncivil treatment;
- 38 percent intentionally let their work quality drop.

Workplace incivility costs money and opportunities. Increased absences result in lost time, replacement costs, higher demands on co-workers that are present. In extreme cases, incivility has legal costs, loss of employee time and loss of management time. Incivility leading to turnover has recruitment and training costs. The upshot of incivility is the creation of a toxic workplace.

However, most organizations do not have procedures in place to deal with such experiences or events. An increasing number of organizations are now paying attention to workplace incivility. Their goals are to build a culture of civility, respect and engagement.

Leiter, Laschinger, Day, Gurnham and Latimer (2009) describe research involving both data collection and intervention in hospital settings designed to increase workplace civility. This project was called CREW, the Civility, Respect and Engagement at Work project, and was carried out in 45 hospitals. It began with a survey in which employees rated the civility and support of mangers and co-workers. Then trained staff met with groups of employees in half-hour long sessions to go over and discuss issues that were raised. Employees met weekly to discuss issues raised in the survey and how it affected their work. The focus was on identifying the ways they now wanted to interact with each other. Civil behaviors included paying attention to others, acknowledging, listening, being considerate and giving praise. A civility workshop was developed that encouraged nursing staff to think before acting, and consider how words and actions affected others. Continuing reminders from top management, the development of civility policies with clear accountabilities, and identifying ways to monitor these policies were also included.

A follow-up survey indicated a drop in levels of perceived stress by 15 percent by groups that did the CREW program compared to groups that did not, a 10 percent increase in views that managers behaved with more civility, team members treated each other with more respect, reports of co-worker incivility dropped by 30 percent and absences fell 15 percent.

Osatuke, Mohr, Ward, Moore, Dryenforth and Bellan (2009) also reported benefits from an intervention program undertaken in several US Veterans Administration hospitals.

Dealing with Toxic Personalities

Kusy and Holloway (2009) identify three approaches to addressing toxic individuals and their contributions to making organizations themselves toxic: total organizational, tackling work teams and directly intervening with toxic individuals. Total organization interventions typically would consider organizational policies, how performance appraisals might be used to surface important concerns, leadership development efforts that identify toxic behaviors and highly other attitudes and skills, the incorporation of 360-degree feedback processes and skip-level evaluations if an individual feels that they can get "better" help from someone other than their direct supervisor. Running through all these interventions is the articulation and embedding of important values in the organization's culture. Team-based interventions focus on team member selection, team norms levels of team participation, 360-degree team assessments, and the articulation and embedding of core values in team leadership and team members. Individual-level strategies involve the use of targeted feedback, performance evaluation, coaching, and if all else fails, termination.

The Importance of Character

I remember reading a quotation from a successful individual that went something like this:

Given the choice between high levels of skill and high levels of character, go with character.

Here are some examples of why character matters. Jackson (2004) provides other examples of individual and organizational character that underpin reputational capital; reputational capital offering considerable competitive advantages.

A Toronto university graduate in law applied for the opportunity to practice law in Ontario. He was denied this opportunity because the licensing body found him failing the test of "good character" (Robson, 2011). This individual did exceptionally well in his educational programs but he behaved inappropriately in his role on a condominium board (threatening to other board members, use of profanity in describing a condo board member's wife and child, made insulting remarks about tenants living in the building, and forged a letter accusing a condo board member of receiving kickbacks).

And here is more bad news about lawyers and law firms (Popplewell, 2011). Lawyers from a firm specializing in labor relations sponsoring a party for students from across Canada on January 2, 2009, at a Toronto nightclub engaged in lap dances, inappropriate touching and drunkenness. A female junior lawyer with the firm filed a sexual harassment complaint in keeping with the firm's sexual harassment policies. Since this event, three layers have left the firm and one filed a lawsuit against other firm members. The female junior lawyer has left the firm, and the firm indicated that it would no longer participate in such events.

Reputation, individual and organizational, matters more today than it ever has (Jackson, 2004). The public today has a low opinion of organizations doing the right thing. Individuals now have higher expectations of organizational leaders and of organizations themselves. Information on the behavior of individuals and organizations can now be obtained 24/7. Assessments/ratings of the reputation of organizations are now appearing more frequently and are being undertaken by more sources. It is also important to note that reputation is different from image and identity. Jackson, emphasizing integrity and fair play as key elements of corporate reputation, lists several benefits of the development of reputational capital, providing company examples as well.

Expressing and Acting on our Values

In a time of universal deceit telling the truth is a revolutionary act.

George Orwell

Individual values emerged as important factors in thinking about both human frailties and toxic organizations. Consider the following questions. How and when do individuals acquire their values? Can ethics be taught to business students? Do people generally know right from wrong?

Gentile (2010a, 2010b) contends that most people know right from wrong, what is unethical and/or illegal, and what behavior is in a potential "grey" area. Yet in spite of this "knowledge," some people become caught in ethical dilemmas, some watch/ observe unethical behavior in their workplaces, and some engage in unethical and/or illegal behavior. Gentile believes people fall on to a normal distribution—a bell curve—of voicing and acting on their ethical values. A few individuals always voice and act on their ethical values, a few individuals always act in unethical and/or illegal ways, and the vast majority of individuals fall somewhere in between. If more employees gave voice to and acted on their values, organizations would be less toxic (Kusy & Holloway, 2009, Rate & Sternberg, 2007) and more effective (Argyris, 1993; Argyris & Schon, 1996).

Most efforts that teach ethics present considerable content on becoming aware of ethical issues, and considerable content on analyzing issues/situations for possible ethical dimensions, but present considerably less content on action—what would you do (Gentile, Piper & Parks, 1993)?

Gentile has developed a program for students and organizational employees described in her book *Giving Voice to Values: How to Speak your Mind When You Know What is Right*. She lists five learnings obtained during the preparation of the curriculum described in this book.

1. Most ethical choices are not dilemmas; the right course of action or decision is almost always clear.
2. There were times when individuals acted on their values and other times when they did not; these were not "good" people or "bad" people.
3. Individuals can learn to voice their values more often and more successfully if they understand the factors that make this possible (for example, fears, possible punishments).
4. Individuals are better off developing potential ways to deal with their rationalizations for not doing the right things than by analyzing the right thing to do and the rationalizations for not doing it.
5. The key questions then become, "If I acted on my values what would I do and say, to whom, in what way, and in what sequence?"

She has developed a skills-based model of seven principles that underlies her thinking.

1. *Values*—identifying and agreeing on what is core and fundamental to one's work.
2. *Choice*—recognizing that there are options and that everyone has the experience of making difficult choices.
3. *Normality*—acknowledging that conflict about values is to be expected and avoiding demonizing those with whom one disagrees.
4. *Purpose*—defining one's role and being explicit about one's aims.
5. *Self-knowledge and alignment*—challenging one's perception or characterization of self with reference to personal strength and previous successes.
6. *Voice*—developing and practicing "scripts" that enable individuals to speak out and confront conflict about values or ethics.
7. *Reasons and rationalizations*—anticipating the reaction of those with whom we disagree and developing effective and relevant responses.

Costs of Inadequate Sleep

Kessler and Walsh (2011) estimate that insomnia costs the average US worker 11.3 days or $2,250 in lost productivity annually. The national cost is $63.2 billion. These figures are based on a survey of 7,428 employees who were asked about their sleep habits and work performance. Twenty-three percent of the respondents were deemed to have insomnia.

Companies Having a Higher Purpose

About eight years ago, Susan and I were attending a conference in Granada, Spain and remember walking on the first day there from our hotel to the conference venue. En route we passed a large ad for Dove soap which featured four women, not the Victoria Secrets model types wearing skimpy underwear, but rather typical women, a bit plump, wearing what as a man I would guess to be more comfortable underwear. We commented on this immediately. Little would I know that a few days ago (March 13, 2012) I saw another Dove ad with more women in a story about successful firms, their success being based on having a higher purpose. Stengel (2012), using company examples, shows how companies having a higher purpose or ideals engage both employees and consumers; these companies stand for something compelling. He observed 50 brands (companies) that were performing well above average in 2006. Their core ideals fell into five categories.

1. *Eliciting joy*—brand activates happiness, wonder and limitless possibilities.
2. *Enabling connections*—helped people connect with each other, and the world, in meaningful ways.
3. *Inspiring experimentation*—helped people explore new horizons and have new experiences.
4. *Evoking pride*—gave people a feeling of increased confidence, strength, security and vitality.
5. *Impacting society*—challenged the status quo, and changed or redefined business categories. The Dove ad that we saw redefined "real beauty," challenging the status quo.

Organizations need to look at their brand and products and see which of these five ideals best fits. Successful organizations try to make a difference in people's lives.

Hamel (2012) identifies five crucial issues facing organizations today: values, innovation, adaptability, passion and organizational ideology. Passion is more likely to exist in organizations having a higher purpose. In addition, values supporting stewardship, benefitting clients and society instead of greed, morally questionable acts and personal gain, are likely to increase both innovation and passion.

Employee Wellness Programs

A study of police in the UK found that 44 percent were overweight, 14 percent were obese and 1 percent morbidly obese (Allick, 2012). Recruits undergo a fitness test before entering policing, but are never again retested. The study recommended annual fitness testing, and pay reductions for officers who fail the test three years in a row.

As stated above, we believe that healthy employees are a major factor in creating healthy organizations. Reducing the impact of human frailties on the workplace and levels of organizational toxicity contribute to both.

An increasingly common intervention in organizations involves the development of employee wellness programs. Employee wellness programs have been found to have significant benefits to employees and employing organizations. The development of corporate wellness programs is supportive of efforts in the recently emerging field of occupational health psychology to create workplaces that promote and maintain healthy lifestyles and high levels of both emotional and physical well-being.

Benefits include the following;

- decreased health care and health insurance costs;
- more satisfied employees;
- healthier employees;
- reduced absenteeism;
- increased productivity;
- increased employee commitment and loyalty;
- reduced presenteeism.

Employees reported less tobacco use, less sedentary lifestyles, lower blood pressures, lower cholesterol levels and weight loss. Other studies indicated higher morale, higher job satisfaction, greater work productivity, greater energy levels, higher levels of physical fitness, more work–life balance, better stress management approaches and more attention at work.

A corporate wellness program includes many of the following: a health wellness newsletter, health and wellness handouts, annual flu vaccinations, health risk assessments, employee biometric assessments (for example, cholesterol, blood pressure, flexibility, body mass index), tobacco cessation seminars. nutrition education seminars, stress management sessions, disorder management programs, targeted intervention education (cholesterol, high blood pressure, diabetes, nutrition), work–life integration sessions, employee assistance programs, wellness trainers and heath coaches.

Berry, Mirabito and Baun (2010) identified six factors to be critical to the success of a corporate wellness program:

- engaged leadership at many levels;
- linking the corporate wellness initiative with the organization's identity and objectives;
- a program focus that was broad, relevant and of high quality;
- easy and wide accessibility;
- partnership with both internal and external stakeholders;
- effective communication.

A survey conducted in the Chicago area by Aon Hewitt and Rush Health of 361 organizations found that an increasing number of organizations have launched corporate wellness programs, targeting lifestyle habits to improve the health of their employees. Employers increasingly tie incentives to health screening results, reporting improved health outcomes. Wellness initiatives are being undertaken to boost productivity and reduce indirect medical costs. Wellness activities included risk identification tools such as health risk assessments, questionnaires and screenings for blood pressure and cholesterol; behavior modification programs involving coaching, smoking cessation, weight management and nutrition programs; initiating group walking programs; a larger selection of healthy eating options in their cafeterias; and monitoring of outcomes such as participation levels and attrition, satisfaction, changes in health behaviors and outcomes.

Eighty-one percent of organizations addressed lifestyle habits such as physical activity, smoking and weight management initiatives. Among specific conditions, a focus on preventing or controlling diabetes was most common with 72 percent of organizations addressing this, followed by high blood pressure, heart disease and obesity. Ninety-five percent of responding organizations targeted at least one lifestyle habit with 81 percent addressing at least one specific health condition (40 percent of the responding organizations offered incentives for taking part and completing lifestyle modification programs such as stopping smoking or losing weight).

Lowe (2011) suggests that integrating health promotion efforts, employee wellness programs and cultural change initiatives targeting at increasing workplace vibrancy can achieve both healthy employees and successful organizations.

Supporting Women's Career Advancement

Organizations today are facing a "war for talent" (Michaels, Handfield-Jones & Axelrod, 2001). Advancing qualified women into responsible and higher-level jobs has become a key business issue; organizations and society in general cannot to waste the education and talents of half the population. Yet though more women have obtained the necessary work experiences, and more women than men graduate for particular university programs, the number of women at senior organizational levels continues to remain small with little change from year to year. It is still a novelty when a women is appointed to a major organizational position (Davidson & Burke, 2011). We know a lot about the barriers faced in developing successful careers (Catalyst, 1998; Vinnicombe, Burke, Moore & Blake-Beard, 2012). These include: bias and discrimination, sexual harassment, difficulties in working long hours, perceived unwillingness to relocate, greater responsibility for home and family functioning, and working in masculine organizational cultures.

We have developed a better understanding of what organizations need to do to support women's career advancement. Most of this knowledge is based on organizational efforts undertaken in North America, the UK and Scandinavia; in most other countries, organizations are doing little or nothing in this regard.

First, several types of work experiences have been shown to be associated with women's career satisfaction and advancement (Burke 2002). These include:

- *Particular work experiences*—support and encouragement by one's organization, access to training and development opportunities, feeling accepted by one's organization, and the absence of tension from overload and ambiguity from being a woman.
- *Developmental jobs*—challenge, receiving feedback, setting stretch goals and having bottom-line responsibilities.
- *Developmental relationships*—mentoring, networking.
- *Alternative work arrangements*—flexible work hours, teleworking, reduced work loads, compressed work week.

Although interest in advancing women is increasing, tangible progress has been slow. Many senior executives only pay lip service to this goal. And companies introduce isolated initiatives (for example, gender awareness training, mentoring) without examining their existing organizational cultures. Thus, organizations, to be successful, are now introducing organization-wide change efforts. Wittenberg-Cox and Maitland (2008) suggest the following elements of an initiative to build "gender bilingualism:"

- senior management must be convinced that this is a key business issue;
- training needs to offered to senior managers to be inclusive of men and women and fluent in the differences between women and men—through awareness training, mentoring, and coaching;
- empowering women to succeed by identifying messages in organizational culture, organizational politics, and the criteria used in executive decision making about careers, promotions and development;
- removing biases in recruitment, pay, the identification of high-potential managers and professionals, succession planning, and performance evaluation.

The retention of women would be increased by:

- acknowledging the loss of women and determining the size and costs of this loss;
- determining the reasons why this occurs, and comparing these reasons for both men and women;
- acknowledging potential difference in men's and women's career paths;
- recognizing and acknowledging the role of the organization's structure, culture and systems in this process;
- introducing changes that address the causes of these leaks.

Increases in the promotion of women would be achieved through:

- identifying the level in the organization at which the numbers/percentages of women begins to drop;
- determining the reasons for this drop;
- identifying the leadership profile desired in the future and review performance appraisal systems to ensure these can be achieved;
- setting targets for women in leadership development programs, on lists of high potentials and on succession planning lists;
- holding mangers accountable for developing and promoting women;
- measuring progress in the various business departments to identify obstacles and support progress.

Catalyst (1998) identified several characteristics of successful organizational change efforts that supported women's career advancement. These were:

- having a strong foundation—linking motivation and reasons for initiating change to business results and performance;
- guaranteeing support from the highest levels in the organization;
- developing a clear communication plan linking organizational change efforts to business needs;
- developing measures to assess results and progress;
- taking a long-range view;
- increasing support for the initiative through education and training;

- holding mangers accountable;
- celebrating small wins.

Improving Work–life Integration

Managerial and professional men and women are now working longer hours in many countries, for a variety of reasons (Hewlett & Luce, 2006) As a result, more men and women have become concerned about the effects of these long hours on their own well-being, their families, their work satisfaction and their work performance (Burke, 2006 ; Burke & Cooper, 2008). Work–life concerns apply similarly to both men and women.

Organizations need to be interested in work–life integration since work–life conflict has been shown to be associated with adverse individual and organizational outcomes (Byron, 2005; Michel, Kotrba, Mitchelson, Clark & Baltes, 2011). The latter includes higher levels of absenteeism, turnover, dissatisfaction and diminished job performance.

Initially, addressing the consequences of work–family conflict emphasized individual coping and the use of social support from family, friends and co-workers—it was the employee's problem. But given the pervasiveness of work–family conflict, organizations are increasingly offering various formal programs to help their employees integrate their work and family lives. Some of these programs include: onsite childcare, flexible work schedules or flex-time, telecommuting, job sharing, part-time work, leaves of absence, sabbaticals and working the required hours in fewer days There is research evidence that these programs help (Baltes, Briggs, Huff, Wright & Neuman, 1999; Eby, Casper, Lockwood, Bordeaux & Brinely, 2005).

But many managers and professionals do not use these programs because of the "stigma" attached to their use; such employees are not committed (Judiesch & Lyness, 1999). In addition, mangers do not support the use of these programs (Kossek, Barber & Winters, 1999). Thus a supportive organizational culture is necessary for achieving positive benefits. A supportive organizational culture acknowledges and supports employees' personal and family situations affording flexibility, tolerance and support for personal and family needs and obligations (Allen, 2001; Thompson, Beauvais & Lyness, 1999). There is emerging evidence that the presence of such supportive organizational cultures is associated with more positive employee, family and work outcomes (Allen, 2001; Lapierre & Allen, 2006; Mesmer-Magnus & Viswesvaran, 2006; Thompson, Beauvais & Lyness, 1999).

Major and Morganson (2011) suggested three related important organization's initiatives that are supportive of work–life integration. These were: undertaking job analyses to identify characteristics of jobs that impede or enhance work–family integration, training supervisors in family supportive behaviors, and evaluating supervisors on the extent to which their subordinates achieve work–family integration.

Organizational Actions That Address Human Frailties and Toxicity

Here are some suggestions of what steps organizations might take to manage the fallout from human frailties and organizational toxicity:

- implement a more stringent approach to employee recruitment and selection;
- utilize employee orientation and employee early socialization programs to make all employees aware of expected attitudes and behaviors;
- reinforce organizational expectations in all employee training and development efforts;
- use performance appraisal information, performance monitoring, employee feedback and individual coaching to address potential concerns early;
- terminate employees found to be "guilty" of serious breaches in expected behaviors (for example, sexual harassment, theft);
- utilize audits of employee work experiences and dissatisfaction;
- offer lifestyle programs to support physical fitness and wellness efforts on the part of all employees;
- make employee assistance programs either on- or off-site available to employees with pressing needs.

In addition to these organization-focused initiatives, there are other efforts being undertaken in the broader society to address these risks. These include the following:

- more universities and colleges are now offering courses on personal and career development;
- more organizations are offering in-house programs on the support of talent;
- more individuals are aware of the costs of objective success (money, promotions);
- more individuals are interested in achieving a more satisfying life;
- individuals now have more options in the types of jobs and sectors in which they might work (green organizations, socially responsible organizations, non-profit organizations, small and medium-sized businesses);
- more women in the workforce (the percentages of women and of men now in the workforce have become equal in some developed countries) have required a rethinking of some common organizational assumptions;
- more lists of the "100 best places to work" have surfaced indicating what leading employers are providing to attract and retain talent;
- more organizations have become aware of the toll of a singular focus on work on both performance and well-being;
- more organizations are having to come to grips with a potential talent shortage over the next decade such that more employers will have to offer "rewards" that employees value if they (organizations) are to be successful;
- MBA and executive education programs more generally need to revamp the ways that leadership and ethics are "taught." The education system at lower levels (that is, younger students) need to focus more on character, courage and virtue.

We invite the readers of this volume to also look at their local newspapers, particularly those giving coverage to business, to identify examples on human frailties in the workplace and examples of toxicity in organizations.

This volume assembles current thinking on how workplaces can deal with human frailties to both reduce their occurrence and their costs and to make organizations less toxic in the process. Our objective is to increase both the health of organizations and the health of their employees. We believe that healthy individuals and healthy organizations go together. This collection focuses on what workplaces can do to reduce the prevalence and costs of human frailties and to reduce levels of organizational toxicity. Thus it complements the growing number of books that tackle human frailties; those some have called "self-help" books (for example, Caligiuri, 2010; Nash & Stevenson, 2004). We know how to create workplaces that develop effective leaders (Boyatzis, Smith & Blaize, 2006); that support the development and advancement of women and members of minority groups (for example, Catalyst, 1998; Dipboye, 2010; Jayne & Dipboye, 2004); that encourage work–family integration (for example, Hall & Harrington, 2007; Friedman, 2008; Kofodimos, 1993), that increase levels of courage and candor (Comer & Stephens, 2004), that support effective organizational restructurings and cost-cutting efforts without damaging people (Cascio, 2002; Ludy, 2009), that help individuals caught in job-person mismatches (Ibarra, 2002), that build safe workplaces (Burke, Clarke & Cooper, 2011; Cartwright, 2011; Clarke, 2010; Dekker, 2006; Taylor, 2010); that build ethical workplace cultures (Agle, 2005; Howard & Korver, 2008; Schabracq & Smit, 2007; Schwartz, 2011a, 2011b; Stevens, 2009); that increase levels of civility (Osatuke, Mohr, Ward, Moore, Dryenforth & Bellan, 2009); that contribute to the emotional and physical well-being of employees (Csikszentmihalyi, 2003; Fredrickson, 2009; Frost, 2004; Loehr & Schwartz, 2003; Schwartz, 2007; Seldman & Seldman, 2008); and achieve results (Amabile & Kramer, 2011; Boudreau, 2011; Fitz-Enz, 2011; Katzenbach & Khan, 2011; Subramony, 2009) and that build reputational capital (Jackson, 2004). We also can do a better job anticipating crises (Bazerman & Watkins, 2008; Bonner, 2011; Gerstein, 2008). The remainder of this collection illustrates initiatives taken by organizations to reduce levels of organizational toxicity.

Overview of the Contents

In Part I, Ronald Burke sets the stage for the chapters that follow by reviewing important concepts and contributions and connecting this volume with others in the Gower Series on Psychological, Behavioral and Social Risk in Organizations. He begins with examples of human frailties and organizational toxicity taken from various media reports and work and life experiences of employees more generally. Leadership emerges as a major factor in the prevalence and effects of both human frailties and toxic organizations. Toxic leadership, the toxic triangle, leader pathologies and "dark side" personality traits are reviewed. Workplace incivility is then considered. Attention is devoted to ways of increasing employee voice in ethics and values and supporting both healthy individuals and healthy workplaces. He concludes with examples of organizational initiatives that tackle both human frailties and levels of organizational toxicity.

The four chapters in Part II highlight desirable individual and organizational outcomes, elements of both healthy individuals and healthy organizations. Arnold Bakker, Wido Oerlemans and Lieke Ten Brummelhuis review ways that individuals and organizations can foster work engagement. The concept of work engagement has received considerable academic interest and organizational support. Work engagement is viewed as a positive, active psychological state characterized by vigor, dedication and absorption. They begin by examining antecedents and outcomes of work engagement for both individuals and organizations. Then they consider aspects of the intervention process (for example, what are its goals, diagnosis, design of the intervention, implementation and evaluation of the intervention). They identified seven possible interventions with potential to foster work engagement. These were: the Job Demands Resources model, job crafting, psychological capital, strengths-based approaches, new ways of working initiatives and work–life support programs. Each of these interventions have been shown to increase levels of work engagement.

Eva Demerouti and Clive Fullagar begin by reviewing the history of the concept of flow going back to Csikszentmihalyi's work in the early 1960s. He observed that people did things for intrinsic reasons. Only recently has attention been devoted to flow at work. Flow at work embodies absorption, enjoyment and intrinsic motivation. The experience of flow varies depending on the nature of the situation and the task being performed. Flow, however, also has some trait like properties (for example, achievement motivation). Preconditions of flow include: challenge–skill balance, goal clarity and feedback. Certain job characteristics facilitate flow as well (for example, skill variety, autonomy) Job resources also support flow (for example, social support, supervisory coaching). Flow, in turn, influences levels of organizational, job and personal resources of the individual. Flow is associated with a variety of consequences: positive emotions and higher levels of performance. They offer five interventions that organizations can initiate to enhance the experience of flow: high challenge–high skill interventions, providing job resources, job crafting, goal setting and increase positive emotional experiences of employees while at work.

Adrian Furnham considers passion in organizations. Passion is rarely examined in work psychology textbooks. This is beginning to change with the emergence and growth of positive psychology and positive organizational scholarship. He begins by reviewing research on related concepts such as intrinsic motivation, fun, zest and thriving. He then considers the research program undertaken by Vallerand on the psychology of passion. Vallerand distinguishes healthy harmonious passion from unhealthy obsessive passion. Passion is revealed at work by high levels of energy and vigor, the experience of flow, happiness and an emphasis on strengths and virtues instead of personal weaknesses. He concludes with some thoughts of fostering passion at work. These include the use of stretching goals, the use of novelty and stimulating questioning, turning work into play, encouraging co-operation and celebrating employee accomplishments. Management style and philosophy are central to all of these proposals.

Fred Walumbwa and Amanda Christensen highlight the importance of social capital, the sum of goodwill and resources available to individuals and teams from their social networks. Social capital enhances both individual and organizational health and functioning. They review several dimensions of social capital: structural, cognitive and relational. They summarize the evolution of social capital research as well. Though the basic ideas in this evolution have remained fairly constant, various perspectives on social capital were noted. They show how structural, cognitive and relational social capital explain individual and organizational phenomena. They conclude with practical implications for managers. Managers can encourage employees to cultivate and maintain their social networks, managers can join with their team members in social activities, managers can permit their employees to engage in "water cooler" time during their work days, and support the building of relationships across work teams.

The chapters in Part II focus on individual resources, individual differences that enhance health and well-being. Christina Nerstad, Glyn Roberts and Astrid Richardsen, using Achievement Goal Theory (AGT), look at person–situation dynamics and individual well-being at work. AGT is a motivational theory that takes individual goals and the organizational context into account. Individuals can be mastery or performance-oriented, with mastery orientation being more strongly related to actual performance. The organization's motivational climate reflects individual perceptions of criteria of success or failure represented by policies, procedures and practices in the work environment. In addition, mastery-oriented individuals have been shown to be at lower risk of developing burnout symptoms and have higher levels of work engagement. In a longitudinal study of 1,081 Norwegian engineers and technologists, they found that motivational climates influenced individual goal orientations, specifically mastery, to a greater extent than it supported a performance orientation. And a mastery orientation was related to job performance. In additions, motivational climate was a stronger predictor of both burnout and engagement than were individual motivational orientations. Mastery orientations were associated with both burnout and engagement levels, in opposite directions. Mastery climate may also serve as buffer against burnout. Organizations need to create working conditions in which employees can develop their mastery orientations. Possible initiatives include developing meaningful and interesting jobs, allowing employees opportunities to make choices and participate in decision making, offering rewards that support, not bribe, achievement, providing employee feedback on mastery, creativity and effort, and allowing employees the time needed to develop these skills.

Richard Boyatzis considers the role of Positive Emotional Attractors (PEAs) and Negative Emotional Attractors (NEAs), forces for good and for evil, in the behaviors of individuals, work teams, leaders and organizations. Both PEA and NEA exist within each of us and in our teams and organizations. He first describes PEA and NEA and their consequences for emotions, attitudes and behavior. Both PEA and NEA have their bases in human biology. PEA and NEA reflect two basic needs: thriving and surviving, thus both are needed. Ideally PEA and NEA should be balanced. Both PEA and NEA are contagious and spread to others. Boyatzis lays out the benefits of PEA and identifies four factors in its arousal: creating a shared vision or purpose, expressing compassion, combining a shared vision with a positive mood, and playfulness. Although NEA is needed, the best balance is when PEA is emphasized over NEA: NEA resembles individual and organizational toxicity. This state produces healthy individuals and healthy organizations.

Roy Lubit examines narcissism in the workplace; there is evidence that narcissism has increased in individuals over the past two decades. Narcissists are arrogant, overconfident, prone to excessive risk taking and willing to use others to further their own aspirations. Yet narcissists are able to successfully climb corporate ladders despite the damage they do to people and their organizations. Lubit begins by defining narcissism and how narcissists advance in their workplaces. Narcissism is more than high self-esteem. They succeed because others take their confidence for competence, and they are good at organizational politics. Over time, however, narcissists do damage to staff, resulting in low morale, high turnover and poor decisions resulting in the eventual undoing of narcissists. He then addresses what individuals can do to cope with their own narcissism (for example, understanding the downside of narcissism, identifying particular narcissistic behaviors that damage important outcomes, why putting work ahead of self and family is problematic). He then considers what organizations can do, the most important action being to avoid hiring and promoting them. This requires a more sophisticated approach to selection and appraisal. Irreplaceable narcissistic mangers need to be kept away for subordinates who they can damage, and be monitored, given feedback, and given coaching by consultants or executive coaches. Replaceable mangers should be confronted, given help and opportunities to change;

if they do not change they should be terminated. Individuals with narcissistic bosses should avoid them as much as possible, avoid confronting them, be tactful, document their negative behaviors, and if things do not get better, move to another position. Individuals with narcissistic peers and narcissistic subordinates should "watch their backs," take credit for legitimate work accomplishments, ignore their boasting and make sure your superior knows what you are doing and why.

Part IV examines organizational resources supportive of individual and organizational health. Jill Flint-Taylor and Ivan Robertson review current trends in both research and practice in organizations' approaches to assessment, selection and development. They focus on three overlapping issues: ensuring that employees are prepared for current and future roles; that employees have positive effects on organizational health and performance; and that leaders have positive effects on their employees' health and performance and on the teams they lead. The first issue emphasizes person–job fit, with attention devoted to assessment and development needs. They consider competencies, emotional intelligence, resilience and positive emotions. They then examine employee contributions in terms of work engagement, counter-productive work behavior, work attitudes and organizational citizenship behaviors. This is followed by a consideration of leader impact on their teams and organizations. They review a number of methods for assessing competencies and behaviors such as measures of personality, attitudes and values, situational judgments, competence-based interviews and self assessments. In addition, development interventions to strengthen person–job fit are also included (for example, resilience, engagement) .The identify a gap between research and practice in these areas and see that both researchers and practitioners hold responsibility for it.

Paul Fairlie examines the role of meaningful work on employee well-being. He begins by defining meaningful work as "job and other workplace characteristics that facilitate the attainment or maintenance of one or more dimensions of meaning." He developed the Meaningful Work Inventory (MWI) to measure eight global work characteristics under four broader facets: self-actualizing work, social impact, personal accomplishment and career advancement. He reports findings from three studies, the first two supporting the development of the MWI. The first study identified significant relationships between individual dimensions of meaningful work with depression or anxiety symptoms. The second study reported significant correlations between MWI dimensions and physical and mental health days off work. These two studies yielded the final version of the MWI which was then used in the third study as a predictor of work engagement, burnout, depression, stress and anxiety. In regression analyses, MWI scores accounted for a significant amount of explained variance in work engagement, emotional exhaustion and depression. He concludes with practical implications. First, meaningful work can be measured using employee surveys and discussed. Second, employees can be made aware of those meaningful work dimensions they currently experience. Third, supervisory training can be used to increase behaviors likely to be associated with higher levels of meaningful work. Fourth, employees can participate in career development workshops to help them achieve their work and career goals, since career advancement is one element of meaningful work.

Robert Dipboye, Barbara Fritzsche and Lindsay Dhanani consider the relationship of workplace discrimination and employee health, offering powerful employee vignettes of their experiences. These individuals pursued court cases against their employers and won financial settlements. Organizations should be interested in addressing workplace discrimination for reasons other than to avoid financial costs. Discrimination can damage the health and well-being of employees. They review research showing that discrimination based on gender, race and sexual orientation has negative psychological and physical health consequences. Even subtle discrimination has negative effects; it doesn't have to be blatant to be damaging. The experience of workplace discrimination increases levels of individual stress which, in turn, diminishes health and well-being. Individuals can cope, however, with discrimination, and adaptive coping has been shown to reduce the negative effects of discrimination. Social support can also prove useful. It makes more sense however to address the work environment and they describe interventions targeted at the perpetrators, the victims and the organizational environment itself. They identify characteristics of interventions found to have value in addressing workplace discrimination.

Vicki Magley, Louise Fitzgerald, Jan Salisbury, Fritz Drasgow and Michael Zickar review how training interventions can reduce the incidence of sexual harassment in organizations. Sexual harassment training is rarely evaluated. They begin by discussing sexual harassment training importance and factors associated with interest in these efforts. Sexual harassment training efforts address their goals in a variety of ways such as communication and sensitization to the costs of sexual harassment. They then consider the few previous evaluations of sexual harassment training concluding that research shortcomings limit their overall usefulness. They emphasize the value of both research design and having realistic goals in evaluation efforts. They describe the evaluation of two organization's sexual harassment training efforts in some detail. In both, pre- and post-intervention training data were collected. Elements of the training programs are outlined as well. Control groups were also employed resulting in a four-group design. Women were found to view their organizations as more tolerant of sexual harassment than were men, and women saw harassment as a more serious problem than did men. Interestingly, only small percentages of both women and men thought the training would change behavior or reduce sexual harassment. These findings, and others they report, highlight how complex and difficult it is to bring about widespread organizational change. Their results also indicate that training is only one part, and likely a small part, of a successful intervention. Training is a necessary but not sufficient initiative to bring about desired changes. Organizations need to be ready and open to change and addressing the cynicism of previously unsuccessful change initiatives needs to be addressed.

Amanda Griffiths, Alex Knight and Nor Diana Mohd Mahudin consider how healthy organizations can address an aging workforce. A shortage of skilled workers makes the retention of older employees a key business issue. More employees will choose to work longer. The quality of one's working life impacts health and well-being during one's working life as well as following retirement. Poor quality work (low autonomy, long working hours and overtime) influence both retirement and intention to retire decisions.

Job stress also affects these decisions, though older employees tend to report lower levels of stress than do middle-aged employees. This finding, however, may reflect the fact that older employees are the "survivors" and likely to be healthier. Older employees report difficulties with high physical demands, time pressures and shiftwork, as well as poor supervision, organizational politics and low levels of social support. They illustrate, using BT, a large communications service provider in the UK, a set of policies supportive of older employees. They conclude with a list of policies and programs consistent with the needs of older employees. These include: adequate rest breaks, reducing hours worked, work at home options, opportunities of development, a respectful workplace culture and flexible options on retirement.

Sharon Clarke, Sara Guediri and Elinor O'Connor review the latest thinking and research evidence for creating a sage and health work environment. Accidents, whether in mining, construction, trucking and health care, continue to be a daily occurrence. Accident rates however have fallen but at increasingly slower rates. The concept of "safety climate" has been shown to be associated with better safety behaviors and outcomes. In addition, workplace stress has also been associated with more workplace accidents. The authors also consider possible antecedents of safety climate. Antecedents have included leadership style, quality of leader-employee relationship, trust in leaders and co-worker relationships. Employee satisfaction, belongingness and self-determination were associated with better safety behaviors and outcomes. They conclude with an overview of interventions and recommendations for organizations.

Mark Schwartz writes that an ethical corporate culture has at least two inter-related foundational elements: an explicit set of core values and an ethical tone set by senior leadership. He describes efforts by a large Canadian financial organization to inculcate values-based leadership based on a set of core ethical values following several embarrassing scandals and negative publicity. Beginning with a general definition of corporate culture, Schwartz then defines an "ethical" corporate culture. Ethical corporate cultures lead to ethical behaviors which in turn lead to financial performance. He describes his work with this organization that desired to instill ethical core values throughout the organization. Senior leadership identified three core values: trust, teamwork and accountability. Schwartz developed and delivered a Leadership Workshop Seminar to over 600 of the firm's most senior executives. This workshop was a useful start to embedding ethical core (and other) values in the firm's policies, practices and processes. But some participants remained cynical about this exercise. Schwartz indicates the activities in the workshop and some of the important learnings that were achieved.

Finally, Fikry Issac and Scott Ratzan describe the corporate wellness program developed at Johnson and Johnson. They conclude that for every dollar invested in wellness they see a return of about $4 in reduced health care costs, lower levels of absenteeism and higher productivity. They stress helping employees and their families obtain a greater sense of personal well-being and fulfillment, including disease prevention. Four beliefs underlie their efforts: health includes well-being, promotion of prevention and engagement worldwide, committing to a culture of health, and that investments in people intersects with their investments in their jobs. They provide specific examples under each of the four beliefs. Some examples include: increasing health literacy of employees by providing resources and information so they can gain greater control of their lives; taking an active role in promoting prevention and engagement in international settings; providing financial rewards to employees making health improvements; supporting and paying for employee participation in Weight Watchers, making pedometers available, and creating tobacco-free workplaces; belief that employee health leads to business health; evaluating outcomes; and encouraging "health champions' who serve as healthy examples.

References

Adebowale, V., & Reed, S. (2010) Case studies on substance abuse in the workplace. In R. J Burke & C. L. Cooper (eds) *Risky Business. Psychological, Social and Financial Costs of High Risk Behavior in Organizations*. Farnham: Gower. pp. 155–175.

Agle, B. (2005) Somebody I look up to: ethical role models in organizations. *Organizational Dynamics*, 5, 313–330.

Albion, M. (2000) *Making a Life, Making a Living: Reclaiming Your Purpose and Passion in Business and in Life*. New York: Warner Books

Albrecht, C. C., Sanders, M. L., Holland, D. V., & Albrecht, C. (2011) The debilitating effects of fraud in organizations. In R. J. Burke, E.C. Tomlinson & C. L. Cooper (eds) *Crime and Corruption in Organizations: Why It Occurs and What to Do About It*. Farnham: Gower. pp. 163–186.

Allen, T. D. (2001) Family-supportive work environments: the role of organization perceptions. *Journal of Vocational Behavior*, 58, 414–435.

Allen, T. D., Johnson, H.-A. M., Xu, X., Bioga, A., Rodopman, O. B., & Ottinot, R. C. (2009) Mentoring and protégé narcissistic entitlement. *Journal of Career Development*, 35, 385–405.

Allick, C. (2012) Beefy British bobbies may face pay cuts: government report urges annual fitness test. *Toronto Star*, March 17, A23.

Amabile, T. M., & Kramer, S. J. (2011) *The Progress Principle: Using Small Wins to Ignite Joy, Engagement, and Creativity at Work*. Boston, MA: Harvard Business School Press.

Anand, V., Ellstrand. A. Rajagopalan, A., & Joshi, M. (2009) Organizational responses to allegations of corporate corruption. In R. J. Burke & C. L. Cooper (eds) *Research Companion to Corruption in Organizations*. Chichester: Edward Elgar. pp. 217–239.

Argyris, C. (1993) *Knowledge for Action: A Guide to Overcoming Barriers to Organizational Change*. San Francisco, CA: Jossey Bass.

Argyris, C., & Schon, D. (1996) *Organizational Learning II: Theory, Method and Practice*. Reading, MA: Addison Wesley.

Ashforth, B. (1994) Petty tyranny in organizations. *Human Relations*, 47, 755–778.

Ashforth, B. (1997) Petty tyranny in organizations: a preliminary examination of antecedents and consequences. *Canadian Journal of Administrative Sciences*, 14, 216–240.

Babiak, P. (1993) When psychopaths go to work: a case study of an industrial psychopath. *Applied Psychology*, 44, 171–188l

Babiak, P., & Hare, R. (2006) *Snakes in Suits*. New York: Regan Books.

Bakan, J. (2004) *The Corporation: The Pathological Pursuit of Profits and Power*. New York: Free Press.

Baker, D. (2010a) *False Profits: Recovering from the Bubble Economy*. San Francisco, CA: Berrett-Koehler.

Baker, D. (2010b) *Plunder and Blunder. The Rise and Fall of the Bubble Economy*. San Francisco, CA: Berrett-Koehler.

Baltes, B. B., Briggs, T. E., Huff, J. W., Wright, T. A., & Neuman, G. A. (1999) Flexible and compressed work week schedules: a meta-analysis of their effects on work-related criteria. *Journal of Applied Psychology*, 84, 496–513.

Barling, J., Kelloway, E. K., & Frone, M. K. R. (2005) *Handbook of Work Stress*. Thousand Oaks, CA: Sage.

Barnes, C. M., Schaubroeck, J, Huth, M., & Ghumman, S. (2011) Lack of sleep and unethical conduct. *Organizational Behavior and Human Decision Processes*. 115, 160–180.

Baron-Cohen, S. (2011) *Zero Degrees of Empathy: A New Theory of Human Cruelty*. London: Allen Lane.

Barreto, M., Ryan, M. K., & Schmitt, M. T. (2009) *The Glass Ceiling in the 21st Century: Understanding Barriers to Gender Equality*. Washington, DC: American Psychological Association.

Bassi, L., Frauenheim, E., McMurrer, D., & Costello, L. (2011) *Good Company: Business Success in the Worthiness Era*. San Francisco, CA: Berret-Koehler.

Bazerman, M. H., & Tenbrunsel, A. E. (2011) *Blind Spots: Why We Fail to Do What's Right and What to Do About It*. Princeton, NJ: Princeton University Press.

Bazerman, M. H., & Watkins, M. D. (2008) *Predictable Surprises*. Boston, MA: Harvard Business School Press.

Belfort, J. (2007) *The Wolf of Wall Street*. New York: Bantam Books.

Belfort, J. (2010) *Catching the Wolf of Wall Street*. New York: Bantam Books.

Bennett, A. D., & Randolph, S. E. (2011) Is everyone disabled under the ADA? An analysis of the recent amendments and guidelines for employers. *Employee Relations Law Journal*, 36, 3–14.

Bergman, J. Z., Westerman, J. W., & Daly, J. P. (2010) Narcissism in management education. *Academy of Management Learning and Education*, 9, 119–131.

Berry, L. L., Mirabito, A. M., & Baun, W. B. (2010) What's the hard return on employee wellness programs? *Harvard Business Review*, 88, 104–112.

Bitti, M. T. (2011) Leadership matters. *National Post*, January 11, FP10.

Bogle, J. C. (2005) *The Battle for the Soul of Capitalism*. New Haven, CT: Yale University Press.

Bogle, J. C. (2009) *Enough: True Measures of Money, Business and Life*. New York: John Wiley.

Boivie, S., Lange, D., McDonald, M. L., & Westphal, J. (2011) Me or we: the effects of organizational identification on agency costs. *Academy of Management Journal*, 54, 561–576.

Bones, C. (2011) *The Cult of the Leader*. San Francisco, CA: Jossey-Bass.

Bonner, A. (2011) *An Ounce of Prevention*. Toronto: Sextant Publishing.

Boudreau, J. W. (2011) *Retooling HR: Using Proven Business Tools to Make Better Decisions about Talent*. Boston, MA: Harvard Business Press.

Boyatzis, R. E., & McKee, A. (2005) *Resonant Leadership: Renewing Your Self and Connecting with Others through Mindfulness, Hope and Compassion*. Boston, MA: Harvard Business School Press.

Boyatzis, R. E., Smith, M., & Blaize, N. (2006) Developing sustainable leaders through coaching and compassion. *Academy of Management Learning and Education*, 5, 8–24.

Bronson, P. (2005) *What Should I Do with My Life: The True Story of People Who Answered the Ultimate Question*. New York: Ballantine.

Burke, R. J. (2002) Career development of managerial women. In R. J. Burke & D. L. Nelson (eds) *Advancing Women's Careers*. Oxford: Blackwell. pp. 139–160.

Burke, R. J., (2006) *Research Companion to Corruption in Organizations*. Chichester: Edward Elgar.

Burke, R. J. (2009a) Corruption in organizations: causes, consequences and choices. In R. J. Burke & C. L. Cooper (eds) *Research Companion to Corruption in Organizations*. Chichester: Edward Elgar. pp. 1–32.

Burke, R. J. (2009b) Greed. In R. J., Burke & C. L. Cooper (eds) *Research Companion to Corruption in Organizations*. Chichester: Edward Elgar. pp. 33–59.

Burke, R. J. (2010a) Work hours, work intensity and work addiction: weighing the costs. In R. J. Burke & C. L. Cooper (eds) *Risky Business: Psychological, Social and Financial Costs of High Risk Behavior in Organizations*. Farnham: Gower. pp. 67–105.

Burke, R. J. (2010b) Human frailties and toxic organizations. In R. J. Burke & C. L. Cooper (eds.) *Risky Business: Psychological, Social and Financial Costs of High Risk Behavior in Organizations*. Farnham: Gower. pp. 3–64.

Burke, R. J. (2010c) Psychologically intimate, romantic, and sexually intimate relationships in the workplace. In R. J. Burke & C. L .Cooper (eds) *Risky Business: Psychological, Social and Financial Costs of High Risk Behavior in Organizations*. Farnham: Gower. pp. 205–237.

Burke, R. J. (2011) Show me the money. In R. J. Burke, E. C. Tomlinson & C, L. Cooper (eds) *Crime and Corruption in Organizations: Why it Occurs and What to Do about It*. Farnham: Gower. pp. 69–96.

Burke, R. J., Clarke S., & Cooper, C. L. (2011) *Occupational Health and Safety*. Farnham: Gower.

Burke, R. J., & Cooper, C. L. (2009) *Research Companion to Corruption in Organizations*. Chichester: Edward Elgar.

Burke, R. J., & Cooper, C. L. (2008) *The Long Work Hours Culture: Causes, Consequences and Choices*. Bingley: Emerald Publishing.

Burke, R. J., & Cooper, C. L. (2010) *Risky Business: Psychological, Social and Financial Costs of High Risk Behavior in Organizations*. Farnham: Gower.

Burke, R. J., Martin, G., & Cooper, C. L. (2011) Corporate Reputation: Managing Opportunities and Threats. Farnham: Gower.

Burke, R. J., & Mattis, M. C. (2007) *Women and Minorities in Science, Technology, Engineering and Mathematics: Upping the Numbers*. Chichester: Edward Elgar.

Burke, R. J., Tomlinson, E. C., & Cooper, C. L. (2011) Crime and Corruption in Organizations: Why it Occurs and What to Do about It. Farnham: Gower.

Byron, K. (2005) A meta-analytic review of work-family inerference and its antecedents. *Journal of Vocational Behavior*, 67, 169–198.

Caligiuri, P. (2010) *Get a Life, Not a Job. Do What You Love and Let Your Talents Work For You*. Upple Saddle River, NJ: FT Press.

Cameron, K. S., Dutton, J. E., & Quinn, R.E. (2003) *Positive Organizational Scholarship: Foundations of a New Discipline*. San Francisco, CA: Berrett-Koehler.

Campbell, W. K., & Foster, C. A. (2002) Narcissism and commitment in romantic relationships: an investment model analysis. *Personality and Social Psychology Bulletin*, 28, 484–495.

Campbell, W. K., Goodie, A. S., & Foster, J. D. (2004) Narcissism, confidence, and risk attitude. *Journal of Behavioral Decision Making*, 17, 297–311.

Cangemi, J. P., & Pfohl, W. (2009) Sociopaths in high places. *Organization Development Journal*, 27, 85–96.

Carnes, R. (2001) *Out of the Shadows: Understanding Sexual Addiction*. 3rd edition. Center City, MN: Hazelden.

Cartwright, S. (2010) Job demands, resources and psychological and physical well-being: critical factors which may make some jobs more stressful than others. In R. J. Burke & C. L. Cooper (eds) *Risky Business: Psychological, Social and Financial Costs of High Risk Behavior in Organizations*. Farnham: Gower. pp. 263–285.

Cascio, W. F. (2002) *Responsible Restructuring: Creative and Profitable Alternatives to Layoffs*. San Francisco, CA: Berrett-Koehler.

Catalyst (1998) *Advancing Women in Business: Best Practices from the Corporate Leaders*. San Francisco, CA: Jossey-Bass.

Ceci, S. J., & Williams, W. M. (2007) *Why Aren't More Women in Science? Top Researchers Debate the Evidence*. Washington, DC: American Psychological Association.

Charan, R., & Colvin, G. (1999) Why CEOs fail. *Fortune*, 139, 68–75.

Chatterjee, A., & Hambrick, D. C. (2007) It's all about me: narcissistic chief executive officers and their effects on company strategy and performance. *Administrative Science Quarterly*, 52, 351–386.

Clarke, S. (2010) Managing the risk of workplace accidents. In R. J. Burke & C. L. Cooper (eds) Risky Business: Psychological, Social and Financial Costs of High Risk Behavior in Organizations. Farnham: Gower. pp. 403–431.

Cloud, H. (2008) *The One-life Solutions: Reclaim your Personal Life While Achieving Greater Professional Success*. New York: Collins Business.

Comer, M. J., & Stephens, T. E. (2004) *Deception at Work: Investigating and Countering Lies and Fraud Strategies*. Farnham: Gower.

Conger, J. (1990) The dark side of leadership. *Organizational Dynamics*, 19, 44–55.

Cowen, A. P., & Marcel, J. J. (2011) Damaged goods: board decisions to dismiss reputationally compromised directors. *Academy of Management Journal*, 54, 509–527.

Csikszentmihalyi, M. (2003) *Good Business: Leadership, Flow, and the Making of Meaning*. New York: Viking.

Davidson, M. J., & Burke, R. J. (2011) *Women in Management Worldwide: Progress and Prospects*. Farnham: Gower.

Dekker, S. (2006) *The Field Guide to Understanding Human Error*. Aldershot: Ashgate.

Desai, S., Brief, A. & George, J. (2010) *When Executives Rake in Millions: Meanness in Organizations*. Paper presented at the 23rd Annual International Association of Conflict Management Conference, Boston, June.

Detert, J. R., & Edmondson, A. C. (2011) Implicit voice theories: taken-for-granted rules of self-censorship at work. *Academy of Management Journal*, 54, 461–488.

Diener, E., & Seligman, M. F. P. (2004) Beyond money: toward an economy of well-being. *Psychological Science in the Public Interest*, 5, 1–31

Dillon, P., & Cannon, C. M. (2010) *Circle of Greed: The Spectacular Rise and Fall of the Lawyer Who Brought Corporate America to its Knees*. New York: Broadway.

Dipboye, R. L. (2010) Discrimination as high risk behavior in the workplace. In R. J. Burke & C. L. Cooper (eds) *Risky Business: Psychological, Social and Financial Costs of High Risk Behavior in Organizations*. Farnham: Gower. pp. 177–203.

Dotlich, D. L., & Cairo, P. C. (2003) *Why CEOs Fail*. San Francisco, CA: Jossey-Bass.

Drago, R. W. (2007) *Striking a Balance: Work, Family, Life*. Boston, MA: Dollars & Sense.

Eby, L., Casper, W., Lockwood, A., Bordeaux, C., & Brinely, A. (2005) Work and family research in IO/OB: content analysis and review of the literature (1980–2002). *Journal of Vocational Behavior*, 66, 124–197.

Einarsen, S., Aasland, M. S., & Skogstad, A. (2010) The nature and outcomes of destructive leadership behavior in organizations. In R. J. Burke & C. L. Cooper (eds) *Risky Business: Psychological, Social and Financial Costs of High Risk Behavior in Organizations*. Farnham: Gower. Farnham: Gower. pp. 323–349.

Fatah, S. (2011) Sand against corruption inspires India. *Toronto Star*, August 18, A21.

Ferguson, M. J. (2011) You cannot leave it at the office: spillover and crossover of coworker incivility. *Journal of Organizational Behavior*, 33, 571–588.

Ferris, G. R., Zinko, R., Brouer, R. L., Buckley, M. R., & Harvey, M. G. (2007) Strategic bullying as a supplementary, balanced perspective on destructive leadership. *The Leadership Quarterly*, 18, 195–206.

Financial Post (2011) Lawsuit accuses Deere of sex bias in hiring, seeks class-action status. *Financial Post*, March 17, FP6.

Finkelstein, S. (2003) *Why Smart Executives Fail*. New York: Penguin

Fitz-Enz, J. (2011) *The New HR Analytics: Predicting the Economic Value of Your Company's Human Capital Investments*. New York: AMACOM.

Ford, D. (2008) *Why Good People Do Bad Things: How to Stop Being Your Own Worst Enemy*. New York: HarperCollins.

Fredrickson, B. (2009) *Positivity: Groundbreaking Research Reveals How to Embrace the Hidden Strength of Positive Emotions, Overcome Negativity, and Thrive*. New York: Crown.

Freeman, R. E., Moriarty, B., & Stewart, L. A. (2009) Ethical leadership. In R. J. Burke & C. L. Cooper (eds) *Research Companion to Corruption in Organizations*. Chichester: Edward Elgar. pp. 192–205.

Friedman, S. D. (2008) *Total Leadership: Be a Better Leader, Have a Richer Life*. Boston, MA: Harvard Business School Press.

Friedman, S. D., & Greenhaus, J. H. (2000) *Work and Family-allies or Enemies? What Happens when Business Professionals Confront Life Choices*. New York: Oxford University Press.

Friesen, J. (2011) Toronto law firms lack diversity: new report finds less than seven percent of high ranking legal professionals are visible minorities. *Globe and Mail*, June 8, A12.

Frost, P. J, (2004) Handling toxic emotions: new challenges for leaders and their organization. *Organizational Dynamics*, 33, 111–127.

Furnham, A. (2004) *The Incompetent Manager*. London: Whurr.

Furnham, A. (2007) Personality disorders and derailment at work: the paradoxical positive influence of pathology in the workplace. In J. Langan-Fox, C. L. Cooper & R. J. Klimoski (eds) *Research Companion to the Dysfunctional Workplace*. Chichester: Edward Elgar. pp. 22–39.

Gaines-Ross, L. (2010) Reputation warfare. *Harvard Business Review*, 88, 70–76.

Gandz. J., Crossan, M., & Seijts, G. (2010) *Leadership on Trial: A Manisfesto for Leadership Development*. London, ON: Richard Ivey School of Business.

Gentile, M. (2010a) *Giving Voice to Values: How to Speak Your Mind When You Know What's Right*. New Haven, CT: Yale University Press.

Gentile, M. (2010b) Turning values into action. *Stanford Social Innovation Review*, 8, 42–47.

Gentile, M., Piper, T. P., & Parks, S. (1993) *Can Ethics be Taught: Perspectives, Challenges and Approaches at Harvard Business School*. Boston, MA: Harvard Business School Press.

George, W. (2003) *Authentic Leadership: Rediscovering the Secrets to Creating Lasting Value*. San Francisco, CA: Jossey-Bass.

Gerstein, M. (2008) *Flirting with Disaster: Why Accidents are Rarely Accidental*. New York: Union Square Press.

Ghodse, H. (2005) *Addiction at Work: Tackling Drug Use and Misuse in the Workplace*. Aldershot: Gower.

Gibbs, N. (2011) Sex, lies, arrogance: what makes powerful men behave so badly? *Time Magazine*, May 19, 45–46.

Gino, F., Schweitzer, M. E.,. Mead, N. L., & Ariely, D. (2011) Unable to resist temptation: how self-control depletion promotes unethical behavior. *Organizational Behavior and Human Decision Processes*, 115, 191–203.

Glad, B. (2002) When tyrants go too far: malignant narcissism and absolute power. *Political Psychology*, 23, 20.

Glasbeek, H. (2002) *Wealth by Stealth: Corporate Crime, Corporate Law, and the Perversion of Democracy*. Toronto: Between the Lines.

Glasso, L., Vie, T. L., & Hoel, H. (2010) Bullying in the workplace. In R. J. Burke & C. L. Cooper (eds) *Risky Business: Psychological, Social and Financial Costs of High Risk Behavior in Organizations*. Farnham: Gower, pp. 351–373.

Globe and Mail (2011) Scandal over dubious surgery research rocks medical world. *Globe and Mail*, March 4, 2011. A17.

Griffin, S. P. (2011) Gaming the Game. The Story Behind the NBA Betting Scandal and the Gambler Who Made it Happen. Fort Lee, NJ: Barricade.

Hall, D. T., & Harrington, B. (2007) *Career Management and Work-life Integration: Using Self-assessment to Navigate Contemporary Careers*. Thousand Oaks, CA: Sage Publications.

Hamel, G. (2012) *What Matters Most*. San Francisco, CA: Jossey-Bass.

Hare, R. (1993) *Without Conscience: The Disturbing World of the Psychopaths Among Us*. New York: Simon & Schuster.

Harris, K. J., Kacmar, K. M., & Zivnuska, S. (2007) An investigation of abusive supervision as a predictor of performance and the meaning of work as a moderator of the relationship. *The Leadership Quarterly*, 18, 252–273.

Heffernan, M. (2011) *Wilful Blindness: Why We Ignore the Obvious at Our Peril*. Toronto: Doubleday Canada.

Henriques, D. (2011) *The Wizard of Lies: Bernie Madoff and the Death of Trust*. New York: Times Books.

Hewlett, S. A., & Luce, C. B. (2006) Extreme jobs: the dangerous allure of the 70 hour workweek. *Harvard Business Review*, December, 49–59.

Higgs, M. (2009) The good, the bad and the ugly: leadership and narcissism. *Journal of Change Management*, 9, 163–178.

Hill, P. W., & Youney, G. (1998) Adaptive and maladaptive narcissism among university faculty, clergy, politicians and librarians. *Current Psychology*, 17, 249–262.

Hochschild, A. R. (1997) *The Time Bind: When Work Becomes Home and Home Becomes Work*. New York: Metropolitan Books.

Hogan, R., & Hogan, J. (2001) Assessing leadership: a view from the dark side. *International Journal of Selection and Assessment*, 9, 40–51.

Holbrook, E. (2011) A decade of discrimination. *Risk Management*, 58, 18–19.

Hollis, J. (2007) *Why Good People Do Bad Things: Understanding Our Darker Selves*. New York: Gotham.

Howard, R. A., & Korver, C.D. (2008) *Ethics for the Real World: Creating a Personal Code to Guide Decisions in Work and Life*. Boston, MA: Harvard Business School Press.

Huffington, A. (2003) *Pigs at the Trough: How Corporate Greed and Political Corruption are Undermining America*. New York: Crown Publishers.

Ibarra, H,. (2002) How to stay stuck in the wrong career. *Harvard Business Review*, December, 40–47.

Immen, W. (2011a) Kicking bad habits for the good of your career. *Globe and Mail*, June 24, B15.

Immen, W. (2011b) Duking it out with bad managers: "Bad apples" often tolerated if they get results but they're headaches for human resources. *The Globe and Mail*, Report on Business, January 21, B14.

Jackson, K. T. (2004) *Building Reputational Capital: Strategies for Integrity and Fair Play that Improve the Bottom Line*. Oxford: Oxford University Press.

Jayne, M. E. A., & Dipboye, R. L. (2004) Leveraging diversity to improve business performance: research findings and recommendations for organizations. *Human Resource Management*, 43, 409–424.

Jordan-Meier, J. (2011) *The Four Stages of Highly Effective Crisis Management: How to Manage the Media in the Digital Age*. Boca Raton, FL: CRC Press.

Judge, T. A., & LePine, J. A. (2007) The bright and dark sides of personality: Implications for personnel selection in individual and team contexts. In. J. Langan-Fox, C. L. Cooper & R. J. Klimoski (eds) *Research Companion to the Dysfunctional Workplace*. Chichester: Edward Elgar. pp. 332–355.

Judge, T. A., LePine, J. A., & Rich, B. L. (2006) Loving yourself abundantly: relationship of the narcissistic personality to self and other perceptions of workplace deviance, leadership, and task and contextual performance. *Journal of Applied Psychology*, 91, 762–776.

Judge, T. A., Piccolo, R.F., & Kosalko, T. (2009) The bright and dark sides of leader traits: a review and theoretical extension of the leader trait paradigm. *The Leadership Quarterly*, 20, 855–875.

Judiesch, M. K., & Lyness, K. S. (1999) Left behind? The impact of leaves of absence on managers' career success. *Academy of Management Journal*, 42, 641–651.

Kaiser, R. B., & Hogan, R. (2007) The dark side of discretion: leader personality and organizational decline. In R. Hooijberg, J. Hunt, J. Antonakis, & K. Boal (eds) *Being There Even When You Are Not: Leading through Strategy, Systems and Structures. Monographs in Leadership and Management*. London: Elsevier. pp. 1177–1197.

Kasser, T. (2002) *The High Price of Materialism*. Cambridge, MA: MIT Press.

Katzenbach, J. R., & Kahn, Z. (2011) *Leading Outside the Lines*. San Francisco, CA: Jossey-Bass.

Kellerman, B. (2004) *Bad Leadership*. Boston, MA: Harvard Business School Press.

Kessler, R. C., Berglund, P. A., Coulouvrat, C., Hajak, G., Roth, T., Shahly, V., Shillington, J. J., & Walsh, J. K. (2011) Insomnia and the performance of US workers: results from the American Insomnia Survey. *Sleep*. 39, 1161–1171.

Kesterton, M. (2011) When teachers go bad. *Globe and Mail*, July 19, L7.

Kesterton, M. (2012) When scientists go bad. *Globe and Mail*, March 8, L7.

Kets de Vries, M. F. R. (1993) Leaders, Fools, and Impostors. San Francisco, CA: Jossey-Bass.

Kets de Vries, M. F. R. (2006) The spirit of despotism: understanding the tyrant within. *Human Relations*, 59, 195–220.

Kets de Vries, M. F. R. (2010) Thought leader interview. *Strategy and Business*, 59, 91–100.

Killinger, B. (1991) *Workaholics: The Respectable Addicts*. Toronto: Key Porter Books.

Kingston, A. (2011) Standing up to bad boys. *Maclean's*, June 13, 28–31.

Kofodimos, J. (1993) *Balancing Act: How Managers Can Integrate Successful Careers and Fulfilling Personal Lives*. San Francisco, CA: Jossey-Bass.

Korman, A. K., & Korman, R. (1980) *Career Success and Personal Failure*. Englewood Cliffs, NJ: Prentice Hall.

Kossek, E. E., Barber, A. E., & Winters, D. (1999) Using flexible schedules in the managerial world: the power of peers. *Human Resource Management Journal*, 38, 33–46.

Krugel, L. (2011) Niko fined $9.5M for Bangladeshi bribe. *Toronto Star*, June 25, B3.

Kusy, M., & Holloway, E. (2009) *Toxic Workplace! Managing Toxic Personalities and Their Systems of Power*. New York: John Wiley.

Kyrios, M., Nedeljkovic, M., Moulding, R., & Doron, G. (2007) Problems of employees with personality disorders: the exemplar of obsessive-compulsive personality disorder (OCPD). In J. Langan-Fox, C. L. Cooper & R. J. Klimoski (eds) *Research Companion to the Dysfunctional Workplace*. Chichester: Edward Elgar. pp. 40–57.

Lammers, J. & Stapel, D. A. (2009) How power influences moral thinking. *Journal of Personality and Social Psychology*, 97, 279–289.

Lammers, J., & Stapel, D. A. (2011) Power increases dehumanization. *Group Processes and Intergroup Relations*, 14, 113–126.

Lammers, J., Stapel, D. A., & Galinsky, A. D. (2010) Power increases hypocrisy: moralizing in reasoning, immorality in behavior. *Psychological Science*, 21, 737–744.

Lammers, J., Stoker, J. I., Jordan, J., Pollmann, M. M. H., & Stapel, D. A. (2011) Power increases infidelity among men and women. *Psychological Science*, 22, 1191–1197.

Langan-Fox, J., Cooper, C. L., & Klimoski, R. J. (2007) Research Companion to the Dysfunctional Workplace. Chichester: Edward Elgar.

Langan-Fox, J., & Sankey, M. (2007) Tyrants and workplace bullying. In J. Langan-Fox, C. L. Cooper & R. J. Klimoski (eds) *Research Companion to the Dysfunctional Workplace*. Chichester: Edward Elgar. pp. 58–74.

Lapierre, L. M., & Allen, T D. (2006) Work-supportive family, family-supportive supervision, use of organizational benefits, and problem focused coping: implications for work-family conflict and employee well-being. *Journal of Occupational Health Psychology*, 11, 169–181.

Lefkowitz, J. (2009) Individual and organizational antecedents of misconduct in organizations: what do we (believe that we) know, and on what bases do we (believe that we) know it? In R. J. Burke & C. L. Cooper (eds) *Research Companion to Corruption in Organizations*. Chichester: Edward Elgar. pp. 60–91.

Leiter, M. P., Laschinger, H. K. S., Day, A., Gurnham, M. E., & Latimer M. (2009) CREW: *Enhancing Mental Health through Workplace Civility*. Paper presented at the 4th Annual Canadian Congress for Research on Mental Health and Addictions in the Workplace.

Leonard, A. (2010) *The Story of Stuff: How Our Obsession with Stuff is Trashing the Planet, Our Communities, and Our Health—and a Vision for Change*. New York: Free Press.

Lester, D. (2011) Violence in the workplace. In R. J. Burke, S. E. Clarke, & C. L. Cooper (eds) *Occupational Health and Safety: Psychological and Behavioral Challenges*. Farnham: Gower. pp. 178–195.

Lewis, M. (1989) *Liars Poker*. New York: Norton.

Lewis, M. (2010) *The Big Short: Inside the Doomsday Machine*. New York: Norton.

Lipman-Blumen, J. (2005) *The Allure of Toxic Leaders: Why We Follow Destructive Bosses and Corrupt Politicians—and How We Can Survive Them*. Oxford: Oxford University Press.

Loehr, J., & Schwartz, T. (2003) *The Power of Full Engagement: Managing Energy, Not Time is the Key to High Performance and Personal Renewal*. New York: Free Press.

Lowe, G. (2011) *Creating Healthy Organizations: How Vibrant Workplaces Inspire Employees to Achieve Sustainable Success*. Toronto: University of Toronto Press.

Lubit, R.H. (2002) The long-term organizational impact of destructively narcissistic managers. *Academy of Management Executive*, 16, 127–138.

Lubit, R. H. (2004) *Coping with Toxic Managers, Subordinates and Other Difficult People*. Upper Saddle River, NJ: Prentice Hall.

Ludy, P. J., (2009) *Profit Building: Cutting Costs without Cutting People*. San Francisco, CA: Berrett-Koehler.

Maccoby, M. (2000) Narcissistic leaders: the incredible pros, the inevitable cons. *Harvard Business Review*, January–February, 4–12.

Maccoby, M. (2004) *The Productive Narcissist: The Promise and Peril of Visionary Leadership*. New York: Broadway Books.

Madrick, J. (2011) *Age of Greed: The Triumph of Finance and the Decline of America, 1970 to the Present*. New York: Knopf.

Magley, V. J., Bauerle, T. J., & Walsh, B. J. (2010) Sexual harassment in the workplace. In R. J. Burke & C. L. Cooper (eds) *Risky Business: Psychological, Social and Financial Costs of High Risk Behavior in Organizations*. Farnham: Gower. pp. 239–261.

Mainero, L. A., & Sullivan, S. E. (2006) *The Opt-out Revolution: Why People are Leaving Companies to Create Kaleidoscope Careers*. Mountain View, CA: Davies-Black.

Major, D. A., & Morganson, V. J. (2011) Applying industrial-organizational psychology to help organizations and individuals balance work and family. *Industrial and Organizational Psychology*, 4, 398–401.

Martin, R. (2011) *Fixing the Game*. Boston, MA: Harvard Business Review Press.

McKeon, S., & Cain, M. (2011) Cleared for takeoff? CEO personal risk-taking and corporate policies. *Social Science Research Network*, May, 1.

McLean, B., & Elkind, P. (2005) *The Smartest Guys in the Room*. New York: Penguin.

Mesmer-Magnus, J. R., & Viswesvaran, C. (2006) How family-friendly work environments affect work-family conflict: a meta-analytic examination. *Journal of Labor Research*, 27, 555–574.

Michaels, E., Handfield-Jones, H., & Axelrod, B. (2001) *The War for Talent*. Boston, MA: Harvard Business School Press.

Michaelson, A. (2009) *The Foreclosure of America: The Inside Story of the Rise and Fall of Countrywide Home and the Mortgage Crisis, and Then Default of the American Dream*. New York: Berkeley Books.

Michel, J. S., Kotrba, L. M., Mitchelson, J. K., Clark, M. A., & Baltes, B. B. (2011) Antecedents of work-family conflict: a meta-analytic review. *Journal of Organizational Behavior*, 32, 689–725.

Miller, J. A., & Shales, T. (2011) *These Guys Have All the Fun: Inside the World of ESPN*. New York: Little, Brown and Company.

Milliken, F. J., Morrison, E. W., & Hewlin, P. F. (2003) An exploratory study of employee silence: issues that employees don't communicate upward and why. *Journal of Management Studies*, 40, 1453–1476.

Moore, M. J. (2011) JPMorgan pays to settle SEC's CDO probe. *Globe and Mail*, June 22, B13.

Morrison, E. W., & Milliken, F. J. (2000) Organizational silence: a barrier to change and development in a pluralistic world. *Academy of Management Review*, 25, 706–725.

Namie, G.& Namie, R. (2011) *The Bully-free Workplace: Stop Jerks, Weasels and Snakes from Killing your Organization*. New York: John Wiley.

Nash, L., & Stevenson, H. (2004) *Just Enough: Tools for Creating Success in Your Work and Life*. New York: John Wiley.

National Post (2011a) John Galliano trial—defending an admiration for Adolf Hitler might be a toughie. *National Post*, March 4, 2011, AL3.

National Post (2011b) German minister resigns over plagiarism. *National Post*, March 2, A9.

Naylor, R. T. (2011) *Crass Struggle: Greed, Glitz, and Gluttony in a Wanna-have World*. Montreal: McGill-Queens University Press.

Offerman, L. (2004) When followers become toxic. *Harvard Business Review*, 84, 454–460.

O'Neill, J. R. (2004) *The Paradox of Success: When Winning at Work Means Losing at Life*. New York: Tarcher/Penguin.

Osatuke, K., Mohr, D., Ward, C., Moore, S. C., Dryenforth, S., & Bellan, C. (2009) Civility, respect, engagement in the workplace (CREW). *Journal of Applied Behavioral Science*, 45, 384–410.

Padilla, A., Hogan, R., & Kaiser, R. B. (2007) The toxic triangle: destructive leaders, susceptible followers, and conducive environments. *The Leadership Quarterly*, 18, 176–194.

Parker, G. (2011) A dirty business: going after financial-sector crime. *The New Yorker*, June 27, 42–55.

Patterson, K., Grenny, J. Maxfield, D., McMillan, R., & Switzer, A. (2011) *Change Anything: The New Science of Personal Success*. New York: Business Plus.

Paulus, D. L., & Williams, K. M. (2006) The dark triad of personality: narcissism, Machiavellianism, and psychopathy. *Journal of Research in Personality*, 36, 556–563.

Pearson, C. M., Anderson, L., & Wegner, J. (2001) When workers flout convention: a study of workplace incivility. *Human Relations*, 54, 1387–1419.

Pearson, C. M., & Porath, C. L. (2008) The cost of bad behavior—how incivility damages your business. *Journal of Empirical Legal Studies*, 5, 239–273.

Pearson, C. M., & Porath, C. L. (2009) *The Cost of Bad Behavior: How Incivility is Damaging Your Business and What to Do About It*. New York: Portfolio.

Penney, L. M., & Spector, P. E. (2002) Narcissism and counterproductive work behavior: Do bigger egos mean bigger problems? *International Journal of Selection and Assessment*, 10, 126–134.

Peterson, C., & Seligman, M. E. P. (2004) *Character Strengths and Virtues: A Handbook and Classification*. Washington, DC and New York: American Psychological Association and Oxford University Press.

Pinder, C. C., & Harlos, K. P (2001) Employee silence: quiescence and acquiescence as responses to perceived injustice. *Research in Personnel and Human Resource Management*, 20, 331–369.

Popplewell, B. (2011) "Night of debauchery" haunts T.O. law firm. *Toronto Star*, April 6, A1, A7.

Porath, C. L., & Erez, A. (2007) Does rudeness really matter? The effects of rudeness on task performance and helpfulness. *Academy of Management Journal*, 50, 1181–1197.

Porras, J., Emery, S., & Thompson, M. (2007) *Success Built to Last: Creating a Life That Matters*. New York: Plume.

Pozner, J. E. (2008) Stigma and settling up: an integrated approach to the consequences of organizational misconduct for organizational elites. *Journal of Business Ethics*, 80, 141–150.

Rate, C. R, & Sternberg, R. J. (2007) When good people do nothing: a failure of courage. In J. Langan-Fox, C. L. Cooper & R. J. Klimoski, (eds) *Research Companion to the Dysfunctional Workplace*. Chichester: Edward Elgar. pp. 3–21.

Rayment, J., & Smith, J. (2010) *MisLeadership: Prevalence, Causes and Consequences*. Farnham: Gower.

Roberts, J. A. (2011) *Shiny Objects: Why We Spend Money We Don't Have in Search of Happiness We Can't Buy*. New York: HarperOne.

Robson, D. (2011) Would-be lawyer fails test of "good character". *Toronto Star*, April 5, A1, A5.

Roman, P. M., & O'Brien, L. A. (2010) Dangerous concoctions: alcohol, employment and the family. In R. J. Burke & C. L. Cooper (eds) *Risky Business: Psychological, Physical and Financial Costs of High Risk Behavior in Organizations*. Farnham: Gower.

Rosen, L. S., & Rosen, M. (2011) *Swindlers*. Toronto: Madison

Rosenthal, S. A., & Pittinsky, T. L. (2006) Narcissistic leadership. *The Leadership Quarterly*, 17, 617–633.

Rothstein, M., & Burke, R. J. (2010) *Self-assessment and Leadership Development*. Chichester: Edward Elgar.

Sainforth, F., Kapsh, B., Broske, B. L., & Smith, M. J. (2001) Applying quality improvement principles to achieve healthy work organizations. *Journal of Quality Improvement*, 27, 465–483.

Schabracq, M. J., & Smit, I. E. (2007) Leadership and ethics: the darker side of management. In J. Langan-Fox, C. L. Cooper & R. J. Klimoski (eds) *Research Companion to the Dysfunctional Workplace*. Chichester: Edward Elgar. pp. 110–124.

Schabracq, M. J., Winnubst, J. A. M., & Cooper, C. L. (2003) *The Handbook of Work and Health Psychology*. 2nd edition. New York: John Wiley.

Schaubroeck, J., Walumbwa, F. O., Ganster, D. C., & Kepes, S. (2007) Destructive leader traits and the neutralizing influence of an "enriched" job. *The Leadership Quarterly*, 18, 236–251.

Schiller, B. (2011) Corruption stars in "Hall of Shame". *Toronto Star*, August 8, A2.

Schlimm, D. (2011) *Influencing Powerful People: Engage and Command the Attention of the Decision-makers to Get Why You Need to Succeed*. New York: McGraw Hill.

Schyns, B., & Hansbrough, T. (2010) *When Leadership Goes Wrong: Destructive Leadership, Mistakes, and Ethical Failures*. Charlottte, NC: Information Age Publishing, Inc.

Schwartz, H. S. (1991) Narcissism project and corporate decay: the case of General Motors. *Business Ethics Quarterly*, 1, 249–268.

Schwartz, M. S. (2011a) How to minimize corruption in business organizations: developing and sustaining an ethical corporate culture. In R. J. Burke, E. C. Tomlinson & C. L. Cooper (eds.) *Crime and Corruption in Organizations: Why it Occurs and What to Do about It*. Farnham: Gower. pp. 273–296.

Schwartz, M. S. (2011b) *Corporate Social Responsibility: An Ethical Approach*. Toronto: Broadview Press.

Schwartz, T. (2007) Manage your energy, not your time, *Harvard Business Review*, October, 63–73.

Seldman, M., & Seldman, J. (2008) *Executive Stamina: How to Optimize Time, Energy and Productivity to Achieve Peak Performance*. New York: John Wiley.

Seligman, M. (2002) *Authentic Happiness: Using the New Positive Psychology to Realize Your Potential for Lasting Fulfillment*. New York: Free Press.

Shaeffer, B. (1997) *Is it Love or is it Addiction?* 2nd edition. Center City, MN: Hazelden.

Shain, M., & Kramer, D. M. (2004) Health promotion in the workplace: framing the concept; reviewing the evidence. *Occupational and Environmental Medicine*, 61, 613–618.

Shapiro, D. L., & Von Glinow, M. A. (2007) When bad leaders stay in good places. In J. Langan-Fox, C. L. Cooper & R. J. Klimoski (eds) *Research Companion to the Dysfunctional Workplace*. Chichester: Edward Elgar. pp. 90–109.

Shulman, T. D. (2010) Biting the hand that feeds: rhe employee theft epidemic—a human face on theft. In R. J. Burke & C. L. Cooper (eds) *Risky Business: Psychological, Social and Financial Costs of High Risk Behavior in Organizations*. Farnham: Gower. pp. 433–445.

Smith, Y. (2010) *Econned: How Unlimited Self-interest Undermined Democracy and Corrupted Capitals*. New York: Palgrave McMillan.

Sorkin, A. (2011) *Too Big to Fail*. New York: Penguin.

Stengel, J. (2012) *Grow: How Ideals Power Growth and Profit in the World's Greatest Companies*. New York: Crown Business.

Stevens, B. (2009) Corporate ethical codes as a vehicle of reducing corruption in organizations. In R. J. Burke & C. L. Cooper (eds) *Research Companion to Corruption in Organizations*. Chichester: Edward Elgar. pp. 252–268.

Subramony, M. (2009) A meta-analytic investigation of the relationship between HRM bundles and firm performance. *Human Resource Management*, 48, 745–768.

Sutton, R. I. (2010) *Good Boss, Bad Boss: How to be the Best...and Learn from the Worst*. New York: Business Plus.

Sutton, R. I. (2007) *The No Asshole Rule: Building a Civilized Workplace and Surviving One that Isn't*. New York: Business Plus.

Taylor, J. B. (2010) *Safety Culture: Assessing and Changing the Behavior of Organizations*. Farnham: Gower.

Tepper, B. J. (2000) Consequences of abusive supervision. *Academy of Management Journal*, 43, 178–190.

Tepper, B. J. (2007) Abusive supervision in work organizations: review, synthesis, and directions for future research. *Journal of Management*, 33, 261–289.

Thompson, K. W. (2010) *The Effects of Supervisors' Narcissistic Entitlement on Job Tension and Depressed Mood at Work*. Paper presented at the Annual Meeting of the Academy of Management, Montreal, August.

Thompson, C. Beauvais, L. L., & Lyness, K. S. (1999) When work-family benefits are not enough: the influence of work-family culture on benefit utilization, organizational attachment, and work-family conflict. *Journal of Vocational Behavior*, 54, 392–415.

Timofeyev, Y. (2011) How Corruption affects social expenditures: evidence from Russia. Working paper, Volgograd: Volgograd State University.

Tobutt, C. (2011) *Alcohol at Work: Managing Alcohol Problems and Issues in the Workplace*. Farnham: Gower.

Tomlinson, E. C. (2009) Reducing employee theft: weighing the evidence on intervention. In R. J. Burke & C. L. Cooper (eds) *Research Companion to Corruption in Organizations*. Chichester: Edward Elgar. pp. 231–251.

Toronto Star (2011a) Dangerous driving behind thousands of cargo crashes. *Toronto Star*, June 27, A8.

Toronto Star (2011b) Medical dean resigns over plagiarism. *Toronto Star*, June 18, A23.

Toronto Star (2012) Senior RCMP officer given reprimand. *Toronto Star*, Febuary 10, A8.

Twenge, J. M. (2006) *Generation Me: Why Today's Young Americans are More Confident, Assertive Entitled—and More Miserable than Ever Before*. New York: Free Press.

Twenge, J. M., & Campbell, W. K. (2009) *The Narcissism Epidemic: Living in the Age of Entitlement*. New York: Free Press.

Twenge, J. M., Konrath, S., Foster, J. D., Campbell, W. K., & Bushman, B. J. (2008) Egos inflating over time: a cross-temporal meta-analysis of the Narcissistic Personality Inventory. *Journal of Personality*, 76, 875–901.

Underhill, P. (2008) *Why We Buy: The Science of Shopping: Updated and Revised for the Internet, the Global Consumer and Beyond*. New York: Simon & Schuster.

Van Cleeve, R. (2010) *Unplugged: My Journal into the Dark World of Video Game Addiction*. Deerfield Beach, FL: Health Communications Inc.

Velez-Mitchell, J., & Mohr, S. (2011) *Addict Nation: An Intervention for America*. Deerfield Beach, FL: Health Communications Inc.

Vinnicombe, S., Burke, R. J., Moore, L., & Blake-Beard, S. (2012) *Handbook of Research on Promoting Women's Careers*. Chichester: Edward Elgar.

Vinnicombe, S., Singh, V., Burke,R. J., Bilimoria, D., & Huse, M. (2008) *Women on Corporate Boards of Directors: International Research and Practice*. Chichester: Edward Elgar.

Wallace, K. (2011) You can blame genetics for your cheating heart: Cheaters more likely to have thrill-seeking gene. *Toronto Star*, June 17, A1, A17.

Wallace, H. M., & Baumeister, R. F. (2002) The performance of narcissists rises and falls with perceived opportunity for glory. *Journal of Personality and Social Psychology*, 82, 819–834.

Weimer, D. A., & Thornton, E. (1997) Slow healing at Mitsubishi: it's clearing up sexual harassment charges, but ill will lingers. *Business Week*, 3545, September 22, 74–76.

Whybrow, P. C. (2005) *When More is Not Enough*. New York: W.W. Norton.

Wiltermuth, S. S. (2011) *Cheating More When the Spoils are Split*. Los Angeles, CA: Marshall School of Business, University of Southern California.

Wittenberg-Cox, A. (2010) *How Women Mean Business: A Step by Step Guide to Profiting from Gender Balanced Business*. New York: John Wiley.

Wittenberg-Cox, A., & Maitland, A. (2008) *Why Women Mean Business: Understanding the Emergence of our Next Economic Revolution*. New York: John Wiley.

Wright, T., & Conley, H. (2011) *Gower Handbook of Discrimination at Work*. Surrey: Gower Publishing.

Young, S. M., & Pinsky, D. (2006) Narcissism and celebrity. *Journal of Research in Personality*, 40, 463–471.

Yu, T. Y., Sengul, M., & Lester, R. H. (2008) Misery loves company: the spread of negative impacts resulting from an organizational crisis. *Academy of Management Review*, 33, 452–472.

Zimbardo, P. (2007) *The Lucifer Effect: Understanding How Good People Turn Evil*. New York: Random House.

Zyglidopoulos, S. C., & Fleming, P. (2009) The escalation of corruption in organizations. In R. J. Burke & C. L. Cooper (eds) *Research Companion to Corruption in Organizations*. Cheltenham: Edward Elgar. pp. 104–120.

Optimal Individual and Organizational Outcomes

2 *Becoming Fully Engaged in the Workplace: What Individuals and Organizations can do to Foster Work Engagement*

ARNOLD B. BAKKER,[1] WIDO G. M. OERLEMANS AND
LIEKE L. TEN BRUMMELHUIS

Work engagement is most often defined as a positive, active psychological state that is characterized by vigor, dedication and absorption (Bakker, Schaufeli, Leiter & Taris, 2008; Schaufeli & Bakker, 2010). Engaged employees are full of energy. In addition, they have a very positive attitude toward their work—they are enthusiastic about what they are doing. Engaged employees often forget about the time because they are fully immersed in their work activities. Employee work engagement has become very popular in science and practice, because the empirical evidence indicates that it is predictive of many important organizational outcomes (Demerouti & Cropanzano, 2010). Examples of these outcomes include increased creativity, better in-role performance, reduced company-registered sickness absenteeism, increased organizational citizenship behaviors, better financial results at the company level and increased client satisfaction.

During the past decade, researchers have also identified a wide range of predictors of work engagement. Although some studies have identified stable personality factors like extraversion, emotional stability and conscientiousness as predictors of engagement (for example, Langelaan, Bakker, Schaufeli & Van Doornen, 2006), most studies have focused on state personal or job resources. Personal resources like optimism and self-efficacy have predictive value for engagement, because such positive self-evaluations signal that one has the ability to control and impact upon the environment successfully (Hobfoll, Johnson, Ennis & Jackson, 2003). Thus, individuals with many personal resources are engaged because they are intrinsically motivated to pursue their goals. Further, job resources like job control, performance feedback and skill variety predict engagement because these resources

1   Arnold B. Bakker, Erasmus University Rotterdam, Department of Work and Organizational Psychology, Woudestein, T12-47, P.O. Box 1738, 3000 DR Rotterdam, The Netherlands. Phone: +31 10 408 8853. www.arnoldbakker.com, email: bakker@fsw.eur.nl.

satisfy basic psychological needs. In addition, job resources help employees to cope with their job demands, attain their goals and learn something. Moreover, job resources are most important for engagement when job demands are high (Bakker, Hakanen, Demerouti & Xanthopoulou, 2007)—job resources seem to turn job demands into challenges.

Organizations have become increasingly interested in how to develop employee engagement. Although to date only very few interventions to improve engagement exist and have been tested (Schaufeli & Salanova, 2007), it is useful to discuss interventions that have the potential to develop, embed and sustain engagement in organizational settings. In this chapter, we will outline seven strategies to improve employee engagement. Some of these strategies can be considered as organizational interventions, like efforts to optimize the work environment and employee work–life balance. Other strategies can be seen as individual interventions, like efforts to optimize employees' personal resources or to ask them to engage in proactive job crafting behaviors. Before we start describing these engagement interventions, we will first outline some important preconditions for interventions and briefly discuss the intervention process itself.

Intervention Process

The success of an intervention is not only dependent on its quality, but also on the organization of the intervention and the process. An important initial step is to assure organizational commitment. Commitment to work engagement requires senior leadership endorsement that is ideally realized by acknowledging engagement as a core value. This may also imply that management is willing to make a considerable financial investment in engagement. Further, when implementing an intervention one may follow Van Strien's (1997) regulative cycle. The first phase in this cycle is the formulation of the goal of the intervention (for example, engaged, creative employees, low absence, high performance). The second phase is the diagnosis. In this phase, an analysis is made of the situation: what is the level of employee engagement and what are its most important drivers? This phase should result in a diagnosis of the most important causes of engagement. For example, at the organizational level, this phase could indicate that the most important predictors of engagement are autonomy, opportunities for growth and skill variety. If the absolute levels of these three resources are low, then the focus should be on a structural increase of these resources. At the individual, employee level, personal resources such as self-efficacy and resilience and job resources like social support and supervisory coaching may be important predictors of engagement. The conclusion will be that these factors should be optimized at the personal level.

The third phase in the regulative cycle is the design of the intervention—this is called the action plan (Van Strien, 1997). What will be done to influence the job and personal resources? What are the means to realize this? Phase four is the implementation of the plan or the intervention itself. In this phase, the plans that were made in the previous step are implemented. There will be monitoring of the progress by conducting assessments. Regular employee surveys provide a means of monitoring engagement and its fluctuations across locations, departments and teams. In the final, fifth phase, the project is evaluated. This phase answers the question, "How well did our intervention accomplish the objectives that were planned?" Was the intervention effective? How efficient was it?

Kompier, Cooper and Geurts (2000) analyzed nine workplace interventions and identified several process variables that contributed to the success of the interventions. Interventions were more successful in sustaining employee well-being when: organizations used a stepwise and systematic approach; there was a clear structure (tasks, responsibilities); consultants or researchers used a participative approach; management and representatives of employees co-operated; employees were recognized as "experts;" the responsibility of management was emphasized; and when monitoring and intervention were combined. In addition, crucial variables that contributed to the success of the interventions were proper risk assessment using adequate instruments; assessment for the company as a whole but also at the level of departments and job positions; and using clear facts and figures to convince top management. Let's now turn to the seven possible strategies that can be used to increase employee work engagement.

Interventions

JD–R INTERVENTION

The Job Demands–Resources (JD–R) model (Bakker & Demerouti, 2008; Demerouti & Bakker, 2011; Demerouti, Bakker, Nachreiner & Schaufeli, 2001) assumes that whereas every occupation may have its own specific working characteristics, these characteristics can be classified in two general categories (that is, job demands and job resources), thus constituting an overarching model that may be applied to various occupational settings, irrespective of the particular demands and resources involved. The central assumption of the JD–R model is that job strain develops—irrespective of the type of job or occupation—when job demands are high and when job resources are limited. In contrast, work engagement is most likely when job resources are high—also in the face of high job demands (Bakker, Hakanen, Demerouti & Xanthopoulou, 2007; Hakanen & Roodt, 2010).

These findings imply that the JD–R model can be used as a tool for human resource management. In close collaboration with human resource managers and consultants, the model has now been applied in over 200 different organizations in The Netherlands and in other countries. Because every occupation may have its own unique drivers of work engagement, we have started to use a two-stage procedure in our organizational research with the model. The first *qualitative* phase of the research includes explorative interviews with job incumbents from different layers of an organization (for example, representatives from management, staff and shop floor). The interviews, which last approximately 45 minutes, include open questions about the jobs of the interviewees. The incorporation of a qualitative phase in the research is valuable because it potentially generates knowledge about unexpected, organization-specific job demands and job resources that will be overlooked by highly standardized approaches (Bakker & Demerouti, 2007).

In the second phase of the research, the job demands and job resources potentially associated with work engagement are operationalized with validated scales and incorporated in a tailor-made questionnaire. All employees from an organization are then invited to fill out this questionnaire. This enables a *quantitative* analysis of the job demands and job resources that have been identified qualitatively and that potentially play a role in the development of engagement. The analysis usually concentrates on differences between departments and job positions, in terms of job demands, resources, engagement and its consequences. In some projects, managers participate in engagement workshops before the start of the study, so that they can learn how to use the information that will become available. The sub-group analyses can provide clear indications for interventions to foster engagement in the workplace, since they highlight the strengths and the weaknesses of departments and job positions. Tailor-made interventions are then possible, aimed at reducing the identified (hindrance) job demands, and increasing the most important job resources, which, in turn, may increase the likelihood of work engagement and high job performance.

In addition, we have developed Internet applications of the JD–R model—called the *JD–R Monitor* and the *Engagement App*—in which employees who fill in an electronic version of the questionnaire receive online and personalized feedback on their computer or smartphone about their most important job demands and resources. For example, the feedback includes histograms of the specific demands and resources identified as important for engagement in the study, and the participants' scores are compared with a benchmark (comparison group). In addition, the feedback mode is interactive, such that participants can click on the histograms and receive written feedback about the meaning of their scores on the demands and resources. In a similar way, feedback about work engagement has been included in these web-based tools. The final PDF report that can be generated at the end of the program is used as input for interviews with human resources managers and personal coaches. In this way, it becomes possible to optimize the working environment for individual employees.

JOB CRAFTING INTERVENTION

Employees may actively change the design of their jobs by choosing tasks, negotiating different job content and assigning meaning to their tasks or jobs (Parker & Ohly, 2008). This process of employees shaping their jobs has been referred to as job crafting (Wrzesniewski & Dutton, 2001). Job crafting is defined as the physical and cognitive changes individuals make in their task or relational boundaries. Physical changes refer to changes in the form, scope or number of job tasks, whereas cognitive changes refer to changing how one sees the job. Berg, Wrzesniewski and Dutton (2010) offer some examples of making "physical changes" to one's job. For instance, they interviewed a maintenance technician who told that he crafts his job in the form of taking on additional tasks. After being in the organization for some time, he started to proactively help newcomers to learn the job. Because he turned out to be good at this, he became formally responsible for the training of new employees. Berg and colleagues also cite a customer service representative who reframed the perception of the job as a meaningful whole that positively impacts others rather than a collection of separate tasks (that is, cognitive change as a form of job crafting): "Technically, [my job is] putting in orders, entering orders, but really I see it as providing our customers with an enjoyable experience, a positive experience, which is a lot more meaningful to me than entering numbers." (p. 167).

Changing relational boundaries means that individuals have discretion over whom they interact with while doing their job. According to Wrzesniewski and Dutton (2001), job crafting focuses on the processes by which employees change elements of their jobs and relationships with others to revise the meaning of the work and the social environment at work. Thus, job crafting is about *changing* the job in order to experience enhanced meaning of it. As a consequence, employees may be able to increase their person–job fit and thereby increase their work engagement. Tims, Bakker and Derks (2012) indeed showed that colleague-ratings of job crafting were positively related to employee work engagement. Thus, employees who increased their job resources, for example, asked for feedback from their supervisor and mobilized their social network, were most likely to be energetic and dedicated to their work. Additionally, workers who increased their own job demands in order to create a challenging work environment were most likely to be engaged. For example, the more often individuals proactively volunteered to be involved in projects, the more likely it was that they were identified by their colleagues as engaged at work.

A job crafting intervention could be designed as follows. Participants who are enrolled in the program are instructed through the Internet and are followed over the course of four weeks. At the start of each week, they receive an e-mail explaining the goal of the program: "The goal of this assignment is to ensure that your work fits (even) better with your specific knowledge, skills, and personal needs. You will do this by personally changing your work or your work environment. Perhaps you have not looked at your work like this before, but research shows that it is possible to derive more satisfaction from life if you proactively align your work with your skills and needs. Please try to use this way of working during this week." Participants can be provided with examples, such as changing the way they work, when they work, with whom they work (clients, colleagues), changing the frequency of feedback and coaching, simplifying their work vs. looking for more challenges and carrying out additional tasks. The instruction could additionally provide clear examples of employees in certain jobs who mobilized their job resources or increased/reduced their job demands. To facilitate the job crafting behaviors, participants can be asked to list up to seven aspects of their work they would like to change during the upcoming week. In addition, they can be asked—for example, via e-mail or smartphone, or initiated by a personal coach—to indicate for each activity how and when they intend to engage in job crafting. Such implementation intentions will facilitate the success of the job crafting intervention.

PSYCAP INTERVENTION

Psychological capital (PsyCap) has been defined as "an individual's positive psychological state of development characterized by: (1) having confidence (self efficacy) to take on and put in the necessary effort to succeed at challenging tasks; (2) making a positive attribution (optimism) about succeeding now and in the future; (3) persevering toward goals, and when necessary, redirecting paths to goals (hope) in order to succeed; and (4) when beset by problems and adversity, sustaining and bouncing back and even beyond (resilience) to attain success" (Luthans, Youssef & Avolio, 2007, p. 3). Sweetman and Luthans (2010) have outlined why PsyCap should be related to work engagement. Employees high in PsyCap are characterized by their tenacity and persistence, driven by their belief in future success. Additionally, they continue to provide hope for goal achievement, even in the face of new challenges, and expect good things to happen to them.

In their studies among highly skilled Dutch technicians, Xanthopoulou, Bakker, Demerouti and Schaufeli (2007, 2009a) examined the role of a slightly different operationalization of PsyCap (self-efficacy, organizational-based self-esteem and optimism— these factors are called personal resources) in predicting work engagement. Results showed that engaged employees are highly self-efficacious; they believe they are able to meet the demands they face in a broad array of contexts. In addition, engaged workers have the tendency to believe that they will generally experience good outcomes in life (optimism), and believe they can satisfy their needs by participating in roles within the organization (organizational-based self-esteem). In short, engaged workers have psychological capital that helps them to control and impact upon their work environment successfully. Diary studies have indicated that daily levels of PsyCap are positively related to work engagement and indirectly to job performance (Xanthopoulou, Bakker, Heuven, Demerouti & Schaufeli, 2008) and financial returns (Xanthopoulou, Bakker, Demerouti & Schaufeli, 2009b).

Peterson, Luthans, Avolio, Walumbwa and Zhang (2011) have shown that positive change in psychological capital is related to positive change in supervisor-rated performance and financial performance (that is, individual sales revenue). Since research also indicates that changes in work engagement are related to job performance (Bakker, 2011), these findings suggest that PsyCap is malleable and can be increased in order to improve work engagement and performance. PsyCap can indeed be developed through targeted interventions (Luthans, Avey, Avolio, Norman & Combs, 2006; Luthans, Avey & Patera, 2008), which consequently has a positive impact on participants' on-the-job performance (Luthans, Avey, Avolio & Peterson, 2010).

For example, in the latter study, Luthans and his colleagues (2010) assigned participants randomly to treatment ($N = 153$) or control ($N = 89$) groups. The treatment groups received a two-hour training intervention conducted by training facilitators that utilized a series of exercises and group discussions designed to impact the participants' level of efficacy, hope, optimism and resilience, individually and overall in terms of their PsyCap. In the intervention training, the facilitators used a series of writing, discussion and reflective exercises specific to each of the four PsyCap constructs to impact PsyCap development. Examples of the exercises used included one that focused on broadening the hope-oriented self-regulating capacity and pathways thinking toward a specific goal. First, each participant was asked to consider and then write down personal goals. The facilitator led participants through a series of techniques to set and phrase goals to increase agentic capacity (Bandura, 2008). This included parceling large goals into manageable units, thereby also increasing efficacy over smaller sub-goals. Next, participants were asked to considering multiple pathways to accomplishing each goal and to share those pathways in small discussion groups within the intervention session. In other words, the participants acted as models for each other. Thus, the capacity for pathway generation was expected to be increased through vicarious learning and in turn to enhance participants' level of efficacy in utilizing the hope application of deriving multiple pathways to accomplish a given goal. In addition, by increasing their efficacy to accomplish the goal, the participants were expected to increase their positive expectations of goal accomplishment (that is, their optimism). For more details on the psychological capital intervention, we refer to Luthans, Avey, Avolio & Peterson (2010).

STRENGTHS-BASED INTERVENTION

It is well conceivable that the degree to which employees feel engaged towards their jobs is—at least in part—dependent on the match between individual strengths possessed by employees, and the degree to which they can draw from their strengths in their daily work activities. Individual strengths can be defined as positive traits reflected in thoughts, feelings and behaviors (Park, Peterson & Seligman, 2004). Examples are curiosity, bravery, kindness and gratitude. Strengths exist in degrees and can be measured as individual differences. Uniform tools for assessing an individual's strengths have already been developed, such as the Virtues-in-Action Classification of Individual Strengths (VIA-IS; Peterson & Seligman, 2004). This test identifies 24 strengths that people may possess to various degrees such as leadership, love of learning and creativity.

Strengths-based interventions may focus on individual strengths, such as reflecting on times when a person was at his/her best and the strengths he/she used then; identifying signature strengths; or a combination of identifying and using strengths in a new way (Seligman, Steen, Park & Peterson, 2005). Another example is the reflected best self-exercise that helps people learn more about their unique talents by asking others in their surroundings to provide examples of moments when they were at their best (Roberts, Dutton, Spreitzer, Heaphy & Quinn, 2005). It has been argued that working with one's strengths is fulfilling and engaging, and induces a feeling of acting in an authentic manner and being true to oneself (Peterson & Seligman, 2004). For those reasons, using strengths may contribute to enhanced work engagement.

Although strengths-based interventions within the context of work have—to the best of our knowledge—not yet been performed, research on well-being in general has produced some promising findings. For example, in one strength-based intervention, participants were asked to first identify their top individual strengths (with the VIA-IS). Subsequently, participants were encouraged to use one of their top character strengths in a new or different way every day for at least one week (Seligman et al., 2005). Participants were randomly assigned to an experimental group ($N = 66$) or a placebo control group ($N = 70$), and were followed over the course of six months. Results showed that this intervention led to significant increases in happiness and significant reductions of depressive symptoms at one week, one month, three months and six months follow-up, with effects being more pronounced for those who kept on using their strengths in their everyday lives after the initial intervention that lasted for only one week. Importantly, positive effects—of strengths on happiness and reduced depressive symptoms—only appeared when people were specifically encouraged to use one of their top strengths in their everyday lives. Another version of this intervention—where people only identified their strengths—did neither result in significant increases in happiness, nor in reduced depressive symptoms (Seligman, Steen, Park & Peterson, 2005).

There may be various ways to "translate" strengths-based interventions to a workplace context. For instance, one option is to identify what kind of strengths are required for particular types of jobs and thereafter assess the degree to which employees fit the strengths needed to perform such specific job activities. Thus, a better match between job types and employee strengths should lead to higher employee engagement. Another way to go is to provide individual feedback to employees (for example, through online modules) about their most important strengths. Thereafter, an option would be to give employees more insight with regard to the frequency with which they use their top character strengths on a daily basis while performing work-related activities (for example, through keeping a work-related diary). If it turns out that employees are insufficiently using their strengths, a next step would be to provide employees with specific pathways that lead them to use their strengths within the work context in a new way. This may lead employees to (re)consider how to use their strengths in specific types of job-related activities, which, in turn, may enhance their level of work engagement.

HAPPINESS INTERVENTIONS

More than 90 percent of all people agree with the statement "a happy worker is a productive worker" (Fisher, 2003). Compared to unhappy workers, happy workers are more active, energetic, interested, sympathetic to their colleagues and persistent in the face of difficulties. Meta-analyses indeed show that there is a relationship between happiness and job performance (Bakker & Oerlemans, 2011; Judge, Thorensen, Bono & Patton, 2001; Lyubomirsky, King & Diener, 2005). Moreover, happiness is positively related to work engagement—engaged employees often experience positive emotions during work including happiness, joy and enthusiasm (Bakker, Schaufeli, Leiter & Taris, 2008). Work engagement, in turn, leads to higher levels of job performance (Demerouti & Cropanzano, 2010).

Thus, one way to improve work engagement may be to improve employee happiness. Various activity-based interventions developed within the field of positive psychology appear to have positive effects on happiness in general, and might thus also be considered as useful for increasing happiness at work. Specific examples are activities aimed at expressing gratitude, performing acts of kindness, optimistic thinking, engaging in sports/exercise and spiritual activities such as yoga or mindfulness (for an overview, see Lyubomirsky, 2008). For example, Lyubomirsky, Tkach and Yelverton (2003) studied the effect of two positive interventions: "practicing random acts of kindness" (Study 1) and "counting one's blessings" (Study 2). In Study 1, students were instructed to practice random acts of kindness during a six-week period. This could be anything ranging from helping out a friend to visiting a sick relative or expressing thankfulness to a loved one. Compared to a control group (no treatment), the intervention group showed a significant increase in well-being. In Study 2, students were asked to complete several exercises during a six-week period. During these exercises, they had to write down their blessings. For example, "having nice friends" or "passing a difficult exam." Results indicated that students' level of well-being in the experimental condition increased significantly (relative to a control group) when they performed the exercise once a week. Other positive interventions, such as writing gratitude letters, remembering positive experiences and practicing optimistic thinking have been shown to be effective in increasing well-being in student samples as well (for example, Ruini, Belaise, Brombin, Caffo & Fava, 2006).

Importantly, the effectiveness of such happiness interventions is likely dependent on personal interests, values and personality (Lyubomirsky, Sheldon & Schkade, 2005). For example, extroverts may benefit most from an activity that requires regular contact with others (for example, acts of kindness toward others). People have to invest considerable time and effort in performing a particular activity to yield sustained happiness change. As a consequence, it is recommended that persons first identify what kind of activities will likely be inherently joyful, interesting, and thus "autotelic" in nature (for example, Deci & Ryan, 2000).

One way to identify the kind of activities that are joyful and interesting would be to let people systematically reflect on their (work) day by filling out a diary based on a Day Reconstruction Methodology (DRM) (Kahneman, Krueger, Schkade, Schwarz & Stone, 2004; Oerlemans, Bakker & Veenhoven, 2011). The DRM combines elements of experience sampling and time diaries, and is designed specifically to facilitate accurate emotional recall. Respondents are first asked to fill out a time diary summarizing episodes that occurred in the preceding day. In particular, respondents describe each episode of the day by indicating when the episode began and ended, what they were doing, where they were and with whom they were interacting. To ascertain how employees feel, participants are asked to report the pleasure and intensity of their feelings in accordance with the circumplex model of affect (Russell, 2003). For instance, through a DRM approach, employees can receive specific feedback on a) what kind of work-related activities they spend most of their time, and b) what kind of work-related activities are most joyful and interesting to perform. This kind of information may help employees planning their workday such that most time is spent on work-related activities that are most joyful, interesting and rewarding for them. Giving people accurate and daily feedback on what kind of (work) activities they find most interesting and joyful may be a vital aspect in improving employee work engagement.

New Ways of Working

In order to create inspiring work environments, an increasing number of organizations have started to redesign the approach of work, organizing work in a more flexible way. Central to this new approach is that employees decide themselves when they work (schedule flexibility), where they work (telecommuting), and via which communication medium (smartphone, e-mail, videoconference) they work (Baarne, Houtkamp & Knotter, 2010). These flexible work designs, also referred to as "new ways of working" (NWW) are thought to boost employee work engagement because NWW offer employees more control over their work process and facilitate efficient communication between co-workers (Gajendran & Harrison, 2007). Employees are allowed to schedule their work in a way that suits their personal situation best. For instance, one employee may choose to start the working day at home, avoiding traffic jams. Another employee may use a different time schedule, enabling him or her to bring and pick up children from school. The increase in autonomy is likely to enhance engagement. Also, employees using NWW stay connected with co-workers by online communication. This efficient work design enables employees to keep pace at work and to communicate quickly with peers, whereby they remain in an engaged work mode (Bakker, Hakanen, Demerouti & Xanthopoulou, 2007; Haddock, Zimmerman, Ziemba & Lyness, 2006).

Empirical studies evaluating the effects of NWW are thus far scarce. There is, however, preliminary support for the idea that NWW enhance employee engagement (Ten Brummelhuis, Bakker, Hetland & Keulemans, 2012). In a daily study among employees from a telecom company, Ten Brummelhuis and her colleagues found that employees reported higher levels of work engagement on days on which they worked according to the NWW work style. This effect could be ascribed to better interpersonal communication. Availability for peers, as well as communication efficiency and communication quality, were higher when employees used NWW. In line with these findings, other researchers have also found that e-mail and smartphone use contributed to social bonding among co-workers, and better task coordination (Lee & Kossek, 2004; Walther, 1995). These optimized work conditions are likely to foster engagement (Bakker & Demerouti, 2008).

NWW thus seem to be a good candidate for an engagement intervention. NWW as an intervention is in itself simple. Managers allow employees to choose their work schedule and the location of their work. However, to make NWW a success, several preconditions should be met.

1. Facilitate by technology. The flexible NWW work design is only possible when backed up by adequate and appropriate office space (at home, in the office or at the client's office). In the office, open flex spaces, suitable for all employees who bring their own laptop, phone and suitcase, are most common. Most importantly, employees are supported by new media technology, including laptops, smartphones and teleconference rooms.
2. Everyone is in. It is important that the management in all layers of the organization support the new work design. Most preferably, the management (including the CEOs) adopts the new work style as well. This may imply that managers also use flexible, open office space.
3. Clear guidelines. Common guidelines and kick-off workshops are indispensible for a good implementation of NWW. A company policy helps to clarify the content of the new work design. Also, during workshops, it is explained what is expected from employees, and what are the exact NWW "rules."
4. Co-worker expectancies. At the group level, it is advisable to make agreements about work schedules and communication. Team members may synchronize their schedules as much as possible, and express their expectancies about the online or face-to-face availability of peers.
5. Communicate smart. A possible side effect of NWW is that the increased online communication brings about interruptions during work tasks. A solution is to introduce non-interruption hours, during which employees work off-line on important tasks.
6. Improve. Finally, evaluation is important for all interventions. Likewise, employees may provide their feedback about the pros and cons of NWW. This allows for further fine-tuning of NWW.

Inclusive Work–life Support

Today, work and family life are inextricably bound up with each other (Voydanoff, 2002). On the one hand, research has shown that employees' family life is beneficial for work when, for example, positive mood spills over from one domain to the other. On the other hand, combining work and family roles may also cause role conflict and feelings of stress (Greenhaus & Beutell, 1985; Wayne, Grzywacz, Carlson & Kacmar, 2007). When employees bring these feelings of stress to the work floor, it is more difficult to get fully immersed, and dedicated to work. The work–family literature puts engagement at work in a somewhat new perspective. Whereas work engagement has commonly been explained by work characteristics, work–family research indicates that on top of that, family factors influence engagement at work (Ten Brummelhuis, Bakker & Euwema, 2010).

In general, previous studies have shown that demanding aspects of family life (for example, care for newborns, family task overload) diminish energy and engagement at work, while rewarding family aspects (for example, support from the partner) enhance engagement at work (Montgomery, Peeters, Schaufeli & Den Ouden, 2003; Ten Brummelhuis, Van der Lippe & Kluwer, 2010). The impact family life may have at work is underlined by research on crossover effects among co-workers. In a study on co-worker dyads, it was found that family-to-work interference of individual employees diminished not only their own engagement at work, but also co-workers' work engagement (Ten Brummelhuis, Bakker & Euwema, 2010).

To facilitate advantageous effects, while preventing possible disadvantageous effects of employees' family life on work, organizations increasingly implement work–life policies. These policies include options designed to give workers greater flexibility in scheduling (flextime and telecommuting); to assist them with their parenting duties (childcare facilities); and to offer emotional support (supportive leadership and organizational culture) (Anderson, Coffey & Byerly, 2002; Lapierre & Allen, 2006). Work–life policies have been evaluated in detail in previous studies (for overviews see Bailey & Kurland, 2002; Baltes, Briggs, Huff, Wright & Neuman, 1999; Gajendran & Harrison, 2007; Glass & Finley, 2002). Research suggests that more pragmatic interventions (flexibility and childcare support) are somewhat successful in helping employees manage the often competing demands of work and family (Mesmer-Magnus & Viswesvaran, 2006), though comparatively less so than the benefits achieved by emotional support such as the presence of a supportive supervisor and family-supportive work cultures (Allen, 2001; Thompson, Beauvais & Lyness, 1999).

Therefore, presumably most progress can be made when work–life interventions aimed at fostering work engagement focus on the organizational culture. Such cultures are characterized by offering employees understanding, advice and recognition for the life roles they may have beyond work (Van Daalen, Willemsen & Sanders, 2006). For instance, a supportive supervisor may help boost an employee's energy level by discussing family-related problems; reinforce the employee's positive self-image by giving positive feedback; and reduce stress by showing understanding for the employee's family life (Halbesleben, 2006; Lapierre & Allen, 2006).

However, one critical note should be made here. Most support policies focus on employees with a family (partner and children), creating family-responsive work climates (Casper, Weltman & Kwesiga, 2007). The risk of this selective focus is that other sub-groups, such as employees without children and single employees, feel excluded (Grover & Crooker, 1995). Previous studies indeed have shown that single employees are less committed and perform worse when they perceive the organizational culture as family responsive (Parker & Allen, 2001; Ten Brummelhuis & Van der Lippe, 2010). The challenge for managers, then, is to create a work culture that advocates the combination of work and life in general. Such a culture would respect parents' family demands in addition to their work role, without neglecting other life roles that employees with various backgrounds may have.

Conclusion

In this chapter, we discussed seven possible interventions that have the potential to develop, embed and sustain engagement in organizational settings. In addition to organizational interventions aimed at optimizing the work environment (new ways of working; optimizing job demands and resources; inclusive work–life support), we discussed individual interventions including job crafting interventions, interventions aimed at increasing employees' psychological capital (efficacy, hope, optimism and resilience), happiness interventions and strengths-based interventions. Although we need more research on the effectiveness of each of these interventions, we believe they have the potential to foster engagement in the workplace. We hope that this chapter will inspire both practitioners and researchers to put our ideas to the test.

References

Allen, T. (2001) Family-supportive work environments: the role of organizational perceptions. *Journal of Vocational Behavior*, 58, 414–435.

Anderson, S. E., Coffey, B. S., & Byerly, R. T. (2002) Formal organizational initiatives and informal workplace practices: links to work-family conflict and job-related outcomes. *Journal of Management*, 28, 787–810.

Baarne, R., Houtkamp, P., & Knotter, M. (2010) *Het Nieuwe Werken Ontrafeld [Unraveling New Ways of Working]*. Assen, The Netherlands: Koninklijke Van Gorcum/Stichting Management Studies.

Bailey, D. E., & Kurland, N. B. (2002) A review of telework research: findings, new directions, and lessons for the study of modern work. *Journal of Organizational Behavior*, 23, 383–400.

Bakker, A. B., (2011) An evidence-based model of work engagement. *Current Directions in Psychological Science*, 20, 265–269.

Bakker, A.B., & Demerouti, E. (2007) The Job Demands-Resources model: State of the art. *Journal of Managerial Psychology, 22,* 309–328.

Bakker, A. B., & Demerouti, E. (2008) Towards a model of work engagement. *Career Development International*, 13, 209–223.

Bakker, A. B., Hakanen, J. J., Demerouti, E., & Xanthopoulou, D. (2007) Job resources boost work engagement, particularly when job demands are high. *Journal of Educational Psychology*, 99, 274–284.

Bakker, A. B., & Oerlemans, W. G. M. (2011) Subjective well-being in organizations. In K.S. Cameron & G.M. Spreitzer (eds), *The Oxford Handbook of Positive Organizational Scholarship*. New York: Oxford University Press. pp. 178–189.

Bakker, A. B., Schaufeli, W. B., Leiter, M. P., & Taris, T. W. (2008) Work engagement: an emerging concept in occupational health psychology. *Work & Stress*, 22, 187–200.

Baltes, B. B., Briggs, T. E., Huff, J. W., Wright. J. A., & Neuman, G. A. (1999) Flexible and compressed workweek schedules: a meta-analysis of their effects on work-related criteria. *Journal of Applied Psychology*, 84, 496–513.

Bandura, A. (2008) An agentic perspective on positive psychology. In S. J. Lopez (ed.) *Positive Psychology*. Westport, CT: Greenwood. Vol. 1, pp. 167–196.

Berg, J. M., Wrzesniewski, A., & Dutton, J. E. (2010) Perceiving and responding to challenges in job crafting at different ranks: when proactivity requires adaptivity. *Journal of Organizational Behavior*, 31, 158–186.

Casper, W. J., Weltman, D., & Kwesiga, E. (2007) Beyond family-friendly: the construct and measurement of singles-friendly work culture. *Journal of Vocational Behavior*, 70, 478–501.

Deci, E. L., & Ryan, R. M. (2000) The "what" and "why" of goal pursuits: human needs and the self-determination of behavior. *Psychological Inquiry*, 11, 227–268.

Demerouti, E., & Bakker, A. B. (2011) The Job Demands–Resources model: challenges for future research. *South African Journal of Industrial Psychology*, 37, 1–9.

Demerouti E., Bakker, A. B., Nachreiner, F., & Schaufeli, W. B. (2001) The Job Demands–Resources model of burnout. *Journal of Applied Psychology*, 86, 499–512.

Demerouti, E., & Cropanzano, R. (2010) From thought to action: employee work engagement and job performance. In A. B. Bakker & M. P. Leiter (eds), *Work Engagement: A Handbook of Essential Theory and Research*. New York: Psychology Press. pp. 147–163.

Fisher, C. D. (2003) Why do lay people believe that satisfaction and performance are correlated? Possible sources of a commonsense theory. *Journal of Organizational Behavior*, 24, 753–777.

Gajendran, R. S., & Harrison, D. A. (2007) The good, the bad, and the unknown about telecommuting: meta-analysis of psychological mediators and individual consequences. *Journal of Applied Psychology*, 92, 1524–1541.

Glass, J. L., & Finley, A. (2002) Coverage and effectiveness of family-responsive workplace policies. *Human Resource Management Review*, 12, 313–337.

Greenhaus, J. H., & Beutell, N. J. (1985) Sources of conflict between work and family roles. *Academy of Management Review*, 10, 76–88.

Grover, S. L., & Crooker, K. J. (1995) Who appreciates family-responsive human resource policies: the impact of family-friendly policies on the organizational attachment of parents and non-parents. *Personnel Psychology*, 48, 271–288.

Haddock, S. A., Zimmerman, T. S., Ziemba, S. J., & Lyness, K. (2006) Practices of dual earner couples successfully balancing work and family. *Journal of Family and Economic Issues*, 27, 207–234.

Hakanen, J. J., & Roodt, G. (2010) Using the job demands-resources model to predict engagement: analysing a conceptual model. In A. B. Bakker & M. P. Leiter (eds) *Work Engagement: A Handbook of Essential Theory and Research*. New York: Psychology Press. pp. 85–101.

Halbesleben, J. R. B. (2006) Sources of social support and burnout: a meta-analytic test of the conservation of resources model. *Journal of Applied Psychology*, 91, 1134–1145.

Hobfoll, S. E., Johnson, R. J., Ennis, N., & Jackson, A. P. (2003) Resource loss, resource gain, and emotional outcomes among inner city women. *Journal of Personality and Social Psychology*, 84, 632–643.

Judge, T. A., Thorensen, C. J., Bono, J. E., & Patton, G. K. (2001) The job satisfaction–job performance relationship: a qualitative and quantitative review. *Psychological Bulletin*, 127, 376–407.

Kahneman, D., Krueger, A., Schkade, D., Schwarz N., & Stone, A. (2004) A survey method for characterizing daily life experience: the Day Reconstruction Method. *Science*, 306, 1776–1780.

Kompier, M. A. J., Cooper, C. L., & Geurts, S. A. E. (2000) A multiple case study approach to work stress prevention in Europe. *European Journal of Work and Organizational Psychology*, 9, 371–400.

Langelaan, S., Bakker, A. B., Schaufeli, W. B., & Van Doornen, L. J. P. (2006) Burnout and work engagement: do individual differences make a difference? *Personality and Individual Differences*, 40, 521–532.

Lapierre, L. M., & Allen, T. D. (2006) Work-supportive family, family-supportive supervision, use of organizational benefits, and problem-focused coping: implications for work–family conflict and employee well-being. *Journal of Occupational Health Psychology*, 11, 169–181.

Lee, M. D., & Kossek, E. E. (2004) *Crafting lives that work: a six year retrospective on reduced load work in the careers and lives of professionals and managers*. Alfred P. Sloan Foundation Study Feedback Report. Available online at: http://flex-work.lir.msu.edu/.

Luthans, F., Avey, J. B., Avolio, B. J., Norman, S. M., & Combs, G. J. (2006) Psychological capital development: toward a micro-intervention. *Journal of Organizational Behavior*, 27, 387–393.

Luthans, F., Avey, J. B., Avolio, B. J., & Peterson, S. J. (2010) The development and resulting performance impact of positive psychological capital. *Human Resource Development Quarterly*, 21, 41–67.

Luthans, F., Avey, J. B., & Patera, J. L. (2008) Experimental analysis of a web-based training intervention to develop positive psychological capital. *Academy of Management Learning & Education*, 7, 209–221.

Luthans, F., Youssef, C. M., & Avolio, B. J. (2007) *Psychological Capital: Developing the Human Competitive Edge*. Oxford: Oxford University Press.

Lyubomirsky, S. (2008) *The How of Happiness: A Scientific Approach to Getting the Life You Want*. New York: Penguin Press.

Lyubomirsky, S., King, L., & Diener, E. (2005) The benefits of frequent positive affect: does happiness lead to success? *Psychological Bulletin*, 131, 803–855.

Lyubomirsky, S., Sheldon, K. M., & Schkade, D. (2005) Pursuing happiness: the architecture of sustainable change. *Review of General Psychology*, 9, 111–131.

Lyubomirsky, S., Tkach, C., & Yelverton, J. (2003) *Pursuing sustained happiness through random acts of kindness and counting one's blessings: tests of two six-week interventions*. Unpublished manuscript, Department of Psychology, University of California, Riverside.

Mesmer-Magnus, J. R., & Viswesvaran, C. (2006) How family-friendly work environments affect work/family conflict: a meta-analytic examination. *Journal of Labor Research*, 27, 555–574.

Montgomery, A. J., Peeters, M. C. W., Schaufeli, W. B., & Den Ouden, M. (2003) Work-home interference among newspaper managers: its relationship with burnout and engagement. *Anxiety, Stress, & Coping*, 16, 195–211.

Oerlemans, W. G. M., Bakker, A. B., & Veenhoven, R. (2011) Finding the key to happy aging: a day reconstruction study of happiness. *Journal of Gerontology: Psychological Sciences*, 66B, 1–10.

Park, N., Peterson, C., & Seligman, M. E. P. (2004) Strengths of character and well-being. *Journal of Social and Clinical Psychology*, 23, 603–619.

Parker, L., & Allen, T. D. (2001) Work/family benefits: variables related to employees' fairness perceptions. *Journal of Vocational Behavior*, 58, 453–468.

Parker, S. K., & Ohly, S. (2008) Designing motivating jobs: an expanded framework for linking work characteristics and motivation. In R. Kanfer, G. Chen & R. Pritchard (eds), *Work Motivation: Past, Present, and Future*. New York: LEA/Psychology Press. pp. 233–284.

Peterson, C., & Seligman, M. E. P. (2004) *Character Strengths and Virtues: A Handbook and Classification*. Washington, DC: American Psychological Association.

Peterson, S. J., Luthans, F., Avolio, B. J., Walumbwa, F. O., & Zhang, Z. (2011) Psychological capital and employee performance: a latent growth modeling approach. *Personnel Psychology*, 64, 427–450.

Ruini, C., Belaise, C., Brombin, C., Caffo, E., & Fava, G. A. (2006) Well-being therapy in school settings: a pilot study. *Psychotherapy and Psychosomatics*, 75, 331–336.

Roberts, L. M., Dutton, J. E., Spreitzer, G. M., Heaphy, E. D., & Quinn, R. E. (2005) Composing the reflected best-self portrait: building pathways for becoming extraordinary in work organizations. *The Academy of Management Review*, 30, 712–736.

Russell, J. A. (2003) Core affect and the psychological construction of emotion. *Psychological Review*, 110, 145–172.

Schaufeli, W. B., & Bakker, A. B. (2010) Defining and measuring work engagement: bringing clarity to the concept. In A. B. Bakker & M. P. Leiter (eds) *Work Engagement: A Handbook of Essential Theory and Research*. New York: Psychology Press. pp. 10–24.

Schaufeli, W. B., & Salanova, M. (2007) Work engagement: an emerging psychological concept and its implications for organizations. In S. W. Gilliland, D. D. Steiner & D. P. Skarlicki (eds) *Research in Social Issues in Management (Volume 5): Managing Social and Ethical Issues in Organizations*. Greenwich, CT: Information Age Publishers. pp. 135–177.

Seligman, M. E. P., Steen, T. A., Park, N., & Peterson, C. (2005) Positive psychology progress: empirical validation of interventions. *American Psychologist*, 60, 410–421.

Sweetman, D., & Luthans, F. (2010) The power of positive psychology: psychological capital and work engagement. In A. B. Bakker & M. P. Leiter (eds), *Work Engagement: A Handbook of Essential Theory and Research*. New York: Psychology Press. pp. 54–68.

Ten Brummelhuis, L. L., Bakker, A. B., & Euwema, M. C. (2010) Is family-to-work interference related to co-workers' outcomes? *Journal of Vocational Behavior*, 77, 461–469.

Ten Brummelhuis, L. L., Bakker, A. B., Hetland, J., & Keulemans, L. (2012) Do new ways of working foster work engagement? *Psicothema*, 24, 113–120.

Ten Brummelhuis, L. L., & Van der Lippe, T. (2010) Effective work-life balance support for various household structures. *Human Resource Management*, 49, 175–195.

Ten Brummelhuis, L. L., Van der Lippe, T., & Kluwer, E. S. (2010) Family involvement and helping behavior in teams. *Journal of Management*, 36, 1406–1431.

Thompson, C. A., Beauvais, L. L., & Lyness, K. S. (1999) When work–family benefits are not enough: the influence of work-family culture on benefit utilization, organizational attachment, and work-family conflict. *Journal of Vocational Behavior*, 54, 329–415.

Tims, M., Bakker, A. B., & Derks, D. (2012) Development and validation of the job crafting scale. *Journal of Vocational Behavior*, 80, 173–186.

Van Daalen, G., Willemsen, T. M., & Sanders, K. (2006) Reducing work–family conflict through different sources of social support. *Journal of Vocational Behavior*, 69, 462–476.

Van Strien, P. (1997) Towards a methodology of psychological practice: the regulative cycle. *Theory & Psychology*, 7, 683–700.

Voydanoff, P. (2002) Linkages between the work family interface and work, family, and individual outcomes: an integrative model. *Journal of Family Issues*, 23, 138–164.

Walther, J. B. (1995) Relational aspects of computer-mediated communication: experimental observations over time. *Organization Science*, 6, 186–203.

Wayne, J. H., Grzywacz, J. G., Carlson, D. S., & Kacmar, K. M. (2007) Work–family facilitation: a theoretical explanation and model of primary antecedents and consequences. *Human Resource Management Review*, 17, 63–76.

Wrzesniewski, A., & Dutton, J. E. (2001) Crafting a job: revisioning employees as active crafters of their work. *Academy of Management Review*, 26, 179–201.

Xanthopoulou, D., Bakker, A. B., Demerouti, E., & Schaufeli, W. B. (2007) The role of personal resources in the job demands-resources model. *International Journal of Stress Management*, 14, 121–141.

Xanthopoulou, D., Bakker, A. B., Demerouti, E., & Schaufeli, W. B. (2009a) Reciprocal relationships between job resources, personal resources, and work engagement. *Journal of Vocational Behavior*, 74, 235–244.

Xanthopoulou, D., Bakker, A. B., Demerouti, E., & Schaufeli, W. B. (2009b) Work engagement and financial returns: a diary study on the role of job and personal resources. *Journal of Occupational and Organizational Psychology*, 82, 183–200.

Xanthopoulou, D., Bakker, A. B., Heuven, E., Demerouti, E., & Schaufeli, W. B. (2008) Working in the sky: a diary study on work engagement among flight attendants. *Journal of Occupational Health Psychology*, 13, 345–356.

3 *Experiencing Flow in the Workplace and What Individuals and Organizations Can Do to Foster It*

EVANGELIA DEMEROUTI[1] AND CLIVE J. FULLAGAR

The construct of "flow" evolved out of work Mihaly Csikszentmihalyi started as a doctoral student at the University of Chicago in 1965. Csikszentmihalyi was interested in understanding why artists would spend an inordinate amount of time engaged in activities for which there was no extrinsic reward. He concluded that it must be the enjoyment inherent in the task that was intrinsically motivating the artist to engage in a creative process that had no financial benefit and little social recognition (Csikszentmihalyi, 1965). The finding that individuals may perform activities purely for intrinsic reasons was contradictory to the prevailing psychological paradigm—that behavior could only be explained in terms of extrinsic rewards (Csikszentmihalyi, 1988). At about the same time, Abraham Maslow was writing about how the process of work could be rewarding in itself and that individuals engaged in work out of a need for "self-actualization" (Maslow, 1965, 1968). However, little research had been done on identifying the characteristics of work that generated such intense levels of involvement or the psychological components of the state of deep engagement.

In the 1970s, academic interest in the notion of intrinsic motivation began to grow, for example in the work of deCharms (1976), Deci (1975) and Lepper and Greene (1978). This research tended to consist of laboratory studies of children engaged in play activities. The focus was primarily on clarifying the dynamics of intrinsic motivation by understanding the "over-justification" effect whereby extrinsic rewards interfered with involvement in, and enjoyment of, intrinsically motivating behaviors.

It was against this scientific background that Csikszentmihalyi published *Beyond Boredom and Anxiety* in 1975. Whereas previous research had concentrated on identifying the antecedents and consequences of intrinsically motivating behaviors induced in a

1   Evangelia Demerouti, Eindhoven University of Technology, Industrial Engineering and Innovation Sciences, P.O. Box 513, 5600 MB Eindhoven, The Netherlands. Email: e.demerouti@tue.nl.

laboratory setting, Csikszentmihalyi was more concerned with understanding the phenomenology of the subjective experience of intrinsic motivation in natural settings (Csikszentmihalyi, 1975). After interviewing chess players, dancers, rock climbers, surgeons and many others, he found that the psychological state associated with engaged activity was remarkably similar across all domains. He defined this dynamic state as "the holistic sensation that people feel when they act with total involvement" (1975, p. 36). The term "flow" arose from the fact that many of the people that were interviewed described the state as flowing from moment to moment. Csikszentmihalyi (1975) described this state as *autotelic*, from the Greek words "auto" meaning self and "telos" meaning goal. Engagement in the activity was rewarding in and of itself.

Most of the research on flow has focused on voluntary leisure and sporting activities. However research has also shown that the experience of flow is apparent in work-related activities (for example, Csikszentmihalyi, 1975; Csikszentmihalyi & LeFevre, 1989; Demerouti, 2006; Fave & Massimini, 1988; Fullagar & Kelloway, 2009; Nielsen & Cleal, 2010). The subjective experience seems to be consistent across work and play, indicating that it is the quality of the experience that is important and not the nature of the activity (Csikszentmihalyi, 1988). In this chapter we will focus on the experience of flow at work. Specifically, we will (a) expound on the nature of the subjective experience of work-related flow; (b) outline the conditions that are necessary to facilitate flow; (c) describe some of the individual and organizational consequences of this optimal experience; and (d) suggest flow-evoking interventions.

Defining Work-related Flow

Csikszentmihalyi (1990) has defined flow as a state in which people are so intensely involved in an activity that nothing else seems to matter. Both qualitative and quantitative research on flow across a diversity of work and leisure activities has indicated that optimal experience consists of six core subjective components (Csikszentmihalyi, 1990, 1993; Jackson, 1996; Jackson & Marsh, 1996; Nakamura & Csikszentmihalyi, 2002). These are: (a) action-awareness merging in that involvement in the activity becomes spontaneous or automatic; (b) an intense and complete concentration on the task at hand; (c) a sense of control over what one is doing; (d) a loss of self-consciousness or a lack of concern for or about oneself; (e) a transformation of one's perception of time passing; and (f) a sense of enjoyment in the intrinsic motivation of the activity. The literature has also identified three additional components to flow, namely a balance between the challenge of the activity and the skills necessary to perform the activity, the clarity of goals inherent in the task and the feedback that the task provides that enables monitoring of one's actions. However these last three components have been differentiated from the subjective experience of flow in that they are regarded as preconditions necessary to facilitate flow (Csikszentmihalyi & Nakamura, 2010; Nakamura & Csikszentmihalyi, 2002, 2009). They are characteristics inherent in the task rather than subjective experiences of the flow state. We will elaborate on these preconditions of flow later.

Recently, Bakker (2005, 2008) has distilled the prevailing definitions of flow into a three component operationalization of work flow, namely the Work-reLated Flow Inventory (WOLF). Drawing on the flow and work engagement literatures, Bakker (2005, 2008) recognized three states-dimensions as the core elements of the flow experience:

absorption, enjoyment and intrinsic motivation. The first element, *absorption*, refers to total concentration and immersion in the activity (Csikszentmihalyi, 1990; Ghani & Deshpande, 1994; Ghani, Supnick & Rooney, 1991; Lutz & Guiry, 1994; Webster, Trevino & Ryan, 1994). Individuals in flow are so focused on what they do that they forget everything else around them. The second core element of flow is *enjoyment* (Csikszentmihalyi, 1990; Ghani, Supnick & Rooney, 1991; Hoffman & Novak 1996; Trevino & Webster, 1992). Employees who enjoy their work and feel happy make a very positive judgment about the quality of their working life (cf. Veenhoven, 1984). This enjoyment or happiness is the outcome of cognitive and affective evaluations of the flow experience (cf. Diener, 2000). The third and final element, *intrinsic motivation*, refers to the state in which people do what they do "even at great cost, for the sheer sake of doing it" (Csikszentmihalyi, 1990, p. 3; see also Ellis, Voelkl & Morris, 1994; Trevino & Webster, 1992).

Work-related flow, particularly as operationalized by the WOLF, has many conceptual similarities with the concept of work engagement (Schaufeli, Bakker & Salonova, 2006; Schaufeli, Salanova, Gonzales-Romá & Bakker, 2002). Work engagement is defined as "a positive, fulfilling, work-related state of mind that is characterized by vigor, dedication, and absorption" (Schaufeli, Salanova, Gonzales-Romá & Bakker, 2002; Schaufeli, Bakker & Salonova, 2006). However, there are important differences between the two concepts. Work engagement is a chronic involvement in the wide variety of activities that constitute one's job, whereas flow is an intense, acute, involvement in a specific work task (Csikszentmihalyi, 1975; Mills & Fullagar, 2008; Schaufeli & Salanova, 2007). Furthermore, work engagement has been operationalized as a general tendency to become frequently engaged in work tasks. Consequently it is measured as a dispositional construct or the predisposition to become engaged in work (Schaufeli, Salanova, Gonzales-Romá & Bakker, 2002). Flow, on the other hand, has been shown to be a predominantly state-like construct that indicates far greater within-individual than between-individual variance (Fullagar & Kelloway, 2009). The experience of flow varies considerably depending on the nature of the situation and the characteristics of the task being performed (Fullagar & Kelloway, 2009).

However, flow also exhibits trait-like properties. It has been correlated with such dispositional variables as achievement motivation, aestheticism and inquisitiveness (Csikszentmihalyi, Rathunde & Whalen, 1993; Jackson, 1984) and recent operationalizations tend to define it as both a state and trait construct (for example, Jackson & Ecklund, 2004). Perhaps the best resolution to the state-trait debate regarding flow is that dispositional variables moderate the relationship between situational characteristics and state-based flow. Individuals who indicate "autotelic" tendencies are more predisposed to seek out tasks that have high challenge/skill balance and consequently are more facilitative of flow (Adlai-Gail, 1994; Csikszentmihalyi & Rathunde, 1992). This is corroborated by more recent research that has shown that individuals are more susceptible to experience flow when they are high in achievement–orientation study (Eisenberger, Jones, Stinglhamber, Shanock & Randall, 2005) or when they exhibit an ability to persevere with a task and stay focused (Keller & Bless, 2008).

The Preconditions of Flow

There is a general consensus that flow is a state of intrinsic motivation (Keller & Bless, 2008; Keller & Blomann, 2008). Consequently there must be a compatibility between individual characteristics, such as skill level and need for achievement, and situational characteristics, such as the demands of the task and available resources. Flow theory has consistently identified three situational or task-specific preconditions that are necessary for flow to be experienced (Nakamura & Csikszentmihalyi, 2002).

CHALLENGE/SKILL BALANCE

Perhaps the most important precondition of flow is that the challenges (action opportunities) that are perceived in the task should match or balance with the skills (action capabilities) that are necessary to perform the task (Csikszentmihalyi, 1975, 1990, 1997). In addition, the level of the perceived challenges and skills should be at a moderate to high level for flow to be experienced (Massimini & Carli, 1988; Massimini, Csikszentmihalyi & Carli, 1987). According to flow theory (Csikszentmihalyi, 1975) when the task has little challenge and requires a low level of skill, the individual is likely to experience apathy. When challenges far exceed perceived skills, then anxiety is the predominant state. When the performer is over-skilled for the task, boredom is the most likely experience. The necessity of balance between perceived challenge and skill has been generally supported by evidence from several field studies (Eisenberger, Jones, Stinglhamber, Shanock & Randall, 2005; Fullagar, Knight & Sovern, 2009; Haworth & Evans, 1995; Hektner & Asakawa, 2000). In addition, flow has been experimentally induced by manipulating challenge/skill balance in a variety of video game tasks (Engeser & Rheinberg, 2008; Keller & Bless, 2008; Keller & Blomann, 2008; Moller, Meier & Wall, 2010). Nonetheless, there are some contradictions with flow theory. Several studies (for example, Engeser & Rheinberg, 2008; Fullagar, Knight & Sovern, 2009; Haworth & Evans, 1995; Hektner & Asakawa, 2000) have shown that tasks low in challenge and exceeded by skill level are often conducive to flow rather than boredom. These findings would suggest that the relationship between flow and challenge/skill balance may be moderated by the characteristics of the task being studied. For example, flow is more likely to be experienced in low challenge and high skill situations when the task is volitional and leisurely (for example, playing a musical instrument, cooking, knitting) (Csikszentmihalyi, 1988; Fullagar, Knight & Sovern, 2009; Hektner & Asakawa, 2000). Also, the perceived importance of the activity to the performer moderates the relationship between challenge/skill balance and flow (Engeser & Rheinberg, 2008). Easy tasks that are perceived as being meaningful and important to the individual's self-concept and that the individual feels adept at performing are more likely to generate high levels of optimal experience compared to tasks that are not important.

GOAL CLARITY

Flow is also facilitated by tasks that have clear and proximal goals (Csikszentmihalyi, 1990, 1997). This is consistent with goal-setting theory and is based on the premise that all human behavior is goal directed (Locke, Shaw, Saari & Latham, 1981). Both goal-setting theory and flow theory emphasize that goals should be both challenging and specific in order to direct attention and action (Csikszentmihalyi, Abunhamdeh & Nakamura, 2005; Latham & Locke, 1991; Locke, Shaw, Saari & Latham, 1981). As we elaborate below, there is research that suggests that autonomy is an important precursor to flow (Demerouti, 2006;

Fullagar & Kelloway, 2009). Again, this is consistent with goal-setting theory that has shown that when individuals have the opportunity to participate in setting their own goals they perform at a superior level compared to when goals are unilaterally assigned by a boss or instructor (Erez, Earley & Hulin, 1985). However, it is important to note that the purpose of goals as conceptualized by Locke and colleagues on one hand, and by Csikszentmihalyi on the other, are not equivalent. Csikszentmihalyi views the role of goals as "channeling attention" (Csikszentmihalyi, Abunhamdeh & Nakamura, 2005), not as an objective or end to which people strive, as in goal theory (Locke, 1968). For Csikszentmihalyi, goals focus attention on the task at hand, thereby filtering out extraneous stimuli from the individual's consciousness and promoting the experience of flow.

We could find only one study that has investigated the effects of goal-setting on flow (Knight, Fullagar & Waples, 2011). Whereas the setting of specific and challenging goals had a positive effect on the performance of a video-game task, it was found to be detrimental to flow. This is not necessarily inconsistent with flow theory. Knight, Fullagar and Waples (2011) extrinsically assigned specific and challenging goals to one group of participants, while another group was instructed to just "do your best." Flow theory has always emphasized that goals should be primarily inferred from intrinsic factors inherent in the task itself, and should not be extrinsically imposed. Goals that are set by an extrinsic source to the task tend to redirect attention away from task itself and onto an extrinsic performance standard (Csikszentmihalyi, 1997). The process of focusing on an extrinsic performance standard may detract from the experience of flow in a way that is consistent with the overjustification effect (Lepper & Greene, 1978). The over-justification effect occurs when an extrinsic incentive, such as an externally imposed goal, decreases the individual's motivation to perform a task (Deci, 1972). There are two explanations of this effect. Self-perception theory suggests that when an external incentive is imposed there is a shift in motivation to extrinsic factors and less attention is paid to the intrinsic enjoyment of performing the task (Aronson, Akert & Wilson, 2006). Cognitive evaluation theory proposes that the imposition of external goals is perceived as coercive and controlling and diminishes perceptions of self-determination, autonomy and intrinsic motivation (Enzle & Ross, 1978).

FEEDBACK

The final precondition to optimal experience is that the task should provide the individual with feedback regarding performance of the task (Csikszentmihalyi, 1990, 1997). Although no research has been done on this precondition, most research on flow has been undertaken on activities that have inherent feedback mechanisms (for example, athletic performance, rock climbing, musical performance, chess playing and so forth). Feedback is an integral component of goal-setting (Locke, Shaw, Saari & Latham, 1981) and flow (Csikszentmihalyi, 1975), in that without it intrinsic goals cannot sustain motivation and enhance flow. Feedback is particularly important for the more difficult and challenging tasks that are associated with flow. However, for feedback to be effective in generating intrinsic motivation, the individual has to believe that it is his/her own skills, efforts and abilities that are producing successful performance of the task (Thomas & Mathieu, 1994).

Predictors of Flow at Work

Although the majority of research on flow has focused on such leisure activities as sports and artistic endeavors, the experience of flow is more likely to occur in a work setting. It is at work that the conditions that foster flow are more prevalent, such as moderately high challenging tasks that require high skill levels and are goal-directed (Csikzentmihalyi, 1990; Csikzentmihalyi & LeFevre, 1989; Haworth & Hill, 1992; Hektner, Schmidt & Csiksentmihalyi, 2007). Nielsen and Cleal (2010) found three specific work activities to be associated with flow at work; planning, problem solving and evaluation. Each one of these activities provided individuals with the opportunity to use skills and to create structure and clarity in the job.

JOB CHARACTERISTICS

One theory that has been applied to understanding the facets of work that facilitate flow is the Job Characteristics Model (JCM). Hackman and Oldham (1980) suggest that intrinsic motivational states occur when work is experienced as meaningful. This critical psychological state is generated when jobs have certain core characteristics (Hackman & Oldham, 1980). First, the job must have *skill variety*, in that different skills and talents should be utilized to carry out the work. Second, the job should have *task identity* and require the completion of a whole and identifiable piece of work. Third, work should have *task significance*, meaning that it should have a substantial impact on other people or oneself. According to Hackman and Oldham (1976), the two most important and necessary job characteristic for generating intrinsic motivation are *autonomy* and *feedback*. Autonomy refers to the degree of discretion, freedom and independence that an individual has in scheduling work and determining the procedural aspects of the job. Task feedback is the extent to which work activities provide information about the results of performance.

Csikszentmihalyi (1975, 1990) has argued that flow is a critical psychological state that is also associated with high levels of intrinsic motivation. Indeed those same characteristics of work that have been associated with generating high levels of motivation have been found, both theoretically and empirically, to be associated with flow. For instance, Demerouti (2006) found that autonomy, skill variety, job feedback, task identity and task significance, combined as a motivating potential score, were predictive of flow experiences among employees engaged in a variety of work and occupations. Elaborating on this research, Fullagar and Kelloway (2009), in a longitudinal study, studied the predictive validity of each of the five core job characteristics and found that skill variety and autonomy were both significantly associated with momentary flow experiences. Of the five job characteristics autonomy seems to be the most consistently and strongly related to optimal experience (Bakker, 2005, 2008; Mäkikangas, Bakker, Aunola & Demerouiti, 2010; Salanova, Bakker & Llorens, 2006). This is not surprising as employees' freedom in scheduling their work and in determining work methods has repeatedly been found to increase positive affect (for example, Saavedra & Kwun, 2000) and motivation (Fried & Ferris, 1987). However the relationship between autonomy and flow may be moderated by the nature of work and the organizations studied. Recently Nielsen and Cleal (2010) in an experience sampling study found that autonomy and role clarity were more significantly associated with flow among elder care managers than accountancy managers. They explain these differences in terms of the contextual variation in work between organizations (such as role clarity and complexity) that make it difficult for some workers to experience the kind of structured environment that promotes flow.

JOB RESOURCES

Two other theoretical frameworks have been used to understand the antecedents and outcomes of flow; Conservation of Resources theory (COR: Hobfoll, 1989) and the Job Demands–Resources (JD–R) model (Bakker & Demerouti, 2007; Demerouti, Bakker, Nachreiner & Schaufeli, 2001). The central tenet of the COR theory is that individuals are motivated to obtain, maintain and protect certain personal resources that are important to the individual and serve as means to achieve valued outcomes (Hobfoll, 2002). These resources include physical possessions (for example, money, a home), conditions (for example, marital status, close social attachments), energies (for example, knowledge, time) and personal characteristics (for example, self-esteem, self-efficacy). By accumulating resources individuals are not only more capable of withstanding stress, but also more likely to thrive and achieve high levels of subjective well-being (Lyubomirsky, King & Diener, 2005). Applied to flow, COR theory would hypothesize that those individuals who gain more job and personal resources are more likely to experience high levels of work-related flow (Mäkikangas, Bakker, Aunola & Demerouti, 2010). Furthermore, the experience of positive flow states may initiate a gain cycle of resources (Hobfoll, 1989, 2002) that facilitates the accumulation of more job resources.

More recently the JD–R model (Bakker & Demerouti, 2007; Demerouti, Bakker, Nachreiner & Schaufeli, 2001) has argued that certain job resources (for example, physical, psychological, social or organizational aspects of the job) enable the individual to cope with the inherent stress of work and also trigger increased learning, development, positive well-being and performance. In addition to the job resources identified by the JCM (that is, skill variety, task identity, task significance, autonomy and feedback), several other job resources have been found to be conducive to flow. For example flow has been associated with social support, supervisory coaching and opportunities for professional development (Bakker, 2005, 2008; Mäkikangas, Bakker, Aunola & Demerouti, 2010). In a longitudinal study among school teachers, Salanova, Bakker and Llorens (2006) found evidence of an upward spiral in job resources by showing a reciprocal relationship with flow. Social support, innovation orientation and clear goals were found to be related to work-related flow eight months later. Flow, in turn, was also found to be predictive of organizational, job and personal resources.

The Consequences of Flow

Both positive organizational behavior (Luthans, 2002) and positive organizational scholarship (Cameron, Dutton & Quin, 2003) have redirected the focus of organizational psychology to the study of positively-oriented human strengths and an understanding of what makes individuals flourish in organizations. Given that flow is defined as an optimal state, it is not surprising that it should be associated with both hedonic well-being (positive emotions and life satisfaction) and eudaimonic well-being (optimal functioning) (Ryan & Deci, 2001; Ryff, 1989; Ryff & Keyes, 1995).

POSITIVE EMOTIONS

Flow is conceptualized as a state of positive well-being and empirically has been linked to such positive emotions as joy, excitement, happiness and pride (Eisenberger, Jones, Stinglhamber, Shanock & Randall, 2005; Fullagar & Kelloway, 2009). Indeed, perhaps the most consistent consequence of flow is positive affect and a sense of subjective well-being (Bryce & Haworth, 2002; Clarke & Haworth, 1994; Fave & Massimini, 2004; Fullagar & Kelloway. 2009). Recently research that has aimed at identifying the physiological analogs of flow has shown states of high flow exhibit the same physiological characteristics as high arousal, positive, emotions, such as joy (De Manzano, Theorell, Harmat & Ullén, 2010). For example, repeated physiological measures taken of 21 professional classical pianists as they performed music indicated higher activity in muscles associated with smiling, a decrease in heart period and larger respiratory depth (De Manzano, Theorell, Harmat & Ullén, 2010). These psychophysiological reactions to flow have important health implications in that they are associated with lower blood pressure (Theorell, Ahlberg-Hulten, Jodko, Sigala & de la Torre, 1993) and a reduced likelihood of coronary heart disease (Bygren, Konlaan & Johannsson, 1996). More specifically, flow has been shown to regulate those parasympathetic nervous systems that are associated with lower stress (Theorell, Ahlberg-Hulten, Jodko, Sigala & de la Torre, 1993). Flow theory stipulates that anxiety is the antithesis of flow (Csikszenmihalyi, 1975, 1990). Flow is a state of focused attention, whereas anxiety is associated with disintegrated attention (Izard, 1977). There is some emerging evidence that flow and anxiety are indeed mutually exclusive in that the experience of one prevents the other (Fullagar, Knight & Sovern, 2009).

One theoretical framework that explains the mechanisms that link positive states, such as flow, positive emotions and long-term well-being is Fredrickson's broaden-and-build theory (Fredrickson, 1998, 2001). This theory proposes that positive emotions have a twofold adaptive function. First, they broaden our awareness and thought-action repertoires. Second, they help us to build skills and resources that have a lasting impact on our psychological and physical well-being (Fredrickson, 1998; Fredrickson, Cohn, Coffey, Pek & Finkel, 2008). Experimental studies have shown that positive affect induces cognitive behavior that is more innovative (Isen, Johnson, Mertz & Robinson, 1985), flexible (Isen & Daubman, 1984), creative (Isen, Daubman & Nowicki, 1987) and efficient (Isen, Rosenzweig & Young, 1991). Furthermore positive emotions have been found to build important psychological resources, such as optimism and resiliency, that enable individuals to withstand adverse conditions and to cope more effectively with stress (Fredrickson, Tugade, Waugh & Larkin, 2003). In a recent study, flow was specifically found to be significantly and positively associated with energy after work, particularly if individuals were not able to recover from stress during work breaks and were able to detach from work at home (Demerouti, Bakker, Sonnentag & Fullagar, 2012). It would appear that flow states induce positive emotions and these emotions counteract the side-effects of negative emotional arousal (Fredrickson & Levenson, 1998), increase life satisfaction and improve overall well-being (Fredrickson, Cohn, Coffey, Pek & Finkel, 2008).

PERFORMANCE

Moneta (2004) argues that flow theory synthesizes both the hedonic and eudaimonic approaches to well-being. Consistent with eudaimonic perspective, flow is also associated with optimal functioning and there is some empirical evidence to support this (Carli, Delle Fave & Massimini, 1988; Jackson, Thomas, Marsh & Smethurst, 2001). Peak performance refers to a level of performance that is beyond our normal level of functioning (Privette, 1983) and is associated with activities in which the person is deeply involved, highly committed to and emotionally connected with (Privette, 1983). There is a considerable amount of overlap between the concepts of flow and peak performance. Consequently it is not surprising to find that the two concepts are correlated with each other (Jackson & Csikszentmihalyi, 1999). However, most of the research on peak performance has been conducted on athletes self-reports of being "in the zone."

There are some studies that have highlighted the role of optimal experience in promoting workers' performance at different levels, including both in- and extra-role tasks. In-role performance refers to the officially required outcomes and behaviors that directly serve the goals of the organization; extra-role performance comprises discretionary behaviors that promote the effective functioning of an organization without necessarily having a direct influence on an employee's productivity. According to Engeser and Rheinberg (2008), flow should be associated with better performance for two reasons. First, flow is a highly functional state that should in itself foster performance. Second, individuals experiencing flow are more motivated to carry out further activities, and in order to experience flow again, they will set themselves more challenging tasks. Thus, flow could be seen as a motivating force for excellence. Additionally, we have argued above that when in flow, people are very concentrated, and they invest all available energy resources.

Several studies document the relationship between flow and performance (Nakamura & Csikszentmihalyi, 2002). Demerouti (2006) found that flow predicted both kinds of performances among conscientious employees. From a different point of view, Eisenberger, Jones, Stinglhamber, Shanock and Randall (2005) found that achievement-oriented employees perceiving high skills and high challenges in their occupations more frequently engaged in organizational spontaneity, namely extra-role behaviors such as making constructive suggestions, enhancing one's own knowledge and skills in ways that can help the organization, protecting it from potential problems and helping co-workers. Studies among students show that flow is a predictor of academic performance in one's talent area (Csikszentmihalyi, Rathunde & Whalen, 1993; see also Wong & Csikszentmihalyi, 1991). In addition, research on athletes has found a positive relationship between flow and success in competitive sports (Jackson, Kimiecik, Ford and Marsh, 1998; Jackson, Thomas, Marsh & Smethurst, 2001). In an attempt to capture performance in an objective way Bakker, Oerlemans, Demerouti, Bruins Slot and Karamat (2011) examined flow among soccer players. Individual performance was rated by both the players and their coaches. Results of multi-level analyses showed that flow at the team level is higher when the match results in a draw or win than when the match results in loss. Moreover, environmental resources, particularly performance feedback and support from the coach, predicted flow during the soccer game, which, in turn, was positively related to self- and coach-ratings of performance. The findings indicate that common-method variance cannot account for the finding that the environment of soccer players facilitates flow and indirectly performance.

Flow-evoking Interventions

The research reviewed in this chapter indicates that flow can make an important contribution to the field of work and health. Focusing on positive constructs, such as work-related flow, helps us develop an understanding of the salutogenetic components of work and their impact on individuals and organizations (Bringsén, Ejlertsson & Andersson, 2011). Such positive constructs provide an opportunity for a work practice characterized by positive aspects instead of the traditional problem-solving and pathogenic focus. There is growing empirical evidence that the application of a positive frame of reference is a way of promoting the health of employees and improves the opportunity for high-quality work practice. Bringsén, Ejlertsson and Andersson (2011) warn that flow situations are a relatively rare phenomenon, since flow is described as a subjective experience of enjoyment, complete absorption and a moment where capabilities are being stretched to facilitate learning, and increase self-esteem and personal complexity. Nonetheless, it is still useful to design jobs with increased opportunities for flow experience as flow seems to be beneficial for work-related health and organizational behavior.

We suggest five possible interventions that organizations can apply in order to increase the chance that their employees experience flow. These interventions can be applied separately or, even better, in combination.

HIGH CHALLENGES–HIGH SKILLS INTERVENTIONS

Csikszentmihalyi, Abuhamdeh and Nakamura (2005) contend that flow is dependent on maintaining a balance between perceived challenge and perceived skill. The flow theory implies that individuals are happiest when they feel that the challenges are just slightly beyond their capabilities. This stretches an individual and encourages them to develop new skills. If challenges begin to exceed skills by too much, a person becomes anxious, and if skills begin to exceed challenges, they become bored. Supervisors, who have sufficient knowledge of their employee's skills and his/her job function, can play an important role in achieving such a balance of high challenges and high skills. The role of the supervisor includes encouraging the employee to pace a challenge, to break down goals so they are achievable or encourage greater levels of challenge at each point. In this way the supervisor plays the role of mentor for the employee. At the same time, opportunities for skill enhancement should be provided, for instance, through training such that the employee can learn to work within new areas. These may include acquiring new skills or developing existing skills that would help the individual to achieve his or her goals. Initially emphasis should be put on the use of an employee's strengths that might help to improve the match between perceived skill and perceived challenge. Flow-favoring methodology would also suggest that at a later stage, as confidence increases and greater challenge is sought, the supervisor might search for opportunities to work with an employee on improving strengths which are less strong. In order to increase challenges, based on the findings of Nielsen and Cleal (2010) we could suggest that work should be organized such that employees can engage in activities that include problem-solving, planning and evaluation of results.

PROVIDE JOB RESOURCES

The findings of different studies suggest that it seems worthwhile for organizations to promote flow among their employees by creating flow-evoking working conditions through work (re)design approaches. As we showed, job characteristics like task variety, autonomy, job feedback, task identity and task significance can be flow-inducing and can be the target of work (re)design or practices of Human Resources Management. These job characteristics, or more generally job resources that represent motivating characteristics of the job, can be improved with job enrichment practices (Hackman & Oldham, 1980). Job resources make individuals more motivated to be immersed in their activities and thus to experience flow. As each job function has its specific resources and its own job procedures we cannot make any suggestions for interventions that are applicable to the universe of jobs. Rather we can propose a way that this can be achieved.

Typically, the perceived working conditions are measured among employees using self-report questionnaires in order to find out which resources are missing which are also relevant the experience of flow. After specifying the job resources that are the target of the intervention, teams are formed that that have the assignment of making suggestions on how to enhance specific job resources for specific job functions. In order to make realistic suggestions these teams should consist of employees (who can provide insider knowledge on their own job), supervisors (who can evaluate whether and how each suggestion could be realized in the given organizational context) and employees from the same organization but from another department (for example, somebody from the HRM department in order to avoid possible group think). In this way, solutions are suggested to the organization that are both feasible and more likely to be accepted by the employees. The advantage of this way of developing interventions is that the available human capital of an organization is utilized, the involvement of the employees in their job as well as their commitment to the organization can be increased and the suggestions can help increasing the chances that flow is experienced within the specific organizational context.

POSITIVE INTERVENTIONS

As individual characteristics like autotelic personality, self-efficacy and need for achievement are found to be linked to the flow experience, interventions aimed at enhancing such individual characteristics seem relevant also to stimulate flow. Following the zeitgeist of positive psychology, several interventions have been recently developed that increase happiness, personal resources and individual strengths. These interventions have in common that they try to enhance positive experiences of individuals by making them more assertive (Demerouti, van Eeuwijk, Snelder & Wild 2011), stimulating the reflection of positive experiences and characteristics that each individual has (Seligman, Steen, Park and Peterson, 2005) and by exercising ways that facilitate goal accomplishment and self-regulatory capacity (Luthans, Avolio, Avey & Norman, 2006). Such interventions have been found to have long-term effects on enduring well-being (Fredrickson et al, 2008).

GOAL-SETTING

Inherent in the experience of flow is goal-setting as "goals serve to add direction and purpose to behaviour" and their value "lies in their capacity to structure experience" (Csikszentmihalyi, Abuhamdeh & Nakamura, 2005, p. 601). It is important that the goals are clear, that the different goals are congruent with each other and that the individuals have the possibility to participate in setting their own goals. However, it is possible there might be goals important for the organization which can differ from the goals that are important for the individual as a professional member of the organization. The supervisor again can play an important role in the process of goal-setting. Similar to the role of a coach, the supervisor can help employees to clarify the goals, to help them specify the means to achieve the goals and where to direct the effort. For instance, Gevers and Demerouti (in press) found that temporal leadership (for example, leaders who frequently provide temporal reminders to their employees) was beneficial for the experience of absorption but only for individuals with a deadline action pacing style (that is, those who undertake action just before the deadline). For individuals with a steady or U-shaped action pacing style, temporal leadership was not beneficial as these employees were able to be absorbed in an activity without any external temporal stimuli.

A number of different models can be used to assist the process of goal-setting, including SMART (Locke and Latham, 1990) and Graham Alexander's GROW model (Whitmore, 2002). Moreover, the supervisors can help employees to discover new opportunities for flow experiences and encourage activities to be focused in areas where more satisfaction will be found. Last but not least the supervisor can play an important role in enhancing the congruence between individual and organizational goals. This can be achieved through the socialization process of new employees (such that they learn from the beginning what is important for the organization) as well as through opening feedback channels and by praising employees for the achievement of organizational goals. Preferably the coaching role of the supervisor in employee goal-setting is an ongoing process rather than an intervention that occurs once a year during the evaluation interview.

JOB CRAFTING

It is clear that intervening on the conditions and individual characteristics that stimulate flow is important but how can an organization be sure that what is offered to the employees is what they need to experience flow? At this point individual job design approaches come to mind. Recently it is recognized that employees may actively change the design of their jobs by choosing tasks, negotiating different job content and assigning meaning to their tasks or jobs (Parker & Ohly, 2008). This process of employees shaping their job has been referred to as job crafting (Wrzesniewski & Dutton, 2001). Job crafting is defined as the physical and cognitive changes individuals make in their task or relational boundaries. Physical changes refer to changes in the form, scope or number of job tasks, whereas cognitive changes refer to changing how one sees the job. For instance, a maintenance technician was interviewed and told that he crafts his job in the form of taking on additional tasks (Berg, Wrzesniewski & Dutton, 2010). After being for some time in the organization, he started to proactively help newcomers to learn the job. Because he turned out to be good at this, he became formally responsible for the training of new employees.

Job crafting is about changing the job in order to experience enhanced meaning of it. As a consequence, employees may be able to increase their person–job fit and thereby their flow experiences. Tims, Bakker and Derks (2012) indeed showed that job crafting (as rated by the colleagues) was positively related to work engagement. Employees who increased their job resources, for instance asked for feedback from their supervisor and mobilized their social network, were more dedicated to and absorbed in their work. Additionally, employees who increased their own job demands in order to create a challenging work environment were most likely to be engaged. For instance, the more often individuals proactively volunteered to be involved in projects, the more likely it was that they were identified by their colleagues as absorbed in and dedicated to their work.

Van den Heuvel, Demerouti, and Peeters (2012) designed a job crafting intervention that consists of four phases: In the first phase a one-day session with the employees of the organization is given. In this session/course is explained what exactly is meant by job crafting and employees are then trained to identify the opportunities for job crafting. The course concludes with a so-called Personal Crafting Plan (PCP). In the second phase, the employees go themselves to work on keeping the "weekly crafting diary." This is a weekly diary for one month where employees report their crafting activities on each respective week as they were defined in the PCP. Following the executive phase, participants attend a reflection meeting, in which they share their experiences and discuss successes, problems and solutions. This intervention was implemented among 39 employees from a Dutch Police district. It was found that the experimental group reported more developmental possibilities, better relationship with the supervisor, more self-efficacy, more positive emotions and less negative emotions after the training while the control group reported no change on these constructs. Although it was not found that the employees were more absorbed in their work after the intervention, job crafting interventions seem a promising venue for future research and practice as it might initiate a longer-term positive cycle.

Conclusion

With this chapter we attempted to put flow on the research agenda by showing that flow at work is related to concrete working conditions and, in its turn, may influence highly valuable outcomes of organizational behavior, like job performance. As such flow at work represents an important phenomenon of organizational practice that deserves more attention than it gets currently. We suggested several interventions on the organizational, job function and individual level that are aimed at enhancing flow experiences of employees during work. To our view these interventions have the potential to stimulate flow at work. However, future research is necessary to justify the effectiveness of each of these interventions. As has been shown, flow at work seems significant for organizations and warrants consideration in the future from both scientists and practitioners alike.

References

Adlai-Gail, W. S. (1994) *Exploring the autotelic personality.* Unpublished doctoral dissertation, University of Chicago: Chicago, IL.

Aronson, E., Akert, R. D., & Wilson, T. D. (2006) *Social Psychology*. 6th edition. Upper Saddle River, NJ: Pearson Prentice Hall.

Bakker, A. B. (2005) Flow among music teachers and their students: the crossover of peak experiences. *Journal of Vocational Behavior*, 66, 26–44.

Bakker, A. B. (2008) The work-related flow inventory: construction and initial validation of the WOLF. *Journal of Vocational Behavior*, 72, 400–414.

Bakker, A. B., & Demerouti, E. (2007) The Job Demands-Resources model: state of the art. *Journal of Managerial Psychology*, 22, 309–328.

Bakker, A. B., Oerlemans, W., Demerouti, E., Bruins Slot, B., & Karamat A. D. (2011) Flow and performance: a study among talented Dutch soccer players. *Psychology of Sport and Exercise*, 12, 442–450.

Berg, J. M., Wrzesniewski, A., & Dutton, J. E. (2010) Perceiving and responding to challenges in job crafting at different ranks: when proactivity requires adaptivity. *Journal of Organizational Behavior*, 31, 158–186.

Bringsén, A., Ejlertsson, G., & Andersson, I. H. (2011) Flow situations during everyday practice in a medical hospital ward. Results from a study based on experience sampling method. *BMC Nursing*, 10, 3.

Bryce, J. & Haworth, J. T. (2002) Well-being and flow in a sample of male and female office workers. *Leisure Studies*, 21, 249–263.

Bygren, L. O., Konlaan, B. B., & Johansson, S. E. (1996) Attendance at cultural events, reading books or periodicals, and making music or singing in a choir as determinants for survival: Swedish interview survey of living conditions. *British Medical Journal*, 313, 1577–1580.

Carli, M., Delle Fave, A., & Massimini, F. (1988) The quality of experience in the flow channels: comparison of Italian and US students. In M. Csikszentmihalyi, & I. S. Csikszentmihalyi (eds) Optimal Experience: Psychological Studies of Flow in Consciousness. New York: Cambridge University Press. pp. 288–318.

Cameron, K. S., Dutton, J. E., & Quinn, R. E. (eds). (2003). *Positive Organizational Scholarship*. San Francisco: Berrett-Koehler.

Clarke, S. G., & Haworth, J. (1994) "Flow" experience in the daily lives of sixth-form college students. *British Journal of Psychology*, 85, 511–523.

Csikszentmihalyi, M. (1965) *Artistic problems and their solution: An exploration of creativity in the arts.* Unpublished doctoral dissertation, University of Chicago.

Csikszentmihalyi, M. (1975) *Beyond Freedom and Anxiety.* San Francisco, CA: Jossey-Bass.

Csikszenmihalyi, M. (1988) Introduction. In M. Csikszentmihalyi & I. S. Csikszentmihalyi (eds) *Optimal Experience: Psychological Studies of Flow in Consciousness*. New York: Cambridge University Press. pp. 3–14.

Csikszentmihalyi, M. (1990) *Flow: The Psychology of Optimal Experience.* New York: Harper & Row.

Csikszentmihalyi, M. (1993) *The Evolving Self.* New York: Harper & Row.

Csikszentmihalyi, M. (1997) *Finding Flow: The Psychology of Engagement with Everyday Life.* New York: Basic Books.

Csikszentmihalyi, M., Abuhamdeh, S., & Nakamura, J. (2005) Flow. In A. J. Elliot & C. S. Dweck (eds) *Handbook of Competence and Motivation*. New York: Guilford Press. pp. 598–608.

Csikszentmihalyi, M., & LeFevre, J. (1989) Optimal experience in work and leisure. *Journal of Personality and Social Psychology*, 56, 815–822.

Csikszentmihalyi, M., & Nakamura, J. (2010) Effortless attention in everyday life: a systematic phenomenology. In B. Bruya (ed.) *Effortless Attention: A New Perspective in the Cognitive Science of Attention and Action*. Cambridge, MA: MIT Press. pp. 179–190.

Csikszentmihalyi, M., & Rathunde, K. (1992) The measurement of flow in everyday life: toward a theory of emergent motivation. In J. E. Jacobs (ed.), *Developmental Perspectives on Motivation: Volume 40 of the Nebraska Symposium on Motivation.* Lincoln, Nebraska: University of Nebraska Press. pp. 57–97.

Csikszentmihalyi, M., Rathunde, K., & Whalen, S. (1993) *Talented Teenagers: The Roots of Success and Failure.* New York, NY: Cambridge University Press.

de Manzano, Ö., Theorell, T., Harmat, L., & Ullén, F. (2010) The psychophysiology of flow during piano playing. *Emotion*, 10, 301–311.

deCharms, R. (1976) *Enhancing Motivation: Change in the Classroom.* New York: Irvington.

Deci, E. L. (1972) Intrinsic motivation, extrinsic reinforcement, and inequity. *Journal of Personality and Social Psychology*, 22, 113–120.

Deci, E. L. (1975) *Intrinsic Motivation.* New York: Plenum.

Demerouti, E. (2006) Job characteristics, flow, and performance: the moderating role of conscientiousness. *Journal of Occupational Health Psychology*, 11, 266–280.

Demerouti, E., Bakker, A. B., Nachreiner, F., & Schaufeli, W. B. (2001) The job demands–resources model of burnout. *Journal of Applied Psychology*, 86, 499–512.

Demerouti, E., Bakker, A. B., Sonnentag, S., & Fullagar, C. (2012) Work-related flow and energy at work and at home: a study on the role of daily recovery. *Journal of Organizational Behavior*, 33, 276–295.

van den Heuvel, M., Demerouti, E., & Peeters, M. (2012). Succesvol job craften door middel van een groepstraining [Succesful job crafting through group training]. In J. de Jonge, M. Peeters, S. Sjollema & H. de Zeeuw (eds) *Scherp in Werk: 5 Routes naar Optimale Inzetbaarheid.* Assen: Koninklijke van Gorcum BV. pp. 27–49.

Demerouti, E., van Eeuwijk, E., Snelder, M., & Wild, U. (2011) Assessing the effects of a "personal effectiveness" training on psychological capital, assertiveness and self-awareness using self-other agreement. *Career Development International*, 16, 60–81.

Diener, E. (2000) Subjective well-being, the science of happiness and a proposal for a national index. *American Psychologist*, 55, 34–43.

Eisenberger, R., Jones, J. R., Stinglhamber, F., Shanock, L., & Randall, A.T. (2005) Flow experiences at work: for high need achievers alone? *Journal of Organizational Behavior*, 26, 755–775.

Ellis, G. E., Voelkl, J. E., & Morris, C. (1994) Measurement and analysis issues with explanation of variance in daily experience using the flow model. *Journal of Leisure Research*, 26, 337–356.

Engeser, S., & Rheinberg, F. (2008) Flow performance and moderators of challenge-skill balance. *Motivation & Emotion*, 32, 158–172.

Enzle, M. A., & Ross, J. M. (1978) Increasing and decreasing intrinsic interest with contingent rewards: a test of cognitive evaluation theory. *Journal of Experimental Social Psychology*, 14, 588–597.

Erez, M., Earley, P. C., & Hulin, C. L. (1985) The impact of participation on goal acceptance and performance: a two-step model. *Academy of Management Journal*, 28, 50–66.

Fave, A. D., & Massimini, F. (1988) Modernization and the changing contexts of flow in work and leisure. In M. Csikszentmihalyi & I.S. Csikszentmihalyi (eds) *Optimal Experience: Psychological Studies of Flow in Consciousness.* New York: Cambridge University Press. pp. 193–213.

Fredrickson, B. L. (1998) What good are positive emotions? *Review of General Psychology*, 2, 300–319.

Fredrickson, B. L. (2001) The role of positive emotions in positive psychology: The broaden-and-build theory of positive emotions. *American Psychologist*, 56, 218–226.

Fredrickson, B. L., Cohn, M. A., Coffey, K. A., Pek, J., & Finkel, S. M. (2008). Open hearts build lives: Positive emotions, induced through loving-kindness meditation, build consequential personal resources. *Journal of Personality and Social Psychology*, 95, 1045–1062.

Fredrickson, B. L., & Levenson, R. W. (1998) Positive emotions speed recovery from the cardiovascular sequelae of negative emotions. *Cognition and Emotion*, 12, 191–220.

Fredrickson, B. L., Tugade, M. M., Waugh, C. E., & Larkin, G. (2003) What good are positive emotions in crises? A prospective study of resilience and emotions following the terrorist attacks on the United States of September 11th, 2001. *Journal of Personality and Social Psychology*, 84, 365–376.

Fried, Y., & Ferris, G. R. (1987) The validity of the job characteristics model: a review and a meta-analysis. *Personnel Psychology*, 40, 287–322.

Fullagar, C., & Kelloway. E. K. (2009) "Flow" at work: an experience sampling approach. *Journal of Occupational and Organizational Psychology*, 81, 595–615.

Fullagar, C., Knight, P. K., & Sovern, H. (2009) Flow and Performance Anxiety. Paper presented at the 24th Annual Conference of the Society for Industrial and Organizational Psychology. New Orleans, LA, April 2–4, 2009.

Gevers, J. & Demerouti, E. (in press). How supervisors' reminders relate to subordinates' absorption and creativity. *Journal of Managerial Psychology*.

Ghani, J. A., & Deshpande, S. P. (1994) Task characteristics and the experience of optimal flow in human-computer interaction. *The Journal of Psychology*, 128, 381–391.

Ghani, J. A., Supnick, R., & Rooney, P. (1991) The experience of flow in computer- mediated and in face-to-face groups, In J. I. DeGross, I. Benbasat, G. DeSanctis, & C. M. Beath (eds) *Proceedings of the Twelfth International Conference on Information Systems*. New York, New York, December 16–18.

Hackman, J. R., & Oldham, G. R. (1976) Motivation through the design of work. *Organizational Behavior and Human Performance* 16, 250–279.

Hackman, J. R., & Oldham, G. R. (1980) *Work Redesign*. Reading, MA: Addison-Wesley.

Haworth, J., & Evans, S. (1995) Challenge, skill and positive states in the daily life of a sample of YTS students. *Journal of Occupational and Organizational Psychology*, 68, 109–121.

Haworth, J., & Hill, S. (1992) Work, leisure and psychological well-being in a sample of young adults. *Journal of Community and Applied Social Psychology*, 2, 147–160.

Hektner, J., & Asakawa, K. (2000) Learning to like challenges. In M. Csikszentmihalyi & B. Schneider (eds) *Becoming Adult: How Teenagers Prepare for the World of Work*. New York, NY: Basic Books. pp. 95–112.

Hektner, J. M., Schmidt, J., & Csikszentmihalyi, M. (2007) *Experience Sampling Method: Measuring the Quality of Everyday Life*. Thousand Oaks, CA: Sage.

Hobfoll, S. E. (1989) Conservation of resources: a new attempt at conceptualizing stress. *American Psychologist*, 44, 513–524.

Hobfoll, S. E. (2002) Social and psychological resources and adaptation. *Review of General Psychology*, 6, 307–324.

Hoffman, D. L., & Novak, T .P. (1996) Marketing in hypermedia computer-mediated environments: conceptual foundations. *Journal of Marketing*, 60, 50–68.

Isen, A. M., & Daubman, K. A. (1984) The influence of affect on categorization. *Journal of Personality and Social Psychology*, 47, 1206–1217.

Isen, A. M., Daubman, K. A., & Nowicki, G. P. (1987) Positive affect facilitates creative problem solving. *Journal of Personality and Social Psychology*, 52, 1122–1131.

Isen, A. M., Johnson, M. M. S., Mertz, E., & Robinson, G. F. (1985) The influence of positive affect on the unusualness of word associations. *Journal of Personality and Social Psychology*, 48, 1413–1426.

Isen, A. M., Rosenzweig, A. S., & Young, M. J. (1991) The influence of positive affect on clinical problem solving. *Medical Decision Making*, 11, 221–227.

Izard, C. E. (1977). *Human Emotions*. New York: Plenum.

Jackson, D. (1984) *Personality Research Form Manual*. Port Huron, MI: Research Psycohologists Press.

Jackson, S. A., (1996) Toward a conceptual understanding of the flow experience in elite athletes. *Research Quarterly for Exercise and Sport*, 67, 76–90.

Jackson, S. A., & Csikszentmihalyi, M. (1999) *Flow in Sports: The Keys to Optimal Experiences and Performances*. Champaign, IL: Human Kinetics.

Jackson, S. A., & Eklund, R .C. (2004) *The Flow Scales Manual*. Morgantown, WV: Fitness Information Technology, Inc.

Jackson, S. A., Kimiecik, J. C., Ford, S., & Marsh, H. W. (1998) Psychological correlates of flow in sport. *Journal of Sport & Exercise Psychology*, 20, 358–378.

Jackson, S. A., & Marsh, H. W. (1996) Development and validation of a scale to measure optimal experience: the Flow State Scale. *Journal of Sport & Exercise Psychology*, 18, 17–35.

Jackson, S. A., Thomas, P. R., Marsh, H. W., & Smethurst, C. J. (2001) Relationship between flow, self-concept, psychological skill, and performance. *Journal of Applied Sport Psychology*, 13, 129–135.

Keller, J., & Bless, H. (2008) Flow and regulatory compatibility: an experimental approach to the flow model of intrinsic motivation. *Personality and Social Psychology Bulletin*, 34, 196–209.

Keller, J., & Blomann, F. (2008) Locus of control and the flow experience: an experimental analysis. *European Journal of Personality*, 22, 589–607.

Knight, P. A., Fullagar, C., & Waples, C. J. (2011) *Creating Flow to Reduce Stress*. Paper presented at the 2011 Work, Stress, and Health Conference, Orlando, Florida, May 19–22, 2011.

Latham, G. P., & Locke, E. A. (1991) Self-regulation through goal-setting. *Organizational Behavior and Human Decision Processes*, 50, 212–247.

Lepper, M. R., & Greene, D. (1978) *The Hidden Costs of Reward: New Perspectives on the Psychology of Human Motivation*. Hillsdale, NJ: Lawrence Erlbaum.

Locke, E. A. (1968) Toward a theory of task motivation and incentives. *Organizational Behavior and Human Performance*, 3, 157–189.

Locke, E. A., & Latham, G. P. (1990) *A Theory for Goal Setting and Task Performance*. Upper Saddle River, NJ: Prentice-Hall.

Locke, E. A., Shaw, K. M., Saari, L. M., & Latham, G. P. (1981) Goal setting and task performance: 1969–1980. *Psychological Bulletin*, 90, 125–152.

Luthans, F. (2002). The need for and meaning of positive organizational behavior. *Journal of Organizational Behavior*, 23, 695–706.

Luthans, F., Avolio, B. J., Avey, J. B., & Norman, S. M. (2007) Positive psychological capital: measurement and relationship with performance and satisfaction. *Personnel Psychology, 60*, 541–572.

Lutz, R. J., & Guiry, M. (1994) *Intense Consumption Experiences: Peaks, Performances, and Flows*. Paper presented at the Winter Marketing Educators' Conference, St. Petersburg, FL, February.

Lyubomirsky, S., King, L. A., & Diener, E. (2005) The benefits of frequent positive affect: Does happiness lead to success? *Psychological Bulletin*, 131, 803–855.

Mäkikangas, A., Bakker, A. B., Aunola, K., & Demerouti, E. (2010) Job resources and flow at work: modeling the relationship via latent growth curve and mixture model methodology. *Journal of Occupational Health Psychology*, 83, 795–814.

Maslow, A. (1965) Humanistic science and transcendent experience. *Journal of Humanistic Psychology*, 5, 219–227.

Maslow, A. (1968) *Toward a Psychology of Being*. New York: Van Nostrand.

Massimini, F., & Carli, M. (1988) The systematic assessment of flow in daily life. In M. Csikszentmihalyi & I. Csikszentmihalyi (eds) *Optimal Experience: Psychological Studies of Flow in Counscisousness*. New York: Cambridge University Press. pp. 266–287.

Massimini, F., Csikszentmihalyi, M., & Carli, M. (1987) The monitoring of optimal experience: a tool for psychiatric rehabilitation. *Journal of Nervous and Mental Disease*, 175, 545–549.

Mills, M. J., & Fullagar, C. J. (2008) Motivation and flow: toward an understanding of the dynamics of the relation in architecture students. *Journal of Psychology*, 142, 533–553.

Moller, A. C., Meier, B. P., & Wall, R. D. (2010) Developing an experimental indication of flow: effortless action in the lab. In B. Bruya (ed.) *Effortless Attention: A New Perspective in the Cognitive Science of Attention and Action*. Cambridge, MA: MIT Press. pp. 191–204.

Moneta, G. B. (2004) The flow model of intrinsic motivation in Chinese: cultural and personal moderators. *Journal of Happiness Studies*, 5, 181–217.

Nakamura, J., & Csikszentmihalyi, M. (2002) The concept of flow. In C. R. Snyder & J. S. Lopez (eds) *Handbook of Positive Psychology*. New York: Oxford University Press. pp. 89–105.

Nakamura, J., & Csikszentmihalyi, M. (2009) Flow theory and research. In C .R. Snyder & S. J. Lopez (eds) *The Oxford Handbook of Positive Psychology—2nd Edition*. New York: Oxford University Press. pp. 195–206.

Nielsen, K., & Cleal, B. (2010) Predicting flow at work: investigating the activities and job characteristics that predict flow states at work. *Journal of Occupational Health Psychology*, 15, 180–190.

Parker, S. K., & Ohly, S. (2008). Designing motivating work. In R. Kanfer, G. Chen, & R. D. Pritchard (eds) *Work Motivation: Past, Present, and Future*. New York: Routledge. pp. 233–384.

Privette, G. (1983) Peak experience, peak performance, and flow: a comparative analysis of positive human experience. *Journal of Personality and Social Psychology*, 45, 1361–1368.

Ryan, R. M., & Deci, E. L. (2001) On happiness and human potentials: a re-view of research on hedonic and eudaimonic well-being. *Annual Review of Psychology*, 52, 141–166.

Ryff, C. D. (1989) Happiness is everything, or is it? Explorations on the meaning of psychological well-being. *Journal of Personality and Social Psychology*, 57, 1069–1081.

Ryff, C. D., & Keyes, C. L. M. (1995) The structure of psychological well-being revisited. *Journal of Personality and Social Psychology*, 69, 719–727.

Saavedra, R., & Kwun, S. K. (2000) Affective states in job characteristics theory. *Journal of Organizational Behavior*, 21, 131–146.

Salanova, M., Bakker, A., & Llorens, S. (2006) Flow at work: evidence for an upward spiral of personal and organizational resources. *Journal of Happiness Studies*, 7, 1–22.

Schaufeli, W. B., Bakker, A. B., & Salanova, M. (2006) The measurement of work engagement with a short questionnaire: a cross-national study. *Educational and Psychological Measurement*, 66, 701–716.

Schaufeli, W. B., & Salanova, M. (2007) Work engagement: an emerging psychological concept and its implications in organizations. In S. W. Gilliland, D. D. Steiner, & D. P. Skarlicki (eds) *Research in Social Issues Management*. Greenwich, CT: Information Age Publishers. pp. 135–177.

Schaufeli, W. B., Salanova, M., Gonzales-Romá, V., & Bakker, A. B. (2002) The measurement of engagement and burnout: a confirmative analytic approach. *Journal of Happiness Studies*, 3, 71–92.

Seligman, M. E. P., Steen, T. A., Park, N., & Peterson, C. (2005) Positive psychology progress: empirical validation of interventions. *American Psychologist* 60, 410–421.

Theorell, T., Ahlberg-Hulten, G., Jodko, M., Sigala, F., & de la Torre, B. (1993) Influence of job strain and emotion on blood pressure in female hospital personnel during work hours. *Scandinavian Journal of Work, Environment & Health*, 19, 313–318.

Thomas, K. M., & Mathieu, J. E. (1994) Role of attributions in dynamic self-regulation and goal processes. *Journal of Applied Psychology*, 79, 812–818.

Tims, M., Bakker, A. B., & Derks, D. (2012). Development and validation of the job crafting scale. *Journal of Vocational Behavior*, 80, 173–186.

Trevino, L. K., & Webster, J. (1992) Flow in computer-mediated communication. *Communication Research*, 19, 539–573.

Veenhoven, R. (1984).*Conditions of Happiness*. Dordrecht, The Netherlands: Kluwer.

Webster, J., Trevino, L. K., & Ryan, L. (1994) The dimensionality and correlates of flow in human computer interactions. *Computers in Human Behavior*, 9, 411–426.

Whitmore, J. (2002) *Coaching for Performance*. London: Nicholas Brealey Publishing.

Wong, M. M. & Csikszentmihalyi, M. (1991) Motivation and academic achievement: the effects of personality traits and the quality of experience. *Journal of Personality*, 59, 539–574.

Wrzesniewski, A., & Dutton, J. E. (2001). Crafting a job: revisioning employees as active crafters of their work. *Academy of Management Review*, 26, 179–201.

4 *Passion in Organizations*

ADRIAN FURNHAM

Introduction

The word passion rarely appears in psychology textbooks or journal articles. It is not much found, if ever, in the index of differential, clinical or work psychology books. Occasionally there will be a reference to passion in the psychology of love and relationships as well as in the literature on sex. The exception to this is the work of Vallerand (2008) which will be discussed in detail.

Vallerand (2008) defined passion as a "strong inclination toward an activity that people like, find important and in which they invest their time and energy" (p. 1). On the other hand Smilor (1997) defined it as "the enthusiasm, joy, and even zeal that come from the energetic and unflagging pursuit of a worthy, challenging and uplifting purpose" (p. 342). Passion is not thought of as a primary emotion, though it is conceived as a compelling and overwhelming feeling of desire. People can have an enthusiasm for, an extravagant fondness of, or even an almost irrational attachment to, all sorts of things like music, particular possessions and other people.

Other researchers have noted the almost complete neglect of research into various topics in psychology. For instance McManus and Furnham (2010) investigated the concept of *fun* and found five clear types of fun labeled: sociability, contentment, achievement, sensual and ecstatic.

Still others have concentrated on the fulfilling workplace. Hence the concept of thriving at work defined as have a sense of vitality and a sense of learning at work. Spreitzer, Sutcliffe, Dutton, Sonenshein and Grant (2005) were eager to differentiate their concept of *thriving* from other related contructs like *flourishing, flow, self-actualization* and *subjective well-being* (SWB). Their idea is that agentic work behaviors like being task focused, having a sense of exploration and heeding the well-being of others leads to thriving at work which leads to positive outcomes for both the individual and the organization. In three studies Porath, Spreitzer, Gibson and Garnett (2011) developed a measure of thriving at work and provided evidence on convergent, construct and discriminant validity.

The positive psychologists have, however, not been afraid of the word. Indeed, the strengths psychologists have identified what they call *zest* or *passion* or *enthusiasm*: defined as throwing ones whole being (body and soul) into an activity (Martin, 2005; Seligman, 2002). The opposite is boredom and alienation (Eastwood, Cavaliere, Fahlman & Eastwood, 2007).

This chapter is about passion in the workplace. It begins by reviewing some areas of research aligned to the topic of passion though other, related, words and concepts are used. There are however a number of popular books that address the topic. Nancy Anderson, based on her book, *Work With Passion* argues that there are clear indictors of when you are authentically passionate at work. They include the situations when you would do the work even if you did not get paid for it; you are focused on mastering your work, not on the outcome; you are transformed into a better person as you do the work; you are not aware that time is going by; you are paid to be who you are. By contrast, she argues that there are signals that let you know when you are off the passion track. These include: making money is your priority; being concerned about how you look in the eyes of others; being focused on the end result, not the process; taking shortcuts to achieve your objectives; and sacrificing your needs for others' needs even when it is destructive to your emotional and physical health.

This chapter will first examine the literature on intrinsic motivation which seems the logical "forerunner" of the interest in passion at work.

Intrinsic Motivation

There seems little doubt that the literature on passion at and for work grew out of the extensive and long-standing literature on work motivation, more particularly the well-known and widespread distinction between intrinsic and extrinsic motivation.

What is the difference between intrinsic and extrinsic motivation?

It can be illustrated by the following true story.

An academic was working at home. Things were going well, but it was a holiday and the local park nearby was full of children laughing and playing. Their erratic, loud, uncontrollable noise was deeply disturbing. There was no easy alternative for the writer. Closing the windows did little to muffle the sound, only making the room stuffy. There was no other room to decamp to. So what to do, other than ask the children to move on?

A number of possibilities arose: threaten the children or bribe them to go away. The children might accept the bribe but soon return to this lucrative source of dosh.

The academic, however, knew his motivation theory. He wandered outside. Mustering all the charm he could, he gathered the children around him and told them that he had observed them from his office and had admired and enjoyed their noisy games, high-spirited yells and laughter—so much so that he was prepared to pay them to continue. Each child was given £1.

Of course they continued. The wise old don did the same the next day and the next. But on the fourth day, when the expectant children gathered around, he explained that for various reasons he had no money so he could no longer continue to "subsidise" their play. Speaking on behalf of the others, the oldest child said that if he thought the children were going to carry on playing for nothing he was sadly misinformed, and they left.

What the writer knew was that the essence of play is intrinsically satisfying. It is a preposterous idea to pay people to play because they love and volunteer for the activity. You only have to recompense people for doing things they do not really enjoy: things that are dangerous or mind-numbingly dreary; things that are tiring or stressful. Yet by paying for the play the academic persuaded the children to view it in a different way.

Those who are intrinsically motivated would appear to be more passionate at work. They come for the sheer joy of the activity, not the financial rewards nor security afforded by the job.

Extrinsic motivation refers to pay and conditions. People work for very specific rewards: salary, pension, holidays and so on. The issue that concerns most people is pay/salary/wage. The debate about the power of money to motivate is very old, extremely controversial and quite naturally unresolved (Furnham & Argyle, 1998). Those who believe money is at best a weak motivator point to surveys where money is placed low on the list of the most desirable features of a job (after security, opportunities for advancement, recognition and so on). Those who believe in the power of money point to the way those people such as salesmen, on nearly exclusively performance-related pay, work extremely efficiently and effectively.

However, it is generally agreed that:

- Money is a good motivator for those who need or value it enough. This is not a tautology, although it may seem so. People differ enormously in how much they value the symbolism, power and status of money. The greater the need, the greater the motivational power.
- Money is most effective when it has noticeable effects. Large, lump-sum increases make people feel materially better off, able to buy "luxuries."
- Money motivates when it is actually, and seen to be, rewarding performance. If people see a simple but direct relationship between input (hard work) and output (money), they feel able to control and predict their income. This is true of the individuals or groups working in gain-sharing programs (for example, worker co-operatives) that allow them to participate financially in the productivity gains they achieved.

One topic that never goes away is the ability of money to motivate the average worker. Middle managers believe money is the most powerful motivator. Paradoxically, it is nearly always those who do not have it in their power to motivate with money who believe this to be the case. By contrast, the people who have control over the purse strings may not regard money as very relevant.

If money *is* a powerful motivator or satisfier at work, why has research consistently shown that there is no relationship between wealth and happiness? There are four good reasons why this is so:

- *Adaptation.* Although evidence suggests that people feel "happier" after a pay rise, windfall or lottery win, one soon adapts to this and the effect disappears rapidly.
- *Comparison.* People define themselves as wealthy by comparison with others. However, on moving into more upmarket circles they find there is always someone else who is wealthier.
- *Alternatives.* As economists say, the declining marginal utility of money means that as one has more of the stuff, other things such as freedom and true friendship seem much more valuable.
- *Worry.* Increased income is associated with a shifting of concern from money issues to the more uncontrollable elements of life (such as self-development), perhaps because money is associated with a sense of control over one's fate.

The power of money as a motivator is short-lived. Furthermore, it has less effect the more comfortable the people are. Albert Camus, the author, was right when he said it was a kind of spiritual snobbery to believe people could be happy without money. But given or earning a modest amount, the value of other work–benefits becomes greater.

The money that employees receive in exchange for working in an organization is tied up with many other fringe benefits (insurance, sick leave, holiday, pensions), and they are difficult to separate. If money–pay itself satisfies a variety of important and fundamental needs of employees, it should be/is a good motivator to the extent that good job performance is necessary to obtain it. If employees' needs are complex and not clearly related to income, or if the quality or quantity of work performance is not directly related to reward, it serves as a much weaker motivator.

There is however some extremely interesting and controversial work which suggests not only that intrinsic motivation is far preferable to extrinsic motivation, but that extrinsic rewards are actually demotivating. The most powerful and popular advocate of this is Kohn who suggested that rewards can only create *temporary compliance*, not a fundamental shift in performance.

> *When it comes to producing lasting change in attitudes and behavior, however, rewards, like punishment, are strikingly ineffective. Once the rewards run out, people revert to their old behaviors. Studies show that offering incentives for losing weight, quitting smoking, using seat belts, or (in the case of children) acting generously is not only less effective than other strategies but often proves worse than doing nothing at all. Incentives, a version of what psychologists call extrinsic motivators, do not alter the attitudes that underlie our behaviors. They do not create an enduring commitment to any value or action. Rather, incentives merely—and temporarily— change what we do. (Kohn, 1993, p. 110)*

Later he argued, "As for productivity, at least two dozen studies over the last three decades have conclusively shown that people who expect to receive a reward for completing a task or for doing that task successfully simply do not perform as well as those who expect no reward at all" (Kohn, 1993, p. 111).

Kohn offers six reasons why this seemingly backward conclusion is, in fact, the case:

1. *Pay is not a motivator*—whilst the reduction of a salary is a demotivator, there is little evidence that increasing salary has anything but a transitory impact on motivation. This was pointed out 50 years ago; just because too little money can irritate and demotivate does not mean that more money will bring about increased satisfaction, much less increased motivation.
2. *Rewards punish*—rewards can have a punitive effect because they, like outright punishment, are manipulative. Any reward itself may be highly desired; but by making that bonus contingent on certain behaviors, managers manipulate their subordinates. This experience of being controlled is likely to assume a punitive quality over time. Thus the withholding of an expected reward feels very much like punishment.
3. *Rewards rupture relationships*—incentive programs tend to pit one person against another which can lead to all kinds of negative repercussions as people undermine each other. This threatens good teamwork.
4. *Rewards ignore reasons*—managers sometimes use incentive systems as a substitute for giving workers what they need to do a good job, like useful feedback, social support

and autonomy. Offering a bonus to employees and waiting for the results requires much less input and effort.

5. *Rewards discourage risk taking*—people working for a reward generally try to minimize challenge and tend to lower their sights when they are encouraged to think about what they are going to get for their efforts.
6. *Rewards undermine interest*—extrinsic motivators are a poor substitute for genuine interest in one's job. The more a manager stresses what an employee can earn for good work, the less interested that employee will be in the work itself. If people feel they need to be "bribed" to do something, it is not something they would ordinarily want to do.

This literature essentially says this: one can distinguish between intrinsic motivation to partake in some activity out of sheer enthusiasm, joy, passion and extrinsic motivation which involves offering a range of incentives to do an activity rather than the activity itself. The intrinsically motivated worker is therefore easier to manage, happier and possibly more productive. More controversially it has been suggested that extrinsic rewards like money actually decrease joy and passion and even productivity in the long run.

Passion: the Work of Vallerand

Over a 20-year period, Vallerand and colleagues worked on the psychology of passion. Vallerand (2008) defined passion as a "strong inclination toward an activity that people like, find important and in which they invest their time and energy" (p. 1). The idea is that over time people discover that some activities rather than others seem to satisfy their needs for competence, autonomy and relatedness. They thus become a passionate, self-defining, identity-determining activity into which they put their time and energy. Passion has powerful affective outcomes and relates strongly to the persistence in various activities.

More importantly he distinguished between healthy, harmonious passion (HP) and unhealthy obsessive passion (OP). He suggests HP is the autonomous internalization of an activity into a person's identity when they freely accept the activity as important for them. It is done with volition, and not compunction. HP for an activity is a significant but not overpowering part of identity and in harmony with other aspects of a person's life. On the other hand the drivers of OP are essentially specific contingencies like self-esteem, excitement or self-acceptance. They feel compelled to engage in particular activities because of these contingencies which then come to control them.

OP clearly has an addictive quality about it because it is perhaps the only source of important psychological rewards. In this sense workaholism is a sign of OP not HP.

The theory suggests that HP leads to more *flexible* task engagement which in turn leads to more engagement through the process of absorption, concentration, flow and positive effect. OP on the other hand leads to more *rigid and conflicted* task performance which reduces engagement. HP controls the activity, OP is controlled by it. The former promotes healthy adaptation while the latter thwarts it.

Vallerand, Mageau, Ratelle, Leonard, Blanchard, Koestner, Gagne and Marsolais (2003) developed a scale to measure these two dimensions of passion. Referring to particular activities like reading or team sports, items that reflect HP include, "I am completely taken with this activity" and "This activity reflects the qualities I like about myself" while OP items include, "I am emotionally dependent on this activity" and "My mood depends on me being able to do this activity."

Vallerand and colleagues have reported many experimental studies that help explain the process. Thus Vallerand, Salvy, Mageau, Elliot, Denis, Grouzet and Blanchard (2007) showed HP was directly related to activity investment and predicted deliberate practice and mastery goals which had an important effect on performance outcomes. Thus while HP ultimately leads to positive performance the opposite has been true of OP.

Mageau, Vallerand, Charest, Salvy, Lacaille, Bouffard and Koestner (2009) found that children and adolescents whose environment (schools, parents) supported their autonomous choice of activities were more likely to develop and HP rather than an OP.

Various empirical studies have confirmed many of Vallerand's hypotheses. For instance Philippe, Vallerand and Lavigne (2009) showed that HP but not OP was related to both hedonic and eudaimonic well-being. Further, they showed HP actually increased a person's sense of vitality over time. Similarly in a study of older adults over time Rousseau and Vallerand (2008) showed that HP increased activity engagement which was related to SWB while OP had the opposite effect. In a diary study Mageau and Vallerand (2007) were able to demonstrate how passion moderated the relationship between activity engagement and positive effect.

In a recent study Lafreniere, Belanger, Sedikides and Vallerand (2011) showed people with relatively high self-esteem experienced higher levels of HP (given their use of their adaptive self regulatory strategies) while those with low self-esteem (given their ego fragility and defensiveness) would experience higher levels of OP.

Vallerand has applied his idea successfully to the world of sport (Amiot, Vallerand & Blanchard, 2006; Vallerand, Mageau, Elliot, Dumais, Demers & Rousseau, 2008) where it has been shown that HP is positively, and OP negatively associated with various measures of attainment in various sports. The ideas have also been successfully applied to gambling (Rousseau, Vallerand, Ratelle, Mageau & Provencher, 2002; Wang, Khoo, Liu & Divaharan, 2008).

Inevitably this work has been applied to behavior in the workplace. Vallerand and Houlfort (2003) developed a relatively simple model that suggests HP but not OP predicted psychological adjustment at work. They argue that passion has long-term consequences. OP workers seem akin to workaholics while HP workers show greater job satisfaction and performance. Passion is related to affect at work, work–family conflict, turnover, health and performance. In a neat path analytic study Vallerand, Paquet, Phillipe and Charest (2010) showed HP was positively correlated with work satisfaction which in turn was negatively correlated with burnout, while OP was strongly correlated with conflict which in turn was correlated with burn out.

The question is *how* can organizations encourage HP, rather than OP in their organization? The answer is to "provide employees with a healthy, flexible, and secure working environment, one where their opinion is valued, will create conditions that facilitate the development of HP. Organisational support seems to foster an autonomous–supportive context that allows individuals to internalize the activity in their identity in an autonomous fashion" (Vallerand, Paquet, Phillipe and Charest, p. 193).

Others have been inspired by Vallerand's work. Thus Burke and Fiksenbaum (2009) administered a questionnaire which measured "feeling driven to work because of inner pressure" and "work enjoyment" which they called *passion* and *addiction* to different groups in Australia, Canada and Norway. They found that those who scored higher on passion than addiction were more heavily invested in their work and more job satisfied, while showing less work obsessive behaviors and higher psychological well-being. Equally Gorgievski and Bakker (2010) distinguished between *work engagement* and *workaholism*.

The Manifestations and Correlates of Passion

ENERGY AND VIGOR AT WORK

Job advertisements, especially those aimed at recruiting young graduates for highly pressurized positions, sometimes speak of "high-energy individuals." They might as well add "impervious to sleep deprivation and the effects of weekend working" to the list of desirable characteristics for these high energy burnout careers.

Energy is a hot topic. Whether it be the energy that powers our cars and computers or physical energy to remain alert, active and attentive at the end of the day. Personal energy is equally important and has various components. The *first* is *physical energy* Older people have less energy than younger people. Sick people have less energy than well people. Sleep deprived people are less energetic than the well-rested.

The *second* is *psychological energy*. This has been conceived of in different ways. The Freudians conceived a psychic energy: a force that drives us to want and do things we barely understand. Thus we can be driven to a-rational, irrational, bizarre behaviors because of these unconscious libidinous springs.

Personality factors are also related to energy. Extroverts appear more (socially) energetic but burn up easily with their impulsivity and impatience. Introverts have a much slower-burning fuse and are able to sustain longer periods of attentiveness under conditions of poor arousal. Neurotics waste their energy. They burn it up on the irrelevant and the imaginary. They can easily become anxious, then depressed, by small things. They fritter away their additional nervous energy rather than conserve it for the long haul or the really important. Paradoxically then, they appear to have more energy than their stable opposites but waste it on worry. And they end up exhausted.

Third there is *intellectual energy*. The bright have more intellectual energy: more curiosity, more openness-to-new-experience. They use their energy more efficiently. Indeed one definition of intelligence is about energy efficient brain processing.

There is an academic literature on *vigor*. Shirom (2011) has defined this as physical strength, emotional energy and cognitive liveliness. He argues that genetic, physiological and psychological factors affect vigor which in turn is related to job performance and satisfaction, as well as physical and mental health. He sees vigor as a personal resource, like optimism and self-efficacy, related to energy and the way it can be directed in the workplace. His argument is that vigor predicts interaction with others at work, leadership style as well as group processes and the use of organizational resources to be successful at work.

FLOW

Over 15 years ago a Transylvanian psychologist called Csikszentmihalyi wrote a book called *Flow*. His research involved watching and talking to people who were creative and successful in various fields from rock climbing to rock music. He also introduced a method called experience sampling. People carried a beeper. Eight times a day this went off and carriers were required to write down immediately both what they were doing and how they were feeling.

People felt best, he found, when *engrossed* in some challenging activity. During flow they lost track of time, felt more capable, more sensitive and more self-confident even though the activities may be work-based challenges. The activity was its own reward: intrinsically motivating. Flow banishes depression, distraction and creeping dispiritedness. So what are the preconditions of flow?

Csíkszentmihályi identified the following factors as accompanying an experience of flow:

1. *Clear goals* (expectations and rules are discernible and goals are attainable and align appropriately with one's skill set and abilities). The challenge level and skill level should both be high.
2. *Concentrating*, a high degree of concentration on a limited field of attention (a person engaged in the activity will have the opportunity to focus and to delve deeply into it).
3. A *loss of the feeling of self-consciousness*, the merging of action and awareness.
4. *Distorted sense of time*, one's subjective experience of time is altered.
5. Direct and immediate *feedback* (successes and failures in the course of the activity are apparent, so that behavior can be adjusted as needed).
6. *Balance between ability level and challenge* (the activity is neither too easy nor too difficult).
7. A sense of personal *control* over the situation or activity.
8. The activity is *intrinsically rewarding*, so there is an effortlessness of action.
9. A lack of awareness of *bodily needs* (to the extent that one can reach a point of great hunger or fatigue without realizing it).
10. Absorption into the activity, narrowing of the focus of awareness down to the activity itself, *action awareness merging*.

Vallerand (2008) sees flow as the consequence of (harmonious) passion. Thus for flow to be experienced at work a person needs: a clear goal in mind; reasonable expectations of completing satisfactorily the goal in mind; the ability to concentrate; to be given regular and specific feedback on their performance; to have the appropriate skills to complete the task.

We all know the flow experience both at home and work. One can observe flow in those jobs where people experience greatest work satisfaction. They include mainly artisans—potters and painters, writers and weavers, thatchers and designers. They exercise their talents, work at their own pace and are the opposite of "alienated from the products of their labours." Indeed they are the products of their labor. They are what they produce. They are bound-up in the product. Their identity, their being, is in the product of their talents.

HAPPINESS AT WORK

The word "happiness" means several different things (joy, satisfaction) and therefore many psychologists prefer the term "subjective well-being" (SWB) which is an umbrella term that includes the various types of evaluation of one's life one might make. It can include self-esteem, joy and feelings of fulfilment. The essence is that the person *himself/ herself* is making the evaluation of life. Thus the person herself or himself is the expert here: is my life going well, according to the standards that I choose to use?

It has also been suggested that there are three primary components of SWB: general satisfaction, the presence of pleasant affect and the absence of negative emotions including anger, anxiety, guilt, sadness and shame. More importantly SWB covers a wide scale from ecstasy to agony: from extreme happiness to great gloom and despondency. It relates to long-term states, not just momentary moods. It is not sufficient but probably a necessary criterion for mental or psychological health.

Many researchers have listed a number of myths about the nature and cause of happiness. These include the following which are widely believed but wrong:

- happiness depends mainly on the quality and quantity of things that happen to you;
- people are less happy than they used to be;
- people with a serious physical disability are always less happy;
- young people in the prime of life are much happier than older people;
- people who experience great happiness also experience great unhappiness;
- more intelligent people are generally happier than less intelligent people;
- children add significantly to the happiness of married couples;
- acquiring lots of money makes people much happier in the long run;
- men are overall happier than women;
- pursuing happiness paradoxically ensures you lose it.

The first books on the psychology of happiness started appearing in the 1980s. Then a few specialist academic journals began to appear but it was not until the turn of the millennium that the positive psychology movement was galvanized into action by significant grant money as well as research focus of many famous psychologists. The psychology of happiness attempts to answer some very fundamental questions pursued over the years by philosophers, theologians and politicians. The *first* series of questions are really about definition and measurement of happiness; the *second* are about why certain groups are as happy or unhappy as they are; and the *third* group of questions concern what does one have to do (or not to do) to increase happiness.

Most measurements of happiness are by standardized questionnaires or interview schedules. On the other hand it could be done by informed observers: those people who know the individual well and see them regularly. There is also experience sampling when people have to report how happy they are many times a day, week or month when a beeper goes off and these ratings are aggregate. Yet another is to investigate a person's memory and check for whether they feel predominantly happy or unhappy about their past. Finally there are some, as yet crude, but ever developing physical measures, looking at everything from brain scanning to saliva cortisol measures. It is not very difficult to measure happiness reliably and validly.

The relatively recent advent of studies on happiness, sometimes called SWB has led to a science of well-being (Huppert, Baylis & Keverne, 2005). Argyle (2001) noted that different researchers had identified different components of happiness such as life satisfaction, positive affect, self-acceptance, positive relations with others, autonomy and environmental mastery. It constitutes joy, satisfaction and other related positive emotions.

Myers (1992) noted the stable and unstable characteristics of happy people. They tend to be creative, energetic, decisive, flexible and sociable. They also tend to be more forgiving, loving, trusting and responsible. They tolerate frustration better and are more willing to help those in need. In short they feel good, so do good. Diener (2000) has defined SWB as how people cognitively and emotionally evaluate their lives. It has an evaluative (good–bad) as well as a hedonic (pleasant–unpleasant) dimension.

Positive psychology is the study of factors and processes that lead to positive emotions, virtuous behaviors and optimal performance in individuals and groups. Although a few, mainly "self psychologists," were always interested in health, adjustment and peak performance, the study of happiness was thought to be unimportant, even trivial.

Finding work and leisure activities that really engage your skills and passions help a great deal. Taking regular exercise, and sleeping and eating well helps keep up a good mood. Investing time and care in relationships is a very important feature of happiness. Affirming others, helping others and regularly expressing gratitude for life increases happiness. As does having a sense of purpose and hope that may be best described as faith.

Myers's (1992) suggestions for a happier life are:

"1. **Realise that enduring happiness doesn't come from success.** People adapt to changing circumstances—even to wealth or a disability. Thus wealth is life health: its utter absence breeds misery, but having it (or any circumstances we long for) doesn't guarantee happiness.

2. **Take control of your time.** Happy people feel in control of their lives. To master your use of time, set goals and break them into daily aims. Although we often over estimate how much we will accomplish in any given day (leaving us frustrated) we generally underestimate how much we can accomplish in a year, given just a little progress every day.

3. **Act happy.** We can sometimes act ourselves into a happier frame of mind. Manipulated into a smiling expression, people feel better; when they scowl, the whole world seems to scowl back. So put on a happy face. Talk as if you feel positive self-esteem, are optimistic, and are outgoing. Going through the motions can trigger the emotions.

4. **Seek work and leisure that engages your skills.** Happy people often are in a zone called "flow"—absorbed in tasks that challenge but don't overwhelm them. The most expensive forms of leisure (sitting on a yacht) often provide less flow experience than gardening, socialising, or craft work.

5. **Join the 'movement' movement.** An avalanche of research reveals that aerobic exercise can relive mild depression and anxiety as it promotes health and energy. Sound minds reside in sound bodies. Off your duffs, couch potatoes.

6. **Give your body the sleep it wants.** Happy people live active vigorous lives yet reserve time for renewing sleep and solitude. Many people suffer from a sleep debt, with resulting fatigue, diminished alertness and gloomy moods.

7. **Give priority to close relationships.** Intimate friendships with those who care deeply about you can help you weather difficult times. Confiding is good for soul and body. Resolve to nurture your closest relationship by not taking your loved ones for granted, by displaying to them the sort of kindness you display to others, by affirming them, by playing together and sharing together. To rejuvenate your affections, resolve in such ways to act lovingly.

8. **Focus beyond the self.** Reach out to those in need. Happiness increases helpfulness (those who feel good do good). But doing good also makes one feel good.
9. **Keep a gratitude journal.** Those who pause each day to reflect on some positive aspect of their lives (their health, friends, family, freedom, education, senses, natural surroundings and so on) experience heightened well-being.
10. **Nuture your spiritual self.** For many people faith provides a support community, a reason to focus beyond self, and a sense of purpose and hope. Study after study finds that actively religious people are happier and that they cope better with crises."

Positive psychology (Seligman, 2002; Linley, 2008) shifts the focus to exploring and attempting to correct or change personal weakness to a study of strengths and virtues. Its aim is to promote authentic happiness and the good life and thereby promote health. A starting point for positive psychology for both popular writers and researchers has been to try to list and categorize strengths and values. This has been done though it still excites controversy. Positive psychology has now attracted the interest of economists and even theologians as well as business people. It is a movement that is rapidly gathering "steam" and converts to examine scientifically this most essential of all human conditions.

Health and wellness are, it seems, systematically related to the age, sex, race, education and income states of individuals. We know the following: women report more happiness and fulfilment if their lives feel rushed, rather than free and easy. Women are more likely than men both to become depressed and to express joy. There is very little change in life satisfaction and happiness over the life span. There are social class factors associated with mental health and happiness but these are confounded with income, occupation and education. There is a relationship between health, happiness and income but the correlation is modest and the effect disappears after the average salary level is reached. Better educated people—as measured by years of education—is positively associated with happiness. Occupational status is also linked to happiness with dramatic differences between Class I and V. Race differences in health and happiness in a culture are nearly always confounded with education and occupation. There are dramatic national differences in self-reported happiness which seems to be related to factors such as national income, equality, human rights and democratic systems. Physical health is a good correlate of mental health and happiness but it is thought to be both a cause and an effect of happiness.

How to Foster Passion

There seems abundant evidence that the intrinsically motivated, harmoniously passionate person at work experiences vigor, flow and well-being. The question is how to pick the right people and adopt the optimal management style and corporate culture to maximize it. The literature on intrinsic motivation, passion and flow all suggest similar ideas. These include:

• *Challenge*: Goals need to be set by both worker and supervisor that involve an *optimal amount* of difficulty/challenge in attaining them. People do best when working on meaningful goals where tasks are of intermediate difficulty. They should be *stretching goals* and seen as part of a development plan. Thus let people set personally meaningful goals and targets which related to their self-esteem. Give them feedback so that they can see how they are doing.

- *Curiosity*: Activities that stimulate an employee's attention and interest are best. This means introducing novelty and stimulating questioning that takes them beyond their present skills and knowledge. Changes and challenges stimulate curiosity. The idea is to foster a sense of wonder. It is about job enrichment.
- *Control*: Allowing employees to have a choice in what happens. This sense of, and actual, autonomy is most important. Leadership roles, even temporary ones, create a higher sense of engagement and recognition. People at work need to understand cause-and-effect relationships. They need to know and believe that their effort and outcomes have real and powerful effects. But most importantly they must be able to freely choose what and how they learn.
- *Fun and fantasy*: Using imagination and games to promote learning in the workplace. The idea is to turn work into play.
- *Competition*: Comparing the performance from one employee to another more as a source of feedback than in the spirit of trying to win a competition. This can however have negative consequences if it reduces co-operation.
- *Co-operation*: Encouraging employees to help each other to achieve goals. This means working in self-organized teams. People enjoy helping as much as being helped. Co-operation improves interpersonal skills.
- *Recognition*: Celebrating employees' accomplishments and successes. This means recognizing employees for a job well done and praise for doing a great job. Where possible, praise should be public; gather your team together for a moment and celebrate an accomplishment. Spend your day looking for and recognizing great performance.

The problem with the above of course is that it may not be possible with many jobs. De-skilled, repetitive jobs may not always be economically viable to redesign. However what does seem to be the case is that management style and philosophy itself can go a long way to increasing passion in the work place which has benefits for all.

References

Amiot, C. E., Vallerand, R. J., & Blanchard, C. M. (2006) Passion and psychological adjustment: a test of the person-environment fit hypothesis. *Personality and Social Psychology Bulletin*, 32, 220–229.

Argyle, M. (2001) *The Psychology of Happiness*. London: Routledge.

Burke, R. J., & Cooper, C. L. (2008) *The Long Work Hours Culture: Causes, Consequences and Choices*. London: Emerald Group Publishing Limited.

Burke, R. J., & Fiskenbaum, L. (2009) Work motivations, work outcomes, and health: passion versus addiction. *Journal of Business Ethics*, 84, 257–263.

Diener, E. (2000) Subjective well-being. *American Psychologist*, 55, 34–41.

Eastwood, J. D., Cavaliere, C., Fahlman, S. A., & Eastwood, A. E. (2007) A desire for desires: boredom and its relation to alexithymia. *Personality and Individual Differences*, 42, 1035–1045.

Furnham, A., & Argyle, M. (1998) *The Psychology of Money*. London: Routledge.

Gorgievski, M., & Bakker, A. (2010) Passion for work: work engagement vs workaholism. In S. Albrecht (ed.) *Handbook of Employee Engagement*. London: Edward Elgar. pp. 264–271.

Hodder, M., & Coleman, B. (2007) The contribution of social relationships to children's happiness.

Huppert, F., Baylis, N., & Keverne, B.(Eds) (2005) *The Science of Well-Being*. Oxford: OUP.

Kohn, A. (1993) Punished by rewards. *Hravard Business Review*, September/October, 3–7.

Lafreniere, M-A., Belanger, J., Sedikides, C., & Vallerand, R. (2011) Self-esteem and pssion for activities. *Personality and Individual Differences,*51, 541–544.

Linley, A. (2008) *Average to A+*. Coventry: CAPP Press.

Mageau, G. A., & Vallerand, R. J. (2007) The moderating effect of passion on the relation between activity engagement and positive affect. *Motivation and Emotion*, 31, 312–321.

Mageau, G. A., Vallerand, R. J., Charest, J., Salvy, S-J., Lacaille, N., Bouffard, T., & Koestner, R. (2009) On the development of harmonious and obsessive passion: the role of autonomy support, activity specialisation, and identification with the activity. *Journal of Personality*, 77, 602–646.

Martin, A. J. (2005) Perplexity and passion: further consideration of the role of positive psychology in the workplace. *Journal of Organisational Behaviour Management*, 24, 203–205.

McManus, I. C., & Furnham, A. (2010) "Fun, Fun, Fun": types of fun, attitudes to fun, and their relation to personality and biographical factors. *Psychology*, 1, 159–168.

Myers, D. (1992) *The Pursuit of Happiness*. New York: Avon.

Nevid, J., Rathus, S., & Greene, B. (1997) *Abnormal Psychology in a Changing World*. New Jersey: Prentice Hall.

Phillipe, F. L., Vallerand, R. J., & Lavigne, G. L. (2009) Passion does make a difference in people's lives: a look at well-being in passionate and non-passionate individuals. *Applied Psychology: Health and Well-Being*, 1, 3–22.

Porath, C., Spreitzer, G., Gibson, C., & Garnett, F. (2011) Thriving at work. *Journal of Organizational Behaviour*, 33, 250–275.

Positive Psychology Centre: Frequently Asked Questions. Available online at: www.ppc.sas.upenn. edu/faqs.htm.

Rosenberg, M. (1965) *Society and the Adolescent Self-image*. Princeton, NJ: Princeton University Press.

Rousseau, F. L., & Vallerand, R. J. (2008) An examination of the relationship between passion and subjective well-being in older adults. *International Journal of Aging and Human Development*, 66, 195–211.

Rousseau, F. L., Vallerand, R. J., Ratelle, C. F., Mageau, G. A., & Provencher, P. J. (2002) Passion and gambling: on the validation of the gambling passion scale. *Journal of Gambling Studies*, 18, 45–66.

Seligman, M. (2002) *Authentic Happiness*. New York: Free Press.

Seligman, M., & Rosenhan, D. (2001) *Abnormal Psycholog*. New York: W. W. Norton.

Shirom, A. (2011) Vigor as a positive affect at work. *Review of General Psychology*, 15, 50–64.

Smilor, R. (1997) Entrepreneurship, reflections on a subversive activity. *Journal of Business Venturing*, 12, 341–346.

Spreitzer, G., Sutcliffe, K., Dutton, J., Sonenshein, S., & Grant, A. (2005) A socially embedded model of thriving at work. *Organization Science*, 16, 537–549.

Vallerand, R. J. (2008) On the psychology of passion: in search of what makes people's lives most worth living. *Canadian Psychology*, 49, 1–13.

Vallerand, R. J., & Houlfort, N. (2003) Passion at work: towards a new conceptualization. In S. Gilliand, D Steiner & D Skarlicki (eds) *Emerging Perspectives on Values in Organisations*. Greenwich, CT: IAP. pp. 187–204.

Vallerand, R. J., Mageau, G. A., Elliot, A. J., Dumais, A., Demers, M-A., & Rousseau, F. (2008) Passion and performance attainment in sport. *Psychology of Sport and Exercise*, 9, 373–392.

Vallerand, R. J., Mageau, G. A., Ratelle, C., Leonard, M., Blanchard, C., Koestner, R., Gagne, M., & Marsolais, J. (2003) Les passions de l'âme: on obsessive and harmonious passion. *Journal of Personality and Social Psychology*, 85, 756–767.

Vallerand, R., Paquet, Y., Philippe, F., & Charest, J. (2010) On the role of passion for work in burnout. *Journal of Personality*, 78, 290–311.

Vallerand, R. J., Salvy, S-J., Mageau, G. A., Elliot, A. J., Denis, P. L., Grouzet, F. M., & Blanchard, C. (2007) On the role of passion in performance. *Journal of Personality*, 75, 505–534.

Wang, C. K., Khoo, A., Liu, W. C., & Divaharan, S. (2008) Passion and intrinsic motivation in digital gaming. *CyberPsychology & Behavior*, 11, 39–45.

5 The Importance of Social Capital in the Workplace and How Individuals and Organizations Can Support Its Development

FRED O. WALUMBWA AND AMANDA L. CHRISTENSEN

Organizational life is inherently social. Organizations depend on the co-operation of individuals and the smooth functioning of teams to compete effectively with other organizations (Martin & Bal, 2006). Not only do organizations depend on social dynamics, but so too do individuals. Individuals rely on others in the workplace for advice, information and support. As the saying goes, "it's not what you know, it's *who* you know." Social capital, therefore, is the sum of the goodwill and potential resources available to individuals and groups stemming from their networks of relationships (Adler & Kwon, 2002; Nahapiet & Ghoshal, 1998). It is comprised of the subjective beliefs and symbols embedded in relationships among individuals (Bourdieu, 1986), and is usually conceptualized as network engagement, social norms and trustworthiness (Coleman, 1988; Lee, 2009; Putnam, 2000). This definition recognizes that social ties, such as friendship, may accommodate many purposes, including advice and support (Coleman, 1988).

Kogut and Zander (1992) proposed that organizations can be best understood as social communities and others have argued that relationships are the basis for social action (Bourdieu, 1986; Burt, 1992; Coleman, 1988). Broadly, social capital influences such organizational outcomes as career success (Gabbay & Zuckerman, 1998), helps individuals find jobs (Granovetter, 1973), influences inter-unit resource exchange and product innovation (Tsai & Ghoshal, 1998), motivates the combination and exchange of intellectual capital (Nahapiet & Ghoshal, 1998), enhances communication (Krackhardt & Hanson, 1993), promotes higher organizational survival chances (Uzzi, 1996) and influences inter-firm learning (Kraatz, 1998). In sum, social capital contributes to individual well-being and development (Putnam, 1993), and aggregately, to organizational advantage (Nahapiet & Ghoshal, 1998), and is thus critically important for effective organizational functioning.

The concept of social capital has been studied under many terms such as trust, culture, social exchange, embeddedness and social networks (Adler & Kwon, 2002). Many individual and organizational phenomena are influenced by subjective social processes (Granovetter, 1985). For example, through ties in their social networks (Granovetter, 1973), individuals can gain access to privileged information and career opportunities. Thus, social capital includes both networks of individuals and the tangible and intangible resources available through those networks (Bourdieu, 1986; Burt, 1992). As such, social capital is not necessarily a one-dimensional concept, and is perhaps better examined as one with multiple dimensions (Nahapiet & Ghoshal, 1998). As a way of classifying and organizing types of social capital, Nahapiet and Ghoshal (1998) provided a framework comprising three dimensions of social capital: structural, cognitive and relational. Though several of the features within each dimension overlap, the framework is nonetheless a useful tool for organizing the facets of social capital and will be used as an organizing basis for this chapter.

The first dimension, structural social capital, is used to capture the overall pattern of connections between individuals, that is, "who you reach and how you reach them" (Burt, 1992; Nahapiet & Ghoshal, 1998, p. 244). Through who individuals know and how they are connected to each other, networks can be appropriated to acquire resources and to gain access to opportunities that individuals cannot gain on their own (Burt, 1997). Some people seem to receive all the "luck" when it comes to faster promotions or receiving better projects to work on. Research suggests that such seemingly fortuitous events might not be so much luck but more owing to individuals' networks of relationships (Burt, 1997). The second dimension, cognitive social capital, refers to the shared languages, codes and narratives that groups of individuals develop over time (Nahapiet & Ghoshal, 1998). Through a history of shared interactions, systems of meanings, interpretations and representations emerge over time (Cicourel, 1973). These shared meanings are important in guiding individuals' behavior and providing expectations necessary to navigate group life. Finally, the third dimension, relational social capital, refers to the relations individuals have with each other, such as respect and friendship, that affect their behavior (Nahapiet & Ghoshal, 1998). Though two individuals may hold similar positions in their respective networks, they may differ in the types of relationships they hold with others in their network. Through relationships, individuals gain access to social currency such as sociability, approval and prestige. This dimension encompasses trust (Putnam, 1993), norms (Coleman, 1990), obligations (Burt, 1992) and identification (Merton, 1968).

Organizational life includes all three aspects of social capital discussed above. The purpose of this chapter, therefore, is to present a framework for which individuals and managers can support and build social capital as a means of influencing individual development and well-being. This objective is achieved by first presenting a historical perspective of social capital research and then by reviewing the three main facets of social capital relevant to business and management. However, rather than exhaustively review each dimension, because space considerations do not allow for such an exhaustive review and because this has been done elsewhere (see Lee, 2009, for a recent review), each of the three dimensions will be defined below followed by a broad overview of the main findings related to each dimension. Next, several suggestions for moving the field forward will be presented followed by some practical implications for individuals and organizations.

Roots of Social Capital Research

Research on the theory of social capital stems from many social science fields including sociology, public health, community life, education, and business and management (Coleman, 1988; Lochner, Kawachi & Kennedy, 1999; Nahapiet & Ghoshal, 1998; Putnam, 1993, 2000). Bourdieu (1986) maintained that capital can take on both tangible (such as money and materials) and intangible forms (such as beliefs and expectations) that hold some kind of actual or potential value. As such, Coleman (1988), coming from a sociological perspective, argued that social capital is an intangible form of capital that exists in relationships among individuals.

In Putnam's (1993) paper on social capital and public life, he begins with the parable of two farmers, who, working together, are both better off than when working alone. The farmers are able to work together to harvest one's crop on one day, and the other's crop another day. But when trust is lost, neither farmer helps the other and both crops are lost because there is not enough labor. The twist, however, is in the lost trust. When one individual breaks the trust, the other feels obligated to reciprocate, or at least to no longer trust, and the two become ensnarled in a trap whereby not only are the crops lost, but future interactions are bound to reflect the mutual loss of confidence and trust. A similar story is captured in the prisoner's dilemma, the logic of collective action and the tragedy of the commons. When trust is gone, co-ordination and co-operation fail. When one defects, everyone defects.

How can this dilemma be resolved? Putnam (1993) suggests that the answer lies in social capital. Whereas physical capital is in the form of such tangibles as tools and materials, human capital is less tangible, and is embodied in skills and knowledge. Social capital, however, is still less tangible, and lies in the body of social organization, in the norms, networks and trust that enable co-ordination and co-operation for the greater good (Coleman, 1988; Putnam, 1993). Social capital enhances the benefits of and allows for the co-ordination of physical and human capital (Putnam, 1993). Communities that foster social capital are better equipped to deal with poverty and vulnerability (Moser, 1996), resolve disputes (Varshney, 2000) and adopt new technologies (Isham, 1999). The absence of social capital, however, can be just as detrimental as the presence can be good (Woolcock & Narayan, 2000). Consider the plight of the poor. By not being a member of certain social groups, individuals do not have access to good jobs or decent housing, making it that much harder to obtain a better economic position (Wilson, 1987).

Although the basic ideas underlying social capital remain fairly constant across perspectives, we briefly outline four main perspectives that have been used to examine social capital across several social science disciplines. The four perspectives are communitarian, networks, institutional and synergy (Woolcock & Narayan, 2000). The communitarian view holds that when individuals come together closely in clubs, associations and civic groups, individuals must develop and adhere to moral beliefs, standards of fairness and good spirit (Paldam, 2000). In Haiti, peasant groups look out for their members and help them gain access to land, manage risk and promote mutual aid (White & Smucker, 1998). However, some researchers have suggested that too much collectivity within groups can be damaging when individuals are isolated from other groups, as in the case of gangs or groups without access to important outside resources (Woolcock & Narayan, 2000). Notwithstanding, the communitarian view largely assumes that any community is good community. However, individuals must strike a balance between group loyalty and seeking outside connections, as recognized below.

The second major perspective on social capital, the networks view, recognizes both the upsides and downsides of social capital stemming from close groups. Strong intra-group ties provide important emotional and material resources (Granovetter, 1973), such as emotional intimacy, mutual empowerment and economic development (Patulny & Svendsen, 2007). However, there are also costs when ties are too strong at the exclusion of outside ties. For example, individuals may become isolated from important information or may not have access to resources not available within their group (Burt, 1992). Burt (1992, 1997) and Granovetter (1973) maintained that strong ties that bond individuals carry many benefits, but when coupled with weak ties that bridge different groups, individuals are in much better positions to gain access to a breadth of resources.

A third root of social capital research involves an institutional perspective. This view argues that social capital is the product of political, legal and institutional environments (Woolcock & Narayan, 2000). Whereas the previous two perspectives assume that social capital arises somewhat independently from larger systems, this view maintains that the capacity of individuals and groups to appropriate social capital depends largely on the quality of the formal institutions surrounding them (North, 1990). For example, immigrants' access to international support, language skills and work training depends largely on the institutions in place to support them (Woolcock & Narayan, 2000).

Finally, the fourth view is a blend of the network and institutional views, termed the synergy view (Woolcock & Narayan, 2000). Here, institutions cannot work effectively absent supportive relationships with individuals and groups who reside under them (Evans, 1992). Institutions that protect the rights of individuals and groups are more capable of influencing social capital and providing for the common good. Furthermore, this view maintains that for institutions to be responsive to community needs, the institutions and communities must be embedded together. That is, institutions overseeing, for example, land farming, will produce more positive outcomes when those institutions understand the needs of farmers through interactions with them. Thus, in this view, institutions and networks dually support each other and the development and appropriation of social capital reciprocally influences individuals, communities and institutions (Woolcock & Narayan, 2000).

In summary, social capital stands as a potential solution to enhance mutual co-ordination and co-operation. The development and appropriation of social capital is of benefit to individuals, groups, communities and institutions. Although we have outlined research that spans many social science fields, research also abounds in the business and management field. The following section reviews social capital research that is more specific to the business and management field, using the three main facets of social capital, that is, structural, cognitive and relational, as a guiding framework.

Social Capital in Business and Management

STRUCTURAL SOCIAL CAPITAL

The first of the three dimensions proposed by Nahapiet and Ghoshal (1998), structural social capital, encompasses the *structure* of relations among individuals. That is, this dimension involves the linkages among individuals in a network as a whole and the overall pattern of connections between individuals—or, who you can reach and how you can reach them (Burt, 1992). The structural approach examines how network ties and configurations produce access to resources (Krackhardt, 1990; Scott, 1991).

Information is an important basis for facilitating social action. Coleman (1988) argued that while information is essential to action, it is also costly to obtain. Information is often privileged, that is, individuals often share information with those in their circles or with whom they have close ties. Burt (1992) argued that social networks are able to reduce the cost and time involved in gathering information. Individuals with many network ties have greater access to information and receive information earlier. Individuals with strong ties are more bonded and may receive privileged information, while those with ties that span networks have access to more diverse information (Granovetter, 1973). Therefore, although network ties represent the channels through which information is carried, the configuration of ties represents the flexibility and ease through which information is exchanged. Configuration patterns are assessed through measurements of network size, centrality and constraint. Size is conceptualized as the sum total of all ties in a network (Wasserman & Faust, 1994). Centrality refers to the cohesion of a network, and constraint refers to the extent of structural holes and brokerages in a network (Burt, 1992), that is, the extent of disconnections between non-redundant contacts and those individuals who are positioned to bridge those contacts. Burt (1992) argued that sparse networks with few redundant contacts provide richer information, while dense networks are inefficient and result in less diverse information.

There is some support for the above arguments (see Lee, 2009). For example, Uzzi (1999) found support in the banking industry for the maxim, "a relationship is worth a basis point" (p. 499). Specifically, in a study of commercial transactions between firms and banks, analyses revealed that, when transactions were embedded in relationships, firms had greater access to capital and were able to obtain loans at lower costs. Uzzi argued that embedded ties provided banks with governance benefits, suggesting that trust and expectations of reciprocity resulting from ties made it easier to arrive at unique lending solutions with reduced uncertainty. In another study of private colleges faced with environmental threats, Kraatz (1998) found that strong ties increased communication and information sharing across organizations, resulting in increased adaptability and less uncertainty. Additionally, Kraatz argued that networks promote social learning, more so than other forms of inter-organizational imitation. These results suggest that, in turbulent times, networks enhance social learning, allowing for organizations and groups to adapt and survive. Finally, in a study of startup biotechnology firms, Walker, Kogut and Shan (1997) found that network formation and industry growth were influenced by social capital. Their study showed that firms were more likely to co-operate with each other when they perceived that they were in a psychologically close network, thereby reducing transaction costs. Evidence suggested that social capital helped reproduce the network over time, suggesting that less energy was required to manage existing relationships and more resources could be used to form new relationships.

COGNITIVE SOCIAL CAPITAL

Cognitive social capital, the second dimension identified by Nahapiet and Ghoshal (1998), consists of shared meaning among individuals, including shared language, codes and narratives. Within groups or organizations, individuals come to share an understanding of the context over time. This understanding is reflected in common meanings among communicative elements such as language, vocabulary and collective narratives. Shared language and codes are an important dimension of social capital for two primary reasons. First, when individuals come to share a common language, information is shared more efficiently as parties do not need to constantly interpret others' words. Language is the means by which individuals discuss and exchange information, ask questions and conduct business (Nahapiet & Ghoshal, 1998). Thus, shared language and codes allow for easier access to and flow of information. Second, common meanings in language and codes serve a perceptual function by providing a frame of reference for individuals to quickly observe and interpret external events (Berger & Luckman, 1966).

Myths, stories and metaphors, categorically termed shared narratives, comprise the second facet of the cognitive social capital dimension. Clark (1972) suggested that organizational narratives tie together historical events and preserve rich sets of meanings. Individuals relay important practical and tacit information through narratives. As a form of collective knowing, shared narratives result in bonding and trust among individuals, thereby strengthening a sense of community. Indeed, researchers have recognized that shared communication codes are valuable for firms. For example, knowledge within a firm was argued to be embedded in the organizing principles and co-operative behaviors of groups of individuals within firms (Kogut & Zander, 1992). Social knowledge is embedded in enduring relationships among individuals, and that knowledge is enacted in organizing patterns and capabilities. Thus, knowledge is held not only at the individual level, but also at the collective level in that it is expressed in regularities by which individuals co-operate on a periodic basis.

We offer two empirical examples to illustrate these points. First, in a study of project management teams, Newell, Tansley and Huang (2004) found that a team of members from different departments was unable to fully articulate benefits of their project, and thus, was unable to provide a strong justification to management for their project. From interview data, the researchers concluded that the team had failed to develop common or redundant knowledge, making it difficult to effectively integrate and explore individual members' ideas and concerns regarding the project and to come to a shared understanding for the team to function. Shared understandings facilitate the exploitation and integration of team members' knowledge. Absent shared understandings, individuals have little collective basis for which to integrate information. Second, Kumar and Worm (2003) found evidence that shared understandings helped Danish and Chinese negotiators to overcome interactional difficulties. Specifically, shared language helped create knowledge of appropriate behavioral patterns so that the negotiators knew when to speak and the level of formality expected on behalf of their counterparts. Thus, shared understandings helped ease negotiations between parties of different cultural backgrounds.

RELATIONAL SOCIAL CAPITAL

Relational social capital, the final dimension identified by Nahapiet and Ghoshal (1998), regards assets that are created and leveraged through relationships. Although all three dimensions clearly overlap, each dimension offers an important piece in understanding social capital. Relational social capital has to do with personal relationships that have been developed over time (Granovetter, 1992) and that influence the way individuals behave toward each other (Nahapiet & Ghoshal, 1998). Facets in this realm include trust, norms, obligations and expectations, and identification.

The first aspect of relational social capital as identified by Nahapiet and Ghoshal (1998) is trust. Misztal (1996) defined trust as the belief that "the results of somebody's intended action will be appropriate from our point of view" (pp. 9–10). Trust in an individual is the expectation that his or her actions will be somewhat predictable and fair (Zaheer, McEvily & Perrone, 1998). Trust involves a "leap of faith" that another will not behave opportunistically and will behave reliably, predictably and fairly. Thus, trust promotes inter-group and relational cohesion, co-operative behavior, and opens channels for enhanced communication (Misztal, 1996; Ring & Van de Ven, 1994). Other research (for example, Walumbwa, Luthans, Avey & Oke, 2011) has not only found trust to be critical to the leadership process, but also important for effective organizational functioning by enhancing team behaviors such as organizational citizenship behavior and performance.

Norms, the second element of the relational dimension, arise through consensus of social networks or systems (Coleman, 1988). Norms serve as expected standards of behavior that shape and constrain action within the social context. Norms are often internalized, and in other cases, are externally supported through rewards and socially expressed approval or disapproval. The third element of the relational dimension, obligations and expectations, refers to individuals' duties to each other (Nahapiet & Ghoshal, 1998). Coleman (1988) argues that obligations and expectations are like "credit slips" that individuals owe each other. If one individual does something for another, then the other is expected to reciprocate in the future. Thus, obligations serve as a commitment to repay a social debt, while those who are owed the debt have expectations that their favors will be repaid. This view is supported by extensive research in social exchange relationships (see Cropanzano & Mitchell, 2005, for a review of this literature), which suggests that when individuals are in a high social exchange relationship, they tend to reciprocate by going beyond formal duty, leading to important individual and organizational outcomes such as engaging in more voluntary learning, citizenship behaviors and increased performance (Walumbwa, Cropanzano & Golman, 2011; Walumbwa, Cropanzano & Hartnell, 2009).

The fourth and final aspect identified in the relational dimension is identification. Identification with others occurs when an individual sees him- or herself as belonging with a group of others (Tajfel, 1982), indeed, when one's self-concept becomes implicated with another's. Ashforth and Mael (1989) describe this as a perception of "oneness" with another group. Identification with a group influences concern for the group's outcomes and behaviors that support the common good (Adler & Kwon, 2002). When individuals identify with others, the interests of the others become a primary motivator. A growing body of research also suggests that identification is related to a variety of individual and organizational behaviors necessary for effective organizational functioning (Kark, Shamir & Chen, 2003; Sluss & Ashforth, 2008; Walumbwa, Avolio & Zhu, 2008; Walumbwa & Hartnell, 2011; Walumbwa, Wang, Wang, Schaubroeck & Avolio, 2010). This is because identification is associated with the motivation to achieve goals and induces individuals to take the target's or group's perspectives and to experience them as their own (van Knippenberg, 2000).

To further illustrate this dimension, Gulati (1999) maintained that resources determining alliance formation resided not solely within a firm, but rather in the inter-firm networks in which the firms were located. Alliance formation is risky, and thus, information gathered through the network about other firms' reliability lessens concerns regarding hazards such as free-riding, unpredictability and opportunistic behavior. Indeed, Gulati (1999) found support for the notion that the relationships in which firms were embedded influenced their alliance formations. In another study of business units of a large multi-national company, Tsai and Ghoshal (1998) found that trust was significantly related to the sharing of resources across business units which thereby influenced innovation. The authors argued that not only did trust between partners matter, but so too did a partner's reputation for trustworthiness within the network. Individuals develop reputations over time, and these reputations serve as important information for those in the network. Similarly, Watson and Papamarcos (2002) showed how inter-personal capital, in the forms of trust and communication, among sales professionals influenced organizational commitment. They argued that when individuals trusted those with whom they worked, they could have faith that their efforts toward others would be reciprocated, and thus, their associations at work would be more rewarding. Indeed, analyses showed that trust in management and perceptions of management's reliability of communication had significant effects on employee's commitment to the organization.

In sum, the three main components of social capital, structural, cognitive and relational, are important in understanding and explaining both individual and organizational benefits and performance. The following section provides suggestions for future research and practical implications for managers.

Future Research Directions and Practical Implications

The development and maintenance of social capital is a compelling way in which individuals and organizations can support their own and each other's well-being and development. A cursory review of the social capital literature suggests that research in this area is alive and well, and indeed it is, for this chapter did not have enough space in which to exhaustively review the complete literature. The good news for researchers interested in studying social capital, however, is that there are many unexplored areas as well, a few of which are suggested below.

An assumption underlying some social capital research is the idea that the development of social capital is largely an individual initiative. Some researchers have examined the effects of individuals' reputations on the development of social capital (see Tsai & Ghoshal, 1998), and while social capital is posited to exist within individuals' networks (Burt, 1992), the assumption is largely that individuals have direct control over the development and maintenance of social capital. Research from the leadership field, however, suggests that many leader perceptions are controlled not directly by leaders themselves, but are formed and carried through surrogates, or individuals who act somewhat as substitutes for others in that they relay important information and perceptions about focal individuals (Galvin, Balkundi & Waldman, 2010). In the case of social capital research, the role of surrogates is unexplored (the closest concept is that of reputation; see Tsai & Ghoshal, 1998). It is possible that individuals' positions in their social networks are largely due to information that surrogates pass on about the focal individuals.

Though it is recognized that social capital grows and declines, research on the dynamic nature of social capital is sparse. Walker and colleagues (1997) showed that networks are reproducible, suggesting that high levels of energy are not necessarily needed to manage existing relationships. If this is so, a growth modeling approach might help researchers to understand, empirically, at what points the networks reproduce most quickly and which factors produce the quickest growth spurts. A growth modeling approach would also be helpful in determining the individual difference factors and contexts that allow individuals to become socially embedded in organizations more quickly.

Another area that could use more research attention in the social capital literature is virtual teams research (Walumbwa, Christensen & Hailey, 2011). With technological advancements, more employees work from home and meet only virtually. This presents challenges for individuals in developing social capital and for leaders interested in developing it collectively. In a case study of four virtual teams, Sivunen (2006) found that leaders who set common goals and performance standards were able to engender higher levels of group identification among their team members, helping individuals to work together more effectively and to bring about higher levels of group performance. More research examining the development of social capital in virtual teams would be helpful to both individuals and organizations.

Finally, research on person–team fit could help advance social capital research. Research on social capital assumes that when individuals in groups trust each other, they are more likely to co-operate and work together more effectively. However, research from the person–team fit literature suggests that the complementarity or supplementarity of individual differences affects how group members work together (and presumably the trust that develops or does not develop as a result). For example, Kristof-Brown, Barrick and Stevens (2005) found that individuals whose personality complemented that of other members were more likely to be attracted to the team, whereas, when personalities were too similar, those individuals were less attracted to the team. This suggests that the configuration of individual differences, such as personality, on work teams could potentially affect the development of social capital for individuals.

Research on social capital has many practical implications for managers as well. Managers can influence the development of social capital within their organizations by encouraging employees to tend to their social networks, such as through the use of team-building activities or company-sponsored social outings. Additionally, managers should not build walls between themselves and their teams. By joining employees for lunch or on social outings, managers can build trust between themselves and employees. Watson and Papamarcos (2002) demonstrated a positive link between trust in management and employee's commitment to the organization. Reasons for building trust with employees should go beyond those of the instrumental, however. The experience of unconditional trust between individuals can be an endpoint in itself, providing a basis for confidence in each other's values, forming the foundation for favorable attitudes toward each other, and providing a context of favorable affect in the relationship (Jones & George, 1998). Hence, individuals benefit emotionally and instrumentally when trust prevails and managers should do their best to influence it.

Additionally, to support the development of shared narratives among individuals, managers should allow for some "water cooler" time in employees' work days. What appears to be idle time to some managers may actually be time spent developing and maintaining social capital for employees. Time spent making sense of organizational events or helping others to overcome difficult parts of their work day helps to build bonds among individuals and provides opportunities for individuals to co-develop and pass on organizational cultural scripts, influencing the cognitive aspect of social capital.

Another approach that managers can take to influence the development of social capital is to encourage social ties that span groups, both for themselves and for employees. Both Burt (1992) and Granovetter (1973) argued for the importance of strong intra-group ties, but both also acknowledged the potential downside of ties that are too strong at the exclusion of outside ties. When individuals become isolated from outside groups, they are excluded from potentially important information and from resources not readily available from within their own group. Managers should encourage the formation of ties both within and between groups. Outside ties can be formed through trade organizations, industry roundtables and networking events, and social media sites can be used to help maintain individuals' broader networks.

Finally, stemming from the synergy view as put forth by Woolcock and Narayan (2000), human resource and management groups must be responsive to employees' needs. Organizations and employees are not independent; rather, they are deeply embedded together and thus reciprocally influence the development of social capital and optimal performance at the individual, group and organizational levels. Therefore, human resource and management groups must understand employees' needs by getting to know them so that everyone can dually support each other.

In conclusion, as our review of the social capital research suggests, social capital is a diverse concept. It ranges from network ties and configurations to shared language, codes and narratives to trust, identity, obligations and expectations. The three main components of social capital, structural, cognitive and relational (Nahapiet & Ghoshal, 1998), serve as a guiding framework with which to organize social capital research. The bottom line of social capital research is that individuals and organizations are better off when working together than when working alone. Social capital enhances the benefits of and allows for the co-ordination of physical and human capital (Putnam, 1993), influencing such outcomes as the exploitation and integration of knowledge (Newell, Tansley & Huang, 2004), commitment (Watson & Papamarcos, 2002), innovation (Tsai & Ghoshal, 1998) and organizational survival (Kraatz, 1998). As the business world becomes ever more technologically complex and unpredictable, social capital becomes more critical for individuals and organizations to navigate new frontiers.

References

Adler, P., & Kwon, S. (2002) Social capital: prospects for a new concept. *Academy of Management Review*, 27, 17–40.

Ashforth, B. E., & Mael, F. (1989) Social identity theory and the organization. *Academy of Management Review*, 14, 20–39.

Berger, P. L., & Luckman, T. (1966) *The Social Construction of Reality*. London: Penguin Press.

Bourdieu, P. (1986) The forms of capital. In J. G. Richardson (ed.) *Handbook of Theory and Research for the Sociology of Education*. New York: Greenwood. pp. 241–258.

Burt, R. S. (1992) *Structural Holes: The Social Structure of Competition*. Cambridge MA: Harvard University Press.

Burt, R. S. (1997) The contingent value of social capital. *Administrative Science Quarterly*, 42, 339–365.

Cicourel, A. V. (1973) *Cognitive Sociology*. Harmondsworth, England: Penguin Books.

Clark, B. R. (1972) The occupational saga in higher education. *Administrative Science Quarterly*, 17, 178–184.

Coleman, J. S. (1988) Social capital in the creation of human capital. *American Journal of Sociology*, 94, 95–120.

Coleman, J. S. (1990) *Foundations of Social Theory*. Cambridge, MA: Belknap Press of Harvard University Press.

Cropanzano, R., & Mitchell, M. S. (2005) Social exchange theory: an interdisciplinary review. *Journal of Management*, 31, 874–900.

Evans, P. (1992) The state as problem and solution: predation, embedded autonomy, and structural change. In S. Haggard & R. Kaufman (eds) *The Politics of Economic Adjustment: International Constraints, Distributive Conflicts, and the State*. Princeton, NJ: Princeton University Press. pp. 139–181.

Gabbay, S. M., & Zuckerman, E. W. (1998) Social capital and opportunity in corporate R&D: the contingent effect of contact density on mobility expectations. *Social Science Research*, 27, 189–217.

Galvin, B. M., Balkundi, P., & Waldman, D. A. (2010) Spreading the word: the role of surrogates in charismatic leadership processes. *Academy of Management Review*, 35, 477–494.

Granovetter, M. S. (1973) The strength of weak ties. *American Journal of Sociology*, 78, 1360–1380.

Granovetter, M. S. (1985) Economic action and social structure: the problem of embeddedness. *American Journal of Sociology*, 91, 481–510.

Granovetter, M. S. (1992) Problems of explanation in economic sociology. In N. Nohria & R. Eccles (eds), *Networks and Organizations: Structure, Form and Action*. Boston: Harvard Business School Press. pp. 25–56.

Gulati, R. (1999) Network location and learning: the influence of network resources and firm capabilities on alliance formation. *Strategic Management Journal*, 20: 397–420.

Isham, J. (1999) *The Effect of Social Capital on Technology Adoption: Evidence from Rural Tanzania*. Paper presented at the annual meeting of the American Economic Association, New York.

Jones, G. R., & George, J. M. (1998) The experience and evolution of trust: implications for cooperation and teamwork. *Academy of Management Review*, 23, 531–546.

Kark, R., Shamir, B., & Chen, G. (2003) The two faces of transformational leadership: empowerment and dependency. *Journal of Applied Psychology*, 88, 246–255.

Kogut, B., & Zander, U. (1992) Knowledge of the firm, combinative capabilities and the replication of technology. *Organization Science*, 3, 383–397.

Kraatz, M. S. (1998) Learning by association? Interorganizational networks and adaptation to environmental change. *Academy of Management Journal*, 4, 621–643.

Krackhardt, D. (1990) Assessing the political landscape: structure, cognition, and power in organizations. *Administrative Science Quarterly*, 35, 342–369.

Krackhardt, D., & Hanson, J. R. (1993) Informal networks: the company behind the chart. *Harvard Business Review*, 71, 104–111.

Kristof–Brown, A., Barrick, M. R., & Stevens, C. K. (2005) When opposites attract: a multi-sample demonstration of complementary person–team fit on extraversion, *Journal of Personality*, 73, 935–958.

Kumar, R., & Worm, V. (2003) Social capital and the dynamics of business negotiations between the northern Europeans and the Chinese. *International Studies of Management & Organization*, 29, 94–112.

Lee, R. (2009) Social capital and business and management: setting a research agenda. *International Journal of Management Reviews*, 11, 247–273.

Lochner, K., Kawachi, I., & Kennedy, B. (1999) Social capital: a guide to its measurement. *Health and Place*, 5, 259–270.

Martin, A., & Bal, V. (2006) *The State of Teams: CCL Research Report*. Greensboro, NC: Center for Creative Leadership.

Merton, R. K. (1968) *Social Theory and Social Structure*. New York: Free Press.

Misztal, B. (1996) *Trust in Modern Societies*. Cambridge, UK: Polity Press.

Moser, C. (1996) *Confronting Crisis: A Comparative Study of Household Responses to Poverty and Vulnerability in Four Poor Urban Communities*. Washington, DC: World Bank.

Nahapiet, J., & Ghoshal, S. (1998) Social capital, intellectual capital, and the organizational advantage. *Academy of Management Review*, 23, 242–266.

Newell, S., Tansley, C., & Huang, J. (2004) Social capital and knowledge integration in an ERP project team: the importance of bridging and bonding. *British Journal of Management*, 15, 43–57.

North, D. C. (1990) *Institutions, Institutional Change, and Economic Performance*. New York: Cambridge University Press.

Paldam, M. (2000) Social capital: one or many? Definition and measurement. *Journal of Economic Surveys*, 14, 629–653.

Patulny, R. V., & Svendsen, G. (2007) Exploring the social capital grid: bonding, bridging, qualitative, quantitative. *International Journal of Sociology and Social Policy*, 27, 32–51.

Putnam, R. D. (1993) The prosperous community: social capital and public life. *American Prospect*, 13, 35–42.

Putnam, R. D. (2000) *Bowling Alone: The Collapse and Revival of American Community*. New York: Simon & Schuster.

Ring, P. S., & Van de Ven, A. H. (1994) Developmental processes of cooperative interorganizational relationships. *Academy of Management Review*, 19, 90–118.

Scott, J. (1991) Networks of corporate power: a comparative assessment. *Annual Review of Sociology*, 17, 181–203.

Sivunen, A. (2006) Strengthening identification with the team in virtual teams: the leaders' perspective. *Group Decision and Negotiation*, 15, 345–366.

Sluss, D. M., & Ashforth, B. E. (2008) How relational and organizational identification converge: processes and conditions. *Organization Science*, 19, 807–823.

Tajfel, H. (1982) Social psychology of intergroup relations. *Annual Review of Psychology*, 33, 1–39.

Tsai, W., & Ghoshal, S. (1998) Social capital and value creation: the role of intrafirm networks. *Academy of Management Journal*, 41, 464–476.

Uzzi, B. (1996) The sources and consequences of embeddedness for the economic performance of organizations: the network effect. *American Sociological Review*, 61, 674–698.

Uzzi, B. (1999) Embeddedness in the making of financial capital: how social relations and networks benefit firms seeking financing. *American Sociological Review*, 64, 481–505.

Varshney, A. (2000) *Ethnic Conflict and Civic Life: Hindus and Muslims in India*. New Haven, CT: Yale University Press.

van Knippenberg, D. (2000) Work motivation and performance: a social identity perspective. *Applied Psychology: An International Review*, 49, 357–371.

Walker, G., Kogut, B., & Shan, W. (1997) Social capital, structural holes and the formation of an industry network. *Organization Science*, 8, 109–125.

Walumbwa, F. O., Avolio, B. J., & Zhu, W. (2008) How transformational leadership weaves its influence on individual job performance. *Personnel Psychology*, 61, 793–825.

Walumbwa, F. O., Christensen, A. L., & Hailey, F. (2011) Authentic leadership and the knowledge economy: sustaining motivation and trust among knowledge workers. *Organizational Dynamics*, 40, 110–118.

Walumbwa, F. O., Cropanzano, R., & Goldman, B. M. (2011) How leader–member exchange influences effective work behaviors: social exchange and internal–external efficacy perspectives. *Personnel Psychology*, 64, 739–770.

Walumbwa, F. O., Cropanzano, R., & Hartnell, C. A. (2009) Organizational justice, voluntary learning behavior, and job performance. A test of the mediating effects of identification and leader–member exchange. *Journal of Organizational Behavior*, 30, 1103–1126.

Walumbwa, F. O., & Hartnell, C. A. (2011) Understanding transformational leadership–employee performance links: the role of relational identification and self-efficacy. *Journal of Occupational and Organizational Psychology*, 84, 153–172.

Walumbwa, F. O., Luthans, F., Avey, J. B., & Oke, A. (2011) Authentically leading groups: the mediating role of collective psychological capital and trust. *Journal of Organizational Behavior*, 32, 4–24.

Walumbwa, F. O., Wang, P., Wang, H., Schaubroeck, J., & Avolio, B. J. (2010) Psychological processes linking authentic leadership to follower behaviors. *Leadership Quarterly*, 21, 901–914.

Wasserman, S., & Faust, K. (1994) *Social Network Analysis Methods and Applications*. Cambridge, UK: Cambridge University Press.

Watson, G. W., & Papamarcos, S. D. (2002) Social capital and organizational commitment. *Journal of Business and Psychology*, 16, 537–552.

White, T. A., & Smucker, G. (1998) Social capital and governance in Haiti: traditions and trends. *The Challenges of Poverty Reduction*. Washington, DC: World Bank.

Wilson, W. J. (1987) *The Truly Disadvantaged*. Chicago, IL: University of Chicago Press.

Woolcock, M., & Narayan, D. (2000) Social capital: implications for development theory, research, and policy. *World Bank Research Observer*, 15, 225–249.

Zaheer, A. B., McEvily, V., & Perrone, V. (1998) Does trust matter? Exploring the effects of interorganizational and interpersonal trust on performance. *Organization Science*, 9, 141–159.

PART III

Individual Resources

CHAPTER

6 *Person–Situation Dynamics and Well-Being at Work: An Achievement Goal Theory Perspective*

CHRISTINA G. L. NERSTAD, GLYN C. ROBERTS AND
ASTRID M. RICHARDSEN

The world of work is increasingly dynamic, creating pressure for significant and constant organizational change. Today's work situation is predominantly driven by the technological imperative rather than holistic perspectives that take into account personal, social and cultural issues (Cooper, Dewe & O'Driscoll, 2001). New technology, the globalization of trade, the current economic crisis and the changing needs of today's employees require organizations to adapt in order to remain competitive (Cooper, Dewe & O'Driscoll, 2001; Twenge & Campbell, 2010), leading to substantial reductions in workforce size and increasing unemployment as well as underemployment (Cooper, Dewe & O'Driscoll, 2001). Technological innovations and advances have made it possible for people to be "at work" at virtually any time. As a result, it is becoming increasingly difficult for individuals to separate their job/career from their lives away from the job, including leisure activities and relationships with spouses/partners, children and friends. Accordingly, occupational health psychology has been challenged with the question of how to construct "healthy" organizations and thereby create working environments that enhance employees' work-related health and well-being (Cooper, Dewe & O'Driscoll, 2001).

This topic has become increasingly important and has been approached from several viewpoints including positive psychology (Seligman & Csikszentmihalyi, 2000). However, the increasing emphasis on striving toward excellence, longer working hours, competition with co-workers and striving for perfection, especially among younger workers (Barendsen & Gardner, 2010; Cascio, 2010; Twenge & Campbell, 2010), leads us to ask the question: What can organizations actually do to enhance the health and well-being of their employees? One approach may be to determine what defines success and failure in the workplace, and how this influences employee health and well-being.

In this chapter we present a motivational point of view of the changing nature of work by discussing the salience of the context, or more specifically the criteria of success and failure that defines the motivational climate at work and its relevance to employees' health and well-being. We further discuss whether and how an individual's personal theory of achievement, most commonly defined as his/her dispositional goal orientation, interplays with the situation in influencing health and well-being.

The purpose of this chapter is to present two main approaches to person—situation dynamics and discuss the importance of the person and/or the situation in determining health and well-being outcomes at work. The contribution of our chapter is to present a "novel" approach to understanding and enhancing health and well-being in the workplace based on the dynamic interplay of constructs derived from achievement goal theory (AGT) (Ames, 1992a, 1992b; Nicholls, 1984, 1989).

Achievement Goal Theory

AGT mainly applies to individuals who are in a valued achievement context and are trying to achieve a desired personal or socially constructed goal (Roberts, 2001). Individuals are motivated to achieve success through reaching the goal, and will strive to demonstrate or develop a valued competence and/or avoid demonstrating incompetence in achieving the goal (for example, Nicholls, 1989). The goals define the way individuals approach and react when in an achievement situation and the meaning that they assign to the achievement setting (Roberts, 2012; Roberts, Treasure & Conroy, 2007). Individuals may have different goals (or purposes) for engaging in achievement behavior, whether they involve work, sport or education, but it is the demonstration of competence in order to meet the criteria of success inherent in that goal that is crucial (Nicholls, 1984, 1989).

Nicholls argued that more than one conception of competence exists and that achievement behavior may differ depending on the conception of competence held by the person or perceived to be extant in the environment. Thus, differing conceptions of competence give rise to different criteria of successful achievement (Roberts, 2012). There is a difference between developing competence and demonstrating competence. When developing competence, individuals may not differentiate between ability and effort. The individual is focused on developing task mastery, and success and failure are self-referenced in that developing mastery is regarded as success. When demonstrating competence, individuals may differentiate between ability and effort by focusing on demonstrating superiority to others, and success and failure are other-referenced (Nicholls, 1984, 1989). Achievement behavior at work can therefore be identified utilizing the undifferentiated conception of ability as *mastery involvement* and achievement behavior utilizing the differentiated conception of ability as *performance (or ego) involvement*. These refer to the motivated state of involvement of the employee at any one moment in time. An interesting question then arises: How does one become mastery or performance involved?

According to AGT, one may become mastery or performance involved through a personal dispositional inclination to being mastery or performance involved, called goal orientation. Goal orientation has been defined as a disposition toward developing or demonstrating ability in achievement situations (Nicholls, 1989; Payne, Youngcourt & Beaubien, 2007), but one may also be mastery or performance involved because of the perceived criteria of success and failure extant in the work environment, operationally defined as the motivational climate (Ames, 1992a). The motivational climate and individual dispositional goal orientation may together or separately represent important determinants of the motivated state of involvement shown by employees (Nicholls, 1989; Roberts, Treasure & Conroy, 2007) (see Figure 6.1).

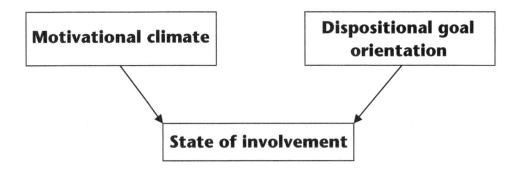

Figure 6.1   Illustration of how a person's state of involvement depends on his or her dispositional goal orientation and the motivational climate

Employees may fluctuate from one state of involvement to the other during work, depending on their perception of the momentary situational cues and/or dispositional tendencies (Gernigon, d'Arripe-Loungeville, Delignères & Ninot, 2004; Roberts, 2001; Roberts, Treasure & Conroy, 2007). An employee may begin a task with strong mastery-involved motivation, but contextual events may make the employee wish to demonstrate superiority to co-workers, and so the employee becomes ego-involved in the task. This indicates that the goal states of involvement are dynamic and may change from moment to moment as information is processed (Roberts, Treasure & Conroy, 2007). In other words, the state of involvement is dynamic and ebbs and flows depending on the perception of the individual.

Because of its dynamic nature, the state of involvement turns out to be particularly challenging to measure (Roberts, 2012). In addition, forcing individuals to consider why they are doing what they are doing may make them more self-aware, possibly resulting in a switch of involvement (Roberts, Treasure & Conroy, 2007). Within industrial and organizational (I/O) psychology there has been a major focus on trait versus state goal orientation (Payne, Youngcourt & Beaubien, 2007); however, there is little empirical evidence showing the importance of both the motivational climate and the dispositional goal orientation in determining employees' state of involvement. AGT research has typically dealt with these personal and situational constructs separately (DeShon & Gillespie, 2005), thereby failing to account for the importance of both in determining an individual's state of goal involvement (Nicholls, 1989). Although acknowledging the relevance of the situation (for example, Button, Mathieu & Zajac, 1996; Janssen & Van Yperen, 2004; Van Yperen, Hamstra & van der Klauw, 2011), organizational research has primarily focused on individual goal orientation, and to some extent on team or group goal orientation (for example, Bunderson & Sutcliffe, 2003).

The interactionist perspective of AGT predicts that goal orientation and the motivational climate are likely to interplay in order to influence individual affective, behavioral and cognitive outcomes (Roberts, 2012; Roberts, Treasure & Conroy, 2007). Still, it is not clear whether the context is more powerful than enduring personal predispositions in creating various work and individual outcomes (Kaplan & Maehr, 2007; Maehr & Zusho, 2009). The research results to date have indicated that dispositional goal orientation may be both stable and changeable (Fryer & Elliot, 2007; Payne, Youngcourt & Beaubien, 2007), suggesting the potential importance of the motivational climate in shaping an individual's goal orientation. Understanding one or the other is not sufficient (DeShon & Gillespie, 2005). To advance the knowledge about how best to stimulate employees' involvement in their work, these aspects need clarification (Roberts, Treasure & Conroy, 2007).

The Person-centered Achievement Goal Theory Perspective

According to the person-centered AGT perspective, goal orientation viewed as a personal disposition is assumed to play a major role in the motivational process (Maehr & Zusho, 2009). This perspective implies that people are likely to have goal tendencies that determine which goal they will endorse in a given work situation (Maehr & Zusho, 2009). Individuals' goal orientation represents a disposition acquired in early childhood, and is assumed to be based on self-schemas. Therefore, goal orientation is viewed as a relatively stable entity (Janssen & Van Yperen, 2004; Kaplan & Maehr, 2007; Maehr & Zusho, 2009) that comprises an individual's personal theory of motivation (Nicholls, 1989).

An individual's personal theory of achievement predisposes him/her to act in a mastery-oriented or performance-oriented manner (Roberts, 2012). The difference between these two goal orientations is that in one performance is aimed at developing or demonstrating mastery and in the other it is aimed at demonstrating superiority over others. In other words, mastery-oriented and performance-oriented individuals are differentiated according to the criteria by which they define or judge their successes and failures.

VandeWalle (1997) and Elliot (1997; Elliot & Church, 1997) differentiated two aspects of performance goal orientation—performance prove (or approach) and performance avoid (or avoidance). Elliot (1999) also presented a distinction between mastery approach and mastery avoidance goals. In these conceptualizations of goal orientation, achievement striving is determined by the way in which individuals define competence with its attendant valence (Roberts, 2012). Therefore, goals are assumed to be the manifestation of needs (Kaplan & Maehr, 2007). This is not in line with the theoretical conceptualizations presented by Nicholls (1984, 1989), which represent a social–cognitive focus on how individuals define success and what it takes to achieve success at work. In this view, it is assumed that the goals themselves are the critical determinants of achievement cognition, affect and behavior, and not the satisfaction of avoidance or approach needs. The concepts of mastery and performance goal orientation, as suggested by Ames (1992a) and others (for example, Maehr & Zusho, 2009), may be more plausible explanations for the relatively stable preferences for one or the other goal orientation.

According to meta-analytical evidence, mastery dispositional goal orientation predicts work performance above and beyond cognitive ability and the Big Five personality dimensions (Payne, Youngcourt & Beaubien, 2007). Performance goal orientation has been found to have virtually no relationship with various outcomes, such as learning or academic performance (Payne, Youngcourt & Beaubien, 2007). In a more recent meta-analysis, it was argued that a mastery orientation may be the most desirable orientation in achievement contexts, including work (Cellar, Stulmacher, Young, Fisher, Adair, Haynes and Riester, 2011). Rawsthorne and Elliot (1999) investigated the relationship between dispositional goal orientation and intrinsic motivation, and found that the pursuit of performance goals undermined intrinsic motivation, while the pursuit of mastery goals enhanced intrinsic motivation. These are interesting and important findings, but where do these goal orientations come from and why are they supposed to determine how employees interpret events in a given situation and process information about them?

In support of the person-centered perspective, a recent study investigated birth order effects on goal orientation among a sample of 375 undergraduate students (Carette, Anseel & Van Yperen, 2011). The results showed that birth order was important for an individual's goal orientation preferences. Firstborns preferred mastery goals whereas second-born siblings preferred performance goals (Carette, Anseel & Van Yperen, 2011). Firstborns may learn to prefer self-referenced conceptions of ability as a result of a mastery focus by parents during early childhood. Second-born children on the other hand may learn to prefer other-referenced conceptions of ability due to parents comparing their competence with that of their older siblings (Carette, Anseel & Van Yperen, 2011).

The person-centered perspective suggests that an individual's goal orientation generates a framework for interpreting and responding to the achievement situations that arise. Depending on their preferred goal orientation, employees will approach their work situation with different perspectives, ask different questions, have different concerns and seek different information (Dweck & Leggett, 1988; VandeWalle, 1997).

The Situated Perspective

The situated AGT perspective (for example, Ames, 1992a, 1992b; Nicholls, 1984, 1989) assumes that achievement goals are a function of the context (Maehr & Zusho, 2009; Treasure & Roberts, 1998). The situation plays an important role in the motivational process in that achievement behavior is influenced by the interplay of goal orientation and the motivational climate (Ames, 1992b; Nicholls, 1989; Smith, Smoll & Cumming, 2009).

The motivational climate at work may be defined as individuals' perceptions of the extant criteria of success and failure emphasized through the policies, practices and procedures in the work environment (Nerstad, Roberts & Richardsen, in press). This is a social–psychological factor that is likely to influence individuals' motivation in general and their goal orientation in particular (Ames, 1992a; Cumming, Smoll, Smith & Grossbard, 2007; Nicholls, 1989). The motivational climate is also described in terms of mastery and performance criteria. A mastery (or task-involving) climate exists when the criteria of success are characterized by aspects such as self-learning, co-operation, task mastery, development and effort (Ames, 1992a, 1992b). A mastery climate is suggested to promote adaptive behavior and well-being, such as being engaged, trying hard and persisting in the face of difficulties.

A performance (or ego-involving) motivational climate, on the other hand, is characterized by demonstrating ability and making normative comparisons, and is suggested to promote maladaptive behavior and ill-health, such as seeking easy tasks, giving up when faced with difficulties and developing burnout (Ames, 1992a; Ntoumanis & Biddle, 1999; Roberts et al., 2007).

Mastery and performance climates influence cognitive, affective and behavioral outcomes in different ways because they represent different conceptions of success. Leaders are crucial in the communication of what is needed to succeed in a work environment (Ames, 1992b). The way in which leaders give feedback about employees' performance will influence their perceptions of the work climate (Dragoni, 2005; Johnson, Shull &

Wallace, 2011) and therefore be a determinant of the motivational climate (Ames & Archer, 1988; Jagacinski & Nicholls, 1984; Pensgaard & Roberts, 2002).

Can the Motivational Climate Shape Dispositional Goal Orientation?

The situated perspective suggests that situational factors may influence goal orientation, or at least that the interplay between the situational structure and the goal orientation will determine the probability of a certain course of action or pattern of behavior (Treasure & Roberts, 1998). However, this may depend on the strength of the situational cues (Dweck & Leggett, 1988). If, for example, the situational cues are strongly in favor of either a performance climate or a mastery climate, dispositions (goal orientations) may be overridden by situational cues. In other words, the weaker the disposition, the more easily it can be altered by situational cues (Dweck & Leggett, 1988; Treasure & Roberts, 1998).

To date, only a few studies have tested the interplay between motivational climate and goal orientation (Roberts, 2012), but these have often been based in domains other than work. One such study was conducted among 700 French pupils, and it was found that the perceived motivational climate had a stronger relationship with intrinsic interest than with dispositional goal orientation (Cury, Biddle, Famouse, Goudas, Sarrazin and Durand, 1996). This indicates that climate may be a stronger predictor of adaptive work behavior and perhaps performance than dispositional factors.

In a more recent study, Chen and Mathieu (2008) conducted an experiment among 104 undergraduate students to investigate the dynamic interplay between the situation and the individual differences in performance trajectories over time. The results indicated that neither dispositional nor situational inducements of mastery and performance goal orientation significantly predicted performance trajectories. However, the participants exposed to a mastery goal condition benefited more (in terms of performance) from performance-oriented feedback. The authors concluded that employees may benefit from combined high levels of mastery and performance orientations. This indicates that dispositional goal orientations may be orthogonal (Nicholls, 1989), that is, a person can be high or low in each or both at the same time (DeShon & Gillespie, 2005; Roberts, 2012). Although the findings of Chen and Mathieu (2008) indicate that individual goal orientations may not be as important for employee motivation and performance as the motivational climate, their findings were based on a student sample and may not be generalizable to real work settings.

Motivational Climate, Achievement Goals and Work Engagement/Burnout

Studies have demonstrated that the motivational climate is directly associated with athletes' performance and perceptions of well-being and ill-health (Lemyre, Hall & Roberts, 2008; Reinboth & Duda, 2004). Typically athletes have been found to perform better and experience a higher level of well-being in a mastery climate than in a performance climate (for example, Valentini & Rudisill, 2006). Reinboth and Duda (2004) found that athletes' perceptions of a performance climate were positively related to burnout, but that perceptions of a mastery climate were not. These findings were supported in a recent study indicating that a mastery climate may temper symptoms of burnout (Smith, Gustafsson & Hassmén, 2010). It is likely that the climate perceptions at work will also have an impact on health and well-being over time.

Burnout, which is defined as a syndrome characterized by exhaustion, cynicism and reduced personal efficacy (Maslach, Jackson & Leiter, 1996), represents employee strain and ill-health. Research on burnout has typically focused on the role of work characteristics, rather than on individual dispositions (Langelaan, Bakker, van Doornen & Schaufeli, 2006). However, personal dispositions may determine the extent to which individuals are exposed to certain kinds of stressful circumstances, which may lead to strain (Alarcon, Eschleman & Bowling, 2009; Cooper, Dewe and O'Driscoll, 2001). Goal orientation may represent a personal disposition that will influence employees' perception of the motivational climate and in turn affect their well-being (Hall, Cawthraw & Kerr, 1997).

Performance-oriented individuals have been found to be at greater risk of developing symptoms of burnout than mastery-oriented individuals (Roberts et al., 2007). Although the empirical evidence has indicated that a mastery climate is associated with low levels of burnout, this relationship may vary depending on the employee's performance orientation. Employees who are performance-oriented and who also perceive their ability to be high will probably experience well-being. However, performance-oriented employees are typically preoccupied with demonstrating their ability to others in order to validate their own self-worth (Jagacinski & Nicholls, 1984; Lemyre, Hall and Roberts, 2008), even if the work climate is more supportive of self-referential criteria of success. In a performance climate, employees who continually perceive that their effort and/or ability are not high enough may experience dysfunctional cognitions and affective responses (Lemyre, Hall and Roberts, 2008; Roberts, 2001). Therefore, performance-oriented individuals in either type of climate may turn out to be at greater risk of experiencing burnout (Retelsdorf, Butler, Streblow & Schiefele, 2010).

On the other hand, a mastery orientation may serve as a protective factor against burnout (Retelsdorf, Butler, Streblow & Schiefele, 2010). In a mastery climate, mastery-oriented employees will probably experience well-being and not be at risk of burnout. In such a climate, performance-oriented individuals may over time become more mastery-oriented and thus be less at risk of burnout. In a performance climate, a high mastery orientation may buffer the negative association with work engagement or the positive relationship with burnout, meaning that the relationship with engagement becomes less negative, while the positive relationship with burnout becomes less positive. Still, this may depend on the strength of the climate (Dweck & Leggett, 1988). Working in a performance climate over a longer period of time may even make the mastery-oriented employee feel frustrated by the constant focus on social comparison. To meet the signaled demands of a performance climate in terms of being successful at work, the mastery-oriented employee may over time switch to becoming more performance-oriented and consequently he/she may have a higher risk of burnout. This is likely especially if their perceived ability is low (Jagacinski & Nicholls, 1984).

Work engagement is a persistent, pervasive and positive affective—motivational state of fulfillment, characterized by vigor, dedication and absorption (Llorens, Schaufeli, Bakker & Salanova, 2007). Work engagement contributes to both the development of the organization's human capital and the creation of competitive advantage (Bakker, Schaufeli, Leiter & Taris, 2008; Rich & Lepine, 2007; Schaufeli & Salanova, 2007).

Work engagement is related to intrinsic motivation, including feelings of enthusiasm, well-being, identification with one's job, high levels of activation, and carrying out an activity because it is rewarding and meaningful in itself (Salanova, Agut & Peiro, 2005; Salanova & Schaufeli, 2008).

With regard to work engagement, there is little empirical evidence on the influence of individual dispositions (Langelaan, Bakker, van Doornen & Schaufeli, 2006), and the importance of goal orientations has not yet been empirically investigated. A mastery orientation has been found to be a strong predictor of intrinsic motivation (Adie & Jowett, 2010; Ferrer-Caja & Weiss, 2000), suggesting that the situational structure may influence related variables, such as engagement. We also know very little about the potential moderating role of goal orientation in the relationship between motivational climate and engagement. It is likely that the relationship between a mastery or a performance climate and work engagement may depend on the levels of performance and mastery orientation.

A Study of Motivational Climate, Goal Orientation and Burnout/Engagement

Given the scarce empirical evidence testing these predictions, we (Nerstad, Richardsen & Roberts, 2011) recently conducted a longitudinal study among 1,081 engineers and technologists to investigate the interplay between the motivational climate at work and the employees' goal orientation, and their impact on burnout and work engagement over time (seven months). In order to be able to test the salience of both the person-centered perspective and the situated perspective we presented competing hypotheses. In line with the person-centered perspective we first hypothesized that dispositional goal orientation would moderate the relationship between perceived motivational climate and work engagement/burnout. In line with the situated perspective we hypothesized that the motivational climate would facilitate a change in goal orientation over time, and that a change (increase/decrease) in goal orientation over time would mediate the relationship between the motivational climate at time 1 and the change (increase/decrease) in work engagement and burnout. To test these hypotheses we conducted a survey. The respondents received an e-mail with a web-based questionnaire asking them about their perceptions of the motivational climate, goal orientation, work engagement and burnout. Research has indicated that perceptions of the motivational climate as well as goal orientation may be perceived differently as a result of age and gender (Abrahamsen, Roberts & Pensgaard, 2008; Payne, Youngcourt and Beaubien, 2007). Based on t-tests, we found that the participants who responded at time 2 differed significantly with regard to education and hours worked per week from those responding only at time 1. We therefore controlled for age, gender, education and hours worked per week.

There were several notable findings. First, in support of the situated perspective, the results indicated a shaping influence of the motivational climate on goal orientation over time. Individuals perceiving a mastery climate at both times indicated an increase in their dispositional mastery orientation, and employees perceiving a performance climate at both times indicated an increase in their dispositional performance orientation. The findings are consistent with the results from other studies (for example, Dweck, 1986; Treasure & Roberts, 1998), suggesting the power of the motivational climate to influence dispositional goal orientation, particularly when goal orientation may be weak. Our findings make conceptual sense because individuals tend to interpret a mastery climate as informational rather than controlling, and because there is a greater focus on the process of achieving in such a climate individuals may become even more mastery-oriented (Treasure & Roberts, 1998). In a performance climate, control is an important aspect and this possibly increases employees' performance orientation because the main focus is always on the outcome, and competition to achieve this outcome is valued and recognized (Treasure & Roberts, 1998).

Second, we found that the perceived motivational climate was a stronger predictor of work engagement and burnout than goal orientation. This finding is much in line with the findings of Newton and Duda (1999), who found that the motivational climate was the major predictor of enjoyment/interest and pressure/tension among relatively young female athletes. In addition, Bakker, Albrecht and Leiter (2011) recently suggested that more attention should be paid to contextual factors that may have an impact on work engagement by facilitating a "climate for engagement." A mastery climate may serve as an important facilitator of work engagement over time. Thus, through developing and enhancing the potential of each employee by emphasizing mastery criteria in the workplace, organizations may increase the engagement of their workforce. This is beneficial because an engaged workforce is more likely to improve or maintain the organization's competitive advantage (Christian, Garza & Slaughter, 2011).

A mastery climate may also serve as a positive "buffer" against burnout, whereas a performance climate leads to emotional exhaustion and cynicism over time. As argued by Cresswell and Eklund (2005, p. 469): "one of burnout's most striking features is its motivational signature." Hence, a performance motivational climate may undermine intrinsic motivation to be task-involved and therefore make individuals prone to burnout by persistently focusing on outcomes and demonstrating superiority to co-workers.

Third, our findings suggested that a mastery climate and mastery orientation interplayed in predicting an increase in work engagement and a decrease in burnout over a period of seven months. We also found that the relationship between a perceived mastery climate and an increase in work engagement and a decrease in experiences of burnout over time was partially mediated by an increase in mastery orientation. These findings seem to be supportive of the situated perspective, and point to the organizational benefits of creating and emphasizing a mastery climate at work, that is, creating working conditions in which employees feel free to develop their abilities and learn to master new tasks. The benefit is to increase performance and enhance health and well-being. Our results are in line with other empirical findings. For example, Lemyre, Hall and Roberts (2008) studied elite winter sport athletes and found that athletes who were performance-oriented and also had a coach and parents who emphasized performance outcomes (thereby facilitating a performance climate) were more at risk of developing symptoms of burnout than mastery-oriented athletes. A mastery climate may decrease experiences of burnout by enhancing a mastery goal orientation and thus employees' work engagement, while a performance climate may increase experiences of burnout by enhancing a performance goal orientation and passionate work engagement may suddenly disappear (Leiter & Maslach, 2001; Schaufeli & Buunk, 2003).

In sum, our findings were more supportive of the situated perspective, which views goal orientations as cognitive schemas that are dynamic and subject to change as the individual processes information regarding his or her task performance (Roberts, 2012).

Some studies (for example, Fryer & Elliot, 2007) have investigated the stability and/ or changeability of goal orientation over time, but not beyond the length of a college semester (Payne, Youngcourt and Beaubien, 2007) nor taking into account the influence of the motivational climate on goal orientation. Thus, according to our findings, it may be critical to consider the salience of the motivational climate in "shaping" goal orientations.

Further, our results suggested that while goal orientation as a dispositional variable has very little impact on the motivational climate and work and well-being outcomes, the motivational climate seems to have the ability to enhance the existing goal orientations that match the contextual structure, but not to change the existing goal orientations that oppose the contextual structure. This leads us to question whether seven months are sufficient in order to achieve a change in goal orientation in opposition to the context. To the extent to which environmental influences remain stable over time, dispositional continuity may be expected (Caspi & Roberts, 1999). Adjustment in environmental influences and in role expectations can affect change, either through punishing inappropriate behavior or rewarding appropriate behavior (Roberts, Walton & Viechtbauer, 2006). For example, if an employee is highly mastery-oriented, but perceives a performance climate at work over a long period of time, meeting the expectations of such a climate by becoming more performance-oriented should result in increased perceptions of success and greater levels of acceptance and social reinforcement if the employee is able to meet the extant performance criteria. Therefore, role expectations at work, emphasized through the motivational climate, may facilitate change in goal orientation by serving as a guide for how employees should act and how they should change their criteria of success and failure and thus their goal orientation. However, the time frame required for such a change to take place is still unclear (Roberts, Walton & Viechtbauer, 2006).

The Facilitation of a "Healthy" Motivational Climate at Work

The evidence so far supports a situated approach to the understanding of employee performance, health and well-being. As such, there are great benefits in facilitating a mastery climate at work (Poortvliet & Darnon, 2010; Ntoumanis & Biddle, 1999; Valentini & Rudisill, 2006). The benefits of a mastery climate are twofold. First, it would influence employees with both a performance goal orientation and a mastery goal orientation to become more mastery-oriented. This in turn would have the impact of making all employees highly engaged and less at risk of burnout. As it is well documented that work engagement and intrinsic motivation have a positive influence on work performance (Christian, Garza and Slaughter, 2011), there are potentially great organizational advantages to creating a mastery work climate (Van Yperen, Hamstra and van der Klauw, 2011).

How one would go about specifically fostering a mastery climate in an organizational setting is not all that clear (DeShon & Gillespie, 2005). However, the findings from sports and education may provide some clues. The strategies demonstrated to be successful are the following: (a) designing meaningful and interesting tasks that include variety, challenge and control; (b) giving each individual opportunities to make choices and to participate in decision making, including deciding upon strategies for completing the task;

(c) giving thorough consideration to how outcomes and striving behaviors are recognized, by avoiding rewards and recognition that are perceived as bribes or methods of control; (d) encouraging the benefits of the differences between individuals by treating everyone in a similar way; (e) privately evaluating each individual based on his/her progress, mastery, creativity and effort; and (f) managing time by allowing those individuals who need more time to develop the necessary skills to perform at a higher level to have more time (Ames, 1992b; Braitwaite, Spray & Warburton, 2011; Deci & Ryan, 2000; Roberts, 2012).

In an organizational setting this may be accomplished through what is emphasized in commitment-based human resource management (HRM) practices. These practices are considered as high performance work practices (HPWPs) (Combs, Yongmei, Hall & Ketchen, 2006; Huselid, 1995). These empower and motivate employees to act, as well as increasing employees' knowledge, skills and abilities (KSAs) (Combs, Yongmei, Hall & Ketchen, 2006). According to Collins and Smith (2006), commitment-based HRM practices can foster social climates of trust, co-operation, and shared codes and language, aimed at enhancing the employee's capabilities. Because a mastery climate is known to focus on aspects such as learning, development, co-operation and self-referenced criteria of success that is consistent with commitment-based HRM practices, it is likely that the commitment-based HRM system serves as an important predictor of work engagement, especially given the emphasis on employee resources and well-being in such practices (Nishii, Lepak & Schneider, 2008).

The supervisor is posited to be the main architect of the motivational climate (cf., Ames, 1992a). Consequently, the achievement patterns of supervisors may direct employees' attention to the preferred achievement priorities, and in that way encourage specific climate perceptions. Supervisors valuing responsibility or concern for the welfare of employees are likely to facilitate a mastery climate and be perceived as supportive. In contrast, supervisors who place more value on normative ability evaluations and extrinsic motivation facilitate a performance climate and may focus more on themselves than being concerned with and supportive of the welfare of others (cf., Ames & Ames, 1984). Thus, for such supervisors, the maintenance of control over employees to boost a personal sense of esteem rather than the esteem of others is valued. Research has convincingly demonstrated that when supervisors are perceived as supportive of their subordinates, through creating a mastery climate as we argue here, then this behavior leads to positive outcomes among employees, such as increased work performance, job satisfaction, lower employee turnover and reduced stress experiences for both the employee and, in turn, the organization (for example, Maertz, Griffeth, Campbell & Allen, 2007; Rhoades & Eisenberger, 2002; Rhoades, Shanock & Eisenberger, 2006).

Given their important role, supervisors should clearly choose the HRM practices used to manage their subordinates carefully, because these practices may shape the organization's social contexts, which in turn may affect what subordinates perceive they have to do to be successful in their work situation. These perceptions are likely to be important determinants of subordinates' attitudes, motivation, well-being and performance, which are significant aspects of ensuring the organization's human capital (employees' collective KSAs) (Huselid, Jackson & Schuler, 1997) and improving the overall quality of the social relationships among the employees, including their relationship with the employer (Lee & Akhtar, 2011). This kind of knowledge may help organizations create management programs to develop and assist line managers in improving their capabilities when communicating their priorities to employees (Dragoni, 2005). This is important because subordinates typically experience the organization to be committed to their well-being when they perceive support from their supervisors, thus motivating them to reciprocate with their supervisors and organization (Gentry, Kuhnert, Mondore & Page, 2007). Whereas managers are primarily interested in output performance, subordinates are mainly interested in creating a productive and pleasant atmosphere (Paauwe, 2004). Both may be achieved through creating a mastery climate with self-referenced criteria of success which may be the result of commitment-based HRM practices and supportive supervisors who are concerned about their subordinates' well-being.

Implications for Research

It may be important for future research to determine the antecedents of the motivational climate at work. The leader has often been seen as the main architect of the motivational climate (Ames, 1992a), but significant others (for example, colleagues) and/or organizational practices may also play an important role in creating such a climate (Janssen & Van Yperen, 2004; Roberts et al., 2007). As we know considerably less about the antecedents of the motivational climate than its outcomes (cf., Kuenzi & Schminke, 2009), we suggest that one line of inquiry for future research might be to investigate HRM practices and/or job designs as potential determinants of the perceived motivational climate at work. Also, there is a need to understand further the relationships between situational and dispositional factors in motivating employees to perform, develop and learn, and future research may contribute to a better understanding of antecedents, moderators and outcomes, thus suggesting specific criteria for facilitating a mastery climate at work.

Conclusion

Based on the theoretical arguments and empirical findings presented in this chapter, we suggest that the elegant, parsimonious and powerful traditional AGT is relevant to understanding the motivational dynamics of the workplace, and that it is important to consider the situated approach in future work setting field research. Given the mounting research evidence emphasizing the importance of a mastery climate in facilitating health and well-being outcomes, organizations are likely to benefit from creating and emphasizing a mastery climate at work. As Nicholls (1989, p. 7) once stated: "... equality of optimum motivation for intellectual development, substantial accomplishment, satisfaction in work, and more productive relationships with our fellows will all be more likely if we become more like little children." What Nicholls meant is that as children do not differentiate effort and ability, and often believe that effort *is* ability, children are in a constant state of mastery involvement. Thus, Nicholls argued that enhanced motivation for all the workforce would be more likely to occur in a mastery climate. In contrast to a performance climate, in which there is a focus on mainly developing the potential of the talented and best performers, a mastery climate facilitates optimal motivation for each employee with the possibility of developing his or her potential at work. This may be important for organizations and their leaders to consider in the facilitation of "healthy" organizations.

References

Abrahamsen, F. E., Roberts, G. C., & Pensgaard, A.-M. (2008) Achievement goals and gender effects on multidimensional anxiety in national elite sport. *Psychology of Sport and Exercise*, 9, 449–464.

Adie, J. W., & Jowett, S. (2010) Meta-perceptions of the coach–athlete relationship, achievement goals, and intrinsic motivation among sport participants. *Journal of Applied Social Psychology*, 40(11), 2750–2773.

Alarcon, G., Eschleman, K. J., & Bowling, N. A. (2009) Relationship between personality variables and burnout: a meta-analysis. *Work & Stress*, 23(3), 244–263.

Ames, C. (1992a) Achievement goals, motivational climate, and motivational processes. In G. C. Roberts (ed.) *Motivation in Sport and Exercise*. Champaign, IL: Human Kinetics. pp. 161–176.

Ames, C. (1992b) Classrooms: goals, structures, and student motivation. *Journal of Educational Psychology*, 84, 261–271.

Ames, C., & Ames, R. (1984) Systems of student and teacher motivation: toward a qualitative definition. *Journal of Educational Psychology*, 76, 535–556.

Ames, C., & Archer, J. (1988) Achievement goals in the classroom: students' learning strategies and motivation processes. *Journal of Educational Psychology*, 80, 260–267.

Bakker, A. B., Albrecht, S. L., & Leiter, M. P. (2011) Key questions regarding work engagement. *European Journal of Work and Organizational Psychology*, 20, 4–28.

Bakker, A. B., Schaufeli, W. B., Leiter, M. P., & Taris, T. W. (2008) Work engagement: an emerging concept in occupational health psychology. *Work & Stress*, 22, 187–200.

Barendsen, L., & Gardner, H. (2010) Good for what? The young worker in a global age. In P. A. Linley, S. Harrington & N. Garcea (eds) *Oxford Handbook of Positive Psychology and Work*. New York: Oxford University Press. pp. 301–312.

Braitwaite, R., Spray, C. M., & Warburton, V. E. (2011) Motivational climate interventions in physical education: a meta-analysis. *Psychology of Sport and Excercise*, 12, 628–638.

Bunderson, J. S., & Sutcliffe, K. M. (2003) Management team learning orientation and business unit performance. *Journal of Applied Psychology*, 88(3), 552–560.

Button, S. B., Mathieu, J. E., & Zajac, D. M. (1996) Goal orientation in organizational research: a conceptual and empirical foundation. *Organizational Behavior and Human Decision Processes*, 67, 26–48.

Carette, B., Anseel, F., & Van Yperen, N. W. (2011) Born to learn or born to win? Birth order effects on achievement goals. *Journal of Research in Personality*, 45, 500–503.

Cascio, W. F. (2010) The changing world of work. In P. A. Linley, S. Harrington, & N. Garcea (eds) *Oxford Handbook of Positive Psychology*. New York: Oxford University Press. pp. 13–24.

Caspi, A., & Roberts, B. W. (1999) Personality continuity and change across the life course. In L. A. Pervin & O. P. John (eds) *Handbook of Personality: Theory and Research* (2nd edition) New York, NY: Guilford Publications Inc. pp. 300–326.

Cellar, D. F., Stuhlmacher, A. F., Young, S. K., Fisher, D. M., Adair, C. K., Haynes, S., & Riester, D. (2011) Trait goal orientation, self-regulation, and performance: a meta-analysis. *Journal of Business Psychology*, 26, 467–483.

Chen, G., & Mathieu, J. E. (2008) Goal orientation dispositions and performance trajectories: the roles of supplementary and complementary situational inducements. *Organizational Behavior and Human Decision Processes*, 106, 21–38.

Christian, M. S., Garza, A. S., & Slaughter, J. E. (2011) Work engagement: a quantitative review and test of its relations with task and contextual performance. *Personnel Psychology*, 64, 89–136.

Collins, C., & Smith, K. G. (2006) Knowledge exchange and combination: the role of human resource practices in the performance of high-technology firms. *Academy of Management Journal*, 49(3), 544–560.

Combs, J., Yongmei, L., Hall, A., & Ketchen, D. (2006) How much do high-performance work practices matter? A meta-analysis of their effects on organizational performance. *Personnel Psychology*, 59, 501–528.

Cooper, C. L., Dewe, P., & O'Driscoll, M. P. (2001) *Organizational Stress: A Review and Critique of Theory, Research, and Applications*. Thousand Oaks, CA: Sage.

Cresswell, S. L., & Eklund, R. C. (2005) Motivation and burnout in professional rugby players. *Research Quarterly for Exercise and Sport*, 76(3), 370–376.

Cumming, S. P., Smoll, F. L., Smith, R. E., & Grossbard, J. R. (2007) Is winning everything? The relative contributions of motivational climate and won–lost percentage in youth sports. *Journal of Applied Sport Psychology*, 19, 322–336.

Cury, F., Biddle, S., Famouse, J.-P., Goudas, M., Sarrazin, P., & Durand, M. (1996) Personal and situational factors influencing intrinsic interest in adolecent girls in school physical education: a structural equation modelling analysis. *Educational Psychology*, 16, 305–315.

Deci, E. L., & Ryan, R. M. (2000) The "what" and "why" of goal pursuits: human needs and the self-determination of behaviour. *Psychological Inquiry*, 11(4), 227–268.

DeShon, R. P., & Gillespie, J. Z. (2005) A motivated action theory account of goal orientation. *Journal of Applied Psychology*, 90, 1096–1127.

Dragoni, L. (2005) Understanding the emergence of state goal orientation in organizational work groups: the role of leadership and multilevel climate perceptions. *Journal of Applied Psychology*, 90, 1084–1095.

Dweck, C. S. (1986) Motivational processes affecting learning. *American Psychologist*, 41, 1040–1048.

Dweck, C. S., & Leggett, E. L. (1988) A social-cognitive approach to motivation and personality. *Psychological Review*, 95, 265–273.

Elliot, A. J. (1997) Integrating the "classic" and "contemporary" approaches to achievement motivation: a hierarchical model of approach and avoidance achievement motivation. In M. L. Maehr & P. R. Pintrich (eds) *Advances in Motivation and Achievement Goals*. Greenwich, Connecticut: JAI. Vol. 10, pp. 143–179.

Elliot, A. J. (1999) Approach and avoidance motivation and achievement goals. *Educational Psychologist*, 34, 169–189.

Elliot, A. J., & Church, M. A. (1997) A hierarchical model of approach and avoidance achievement motivation. *Journal of Personality and Social Psychology*, 72, 218–232.

Ferrer-Caja, E., & Weiss, M. R. (2000) Predictors of intrinsic motivation among adolescent students in physical education. *Research Quarterly for Exercise and Sport*, 71(3), 267–279.

Fryer, J. W., & Elliot, A. J. (2007) Stability and change in achievement goals. *Journal of Educational Psychology*, 99, 700–714.

Gentry, W. A., Kuhnert, K. W., Mondore, S. P., & Page, E. E. (2007) The influence of supervisory-support climate and unemployment rate on part-time employee retention: a multilevel analysis. *Journal of Management Development*, 26(10), 1005–1022.

Gernigon, C., d'Arripe-Loungeville, F., Delignères, D., & Ninot, G. (2004) A dynamical systems perspective on goal involvement states in sport. *Journal of Sport & Exercise Psychology*, 26, 572–596.

Hall, H. K., Cawthraw, I. W., & Kerr, A. W. (1997) Motivation antecedents of precompetitive anxiety in youth sport. *Sport Psychologist*, 11, 24–42.

Huselid, M. A. (1995) The impact of human resource management practices on turnover, productivity, and corporate financial performance. *Academy of Management Journal*, 38, 635–672.

Huselid, M. A., Jackson, S. E., & Schuler, R. S. (1997) Technical and strategic human resource management effectiveness as determinants of firm performance. *Academy of Management Journal*, 40(1), 171–188.

Jagacinski, C. M., & Nicholls, J. G. (1984) Conceptions of ability and related affects in task involvement and ego involvement. *Journal of Educational Psychology*, 76(5), 909–919.

Janssen, O., & Van Yperen, N. W. (2004) Employees' goal orientations, the quality of leader–member exchange, and the outcomes of job performance and job satisfaction. *Academy of Management Journal*, 47(3), 368–384.

Johnson, P. D., Shull, A., & Wallace, J. C. (2011) Regulatory focus as a mediator in goal orientation and performance relationships. *Journal of Organizational Behavior*, 32, 751–766.

Kaplan, A., & Maehr, M. L. (2007) The contributions and prospects of goal orientation theory. *Educational Psychological Review*, 19, 141–184.

Kuenzi, M., & Schminke, M. (2009) Assembling fragments into a lens: a review, critique, and proposed research agenda for the organizational work climate literature. *Journal of Management*, 35(3), 634–717.

Langelaan, S., Bakker, A. B., van Doornen, L. J. P., & Schaufeli, W. B. (2006) Burnout and work engagement: do individual differences make a difference? *Personality and Individual Differences*, 40, 521–532.

Lee, S. Y., & Akhtar, S. (2011) Effects of the workplace social context and job content on nurse burnout. *Human Resource Management*, 50(2), 227–245.

Leiter, M. P., & Maslach, C. (2001) Burnout and health. In A. Baum, T. A. Revenson, & J. E. Singer (eds) *Handbook of Health Psychology*. New Jersey, NJ: Lawrence Erlbaum Associates, Publishers. pp. 415–426.

Lemyre, P. N., Hall, H. K., & Roberts, G. C. (2008) A social cognitive approach to burnout in elite athletes. *Scandinavian Journal of Medicine and Science in Sports*, 18, 221–234.

Llorens, S., Schaufeli, W., Bakker, A., & Salanova, M. (2007) Does a positive gain spiral of resources, efficacy beliefs and engagement exist? *Computers in Human Behavior*, 23(1), 825–841.

Maehr, M. L., & Zusho, A. (2009) Achievement goal theory: the past, present, and future. In K. R. Wentzel & A. Wigfield (eds) *Handbook of Motivation at School*. New York, NY: Routledge. pp. 77–104.

Maertz Jr., C. P., Griffeth, R. W., Campbell, N. S., & Allen, D. G. (2007) The effects of perceived organizational support and perceived supervisor support on employee turnover. *Journal of Organizational Behavior*, 28, 1059–1075.

Maslach, C., Jackson, S. E., & Leiter, M. P. (1996) *Maslach Burnout Inventory Manual* (3rd edition). Palo Alto, CA: Consulting Psychologists Press.

Nerstad, C. G. L., Richardsen, A. M., & Roberts, G. C. (2011) *The Person–situation Interaction Revisited: An Achievement Goal Theory Perspective*. Paper presented at the Academy of Management Annual Meeting, San Antonio, Texas, USA (August 12–16).

Nerstad, C. G. L., Roberts, G. C., & Richardsen, A. M. (in press). Achieving success at work: The development and validation of the motivational climate at work questionnaire (MCWQ). *Journal of Applied Social Psychology*.

Newton, M., & Duda, J. L. (1999) The interaction of motivational climate, dispositional goal orientations, and perceived ability in predicting indices of motivation. *International Journal of Sport Psychology*, 30, 63–82.

Nicholls, J. G. (1984) Achievement motivation: conceptions of ability, subjective experience, mastery choice and performance. *Psychological Review*, 91(3), 328–346.

Nicholls, J. G. (1989) *The Competitive Ethos and Democratic Education*. Cambridge, MA: Harvard University Press.

Nishii, L. H., Lepak, D. P., & Schneider, B. (2008) Employee attributions of the "why" of HR practices: their effects on employee attitudes and behaviors, and customer satisfaction. *Personnel Psychology*, 61, 503–545.

Ntoumanis, N., & Biddle, S. J. H. (1999) A review of motivational climate in physical activity. *Journal of Sport Sciences*, 17, 643–665.

Paauwe, J. (2004) *HRM and Performance: Achieving Long-term Viability*. Oxford, UK: Oxford University Press.

Payne, S. C., Youngcourt, S. S., & Beaubien, M. J. (2007) A meta-analytic examination of goal orientation nomological net. *Journal of Applied Psychology*, 92, 128–150.

Pensgaard, A.-M., & Roberts, G. C. (2002) Elite athletes' experiences of the motivational climate: the coach matters. *Scandinavian Journal of Medicine and Science in Sports*, 12, 54–60.

Poortvliet, P., & Darnon, C. (2010) Toward a more social understanding of achievement goals: the interpersonal effects of mastery and performance goals. *Current Directions in Psychological Science*, 19(5), 324–328.

Rawsthorne, L. J., & Elliot, A. J. (1999) Achievement goals and intrinsic motivation: a meta-analytic review. *Personality and Social Psychology Review*, 3(4), 326–344.

Reichers, A. E., & Schneider, B. (1990) Climate and culture: an evolution of constructs. In B. Schneider (ed.) *Organizational Climate and Culture*. San Francisco, CA: Jossey-Bass. pp. 5–39.

Reinboth, M., & Duda, J. L. (2004) The motivational climate, perceived ability, and athletes' psychological and physical well–being. *The Sport Psychologist*, 18, 237–251.

Retelsdorf, J., Butler, R., Streblow, L., & Schiefele, U. (2010) Teachers' goal orientations for teaching: associations with instructional practices, interest in teaching, and burnout. *Learning and Instruction*, 20, 30–46.

Rhoades, L., & Eisenberger, R. (2002) Perceived organizational support: a review of the literature. *Journal of Applied Psychology*, 87, 698–714.

Rhoades Shanock, L., & Eisenberger, R. (2006) When supervisors feel supported: relationships with subordinates' perceived supervisor support, perceived organizational support, and performance. *Journal of Applied Psychology*, 91(3), 689–695.

Rich, B. L., & Lepine, J. A. (2007) *Job Engagement: More Than Just Old Wine in a New Bottle*. Paper presented at the sixty-seventh annual meeting of the Academy of Management, Philadelphia, Pennsylvania.

Roberts, B. W., Walton, K. E., & Viechtbauer, W. (2006) Patterns of mean-level change in personality traits across the life course: a meta-analysis of longitudinal studies. *Psychological Bulletin*, 132, 1–25.

Roberts, G. C. (2001) Understanding the dynamics of motivation in physical activity: The influence of achievement goals on motivational processes. In G. C. Roberts (ed.) *Advances in Motivation in Sport and Exercise*. Champaign, IL: Human Kinetics.

Roberts, G. C. (2012) Motivation in sport and exercise from an achievement goal theory perspective: after 30 years, where are we? In G. C. Roberts & D. Treasure (eds) *Advances in Motivation in Sport and Exercise*. Champaign, IL: Human Kinetics. Vol. 3, pp. 5–58.

Roberts, G. C., Treasure, D. C., & Conroy, D. E. (2007) Understanding the dynamics of motivation in sport and physical activity. In G. Tenenbaum & R. C. Eklund (eds) *Handbook of Sport Psychology* (3rd edition). New Jersey: John Wiley & Sons, Inc. pp. 3–30.

Salanova, M., Agut, S., & Peiro, J. M. (2005) Linking organizational resources and work engagement to employee performance and customer loyalty: the mediation of service climate. *Journal of Applied Psychology*, 90, 1217–1227.

Salanova, M., & Schaufeli, W. B. (2008) A cross-national study of work engagement as a mediator between job resources and proactive behavior. *The International Journal of Human Resource Management*, 19, 116–131.

Schaufeli, W. B., & Buunk, B. P. (2003) Burnout: an overview of 25 years of research and theorizing. In M. J. Schabracq, J. A. M. Winnubst, & C. L. Cooper (eds) *Handbook of Work and Health Psychology* (2nd edition). West Sussex: John Wiley & Sons Ltd. pp. 383–428.

Schaufeli, W. B., & Salanova, M. (2007) Work engagement: an emerging psychological concept and its implications for organizations. In S. W. Gilliand, D. D. Steiner, & D. P. Skarlicki (eds) *Research in Social Issues in Management*. Greenwich, CT: Information Age Publishers. Vol. 5, pp. 135–177.

Seligman, M. E. P., & Csikszentmihalyi, M. (2000) Positive psychology: an introduction. *American Psychologist*, 55, 5–14.

Smith, A. L., Gustafsson, H., & Hassmén, P. (2010) Peer motivational climate and burnout perceptions of adolescent athletes. *Psychology of Sport and Exercise*, 11, 453–460.

Smith, R. E., Smoll, F. L., & Cumming, S. P. (2009) Motivational climate and changes in young athletes' achievement goal orientations. *Motivation and Emotion*, 33, 173–183.

Treasure, D. C., & Roberts, G. C. (1998) Relationship between female adolescents' achievement goal orientations, perceptions of the motivational climate, belief about success and sources of satisfaction in basketball. *International Journal of Sport Psychology*, 29, 211–230.

Twenge, J. M., & Campbell, S. M. (2010) Generation me and the changing world of work. In P. A. Linley, S. Harrington, & N. Garcea (eds) *Oxford Handbook of Positive Psychology and Work*. New York: Oxford University Press. pp. 25–35.

Valentini, N. C., & Rudisill, M. E. (2006) Goal orientation and mastery climate: a review of contemporary research and insights to intervention. *Estudos de Psicologia*, 23, 159–171.

VandeWalle, D. (1997) Development and validation of a work domain goal orientation instrument. *Educational and Psychological Measurement*, 57, 995–1015.

Van Yperen, N. W., Hamstra, M. R. W., & van der Klauw, M. (2011) To win, or not to lose, at any cost: the impact of achievement goals on cheating. *British Journal of Management*, 22, 5–15.

7

When Pulling to the Negative Emotional Attractor is Too Much or Not Enough to Inspire and Sustain Outstanding Leadership

RICHARD E. BOYATZIS

In the *Stars Wars* movies, the viewer is witness to repeated battles between good and bad. Obi-wan Kenobi and Yoda entice Anakin and later Luke Skywalker to "use the force within you" for good. The contrast is the breath-filled voice of Darth Vader tempting Luke with the benefits of the "dark side." Whether they battle with their minds, light swords or clones, these opposing forces, as the sage Yoda explains to Jedi knights in training, are both within us and the universe. It is a Hollywood version of "yin/yang," eternal forces that exist in context of and in opposition to each other.

The Positive Emotional Attractor (PEA) and Negative Emotional Attractor (NEA) represent analogous states which are both necessary and both present at all times, but often function as if they were diametrically opposing states. The PEA and NEA alternate in a person, dyad, team, organization, community or even country. But the period of time spent when one attractor dominates is different from person to person, situation to situation and time to time. These variations help to explain when and how we are willing to consider learning, change and adaptation, and when we are not.

The emerging field and popularity of positive psychology has replaced our focus on needs and deficiencies with a focus on the positive and the possible. But in this fervor, we may be masking the important role of the negative. This chapter will explore how these states affect leaders, their relationships with others around them, and result in effective or ineffective leaders. Particular attention will be paid to the role of the PEA and NEA in how a leader might inspire others to develop and perform, or not. In other words, this chapter will seek to answer the question: When is arousal of the NEA too much, and when is it not enough? At the heart of this conceptual dilemma and emotional tug-of-war, there are a few trends in research that are relevant but from different fields.

Two Strange Attractors: The Postive Emotional Attractor and Negative Emotional Attractor

As a part of Intentional Change Theory, there are two strange attractors within each of us, or our social organizations (Boyatzis, 2008). These are called the PEA and NEA, as mentioned earlier. They are technically strange attractors as first articulated by Ed Lorenz (1963). That is, they create forces that pull our behavior, attitudes, feelings and such around them, but not into them. This is different than a limit point cycle attractor which, like a black hole, pulls all in its presence into a vortex and a center (Casti, 1994). In this application, once caught in the pull of an attractor, a person's mood, state, feelings, thoughts and behavior cycle within a self-perpetuating loop. It takes a tipping point to move the state into the pull of the other attractor.

Positive emotions have been shown to result in more altruistic, helpful, co-operative and conciliatory behavior (Barsade & Gibson, 2007). These cognitive events then reinforce themselves and trigger positive emotions (Fredrickson & Joiner, 2002). This creates a positive feedback loop. In this way, a person is in the PEA until a tipping point shifts the person into the NEA.

Biological research shows that physiological arousal of the parasympathetic nervous system (PNS) and corresponding neuro-endocrine systems arouses the vagus nerve, which then slows the heart rate and triggers the release of variety of hormones. Oxytocin, primarily in women, and vasopressin, primarily in men, are associated with many physiological, psychological and social benefits (Insel, 1997; Schulkin, 1999; Kemp and Guastella, 2011). For example, oxytocin reduces anxiety and heightens feelings of tenderness, attachment and closeness to others. The opposite of this occurs in the Sympathetic Nervous System (SNS), in which endocrines like epinephrine, norepinephrine, corticosteroid endocrines and cortisol enter the bloodstream and have the effect of limiting cognitive, perceptual and emotional openness and performance (Sapolsky, 2004).

Once positive emotions are aroused, and the related neural activations and hormonal arousals occur, the PEA state would result in a person being more cognitively open. A person's cognitive performance would improve (Ashby, Isen & Turken, 1999; Estrada, Isen & Young, 1994, 1997). They would be more perceptually open and accurate in perceptions of others (Fredrickson & Branigan, 2005; Talarico, Berstein & Rubin, 2008). In the PEA, a person is more emotionally open (Critchley, 2005). In the PEA state, a person is believed to have access to more of their neural circuits, is calmer, and their immune system functions at its best (Boyatzis, Smith & Blaize, 2006). A process of creating hippocampal stem cells into new neural tissue in adult humans is called neurogenesis and is believed to occur in the PEA (Erikson, Perfilieva, Bjork-Eriksson, Alborn, Nordburg, Peterson and Gage, 1998). Meanwhile, in the NEA state, a person has less access to their neural circuits and neurogenesis is inhibited (Boyatzis, Smith & Blaize, 2006).

Strange attractors have been used by other scholars to explain the dynamics of better relationships and positive emotions. For example, Losada and Heaphy (2004) claimed that a dynamic, non-linear system described the relationship between team performance and three characteristics of intra-team interactions. One dimension of their model was the ratio of positive to negative statements within the team. They explained, in a mathematical model, how high performing teams would have a positivity to negativity ratio of 2.9 or above. But their model of strange attractors did not use physiological states as a dimension. The other two dimensions of their model focused on effectiveness and the nature of attribution of participants.

Similarly, Gottman, Murray, Swanson, Tyson and Swanson (2002) used a strange attractor to describe how emotions that are aroused within a married couple determine the health and stability of their marriage. Their research revealed a ratio of 5:1 was crucial for healthy, stable, loving marriages. They had two dimensions similar to the PEA: the ratio of positive to negative emotions aroused (similar to Fredrickson's model); and the degree of emotional intensity in the spouses' attempted influence of their partner.

The need for the three dimensions described by the PEA and NEA becomes clearer from a meta-analysis and mathematical argument by Russell and Carroll (1999). They claimed that positive and negative affect are not merely bi-polar. They believed that a dimension that addresses the intensity of the arousal of emotion is also needed beyond the positive/negative dimension.

In the Boyatzis (2008) model, the PEA and NEA are best represented by three dimensions: (1) a continuum of affect aroused from positive to negative; (2) a continuum of a neural activation and endocrine arousal best labeled as the parasympathetic nervous system to the sympathetic nervous system; and (3) a continuum of the relative degree of intensity in the arousal/activation from low to high. Again, once pulled into the orbit of one of these attractors, the person, team, organization or community will cycle around and within it, in what appears to be a homeostatic state. The intensity, nature of the affect and physiological state will vary in degree (that is, a person can be more or less in the PEA or NEA), but the person will be looping in that state until a tipping point occurs to move him/her into the other state.

Two Basic Needs and the Three Dimensions

The two attractors reflect two basic needs of the human organism: the need to survive and the need to thrive. The drive to survive has emerged through adaption of the human organism over our history. Baumeister, Bratslavsky, Finkenauer and Vohs (2001) reviewed many studies from many fields bringing us to the conclusion that "bad is stronger than good." This includes emotions. They conjecture that is serves the human organisms' long-term survival needs. To survive, we need to protect ourselves from risk and danger. Without surviving, there can be no thriving. As described previously in this paper, the NEA incorporates negative over positive emotional arousal *and* the arousal of the sympathetic nervous system and activation of related neural networks.

The NEA state could be said to reflect the survival need of the human. It enables the human organism to activate itself and prepare to defend against threats. Segerstrom and Miller (2004) showed that the human stress response (that is, activation of the SNS) occurs when we feel something is important (the more important the higher the stress), something is uncertain (the more uncertain the higher the stress), or we feel that people are watching and evaluating us (the more people or time involved in their observations and evaluation, the higher the stress). They also point out, supported by Sapolsky (2004), that humans can activate the stress response by merely anticipating one of these the conditions. In today's society, many of the threats have become symbolic. Between real, symbolic and anticipated conditions, it is likely that people in professional or managerial roles activate the NEA more often than to only help us survive.

The Baumeister, Bratslavsky, Finkenauer and Vohs (2001) review does not conclude that bad is better than good, merely stronger. The popularity of the emerging field of positive psychology can be said to result from our fatigue with excessive NEA arousal. Besides optimism, positive emotions have been proposed as a building block of the alternative human need—the need to thrive. The benefits of positive emotions have been documented in many studies summarized by Fredrickson (2009). Her work has shown that the ratio of positive to negative emotions predicts the cognitive, perceptual and emotional conditions of the parasympathetic nervous system and the PEA.

The human need to thrive is described by Fredrickson (2009) as the need to flourish through her "broaden and build" theory. As described previously in this chapter, the PEA incorporates positive over negative emotional arousal *and* the arousal of the parasympathetic nervous system and activation of related neural networks. The appeal of being in the PEA both provides relief from the burdens of the experience in the NEA *and* allows us to explore and enjoy the alternative to the drive to survive.

The activation of the PEA would bring us into the drive to thrive, while the NEA would bring us into the drive to survive. Balancing these states is essential for a human to both adapt with life and work but also to innovate and expand the possibilities in life. An appropriate balance among the PEA and NEA could affect a person's sense of well-being, as well as their ability to learn, develop and create.

Through the neural mechanism of emotional contagion (Boyatzis, Passarelli, Koenig, Lowe, Mathews, Stoller, and Phillips, 2012; Boyatzis, 2012) and the behavioral mechanism of social contagion (that is, through social processes of mimicry, role modeling and enactment of social norms), the experience of the PEA or the NEA is spread to others and becomes a shared experience. A key paper in the positive psychology and positive organizational scholarship field was Roberts, Dutton, Spreitzer, Heaphy and Quinn (2005) about a person's "best self." This is considered a building block of high-quality relationships, which in turn foster a sense of well-being, better innovation, productivity, organizational commitment and engagement. The benefits and appeal of being in the PEA state expand beyond the individual into his or her relationships and have a PEA arousing effect in teams, organizations, communities and even countries (Barsade & Gibson, 2007; Boyatzis, 2008).

The Benefits of the Positive Emotional Attractor

There appear to be four primary experiences which have been related to arousing the PEA state (Boyatzis & McKee, 2005): (1) creating a shared vision, telos or purpose; (2) expressing compassion; (3) a combination of shared vision and positive mood; and (4) playfulness (Ayan, 2009).

The PEA is the relationship between the leader and those around him/her is often evident in the nature of the relationship. The relationship affects the follower's job satisfaction, organizational commitment, turnover intention, health, effort, learning and development (Bass & Avolio, 1990; Bommer, Rubin & Baldwin, 2004; Gerstner & Day, 1997). The arousal of the PEA affects both parties in these relationships. When the followers enter the PEA, in a positive feedback loop, this arouses the PEA in the leader (Boyatzis, Smith & Blaize, 2006). The emerging field of "follower studies" is balancing the leader-centric nature of most leadership research (Tee, Ashkanasy and Paulsen, 2011).

Previous research and models of effective leadership appear to cause or be associated with similar outcomes as the PEA. For example, transformational leadership research is linked to improved employee satisfaction, organizational commitment, effort, organizational citizenship behavior, turnover intention and task performance (Bass & Avolio, 1990; Bommer, Rubin & Baldwin, 2004). Meanwhile, charismatic leadership theory is similar positive outcomes (Rowold & Laukamp, 2009). It has also been associated with improvements in subjective outcomes such as trust, satisfaction and perception of group performance by followers (Conger, Kanungo & Menon, 2000).

Articulating a shared vision or creating a process in which a shared vision is developed or discussed spreads the arousal of the PEA among groups of people. This is merging from recent research as a powerful force in organizational success. Neff (2011) found that shared vision among the management of a family business was a crucial variable in family business success. Trust, confidence in management and developing a learning network also helped, but shared vision was the most powerful predictor. Overbeke (2010) reported that a shared vision in a family business increased the likelihood that a daughter will become the successor in generational transitions. It built upon the daughter's sense of efficacy and allowed her to overcome the sexism of parents or grandparents.

Shared vision is one of the scales in the Positive Negative Emotional Attractor (PNEA) Survey (Boyatzis, 2008). Clayton (2009) showed that shared vision was the most powerful variable predicting championing behavior, which in turn has been shown to predict effective mergers and acquisitions. Shared vision stimulated increased organizational engagement in IT teams, amplifying the effect of the average level of Emotional Intelligence (EI) competencies shown by the team members (Mahon, 2011).

Another of the scales in the PNEA Survey is shared Positive Mood. Along with shared vision, positive mood experienced by a patient predicted degree treatment adherence for Type II diabetics (Khawaja, 2010). When analyzed along with nine other variables from the current medical literature, it was the most powerful (Khawaja, 2010). Buse (2011) showed that a comprehensive personal vision was the most powerful predictor of whether or not women decide to stay in engineering and science careers.

When the Negative Emotional Attractor is Needed

Despite the dysfunctional aspects of remaining in the NEA for long, arousal of the NEA may serve to facilitate better performance in three ways: (1) in activating the organism (that is, waking up a person and preparing one to defend themselves); (2) providing a balance for the negative effects of excessive or unchecked optimism; and (3) when someone desires to stretch, develop, or harden themselves. The primary benefit to the human of the SNS is activation and preparation or defense (Sapolsky, 2004). Anyone teaching an early morning class to undergraduates can attest to the importance of "activation" to wake them up at times.

The need for balance against unchecked optimism is appearing in economic and neuroscience literature (McNulty & Fincham, 2011). Extreme optimists have been shown to make poorer investment decisions than pessimistic counterparts because they appear to ignore disconfirming information and miss opportunities on the "sell" side of financial investments (Gibson & Sanbonmatsu, 2004). Although the most important benefit of the NEA for a human is to defend itself against threats, a major benefit to help in growth is the experience of stretching or challenging oneself beyond a comfort zone (Norem, 2001). This process of adaptation will activate the body's stress response because the outcome is uncertain and the reason for the growth is either seeking novelty or growth. Optimistic views about one's status may result in complacency and weaken the drive to consider an adaptation (McNulty & Fincham, 2011).

Why We Need the Postive Emotional Attractor More Than the Negative Emotional Attractor

Relationships with resonant leaders create a PEA state. Relationships with dissonant leaders create an NEA state. These effects occur even when the leader or followers recall these moments. In a recent study, fMRI (that is, functional magnetic resonance imaging) results showed that recalling key experiences with resonant leaders activated neural areas such as the bilateral insula, right inferior parietal lobe and left superior temporal gyrus (Boyatzis, Passarelli, Koenig, Lowe, Mathews, Stoller, and Phillips, 2012). They pointed out that these regions are associated with the mirror neuron system and default mode network. These neural networks are key to the process of interpersonal emotional contagion in terms of spreading of emotions from one person to another within seconds or milliseconds (ibid,). They reported that recalling experiences with dissonant leaders negatively activated regions associated with the mirror neuron system and those involved in narrowing attention. At the same time, recalling moments with resonant leaders activated neural systems associated with positive emotions and approach behavior, while recalling moments with dissonant leaders activated neural systems associated with negative emotions and avoidance behavior.

Emotional contagion infects others around the leader (Hatfield, Cacioppo & Rapson, 1994). Like waves expanding from a stone tossed into a pond, the leader's PEA helps to change the mood and openness to new possibilities of those around him/her. Resonant leaders arouse and activate the PEA more often than not, with most of the people around them. Arousal and activation of the NEA causes people to suffer cognitive, perceptual and emotional impairment. Dissonant leader can spread NEA quickly to others. Eventually, the NEA could permeate the organization.

The exchange of emotions is predominantly unconscious through perceptual processes such as how we mimic each other's facial expressions, language and movement (Cattaneo & Rizzolatti, 2009; Iacoboni, 2009). It occurs quickly, often within seconds or parts of a second.

Research shows how emotional contagion from the leader affects others (Lewis, 2000; Cherulnik, Donley, Wiewel & Miller, 2001). For example, Dasborough (2006) reported employees remembered negative events (hassles) more frequently and in more detail and intensity than positive events (uplifts). Bono and Ilies (2006) showed that leaders' expressions of positive emotions affected others' moods. Possibly not surprisingly, they added that the followers' positive moods influenced the perceived effectiveness of the leader.

Using positive emotional contagion builds human capital in the organization. Peterson, Balthazard, Waldman and Thatcher (2008) defined leaders who build psychological capital as those who stimulate "optimism, hope, confidence and resilience" (p. 342). Using quantitative electroencephalogram (qEEG), they showed leaders who emphasize social responsibility, altruism and the empowerment of various stakeholders in communicating a vision (socialized vision) created more psychological capital. And the inverse was true—leaders whose communication was narcissistic, self-interested and manipulating toward a personal, not shared vision decreased the psychological capital in the organization (Waldman, Balthazard, Peterson, Galvin & Thatcher, in press).

If the emotional contagion activates certain networks in the brain known as the Default Mode Network (DMN), which is often now called the "social network" (Raichle & Snyder, 2007; Jack, Dawson, Ciccia, Cesaro, Barry, Snyder and Begany, 2009), it helps us to consider others in our presence and their feelings. In offering a conceptualization of two forms of empathy, Decety and Batson (2007) and Decety and Michalska (2010) commented that the posterior cingulate cortex (PCC, which is considered part of the social network) is more strongly activated during recognition of "other's pain" than during recognition of "self-pain." In the Boyatzis, Passarelli, Koenig, Lowe, Mathews, Stoller, and Phillips (2012) study, negative activation of this region when individuals recalled moments with dissonant leaders and contrasted this to their reactions to resonant leaders both suggested that dissonant leaders move a person's thoughts more toward "self-pain" than toward thinking of others, which would be an understandable defensive response to someone in your presence, who has power, creating a threatening environment.

When the Negative Emotional Attractor is Too Much

Repeated arousal of the NEA will result in the many dysfunctional aspects of chronic SNS arousal discussed earlier and likely lead to cognitive, perceptual and emotional impairment.

Dissonant or negative leaders affect others around them negatively and become toxic (Frost, 2004). When a leader harangue's the organization with threats from the competition or attempts to create a sense of urgency through the likely negative consequences of inaction, the consequences of their behavior may be opposite to their desired effect. People hearing the message and feeling the threat will move into the NEA. Repetition of this arousal or escalation of its severity will likely lead to arousal of the SNS and the resulting cognitive, emotional and perceptual impairment.

Destructive leadership has been described as "a set of behaviors displayed consistently over time that disturbs the organization through counterproductive behaviors aimed at the organization, subordinates, or both" (Einarsen, Aasland & Skogstad, 2007). Organizational environments that tolerate or enable toxic leaders to remain in power erode the ability of the organization to adapt, be resilient and perform at their best (Padilla, Hogan & Kaiser, 2007). Schaubroeck, Walumbwa, Ganster and Kepes (2007) showed that toxic leaders negatively affected employees' personal well-being and commitment to the organization. This effect was strongest when there were no compensating positive aspects of the climate. Tepper (2000) called this "abusive supervision" and showed that, in a sample of a wide variety of jobs, abusive supervision was associated with negative consequences, including decreased job, life satisfaction, organizational commitment, increased work–family conflict and psychological distress.

When the Positive Emotional Attractor is Too Much

Following the earlier comments on the dysfunctional aspects of excessive optimism, we could contend that arousing the PEA too much would result in a person not paying attention to threats or misinterpreting symbolic threats as neutral. The openness of perceptions associated with the activation of the social network, especially the PCC, may result in a person being easily distracted. This lack of focus could cause a person to continue being open to new input and ideas at a time when action convergent thinking and action is needed to be more effective.

In Search of an Experienced Balance

Neither the entreaty to be "firm and stern" from the past nor the latest to be "happy and inspirational" will always help lead organizations to increased resilience, adaptation, performance and growth. Perhaps the common sense wisdom, the seventh century BC philosopher Kleovoulos of "nothing too much," or "nothing in excess" continues to be the best guide for leaders. The relationships created invoke others to add value or the opposite (which may be to lose interest and energy or to detract value).

Using some of the latest research from neuroscience, psychology and management, this chapter attempted to show how arousing the PEA is important to growth and innovation AND arousing the NEA is important to growth and defending against threat. Because of the increased valence of negative emotions and experiences, the best balance is one in which we overemphasize the PEA over the NEA.

References

Ashby, F. G., Isen, A. M., & Turken, U. (1999) A neuropsychological theory of positive affect and its influence on cognition. *Psychological Review*, 106(3), 529–550.

Ayan, S. (2009) Laughing matters: seeing the bright side of life may strengthen the psyche, ease pain, and tighten social bonds. *Scientific American Mind*. April/May, 24–31.

Barsade, S. G., & Gibson, D. E. (2007) Why does affect matter in organizations? *Academy of Management Perspectives*, 21, 36–59.

Bass, B. M., & Avolio, B. J. (1990) *Transformational Leadership Development: Manual for the Multifactor Leadership Questionnaire*. Palo Alto, CA: Consulting Psychologists Press.

Baumeister, R. F., Bratslavsky, E., Finkenauer, C., & Vohs, K. D. (2001) Bad is stronger than good. *Review of General Psychology*, 5, 323–370.

Bommer, W. H., Rubin, R. S., & Baldwin, T. T. (2004) Setting the stage for effective leadership: antecedents of transformational leadership behavior. *Leadership Quarterly*, 15, 195–210.

Bono, J. E., & Ilies, R. (2006) Charisma, positive emotions and mood contagion. *Leadership Quarterly*, 17, 317–334.

Boyatzis, R. E. (2008) Leadership development from a complexity perspective, *Consulting Psychology Journal*, 60(4), 298–313.

Boyatzis, R. E. (2012) Neuroscience and leadership: the promise of insights. *Ivey Business Journal*, online January/February. Available at: http://www.iveybusinessjournal.com/topics/leadership/neuroscience-and-the-link-between-inspirational-leadership-and-resonant-relationships-2.

Boyatzis, R. E., & McKee, A. (2005) *Resonant Leadership: Renewing Yourself and Connecting with Others through Mindfulness, Hope, and Compassion.* Boston, MA: Harvard Business School Press.

Boyatzis, R.E., Passarelli, A.P., Koenig, K., Lowe, M., Mathew, B., Stoller, J., & Phillips, M. (2012) Examination of the neural substrates activated in experiences with resonant & dissonant leaders. *Leadership Quarterly*, 23(2), 259–272.

Boyatzis, R. E., Smith, M. L., & Blaize, N. (2006) Developing sustainable leaders through coaching and compassion. *Academy of Management Journal on Learning and Education*, 5, 8–24.

Buse, K. (2011) *Why they stay: individual factors predicting career commitment for women engineers,* Unpublished Doctoral Qualifying Paper, Weatherhead School of Management, Case Western Reserve University, Cleveland, OH, USA.

Casti, J. L. (1994) *Complexification: Explaining a Paradoxical World through the Science of Surprise.* New York: Harper Collins.

Cattaneo, L., & Rizzolatti, G. (2009) The mirror neuron system. *Archives of Neurology*, 66, 557–560.

Cherulnik, P. D., Donley, K. A., Wiewel, T. S. R., & Miller, S. R. (2001) Charisma is contagious: the effect of leaders' charisma on observers' affect. *Journal of Applied Social Psychology*, 31, 2149–2159.

Clayton, B. (2009) *When practice and theory conflict: do financial incentives influence championing behaviours in mergers and acquisitions?,* Unpublished Doctoral Qualifying Paper, Weatherhead School of Management, Case Western Reserve University, Cleveland, OH, USA.

Conger, J. A., Kanungo, R. N., & Menon, S. T. (2000) Charismatic leadership and follower effects. *Journal of Organizational Behavior*, 21, 747–767.

Critchley, H. D. (2005) Neural mechanisms of autonomic, affective and cognitive integration. *Journal of Comparative Neurology*, 493, 154–166.

Dasborough, M.T. (2006) Cognitive asymmetry in employee emotional reactions to leadership behaviors. *Leadership Quarterly*, 79, 163–178.

Decety, J., & Batson, C. D. (2007) Social neuroscience approaches to interpersonal sensitivity. *Social Neuroscience*, 2, 151–157.

Decety, J., & Michalska, K. J. (2010) Neurodevelopmental changes in the circuits underlying empathy and sympathy from childhood to adulthood. *Developmental Science*, 13(6), 886–899.

Einarsen, S., Aasland, M. S., & Skogstad, A. (2007) Destructive leadership behaviour: a definition and conceptual model. *Leadership Quarterly*, 18, 207–216.

Erikson, P. S., Perfilieva, E., Bjork-Eriksson, T., Alborn, A-M, Nordburg, C., Peterson, D. A., and Gage, F. H. (1998) Neurogenesis in the adult human hippocampus. *Nature Medicine*, 4, 313–317.

Estrada, C. A., Isen, A. M., & Young, M. J. (1994) Positive affect improves creative problem solving and influences reported source of practice satisfaction in physicians. *Motivation and Emotion*, 18(4), 285–299.

Estrada, C. A., Isen, A. M., & Young, M. J. (1997) Positive affect facilitates integration of information and decreases anchoring in reasoning among physicians. *Organizational Behavior and Human Decision Processes*, 72(1), 117–135.

Fredrickson, B. (2009) *Positivity: Groundbreaking Research Reveals How to Embrace the Hidden Strength of Positive Emotions, Overcome Negativity, and Thrive.* New York: Crown.

Fredrickson, B. L., & Branigan, C. (2005) Positive emotions broaden the scope of attention and thought-action repertoires. *Cognition and Emotion*, 19, 313–332.

Fredrickson, B. L., & Joiner, T. (2002) Positive emotions trigger upward spirals toward emotional well-being. *Psychological Science*, 13, 172–175.

Frost, P. J. (2004) Handling toxic emotions: new challenges for leaders and their organization. *Organizational Dynamics*, 33, 111–127.

Gerstner, C. R., & Day, D. V. (1997) Meta-analytic review of leader–member exchange theory: correlates and construct issues. *Journal of Applied Psychology*, 82, 827–844.

Gibson, B., & Sanbonmatsu, D.M. (2004) Optimism, pessimism and gambling: the downside of optimism. *Personality and Social Psychology Bulletin*. 30, 149–160.

Gottman, J. M., Murray, J. D., Swanson, C. C., Tyson, R., & Swanson, K. R. (2002) *The Mathematics of Marriage: Dynamic Non-linear Models*. Cambridge, MA: MIT Press.

Hatfield, E., Cacioppo, J. T., & Rapson, R. L. (1994) *Emotional Contagion (Studies in Emotion and Social Interaction)*. New York: Cambridge University Press.

Iacoboni, M. (2009) Imitation, empathy, and mirror neurons. *Annual Review of Psychology*, 60, 653–670.

Insel, T. R. (1997) A neurobiological basis of social attachment. *American Journal of Psychiatry*, 154, 726–735.

Jack, A., Dawson, A., Ciccia, A. Cesaro, R., Barry, K., Snyder, A., & Begany, K. (2009) *Social and mechanical reasoning define two opposing domains of human higher cognition*. Presented at the Society for Neuroscience Annual Conference in Chicago, 2009. The manuscript is currently under in-depth review in *Science*.

Kemp, A. H., & Guastella, A. J. (2011) The role of oxytocin in human affect: a novel hypothesis. *Current Directions in Psychological Science*, 20(4), 222–231.

Khawaja, M. (2010) *The mediating role of positive and negative emotional attractors between psychosocial correlates of doctor-patient relationship and treatment of Type II diabetes*. Doctoral Dissertation, Case Western Reserve University; Cleveland, Ohio.

Lewis, K. M. (2000) When leaders display emotion: how followers respond to negative emotional expression of male and female leaders. *Journal of Organizational Behavior*, 21, 221–234.

Lorenz, E. N. (1963) Deterministic nonperiodic flow. *Journal of Atmospheric Science*, 20, 130–141.

Losada, M., & Heaphy, E. (2004) The role of positivity and connectivity in the performance of business teams. *American Behavioral Scientist*, 47(6), 740–765.

Mahon, E. (2011) *Factors that drive employee engagement: organizational and individual elements interact to intensify employee engagement*. Unpublished Doctoral Qualifying Paper, Weatherhead School of Management, Case Western Reserve University, Cleveland, OH, USA.

McNulty, J. K., & Fincham, F. D. (2012) Beyond positive psychology: toward a contextual view of psychological processes and well-being. *American Psychologist*, 67(2), 101–110.

Neff, J. (2011) *Non-financial indicators of family firm performance: a portfolio model approach*. Unpublished Doctoral Qualifying Paper, Weatherhead School of Management, Case Western Reserve University, Cleveland, OH, USA.

Norem, J. K. (2001) *The Positive Power of Negative Thinking*. New York: Basic Books.

Overbeke, K. (2010) *Into the family and business nexus: succession and daughters in family owned businesses*. Unpublished Doctoral Qualifying Paper, Weatherhead School of Management, Case Western Reserve University, Cleveland, OH, USA.

Padilla, A., Hogan, R., & Kaiser, R. B. (2007) The toxic triangle: destructive leaders, susceptible followers, and conducive environments. *Leadership Quarterly*, 18, 176–194.

Peterson, S. J., Balthazard, P. A., Waldman, D. A & Thatcher, R. W. (2008) Neuroscientific implications of psychological capital: are the brains of optimistic, hopeful, confident and resilient leaders different? *Organizational Dynamics*, 37(4), 342–353.

Raichle, M. E., & Snyder, A. Z. (2007) A default mode of brain function: a brief history of an evolving idea. *NeuroImage*, 37, 1083–1090.

Roberts, L. M., Dutton, J .E., Spreitzer, G., Heaphy, E. D., & Quinn, R. E. (2005) Composing the reflected best-self portrait: building pathways for becoming extraordinary in work organizations. *Academy of Management Review*, 30, 712–736.

Rowold, J., & Laukamp, L. (2009) Charismatic leadership and objective performance indicators. *Applied Psychology*, 58, 602–621.

Russell, J. A., & Carroll, J. M. (1999) On the polarity of positive and negative affect. *Psychological Bulletin.* 125(1), 3–30.

Sapolsky, R. M. (2004) *Why Zebra's Don't Get Ulcers* (3rd edition). New York: Harper Collins.

Schaubroeck, J., Walumbwa, F. O., Ganster, D. C., & Kepes, S. (2007) Destructive leader traits and the neutralizing influence of an "enriched" job. *Leadership Quarterly*, 18, 236–251.

Schulkin, J. (1999) *Neuroendocrine Regulation of Behavior.* New York: Cambridge University Press.

Segerstrom, S. C., & Miller, G. E. (2004) Psychological stress and the human immune system: A meta-analytic study of 30 years of inquiry. *Psychological Bulletin*, 130(4): 601–630.

Talarico, J. M., Bernstein, D., & Rubin, D. C. (2008) Positive emotions enhance recall of peripheral details. *Cognition and Emotion*, 23(2), 380–398.

Tee, E. Y. J., Ashkanasy, N. M., & Paulsen, N. (2011) *Upward emotional contagion and implications for leadership: from a cognitive, leader-centric approach to an effective, follower-centric model of leadership.* Presentation at the Society of Industrial and Organizational Psychology Annual Meeting, Chicago, April 15, 2011.

Tepper, B. J. (2000) Consequences of abusive supervision. *Academy of Management Journal*, 43, 178–190.

Waldman, D. A., Balthazard, P. A., Peterson, S. J., Galvin, B.M., & Thatcher, R.W. (in press) Linking neuroscience, socialized vision, and charismatic leadership. *Strategic Management Journal.*

8 The Emotional Intelligence Response to Coping with Narcissism in the Workplace

ROY LUBIT

Our society's support for individual initiative and achievement often fosters great accomplishments. It also, however, tolerates and supports the rise to power of individuals with prominent narcissistic personality traits. The driving ambition, ruthlessness and charisma of narcissistic managers fuels their rapid advancement. Their confidence and certainty inspires confidence in others leading superiors and subordinates alike to feel that the narcissistic manager is unusually competent. Willing to sacrifice all other aspects of their lives for the pursuit of power, including the needs of their families, their dedication to their work is outstanding. Masters of organizational politics, they often succeed in taking credit for the work of others, transfer blame for mistakes to others, and build undeserved reputations for themselves (Kernberg, 1998).

At the same time, their arrogance, overconfidence, excessive risk taking and willingness to exploit others eventually does tremendous damage to the organization and those who work with them and for them. Their exploitation of others damages morale and undermines those who are truly best from rising to the top. They will do what is good for themselves, regardless of the impact on the organization. They themselves often crash and burn when they over-reach, taking grave risks which fail, or when people come to realize they are unscrupulously self-promoting, dedicated to themselves, not the company (Lubit, 2002).

This chapter will explore the nature of narcissism, how narcissistic managers are able to survive and prosper in organizations, how they eventually do great damage to themselves and those around them, and what can be done to limit their destructive potential to themselves and others.

Narcissism versus Self-esteem

Psychologically healthy individuals have self-esteem and confidence. Self-esteem is needed to invest in oneself and one's career. Without confidence people are unable to make important decisions and stand up for what they believe in.

Narcissism is not the same as self-esteem or confidence. Self-esteem and confidence arise from a realistic appraisal of one's abilities and value. Self-esteem and confidence do not undermine respect for the rights, needs and abilities of others. In stark contrast, narcissistic individuals have an inflated sense of their value and abilities. Seeing themselves as special, the normal rules of society do not apply to them. Whatever helps them and their agenda is acceptable and appropriate. Exploiting others is perfectly appropriate since others are inferior and their own success is all important. They feel entitled to whatever they desire and tend to feel mistreated if others get in their way. Having an inflated sense of their importance, they devalue others and are unconcerned about the damage they do to others (Kernberg, 1985).

Underneath their arrogant exteriors and grandiosity frequently lies fragile self-esteem. They seek admiration and power to deal with their underlying fragile self-esteem. Hungry and envious, they seek what is not theirs, simply because someone else has it rather than because it has intrinsic value for them (Lubit, 2002).

Unable to care about other people or abstract values, and having no true self-love, they are left with a sense of emptiness. Intense ambition, grandiose fantasies and a search for excitement are abortive attempts to deal with their emptiness and underlying feelings of inferiority (Kernberg, 1986).

Under stress, narcissistic individuals can slide into paranoia (Burstein, 1977). Projecting their unacceptable motives and desires onto others, they can be suspicious, mistrustful, hypersensitive and prone to ascribe evil motives to others. Preoccupied with the hidden motives of others, they exaggerate threats. They look for signs of shameful conduct in others to support their devaluation of others. They trust only a few chosen subordinates, cater to them and demand total devotion in return. Lacking real connections to people, they often use new allies to betray old ones.

Narcissistic individuals come in a variety of types. Some are primarily self-aggrandizing. Some are primarily ruthless. Some are primarily overly controlling and rigid. The amount and type of damage they do depends upon the particular narcissistic personality traits they possess (Lubit, 2003).

Origins of Destructive Narcissism

Knowing how to deal with narcissistic managers depends on various factors including its severity and what underlies it. Psychodynamic theories hold that destructive narcissism arises from growing up in a house with chronically cold, covertly aggressive parents. The primary parenting figure, although functioning well on the surface, is callous and indifferent to the child's desires and exhibits spiteful aggression that injures the child's sense of self. At the same time, the child possesses some quality that others can envy which provides the child with a refuge against feelings of being unloved (Kohut, 1971).

Social learning theory provides another explanation for the development of destructively narcissistic behavior. People's behavior is affected by direct reinforcement (being rewarded or punished for a behavior), by vicarious reinforcement (seeing others rewarded or punished for a given behavior) and by self-imposed standards. From the perspective of social learning theory, narcissistic behavior arises when someone sees others behaving in grandiose and self-centered ways and getting away with it, and by getting away with such behavior oneself. People with great power or glamor often learn to be grandiose and self-centered because those around them treat them with great deference, fawn on them and do not provide negative feedback when they fail to be diplomatic or concerned about the needs of others (Bandura, 1977).

Destructive narcissism can come from either psychodynamic or learning factors or from a combination of them. The most important difference is that learned narcissism is not as locked in as psychodynamically-based narcissism. When confronted with the problems in their behavior, individuals with learned narcissism can often make significant changes. In contrast, individuals with psychodynamically-based narcissism are likely to become enraged, and perhaps paranoid, when confronted with problems in their behavior (Lubit, 2003).

Roger had been a star at work, on the football field and socially. The oldest of several children, his intelligence, good looks and athletic skill won him considerable attention both at home and at school. Neighbors and family friends would frequently see his parents lauding their son's abilities. Roger's experience, however, was that his parents excessively pressured him to achieve, took credit for his accomplishments and never cared about how he was feeling or what he wanted. His parents loved his achievements, not him.

At the same time that they were proud to hold themselves out as the parents of a star, Roger's parents were resentful that they were no longer young and the center of attention. They could be callous and even spiteful when he was not filling their needs to be the parents of a star. When a school psychologist tried to explain to them the difference between loving a child and helping a child to excel they had no idea what he was talking about. Of course they loved him, look at how much time and energy they put into helping him succeed. In the end, Roger felt unloved and unlovable, except for his achievements. He was never quite sure whose achievements they were. His parents acted as if the achievements belonged to them not him.

Roger never learned how or why to be concerned about the feelings of others. No one had attended to his feelings. As a result he did not know how to respond to the feelings and needs of others and he did not care about the feelings and needs of others. While his classmates learned that they needed to be attentive to the feelings of others to have friends, Roger's achievements and looks brought him sufficient popularity that he could treat people poorly and still have lots of people around to go to parties with and to date. Although lots of women fawned on him the relationships were never really close. Since there was always someone in the wings he did not have to worry about a girlfriend leaving due to his self-centeredness.

How Narcissistic Individuals Succeed in Organizations

Despite their weaknesses narcissistic managers have a remarkable ability to survive and flourish within organizations. People often mistake their high levels of confidence with competence. Their enthusiasm is also appealing and their assuredness that they know how to handle things and their will to succeed inspires confidence in those around them. Their unrelenting drive to attain prestige and power, and willingness to sacrifice all other areas of their lives, can bring considerable success to the company and themselves. Moreover, they are also frequently good at organizational politics since they have little attachment to the truth and are able to charm superiors and forge quick, superficial relationships. Although lacking empathic concern for others, narcissistic individuals often have "street smarts" that enable them to assess whom they can manipulate and what levers to pull to manipulate them. They can feign interest in others and play up to their bosses. They are masters at selling themselves (Lubit, 2002; Kets de Vries, 1993; Zaleznik, 1989).[1]

The hesitancy of many people to complain about them to superiors, and their ability to restrain their behavior when dealing with superiors, partially shields them from the normal consequences of their behavior. Subordinates are generally very hesitant to complain to superiors, fearing that the complaint might reflect badly on them, or that narcissistic managers will take revenge, or that complaining will lower them to the narcissistic manager's level. Subordinates and peers often expect that the unscrupulous behavior of the narcissistic manager will eventually come to light and the manager will self-destruct without their taking risky actions. But, since everyone is hesitant to share the negative information, no one person realizes how widespread the problem is, leaving the seriousness of the situation unknown to those with the power to do something about it (Lubit, 2003).

After college Roger went to law school and then joined a large law firm. His charm and outward self-confidence brought him quick success in his firm. People assumed he would be a star and he played the role well. When problems occurred he was generally able to push the blame onto others and when things went well he was generally able to grab the credit for himself. As the fair-haired boy of the firm, partners always gave him the benefit of the doubt.

The Destructive Impact of Narcissistic Individuals on Others

The self-centeredness, arrogance, self-aggrandizement, devaluation of others, ruthlessness, sense of entitlement, lack of values and search for excitement common among narcissistic managers can do significant damage to an organization and those who work in it. Ruthless, they will take what they need when they need it, without concern for fairness, ethics, decency or others. Modern-day disciples of Machiavelli, they believe that all is fair in love, war and business. Injuring others in the pursuit of a personal or corporate objective is seen as acceptable collateral damage, and sometimes as fun.

Their treatment of others can drive away the most talented people. Their willingness to manipulate others to achieve their goals, steal credit for the work of others and scapegoat others leads those around them to overly focus on organizational politics, survival and their frustration, rather than the real work of the organization. Their failure to attend to the needs of those around them for resources, co-operation and information necessary to do their work undermines the efforts of those they deal with. Morale flags as they fail

---

1   Manfred Kets de Vries has asserted that a manager could even be a team player until reaching the position of CEO, and then undergo a major transformation in behavior (Kets de Vries, 1993). Moreover, Abraham Zaleznik has written that destructive narcissism, may not manifest itself before a manager rises to the top position (Zaleznik, 1989).

to provide recognition and praise, show concern for subordinates, and encourage and facilitate their development. Further problems arise as they take all credit for themselves and scapegoat others. People in the business unit begin to focus their energies on political survival and dealing with their frustration with the narcissistic manager, rather than on doing their best work (Lubit, 2002).

Good ideas presented by peers and subordinates are likely to be disparaged or not even presented out of fear of disparagement. Implementation is impaired by both their rapid changes of interest and excessive attention to the grand plan, rather than the less exciting details of implementation (Kernberg, 1998).

Destructively narcissistic managers are also vulnerable to making disastrous business decisions. Seeking glory, they may try to build an empire rather than prudently growing a company. Their personal agendas take precedence over the company's best interests. They can squander company money on extravagances. They also cling to power rather than hand it over to the next generation in a timely fashion (Lubit, 2002).

Roger's peers were angered by his frequent bragging about his abilities, or scapegoating of them, and stealing credit for their work. People did not want to work with him. Women were less tolerant of his self-centeredness. As others were settling down, his going from one relationship to another seemed strange to people rather than enviable.

Self-destruction Through Narcissism

In time, narcissistic managers tend to crash and burn. As they rise up by stepping on others they create enemies rather than allies. Success in modern business, however, requires co-operation from others; others can easily sabotage your plans by failing to give needed co-operation. Their overconfidence and desire for excitement can lead to excessive risk taking which pays off when it succeeds but can also lead to disaster. They are likely to develop a reputation for ruthlessness; loose cannons who fail to develop the company's human resources and care only about themselves.

The fragile self-esteem of individuals with psychodynamically-based narcissism leaves them liable to "narcissistic rage" when challenged or criticized. Narcissistic rage is marked by its high intensity and loss of judgment in which the individual strikes out in ways that can be very damaging to himself and others. Their anger, self-centeredness, devaluation of the needs of others and entitlement wears on friends and family members. Not only do their marriages collapse but their children will abandon them and what friendships remain are likely to be shallow.

The aging process with its decrease in abilities and attractiveness is particularly difficult for destructively narcissistic individuals. By middle age they often devalue things they had once liked. They resent no longer having the joys of youth and feel anger over present and past frustrations. They devalue the ideas and behavior of people who still have hopes and those things that they cannot have or be. Rather than gratitude, they feel humiliation, suspicion and anger toward people they depend on (Zaleznik, 1989).

When Roger finally did marry he quickly grew bored and began to have affairs. He had little patience with his children and could fly into a rage if they did not show him the respect he expected. His wife stayed with him to maintain the family structure, rather than from being in love. As his children grew up they bristled at his self-centeredness, his always wanting to have his way, and ignoring of their needs. Unable to care about others, he felt empty.

Roger focused all of his attention on his advancement within his firm. As time went on he increasingly alienated those around him. While his peers would at times irritate others, they also knew how to repair relationships. Roger did not know how to repair relationships; he only replaced damaged relationships with new ones. People were no longer so awed by him, however, and it was not as easy to replace old relationships with new ones. Eventually, his children and wife grew so disgusted with his self-centeredness that his marriage ended and his children were only willing to have relatively small amounts of contact with him. Sliding into depression his work suffered. Having no reason to put up with the rough sides of his personality he was told to look elsewhere for his future.

Coping with Our Own Narcissism

Even those who are not inherently narcissistic as a result of early childhood emotional trauma can fall vulnerable to learned narcissism. Some people are naturally very empathic and giving. For most of us, however, responsiveness to the needs of others requires effort. In the midst of work stress, work success and controlling millions of dollars, people can easily find themselves with too much on their plate to pay attention to the needs of others for support and nurturance. Complicating the situation, people have a remarkable ability to justify as necessary and fair whatever is in their own interests. The needs of friends and family, as well as the needs of colleagues and subordinates, can easily be trampled on destroying the heart of our lives and the reason most of us work so hard. We can become so engulfed in short-term objectives that we forget why we are doing all of this. We can forget that power and prestige are very nice things to have, but family and friends are fundamental to our lives. People also often sacrifice their own physical health as the desire for greater work success interferes with exercise, sleep, diet and rest. He who dies with the most toys does not win the game of life. It is crucial that we frequently step back and think about how we will view our lives from the vantage point of our retirement, and to think about what we will wish we had done during our lives.

Excess absorption with attaining and maintaining power and glory often leads to self-destruction. Our health declines and decision making and performance deteriorate.

Most of us can become blinded to the needs of those around us if given power, placed under great pressure and denied accurate feedback from subordinates. If we do not pay attention to this potential in ourselves, we may inadvertently behave in damaging ways. We need to be wary of this narcissistic behavior in ourselves and be open to the ideas and criticisms of others. At times counseling may be needed to help us to deal with stress and refocus.

For individuals with longstanding narcissistic issues the situation is harder. Major personality change is difficult, and becomes more difficult as people become older. While wide-ranging personality change is unlikely to occur, people can often curtail those behaviors which do the most damage, significantly improving the situation. The key is to focus on what aspects of our narcissism are doing harm to the things we value. Desire for attention and overestimation of one's own value are generally tolerable if we also pay attention to the needs of others and tone down our self-glorification. Devaluing and ignoring the needs of others is far more serious. With effort people can generally be more attentive to the needs and wishes of others. Although it may not come naturally we can generally force ourselves to do so if we realize the consequences of not doing so and put energy into it. We may devalue the needs of our spouse and children, but realizing that failing to be nice to them could lead to divorce and rejection by our children can lead us to be more careful, just as we may not want to pay taxes but do so because the consequences for failing to pay are so great. Those who are more severe and engage in ruthless behavior toward others need to understand that they are making enemies and building a reputation that is likely to eventually bring them down. The short-term advantage such behavior brings is rarely worth the cost. For those who are most severe this knowledge is unlikely to lead to behavior change since the desire to manipulate and exploit people is not simply an instrumental means to the goal of success. Putting something over on others is the goal.

It is also helpful to place oneself in a position in which our weaknesses are least likely to do us harm. It is sometimes best to work in an organization with a culture tolerant of your style. On the other hand, this can also lead to continuation and reinforcement of problematic behavior. Having a buffer is often helpful. For example, a CEO with rough edges or who fails to attend to details can often benefit from having a COO who takes care of these tasks. Teamwork can sometimes be divided so that the skills of the narcissistic manager are used to their best advantage while people are protected from their rough edges. Certain positions and industries are more likely than others to have high levels of competition and to tempt us to behave ruthlessly. Projects requiring extensive co-operation and group work are more likely to lead to problems than situations in which the narcissistic individual is working more independently.

Organizational Alternatives

Perhaps the most important thing that organizations can do to avoid problems with narcissistic managers is to avoid hiring and promoting them. This requires being aware of the problem and conversant with the signs of narcissism. Rather than being seduced by the charm of a glib applicant and rather than equate high confidence with high competence, one should be alert to the possible presence of narcissistic issues. Behavioral interviewing, in which the individual is asked to talk about a time when a project went well and a time when a project did not go well, can be very helpful. Narcissistic managers are likely to claim that they were the reason for all success and others were the cause of all failure. It is also important to adequately screen important hires, getting 360 degree information (information from subordinates and peers as well as superiors) and thereby finding out how they relate to subordinates as well as superiors. Some companies have top hires interviewed by a psychologist or psychiatrist to evaluate for personality issues that could interfere with their work. Once hired it is important to gather information from subordinates and peers as well as superiors when considering promotions. When problems arise, glib responses to questions should not be accepted. Problems should be investigated with some rigor.

Another important issue is to be careful about the organizational culture. An organization's culture—norms of behavior, values and beliefs—is forged from the role models that leaders provide, the myths and stories leaders tell, what the organization measures and rewards, the criteria used for hiring and promoting people, and the historical norms of behavior and values of the organization. Some cultures are tolerant of narcissistic managers and some are not. Some organizations will not mind self-centered ruthless managers as long as they perform, while others will appreciate their long-term destructive potential and not promote them.

What to do with a narcissistic manager depends upon a variety of factors. One should weigh the value, replaceability and potential harm of a narcissistic manager. If the manager is irreplaceable, or their strengths outweigh even their narcissistic issues and the organization decides to keep the individual, it is important to shield the organization from the most destructive aspects of the individual's narcissism. The first issue is to assess what aspects of this individual's personality are likely to adversely affect the company. Narcissistic managers tend to be risk prone, but not all are. Some are thoughtless and will irritate all they interact with, while others are superficially charming but then exploit others. The organization needs to guard against the particular problems a given manager creates and not all possible problems a narcissistic individual could create. It is useful to place a buffer around a high-level narcissistic manager. For example, an organization with a narcissistic CEO may benefit from appointing a COO who handles the day-by-day affairs of running the organization and interacts with members of the organization, limiting the damage the narcissistic CEO does to morale. Major decisions being made by a narcissistic manager should get more than average review by others to make sure that the plan is not too risk prone and that it is truly designed for the best interests of the organization, rather than the best interests of the manager. The organization may also be able to place the individual in a position in which their weaknesses are unlikely to lead to serious problems.

If the narcissistic traits are limited to self-aggrandizement and desire for attention there is generally little risk other than the annoyance of peers. Ruthlessness, rigidity and failure to develop others and consider the needs of others, however, is another matter.

If a narcissistic manager is replaceable, does not have critical knowledge or contacts, then confronting the behavior in the hope of ameliorating it is a good place to begin. If the manager's narcissism is primarily of the learned variety, confrontation and executive coaching are usually helpful. Confrontation can even ameliorate moderate psychodynamically-based narcissism by strongly reminding the narcissistic manager of the consequences of failing to change. If the destructive narcissism is severe and based on psychodynamic problems and fragile self-esteem, however, confrontation may lead to rage and possibly paranoia and make matters worse. These individuals may be helped to function better by providing them with copious emotional support. A skilled executive coach, providing a combination of empathic support and recommendations on how to work with others, can help a narcissistic manager contain some of the most damaging manifestations of narcissism.

The management of an executive with destructive narcissism can be very difficult. The situation becomes particularly complicated when the executive is difficult to replace in the near future, since confrontation of the behavior in the hope of ameliorating it can precipitate a crisis and be counterproductive. Calling in a consultant skilled in dealing with problems of narcissism, and who can provide a complex mix of confrontation, coaching and support, can significantly ameliorate the situation.

Stress leads to anxiety and depression which decreases self-esteem and ultimately increases the rigidity of the narcissistic managers' problematic personality traits. Treating their depression and anxiety with appropriate medication can help them to be less defensive, more responsive to others, and better able to look at their problematic behaviors and make progress in therapy or executive coaching.

Coping with Destructively Narcissistic Bosses

Working for, or with, narcissistic people brings considerable stress for the various reasons described above. Nevertheless, your attitude and actions can significantly affect your stress level when dealing with such people. Attempting to change their behavior by telling them how their behavior makes you feel will not work and inevitably leads to frustration. It is best to accept that they were so damaged in their emotional development that they lack the ability to empathize and behave reasonably.

Avoiding their rough and sometimes explosive edges is generally the best strategy. It is always a bad idea to argue with their criticism of you, since doing so will only enrage them. Pay attention to what situations lead to problems and avoid them. Avoid gossiping with them, borrowing from them and lending to them since these will make you vulnerable. Obtaining written directions can be helpful, since it decreases the room for uncertainty and complaints against you. Documenting your work can help shield you from unfair criticism that you did not do your job properly. It can also be helpful to document interactions and your work so that if you need to defend yourself to someone higher up you have the means to do so.

It is crucial to behave with unusual levels of tact. It is also important to protect the narcissistic boss from threats to his fragile self-esteem lest he becomes enraged and vengeful. Avoid pointing out his mistakes or unfairness, and above all, do not challenge his authority, power or greatness. Instead, support his self-esteem by showing respect and even admiration for his accomplishments. Avoid talking about your own accomplishments. He does not care how competent you are and how much you may help the organization, he cares about how good you will make him look and feel. Give him credit for your accomplishments. Grandiose managers want to be not only the prima ballerina, but the only person on stage. When things do not go well, rather than noting that problems arose because of things outside of your control, accept responsibility and note what you will do to fix things and that you will handle things differently next time. Unfortunately doing a great job also has its problems since a narcissistic manager will hold onto people he needs rather than letting them advance.

In the long term, it is generally best to move to another position within the company. This is particularly important for very capable individuals, who will be seen as a threat by narcissistic individuals.

Confrontation can sometimes help to improve the behavior of people with learned narcissism, but this needs to come from above, not from below. If a subordinate attempts to confront a superior about their behavior, whether his narcissism is mostly learned or mostly psychodynamic, the reaction will generally be anger and retaliation. It is safest for a subordinate to behave in an admiring manner, which tends to decrease tensions.

Dealing with Destructively Narcissistic Peers

Narcissistic colleagues will take credit for your work, disparage you to others, scapegoat you, and lie and mislead people often with no other reason than the perverse pleasure of being able to deceive others. They also act as if they know the best way to do everything, discount others' input, fail to respect boundaries (enter your office and borrow things without permission), expect favors but rarely do any in return, and give you instructions as if they were your boss. In addition to driving you crazy they can seriously undermine your work and reputation.

It is crucial to watch your back. Remember what people are told when given their Miranda Rights: "Whatever you say can and will be used against you." Do not tell them about your weaknesses and vulnerabilities. Do not expect them to behave fairly or to change. Do not count on them to do their share of work. When the deliverable is not ready because they failed to do their job they will find a way to place the onus on you. Document responsibilities and that you fulfilled yours.

Boasting is best handled by ignoring it. If disparaging remarks are made about you it is generally best simply to state that you do not agree with the criticism. Avoid getting into arguments or retaliatory attacks. They can make you look bad to others and provoke the destructively narcissistic person to launch further attacks.

Be careful to establish credit for your work and ideas before they claim them as their own. To avoid having credit for your work stolen, it is best to avoid sharing ideas with destructively narcissistic individuals until after you have told your supervisor and team of your ideas in writing. When asked for ideas, respond in writing with your name attached.

Avoid getting into arguments or retaliatory attacks. They can make you look bad to others and provoke the destructively narcissistic person to launch further attacks. Do not ask a destructively narcissistic individual for favors, and do not borrow or lend anything. If given orders by a destructively narcissistic colleague, either ignore it or write to your boss to ask for clarification on responsibilities.

Avoid getting in the way of ruthless, narcissistic manager until you have enough power and outside support to stand up to him. If you do not pose a threat to his wishes, he will have no reason to attack you. If you support him, he will want to help you. It may be annoying to go along with his agenda, but it is better than martyring yourself when there is little chance of victory.

It is important to check in frequently with superiors to get support for your actions and to heavily document what you do and why. If you carefully document what you do and keep superiors informed in a timely fashion, it will be much harder for someone to either claim that you failed to do your work or that he deserves credit for it. You can also limit your vulnerability by getting ruthless managers to sign off on actions you expect to take. Then e-mail them and copy others, noting the understanding that the two of you came to.

Ruthless managers are unlikely to attack those they see as powerful. If you have powerful supporters, and people know that you do, ruthless managers will be unlikely to attack you and risk reprisal from above. Ruthless managers will not want to go after someone who has a powerful protector who may turn on them. Finally, having a reputation for winning will inhibit people from trying to joust with you. You develop this reputation by engaging only in battles that you are pretty sure you will win.

Dealing with Narcissistic Subordinates

All of the rules of self-protection for dealing with a narcissistic peer apply to dealing with narcissistic subordinates. They will stab you in the back, use whatever you say about yourself to hurt you and steal credit for your work. Their agenda is not the team's or company's success but their own. Don't get taken in by their flattery and admiration. It will not last.

In giving feedback, provide plenty of positive statements first, or they will totally disregard any criticism as a sign you are unfair and wish to hurt them because you are jealous. Take a coaching stance. Help them to see others as people who can help them, rather than as competitors for promotion.

Conclusion

Narcissistic personality traits are very common. Over the course of your career you will work with many people who have some degree of destructive narcissism. Recognizing the pattern early and knowing how to deal with it can protect you from damage to your career and from huge amounts of stress. There is no quick solution or perfect answer, but there are many things that can be done to ameliorate the problem.

It is also crucial to be aware of your own narcissistic personality traits and the possibility of developing such traits over time. Your own narcissism can sabotage your career, undermine your relationships and family life, and hurt those you care about. Pay attention to how the specific details of your narcissistic traits intersect with the nature of your work and relationships potentially causing damage. The more successful and preoccupied you are and the greater the stress you are facing, the more important it is to pay attention to how you are treating others.

It is crucial to have your long-term goals and values in mind and not undermine them in the service of achieving the success that is supposed to facilitate your long-term goals, rather than be your long-term goal. Pursuing power for power's sake, and money for money's sake, has no value and can be remarkably self-destructive. Seeking 360 degree feedback, being open to the criticism and complaints of those around you and seeking coaching can all be helpful.

References

Bandura, A. (1977) *Social Learning Theory*. Englewood Cliffs, NJ: Prentice-Hall.

Burstein, B. (1977) Some narcissistic personality types. In A. Morrison (ed.) *Essential Papers on Narcissism*. New York: NYU Press. pp. 100–119.

Kernberg, O. (1985) *Borderline Conditions and Pathological Narcissism*. Northvale, NJ: Jason Aronson.

Kernberg, O. (1986) Factors in the psychoanalytic treatment of narcissistic personalities. In A. Morrison (ed.) *Essential Papers on Narcissism*. New York: NYU Press. pp. 213–235.

Kernberg, O. (1998) *Ideology, Conflict and Leadership in Groups and Organizations*. New Haven: Yale University Press.

Kets de Vries, M. (1993) *Leaders, Fools and Imposters*. San Francisco, CA: Jossey-Bass Publishers.

Kohut, H. (1971) *The Analysis of the Self*. New York: International Universities Press.

Kohut, H., & Wolf, E. (1978) The disorders of the self and their treatment: an outline. *The International Journal of Psychoanalysis*, 59, 413–426.

Lubit, R. (2002) The Long Term Organizational Effects of Narcissistic Managers and Executives. *Academy of Management Executive*, Spring, 16, 127–138.

Lubit, R. (2003) *Coping with Toxic Managers and Subordinates: Using Emotional Intelligence to Survive and Prosper*. Upper Saddle River, NJ: Prentice-Hall.

Zaleznik, A. (1989) *Managerial Mystique: Restoring Leadership in Business*. New York: Harper & Row.

PART IV
Organizational Initiatives

9 *Enhancing Well-being in Organizations through Selection and Development*

JILL FLINT-TAYLOR AND IVAN T. ROBERTSON

Previous chapters have explored how personal qualities and behaviors can boost or undermine well-being in organizations. Here we review what this means for organizations' approaches to assessment, selection and development. We look at current trends in research and practice, and also highlight points for consideration by organizations who want to do more in this area.

There are three main strands to the question of how to promote individual and organizational health through selection and development:

- how to ensure that an individual is in the best possible shape for current and future roles;
- how to ensure that employees have a positive impact on general organizational well-being;
- how to ensure that managers and leaders in particular have a positive impact on the well-being and performance of the individuals and teams who report to them.

These strands do overlap, but they are distinct enough for us to explore each in turn. In doing so, we review research and practice in three areas:

- criteria for assessment and development;
- methods for assessing qualities and behaviors (including selection techniques);
- trends in development interventions.

Doing the Groundwork—Criteria for Assessment and Development

INDIVIDUALS AND THEIR ROLES

Achieving the best person–job fit—core requirements of the job

There is an extensive body of research literature on achieving the best fit between an individual and the role (for example, Robertson & Smith, 2001). A poor fit between the person and the requirements of their role is well known to be a major impediment to well-being. It often leads to stress and burnout, but this is not the only potential problem. It can also lead to lack of motivation and disengagement, and to other issues that affect both well-being and performance (Maslach, Schaufeli & Leiter, 2001). It is worth noting at the outset that new evidence is emerging all the time concerning the extent to which well-being impacts on performance, both individual and organizational. This means that interventions designed to enhance employee well-being should also benefit performance-related outcomes, including productivity, customer service, retention of critical skills and talent attraction (for example, Harter, Schmidt and Keyes, 2003).

A good starting point is to define clearly and objectively what qualities and skills are needed for the core role the person is to perform. Over the past 20 years, the competency approach has been widely applied by organizations to identify and define their selection and development criteria (Boyatzis & Saatcioglu, 2008). In common with many elegantly simple but insightful concepts, the competency approach has been used to good effect as well as being abused and over-complicated in the pursuit of sophisticated solutions and commercial interests.

Overall, it has proven to be anything but a fad and has endured to play a major role in bringing character, attitudes, values and other personal qualities into reputable, mainstream assessment practice. Together with concurrent advances in other areas of selection and assessment (see, for example, Chan, 2005) it has healed the split between, on the one hand, the academic view that trait-based constructs could not be used effectively or fairly in the prediction of work performance (Ghiselli & Barthol, 1953), and on the other, the practitioner and recruiting managers' conviction that character is one of the most important areas to explore when hiring or promoting someone.

The competency approach has a sound but specific academic basis in the work of McClelland, Boyatzis and their colleagues (Boyatzis, 1982, 1994). From the outset, however, its main principles were supported by studies in the wider field of selection research, which confirmed the need for assessment criteria that were multi-dimensional and defined in terms of observable behaviors (Borman, 1991, Borman, White and Dorsey, 1995).

All this has led to a situation today where there is widespread understanding within organizations of the need to identify, assess and develop the diverse qualities and skills associated with high performance in a particular role. Some organizations go to great lengths to avoid using the term "competency," preferring to use "capabilities," "qualities" or other similar words. Nevertheless, whatever the term used, there is a high level of consistency in the use of selection and assessment procedures that conform to the competency approach. The approach is also used in the context of learning and development interventions, although perhaps not to quite the same extent.

Later in this chapter we discuss selection and development procedures, but first we take a closer look at identifying selection requirements and development needs. We spend some time on this because the need to define your criteria rigorously applies whether you are selecting for specific role requirements, seeking to enhance employee engagement or developing your talent pool to maximize their long-term impact on organizational well-being and performance.

From competency to emotional intelligence

Fundamental to the competency approach is the recognition that assessing intellectual capacity and technical skills or knowledge will get you only so far. McClelland's interest in motivation and "need for achievement" (NAch) led him to argue that in order to predict how well someone will perform in their role, you need to assess other qualities as well, including characteristics and skills relating to self-awareness, self-control and the effective development and management of relationships. This was the foundation for his work on defining and assessing competencies (McClelland, 1973, 1993) and the idea has been supported by many studies since (for example, Fox & Spector, 2000).

Daniel Goleman (1998) took this work a step further by popularizing the concept of Emotional Intelligence. Although Emotional Intelligence (often known as EI or EQ) is generally thought of as being a separate stream of constructs and activity to that of competency-based assessment and development, a closer look reveals that it is a repackaging and refocusing of the competencies of McClelland and Boyatzis. This is not intended as a negative observation. Goleman picked up the term EI from earlier studies, related it to the findings of large-scale analyses of the characteristics that differentiate superior performers from their colleagues, and wrote in an accessible style about the results. In this way, he persuaded a wider audience of leaders, managers and human resource professionals of the importance of "soft skills" for both individual and organizational success.

The study reported by Goleman used a content analysis approach to identify those behaviors that differentiated superior performers from their "average" colleagues. The data were drawn from the output of in-depth interviews using McClelland's Behavioral Interview, or BEI technique (McClelland, 1998), carried out for purposes of competency definition across many different organizations over several years. The study was not restricted to managerial or leadership roles, and even in the most technical roles it was found that superior performers were differentiated by skills such as empathy, self-awareness and relationship building, more often than by their technical skill or knowledge (Goleman, 1998).

One of the important consequences of introducing the competency approach to selection has been the shift away from highly job-specific assessment criteria to more generic criterion clusters (for example, Teamwork & Collaboration, Achieving Results) with behavioral indicators adjusted to capture the right emphasis for the role in question. This development has been supported by the findings of meta-analytic studies demonstrating the generalizability of the validity of assessment procedures across different roles and organizational contexts (Le, Oh, Shaffer & Schmidt, 2007). These studies are discussed below in relation to selection methodology.

Points to watch when using competencies

When implementing the competency approach, there are two specific aspects to which we would like to draw the practitioner's attention. Firstly, anyone can draft a set of competencies on the back of an envelope, and even gain stakeholder acceptance for the output following a few comments and revisions. However, things usually start to break down when such frameworks are put into practice, with users complaining that they do not provide them with what they need in terms of assessing others or being assessed themselves. For the framework to gain currency among users, and for it to facilitate fair and valid judgements of performance and potential, one or more of a small number of competency analysis techniques must be used. These include the BEI technique, the Critical Incident technique (Flanagan, 1954) and the Repertory Grid interview (Smith, 1980), possibly supplemented by expert panels and focus groups.

Secondly, it is important not to lose sight of the generic, broadly applicable nature of competencies. This is one of the central tenets of McClelland's original proposition— one that has been supported by subsequent research. For example, when a framework is developed using appropriate methodology, factor analytic studies of the competency-based criteria typically produce three main, distinct categories of personal qualities and skills, related to (1) intellectual judgement and capability; (2) self-awareness and interpersonal skills; and (3) personal motivation (Flint-Taylor, Robertson and Gray, 1999). Within these clusters, core personal qualities such as empathy, self-control, achievement orientation and resilience consistently appear in some form or other in almost all frameworks.

The risk, however, is that the need to phrase these qualities in terms of specific, job-related behaviors leads to their generic, character-related nature being masked. Detailed behavioral descriptors are important for valid, objective assessment, as well as for providing a practical steer for development planning. However, in designing and implementing selection procedures it is essential to be aware of their connection to a smaller number of underlying and broadly relevant qualities and personal skills.

In addition, the emphasis on behavioral definitions and indicators is sometimes taken to mean that only behavior is a valid topic of interest or discussion in an assessment and selection context, but this is not the case. It must be remembered that competencies cover a wide range of personal attributes, from personality traits to attitudes, values, abilities, skills and other characteristics (Spencer, McClelland and Spencer, 1990, p. 6):

> *Competencies can be motives, traits, self-concepts, attitudes or values, content knowledge, or cognitive or behavioral skills—any individual characteristic that can be measured or counted reliably and that can be shown to differentiate significantly between superior and average performers, or between effective and ineffective performers.*

These individual characteristics need to be defined in terms of what can be observed through behavior (including verbal communication). However, the behavioral definition is mostly a means to an end, with the end being an assessment of the underlying, enduring attributes that someone will take with them into the role for which they are being selected—and into roles far in the future in the case of graduate recruitment or the assessment of leadership potential.

The competency "industry" has produced many overly complex, layered frameworks that are difficult to implement with any rigor. Nevertheless, the overall outcome of the developments described above has been to facilitate the assessment of the full range of personal skills and qualities needed to achieve a good fit between an individual and the role (or future roles) for which he or she is being selected. This, in turn, makes it more likely that the individual will be able to respond well to the positive, challenge pressures of the job while effectively managing the negative, or hindrance, pressures. Taken across teams and organizations, the benefit to general health and well-being of having the "right people in the right jobs" is clear.

BEYOND JOB PERFORMANCE REQUIREMENTS

While competency indicators such as "balancing competing demands and priorities" or "acting with fairness and consideration toward others" obviously have a general impact on well-being beyond that of person–job fit, most still fall within the scope of the core requirements of an individual's job. In recent years, however, a number of other avenues have opened up that help us understand more broadly how selection and development can help to ensure that people are in good shape to meet the challenges they face at work.

Firstly, there are a number of personal characteristics and skills that may be core requirements for certain roles but that also have a broader relevance when considered from the perspective of general employee well-being. Personal resilience is probably the one currently generating the highest level of interest among both researchers and practitioners. It may also be seen as encompassing other, more specific topics such as behavioral self-regulation (Fein & Klein, 2011), psychological hardiness (Kobasa 1979), attributional style (Seligman, Abramson, Semmel & Baeyer, 1979) and positive psychology (Seligman & Csikszentmihalyi, 2000). Other studies look specifically at health and safety concerns, for example traits associated with a low or high incidence of being involved in accidents at work (Clarke & Robertson, 2008).

Resilience

Personal resilience is also known as emotional or psychological resilience. There are different conceptualizations of the construct, most of which make some reference to the kind of self-belief that enables a person to recover quickly from setbacks and to remain focused and positive in the face of difficult or potentially stressful circumstances (for example, "generalized self-efficacy," Lightsey 2006). Much of the academic literature in this field focuses on the construct of psychological hardiness, defined by Kobasa (1979 p. 1) as "a stronger commitment to self, an attitude of vigorousness toward the environment, a sense of meaningfulness, and an internal locus of control."

Resilience or psychological hardiness is well recognized as a core requirement or success factor for certain roles, particularly in military contexts (Bartone, Roland, Picano and Williams, 2008). Resilience in general, and attributional (explanatory) style in particular, have been demonstrated to be predictors of well-being, retention and financial success in sales roles (Proudfoot, Corr, Guest and Dunn, 2009), although there has been surprisingly little implementation of these findings in selection and development practice. In other contexts, resilience often appears in the form of specific behavioral indicators in competency frameworks, for example, "maintains quality and focus under pressure."

As employees and organizations come under increasing pressure from the pace of change and a tough economic climate, general interest in resilience is growing among leaders and human resource professionals. The idea of promoting resilience through development is gaining currency within organizations, and questions are being asked about whether and how to include it in selection procedures.

For the latter purpose, to comply with the principles of fair and valid selection it seems advisable to incorporate appropriate behavioral indicators of resilience into your selection criteria rather than treating resilience as a separate component of the assessment. This should be done on the basis of evidence from a competency or job analysis showing the direct relevance of personal resilience to the role in question, and taking into account the level and nature of typical challenges to be faced.

Where the relationship between resilience and job performance is indirect, or where there is simply a general desire to raise levels of resilience across the employee population, the best approach may well be to focus the effort and investment on development rather than selection. We'll look at ways of doing this in our discussion of selection and development methods below.

Positive emotions

The recent upsurge of interest in positive psychology provides useful material for those interested in assessing and developing resilience, on the basis that positive attitudes and emotions play an important role in determining who is likely to respond in the most resilient way to setbacks and difficulties. Positive attitudes such as optimism have featured consistently in resilience research over the years. Seligman's work in particular (1990), and the cognitive–behavioral approach (Sheldon, 2011) more generally, have always made a direct and clear link between attitudes (and thoughts/beliefs) on the one hand, and emotional outcomes on the other.

For many years, however, emotions have generally been seen as mediating or accompanying responses, with the main focus being on behavior and outcomes such as maintaining persistence and focus under pressure. This was true in the academic field, where researchers such as Paul Ekman (Ekman & Scherer, 1984) were unusual in making emotions the main subject of their studies. It was also true in organizational practice, where emotions were (and for many still are) seen as being outside the scope of hard-nosed business processes and interventions.

Now, however, emotions are increasingly seen a valid and important subject in their own right by academic researchers, human resource (HR) practitioners (for example, Ashkenasay and Daus, 2002) and the popular press. In particular, the work of Barbara Fredrickson and her colleagues has explored the power of positive emotions such as happiness, contentment, excitement and sense of purpose. The results demonstrate a range of personal and business benefits to achieving a good ratio of positive to negative emotions (for example, Fredrickson & Joiner 2002).

The frequency with which individuals experience positive emotions is determined by a number of factors, some personal and some situational. Personality research, for example, has shown positive emotions such as enthusiasm to be linked to enduring traits that are independent of negative, stress-related emotions such as anxiety or depression. The extent to which someone regularly experiences feelings of enthusiasm can be predicted by their score on the Positive Emotions facet of Extraversion in a Five-Factor measure. People who achieve low scores on this facet may be emotionally stable but fail to draw as much pleasure and benefit from situations that provide others with fun, light relief and happiness (Costa & McCrae, 1985).

All this raises the same questions as discussed above in relation to whether to select for resilience, or to focus on helping people to experience a good level of positive emotion through development interventions.

Person–organization fit

Apart from job requirements and specific well-being related characteristics such as resilience and positivity, it is also important to consider how well an individual is likely to fit into the organization (Cable & Judge 1996, Kristof-Brown, Zimmerman &Johnson, 2005). Again, poor fit with organizational culture and other aspects of the organizational context can have a negative effect on personal well-being as well as on performance.

This is an area of research where attitudes and values have been a major focus of interest (Westerman & Cyr, 2004), although other qualities, such as personality, have also been included. Studies have looked at how person–organization fit affects organizational commitment across the public, non-profit and for-profit sectors (De Cooman, De Gieter, Pepermans & Jegers, 2011; Goulet & Frank 2002), attitudes toward workplace fun (Karl, Peluchette, Hall & Harland, 2005), retention in high-turnover roles (McCulloch & Turban, 2007) and many other well-being related outcomes.

Employee engagement

A concept closely related to both person–job and person–organization fit is that of employee engagement. There is a great deal of interest and activity in this area, to the extent that many organizations have relabelled and redesigned their annual employee surveys to focus on this aspect of employee opinion and satisfaction.

Employee engagement has been described by David MacLeod and Nita Clarke as "a workplace approach designed to ensure that employees are committed to their organization's goals and values, motivated to contribute to organizational success, and are able at the same time to enhance their own sense of well-being" (MacLeod & Clarke, 2009, p. 9). As MacLeod and Clarke discuss in their report, there are many different definitions of the term, and also many different views on how to predict, measure and enhance or develop employee engagement. For our purposes here, the relevant point is that engagement is an outcome of many different factors. Situational factors are obviously very important, but so is the type of personal qualities under discussion in this review. A detailed account of the relationship between well-being and employee engagement can be found in Robertson & Cooper (2011, pp. 27–62).

Employees' impact on organizational well-being

We have explored above a range of factors that need to be assessed and developed in order to ensure that employees are in the best possible shape for current and future roles. In discussing person–organization fit and employee engagement, we begin to move on to an area where the personal characteristics or attributes of individual employees can have a direct impact on team climate and organizational culture.

There are many ways in which this broader impact may make itself felt. Two specific areas of current research interest are counter-productive work behaviors and employee proactivity.

Negative impact characteristics

Counter-productive work behaviors (CWBs) include theft, harassment and talking negatively about the organization to outsiders (many large organizations are currently exercised about how to promote what they term "employee advocacy"). Research on CWBs builds on a long history of work in the field of organizational commitment and organizational citizenship (Organ & Ryan, 1995). The direct relationship between CWB and employee well-being is discussed by Bowling and colleagues (2011), who report on previous findings relating personality (FFM model) to CWB (positive relationships for neuroticism and negative relationships for conscientiousness and agreeableness), and their own findings of moderator effects (examining employee personality traits interacting with each other to influence CWBs).

Positive impact characteristics

CWBs are a useful illustration of the negative impact that individuals can have on the organization as a whole, and of the potential benefit of minimizing this kind of risk through selection and development. Again, however, it is not just a question of focusing on the avoidance of negative characteristics or outcomes. How many of us would recognize the following description?

> As time and technology advance, an increasing number of organizations require employees to meet stable, long-term objectives within transient and unpredictable environments. For example, managers are often expected to meet production benchmarks regardless of budget cuts and shifting product specifications. Frequent changes in top-management teams, lay-offs and technological breakdowns are other examples of dynamic challenges that continually threaten progress in modern organizations. (Thomas, Whitman and Viswesvaran, 2010, p. 275)

In response to these challenges in today's work environment, researchers are exploring the concept of employee proactivity. This is a welcome development for practitioners, who have emphasized it in their selection criteria for many years. Current work in the area goes well beyond the importance of proactive behavior for job performance, however. A recent meta-analytic study of proactivity—broadly defined as "an active facilitation of meaningful personal and/or environmental change" (Thomas, Whitman and Viswesvaran, 2010, p. 276)—found significant relationships between proactivity and performance, satisfaction, affective organizational commitment and social networking. They also found proactivity constructs to be associated with but not limited to personality traits.

Clearly, well-being in organizations would benefit from better understanding of how to select for and develop employee proactivity and other positive qualities that have the potential to influence climate, culture and organizational process.

Managers' and leaders' impact on those who report to them

The nature of management and leadership means that the behavior of people in these roles has a very direct impact on the well-being of those who report to them. This is a topic we have discussed in detail elsewhere (Flint-Taylor, Durose & Wigley, 2011, Robertson & Cooper, 2011, Robertson & Flint-Taylor, 2009, 2007).

For the purposes of this review, the same general principles apply to identifying, assessing and developing the qualities and behaviors for leaders, managers and employees in general. There are, however, a few specific points that it is useful to make in relation to the context of leadership and management roles.

Firstly, there is strong and generalizable research evidence supporting the inclusion of criteria related to impact on others' well-being when assessing and selecting leaders and managers (see in particular Robertson & Cooper, 2011 and Robertson & Flint-Taylor, 2009 for reviews of this evidence).

Secondly, clear guidance is available on what is expected of organizations and managers in this regard. In the UK, the Health and Safety Executive (HSE), in collaboration with the Chartered Institute for Personnel and Development (CIPD), have produced a set of recommended management competencies to support the implementation of their stress Management Standards (Yarker, Donaldson-Feilder, Lewis & Flaxman, 2008). HSE advice on implementing the Management Competencies is flexible and pragmatic. They point out that these competencies are not a separate set of requirements that stand alone from other criteria an organization may be using for selection and development. They should be used to help test and shape competencies or other criteria used by organizations to assess people for managerial roles.

Thirdly, the literature on "derailers" and "dark side" qualities (Burke, 2006) is relevant to understanding the negative impact that leaders and managers have on others, as is the related literature on characteristics "taken to extreme" (Kaplan & Kaiser, 2006). The latter concept refers to the idea that many character or personality related qualities (for example, results orientation) are leadership strengths when exercised in moderation, but risks when used to excess (for example, results at any cost). Our own research has explored this in relation to the FFM (Flint-Taylor, 2008; Flint-Taylor & Robertson, 2007).

Methods for Assessing Qualities and Behaviors

So far we have discussed mainly the move to a broader, more comprehensive and relevant set of assessment criteria for use in selection procedures, and the need to ensure that these are defined clearly and rigorously. The next question is that of what assessment methods to use to predict how a candidate will perform against these criteria and to identify potential strengths and risks to inform development planning and interventions. A comprehensive review of assessment research and practice would be too broad for the purpose of this chapter, so again we will highlight some of the more relevant findings and observations.

We mentioned above the effect that meta-analytic studies have had on assessment practice. This really cannot be overstated. Previously it was believed that a test, exercise or other selection procedure should be validated for each different context in which it might be applied. Now, thanks to the influence of meta-analytic research (see, for example, Schmidt & Hunter, 1998), it is possible to draw on previous research and evaluation studies to inform the design of a new selection procedure, and to have confidence in that procedure even without the opportunity to carry out a full, formal validation exercise. This is particularly valuable in today's fast-moving organizational world, where long-term validity studies are often rendered impossible by high levels of employee turnover, organizational restructuring and changing role requirements.

The generalizability of measures of intellectual ability is one important aspect of meta-analytic research (for example, Bertua, Anderson & Salgado, 2005). However, intellectual ability assessments do not have good validity when it comes to predicting competencies (or EI attributes) in the self-awareness/interpersonal skills category, or in the motivation/results category. For this purpose, measures of personality and attitude have more to offer. Heinsman, De Hoogh, Koopman and Van Muijen (2007) suggest a need for more research to inform the rigorous design and implementation of competency-based assessment.

METHODS

Personality measures

As our discussion so far illustrates, there is good evidence associating personality traits (especially FFM constructs) on the one hand, with well-being related behaviors and outcomes, on the other.

Personality assessment has come a long way since the early 1990s when two influential studies (Barrick & Mount, 1991; Tett, Jackson & Rothstein, 1991) made the case for the Five Factor Model of personality (FFM) and its relevance to work performance and selection design (Digman, 1990, Barrick, Mount & Judge, 2001, Roberts & Hogan, 2001, Borman, 2004, Rothstein & Goffin, 2006, Ones, Dilchert, Viswesvaran & Judge, 2007). This is fortunate, since personality traits underpin many competencies as well as having wider relevance to other workplace outcomes.

Research investigating the predictive relationships between personality and job performance has covered a wide range of topics, including customer service (Baydoun, Rose & Emperado, 2001), sales performance (Barrick, Mount & Strauss, 1993) and honesty–humility related criteria (Ashton & Lee, 2008). Examples of relationships between personality traits and workplace well-being have already been reviewed above (for further discussion see Tett & Christiansen, 2007, Viswesvaran, Deller, & Ones, 2007).

So the questions now are, what measures should organizations use to assess personality and how should these be designed into selection and assessment procedures? This is a very broad area, the detail of which is beyond the scope of this review. The evidence supporting the use of FFM measures (such as the NEO-PI R, Costa & McCrae, 1985, 1992) has been continuing to build over the past 20 years. As is often the case, it took some time for general organizational practice to respond, but FFM measures are now widely used in selection and assessment procedures.

Given the popularity of the Myers-Briggs type-based instrument (MBTI), it is worth noting that reservations have been consistently expressed over the years regarding its use in selection contexts (Nowack, 1996; Pittenger, 1993; 2005).

The SASQ (Seligman's Attributional Style Questionnaire) is a personality-related measure of particular interest to us here, as attributional (or explanatory) style is an attribute of specific relevance to resilience and well-being (Peterson, Semmel, Vonbaeyer, Abramson, Metalsky & Seligman, 1982) and has played an important role in programs proven to improve individual resilience (for example, Proudfoot, Corr, Guest & Dunn, 2009, see below).

Measures of attitudes and values

The measurement of attitudes and values is of particular interest to researchers in the area of person–organization fit. Methodology in this area tends to rely on questionnaires, at both the individual (selection) and organizational (attitude survey) levels, although other measures such as interview are used as well.

There are many commercially available measures of attitudes and values for individual selection. It would, however, be useful to have a more wide-ranging, research-based discussion of this topic, and further investigations of the validity and effectiveness of existing measures, along the lines of Metzger and Wu's (2008) report on the use of a popular commercial instrument for teacher selection (the validity of selecting teachers through beliefs, attitudes and values).

One aspect that has been extensively researched is that of integrity testing. This has produced evidence of the value that personality assessment can add to the prediction of attitude and value related behaviors. It has also shown the broader relevance of integrity test measures for predicting job performance and counterproductive behaviors on the job, such as theft, disciplinary problems and absenteeism (Ones, Viswesvaran & Schmidt, 1993).

Another angle on assessing attitudes is related more to organizational development than to selection or individual development. Saari & Judge (2004) discuss the relationship between employee attitudes and job satisfaction, and identify a gap between scientific research and HR practice in the measurement of attitudes within this context: "There are a number of possible methods for measuring employee attitudes, such as conducting focus groups, interviewing employees, or carrying out employee surveys. Of these methods, the most accurate measure is a well-constructed employee attitude survey." (Saari & Judge, 2004, p. 399–400). The authors go on to provide detailed guidance for practitioners in the design, implementation and interpretation of this kind of employee survey.

Situational judgement measures

Early forms of the situational judgement test (SJT) were designed to assess whether the candidate knew how to respond in specific situations that were critical to successful performance of the job. More recently, research has shown how SJTs can be designed to test a combination of personality, attitudes, values and knowledge. One of the most comprehensive reviews of the SJT method was a meta-analytic study based on 102 coefficients and 10,640 people. This study found that situational judgement tests showed useful levels of validity (p = .34) that were generalizable (McDaniel, Morgeson, Bruhn Finnegan, Campion & Braverman, 2001).

SJTs provide incremental validity when used alongside tests of personality and reasoning ability (O'Connell, Hartman, McDaniel, Grubb & Lawrence, 2007), and clearly have the potential to contribute to selection procedures where personality is only one aspect of the personal qualities to be assessed. In our view, organizations are missing a significant opportunity in failing to tap into the potential of SJTs to help them assess a range of personal attributes relevant to well-being and performance.

Interviews

Competency-based interviews are now widely used especially in selection contexts. The research evidence (Taylor & Small, 2002) supports the use of two techniques in particular: the Behavioral Description Interview (BDI, a variation on the Critical Incident and Behavioral Event techniques) and the Situational Interview (SI, Latham, Saari, Lise, Pursell, Elliot & Campion, 1980). A meta-analysis by Huffcutt and colleagues (Huffcutt, Conway, Roth & Klehe, 2004) found that job complexity influences the validity of SIs, with decreased validity for high-complexity jobs, but does not influence the validity of BDIs. Overall the evidence suggests that the BDI is the more effective of the two approaches.

For organizations using the BDI approach (based on eliciting examples from the candidate's recent experience), it would be worthwhile checking the specifics of your interview design (and the way this is implemented) against the principles associated with ensuring adequate validity and reliability (Robertson & Smith, 2001). A common mistake, for example, is to ask for too many examples, which means the interviewer has insufficient time to gather evidence on each example.

Competency-based interviews are often confused with the structured interview approach, but it is important to recognize the difference. Structured interviews emphasize the need to follow a specific structure, or set of questions, for all candidates. The competency-based BDI technique, on the other hand, draws on a pre-agreed set of eliciting questions to request examples, which are then explored using a specific probing strategy and set of rules rather than set follow-up questions.

One meta-analytic study of particular interest here investigated use of the structured interviewing technique for Organizational Citizenship Behavior (OCB) (Allen, Facteau & Facteau, 2004).

Self-assessment

The value of self-assessment (Jones & Fletcher, 2002) is increasingly accepted by organizations as a way of ensuring good person–job and person–organization fit. An example would be the realistic job preview approach (for example, Caligiuri & Phillips, 2003), which is particularly suitable for high-demand roles that may lead to burnout (stress) or roles where "rust-out" (boredom and disengagement) are likely due to the routine or under-stimulating nature of the work.

MULTI-TRAIT, MULTI-METHOD

Most importantly, just as any assessment process needs to incorporate multiple criteria, so it should also avoid relying too heavily on a single assessment method. Assessment and development centers are classic examples of a multi-trait, multi-method approach (Robertson & Smith, 2001). As competency indicators provide observable, behavioral definitions, these make it possible to use any form of assessment to measure attitudes, values and other attributes—including work sample exercises, group discussions, in-tray exercises and so on.

CURRENT ORGANIZATIONAL PRACTICE

Having reviewed some of the most relevant assessment methods, we come to the question of what organizations' selection and assessment procedures look like in practice. This is the subject of a number of reviews, including those by Zibarras and Woods (2010), Furnham (2008), Carless (2007), Piotrowski and Armstrong (2006) and Bertram (2004).

Most importantly, the evidence from these and other reviews suggests a gap between research and practice in this area. For example, Zibarras and Woods (2010, p. 499) report that: "Overall, a smaller proportion of organizations in this sample reported using formalized methods (e.g., assessment centers) than informal methods (e.g. unstructured interviews)." Such gaps apply as well to the rapidly expanding area of online assessment (used for both selection and development), with researchers such as Sylva and Mol (2009) calling for more studies on this topic.

Specifically, it seems that organizations could make better use of research findings to apply a wider range of assessment methods in a rigorous and fair way, thereby improving their assessment of the character-related qualities, skills and behaviors that impact on well-being.

Trends in Development Interventions

Most of the assessment procedures outlined above can be used to identify priorities for personal development, as well as for recruitment and selection. They may, therefore, form part of training needs analyses at both the individual and organizational level.

Once the needs are identified, there is a vast array of diverse approaches to the design and delivery of developmental interventions. The evaluation of these approaches presents its own particular difficulties, especially when it comes to the kind of long-term behavioral change and performance outcomes that are of interest to us here.

Current trends in training and development practice, and questions relating to its evaluation, are discussed in a survey report by the UK Chartered Institute of Personnel and Development (CIPD) (2011). One of the report's main conclusions is that: "In common with previous years, in-house development programmes and coaching by line managers are seen to be the most effective learning and development practices for employees generally. Coaching by external practitioners and external conferences, workshops and events are reported to be the most effective learning methods for leaders." (2011, p. 3).

The report also notes that: "A greater integration between coaching, organisational development and performance management to drive organisational change is the most commonly anticipated major change affecting learning and development over the next two years, reported by nearly half of organisations" (2011, p. 3).

EMPLOYEE WELL-BEING AND ENGAGEMENT TRAINING INITIATIVES

The current trend for large organizations to invest heavily in employee engagement surveys and similar assessments has led to the proliferation of interventions to address problems and risks identified through the survey results. Many of these are organizational development interventions, but training and development programs for individuals are also included (MacLeod & Clarke, 2009).

The nature and content of these training interventions varies widely according to the need identified by the survey—from training in the use of specific technology and systems to help people cope better with the demands of their jobs, to wellness training, assertiveness workshops and other behavioral skills training and programs designed to effect attitude change or gain support for organizational values.

TRAINING TO ENHANCE PERSON–JOB FIT

Given the broad range of qualities, skills and behaviors that may be required for employees to perform specific roles, the same level of variation in training and development provision applies here.

Our aim in this section is to highlight a few specific findings to illustrate developments of particular relevance to the well-being perspective of this chapter. In particular, we look at coaching and resilience training.

COACHING

To start with, it is interesting to note the emphasis on coaching in the CIPD survey of current trends in learning and development practice. Coaching is a method particularly well suited to providing self-awareness of current and potential strengths, and areas for improvement. It also provides a context and support for the kind of personal development most likely to bring about long-term change in behavior (and in associated attitudes, beliefs and other attributes such as vulnerability to irritability or stress) (Evers, Brouwers & Tomic, 2006; Palmer, Tubbs & Whybrow, 2003).

As the value of the coaching approach becomes increasingly well-recognized, different coaching models continue to emerge. As noted by the CIPD report, line managers are increasingly expected to make one-to-one coaching a part of their core role. Peer coaching or peer mentoring (Holbeche, 1996) is another approach used by some organizations.

The move to accreditation of external coaches is in principle a positive development as a high level of specialist skill is required to facilitate self-awareness, behavior change, the personal management of pressure and personal job and career fulfilment. However, as with any accreditation process, it is important to check out and evaluate the credentials, process and standards of the organizations providing accreditation.

Where an accrediting organization's credentials and so on are sound, this provides reassurance on the methods used by their coaches. It is still important, however, to be aware of the strengths and weaknesses of specific coaching methodologies, particular the most popular. There is, for example, useful research evidence investigating the effectiveness of the Neuro Linguistic Programming (NLP) approach (for example, Glasner-Edwards & Rawson 2010) and the Cognitive Behavioral approach (Sheldon, 2011), two methods considered to be particularly appropriate for behavior change and well-being related outcomes.

In terms of the expectations being placed on line managers to act as coaches, it is essential to ensure that they have the necessary training and support to fulfil this role effectively. Without this, there is likely to be a direct, negative impact on the well-being of both line manager and coachee—in addition to the negative implications for the desired performance outcomes.

RESILIENCE TRAINING

There is growing research evidence in support of resilience training to improve the general well-being of employees, as well as to achieve desired performance outcomes for individuals and organizations (Seligman & Fowler, 2011; Waite 2004; Zetterqvist, Maanmies, Ström & Andersson, 2003). The Cognitive Behavioral approach is at the center of many of these programs. For example, an insurance industry study by Judy Proudfoot and her colleagues (2009) demonstrated how sales and retention could be improved by providing in-depth resilience training for under-performing Financial Advisers (in the two years following the training, 50 percent of participants achieved sales figures above the average for their division, with a further 15 percent performing within 5 percent of the average).

The research of Proudfoot, Seligman and others indicates that resilience training is most effective when implemented as part of a program of training and development that is designed to take account of specific contextual challenges, with opportunities to practice resilience techniques in between sessions. In addition to sales training, other contexts in which resilience training has been implemented and evaluated include call centers. A study by Callaghan and Thompson (2002) reported positive results for a highly integrated selection and training/development program in the call center environment, which is well known to be a potential drain on employees' well-being. In this training, particular emphasis was placed on the development of positive attitude.

Recently, the design of resilience training has been broadened beyond the Cognitive Behavioral approach and positive attitude to incorporate a number of different techniques now known to be effective in producing enduring improvements in individuals' levels of personal resilience. These techniques are summarized in Dennis Charney's "Resilience Prescription"—the result of his study of strategies used by individuals to improve their ability to cope with dangerous and stressful environments (Yehuda, Flory, Southwick & Charney, 2006).

Conclusions

Researchers and practitioners are devoting more attention to outcomes that are associated with individual performance, productivity and organizational success, while conveying important benefits in their own right. This interest in factors such as well-being, engagement and positive citizenship has given rise to new questions for the study and practice of selection and development.

Historically personnel selection and assessment processes have concentrated strongly on job performance as the main criterion. As this chapter shows, it is neither necessary nor desirable to reinvent the wheel by looking for new and separate processes to accommodate the assessment and development of attributes associated with well-being in organizations. Personal resilience, for example, can be found in some form or another in most competency frameworks and assessment processes—although not often under that name. Similarly, in a development context, elements of personal resilience have been taught for many years in assertiveness training courses, although again usually not under the label of "resilience."

Especially given recent advances in the field, there is a good range of robust and effective techniques available to organizations wishing to adapt their selection and development processes to enhance well-being. That is not to say, however, that existing research and practice has this area adequately covered so that no further work is required. When it comes to attributes that are important for well-being, the potential of existing techniques has certainly not been fully realized. This appears to be at least partly explained by a two-way gap between research and practice—a gap that applies even when the criterion is performance and that becomes even wider when the criterion is well-being.

While practitioners clearly need to make wider use of the well-researched methods available for assessing personal attributes and skills, the gap in the other direction mentioned by Heinsman and colleagues (2007) also needs to be addressed. In particular, research psychologists need to support practitioners by improving our understanding of the principles and process of competency-based assessment. As things stand, competency-based assessment practice varies hugely in quality and effectiveness. It also frequently fails to give sufficient emphasis to attitudes and values—partly because practitioners have been taught to focus exclusively on behavior.

In order to enhance well-being through selection and development, it would be particularly useful to improve the assessment of attitudes and values at the individual level (as opposed to that of the organizational survey). As indicated above, attitudes and values appear to be under-represented in assessment procedures even when the criteria of interest are directly performance related. Given the nature of the attributes typically associated with well-being outcomes, as discussed in this chapter, it may well be that the assessment of attitudes and values is even more important in this context. Competency-based assessment could meet this need, but further research and changes to organizational practice will be required to realize its potential.

A similar case could be made for expanding research and practice in relation to development techniques—both generally and more specifically in relation to attitudes and values. For example, it may be that the cognitive–behavioral approach has much broader potential for development than current research and practice would suggest. The core principles and techniques of challenging one's own assumptions and beliefs apply to many different developmental challenges, such as learning to manage conflict in a constructive way, learning to delegate, and improving relationships through the avoidance of stereotyping and other "thinking errors" or false assumptions.

While individual practitioners may exercise their skill, knowledge and judgement to extend the cognitive–behavioral approach and other developmental approaches beyond their standard applications, there is clearly a need for further research and wider implementation in this area. This would help to enhance the development of well-being related attributes, by increasing understanding and use of sound, effective techniques while providing the evidence needed to challenge the practice of less robust approaches.

In general, organizations appear to rely heavily on in-house development programs and coaching by line managers. The existing research suggests that there could be significant benefits for organizations that invest in well-designed coaching programs. Resilience training also has the potential to improve sustainable performance by providing employees with the capacity to cope with the pressures inherent in their roles.

One issue that has a strong and clear impact on well-being at work is the quality of management and supervision that people receive (see Barling and Carson, 2008). Investing in suitable training and development for managers may be one of the most cost-effective ways that organizations can improve the health, well-being and engagement of their people.

Although the research and practice reviewed in this chapter suggest that the way an organization utilizes selection and development processes can pay dividends, it seems fair to point out that there is still some way to go before organizations in general incorporate well-being and engagement criteria fully into their selection and development processes. This is no doubt partly due to the relatively slow uptake of research-based findings (for example, formal selection processes that have been available for many years are still not used routinely) but it may also be linked to two other factors.

The first of these factors is the tendency for researchers to communicate almost exclusively with each other (driven by the need to publish in high impact factor journals) and their tendency to frame research questions in the light of previous research—rather than practical, real-world problems. The second factor may be that at its current stage of development the available research does not yet offer findings that are specific and clear enough to provide clear guidance to practitioners. For example, it is clear that personality factors are important in ensuring a good match between an individual job holder and the specific pressures and challenges to well-being and resilience that are offered by the role. The specific personality characteristics linked to key aspects of resilience and well-being are being investigated but are not yet completely understood. In short, more research is needed!

References

Allen, T. D., Facteau, J. D., & Facteau, C. L. (2004) Structured interviewing for OCB: construct validity, faking, and the effects of question type. *Human Performance*, 17, 1–24.

Andersen, N., Lievens, F., van Dam, K., & Ryan, A.M. (2004) Future perspectives on employee selection: key directions for future research and practice. *Applied Psychology: An International Review*, 53, 487–501.

Ashkenasay, N.M., & Daus, C. (2002) Emotion in the workplace: the new challenge for managers. *Academy of Management Executive*, 16, 76–86.

Ashton, M. C., & Lee, K. (2008) The prediction of honesty humility-related criteria by the HEXACO and five-factor models of personality. *Journal of Research in Personality*, 42, 1216–1228.

Barling, J., & Carson, J. (2008) The impact of management style on mental well-being at work. State-of-Science Review: SR-C3. *Foresight Mental Capital and Well-Being Project*. London, UK: Government Office for Science.

Barrick, M. R., & Mount, M. K. (1991) The Big Five personality dimensions and job performance: a meta-analysis. *Personnel Psychology*, 44, 1–26.

Barrick, M. R., Mount, M. K., & Judge, T. A. (2001) Personality and performance at the beginning of the new millennium: what do we know and where do we go next? *International Journal of Selection and Assessment*, 9, 9–30.

Barrick, M. R., Mount, M. K., & Strauss, J. P. (1993) Conscientiousness and performance of sales representatives: test of the mediating effects of goal setting. *Journal of Applied Psychology*, 78, 715–722.

Bartone, P. T., Roland, R. R., Picano, J. J., & Williams, T. J. (2008) Psychological hardiness predicts success in US army special forces candidates. *International Journal of Selection and Assessment*, 16, 78–81.

Baydoun, R., Rose, D., & Emperado, T. (2001) Measuring customer service orientation: an examination of the validity of the customer service profile. *Journal of Business and Psychology*, 15, 605–620.

Bertram, D. (2004) Assessment in organizations. *Applied Psychology: An International Review*, 53, 237–259.

Bertua, C., Anderson, N., & Salgado, J.F. (2005) The predictive validity of cognitive ability tests: a UK meta-analysis. *Journal of Occupational and Organizational Psychology*, 78, 387–409

Borman, W. C. (1991) Job behavior, performance and effectiveness. In M. D. Dunnette & L. M. Hough (eds) *Handbook of Industrial and Organizational Psychology*. Palo Alto: Consulting Psychologists Press. Vol. 2, pp. 271–326.

Borman, W. C. (2004) Introduction to the special issue: personality and the prediction of job performance: More than the Big Five. *Human Performance*, 17, 267–269.

Borman, W. C., White, L. A., & Dorsey, D. W. (1995) Effects of ratee task performance and interpersonal factors on supervisor and peer performance ratings. *Journal of Applied Psychology*, 80, 167–177.

Bowling, N.A., Burns, G.N., Stewart, S.M., & Gruys, M.L. (2011) Conscientiousness and agreeableness as moderators of the relationship between neuroticism and counterproductive work behaviors: a constructive replication. *International Journal of Selection and Assessment*, 19(3), 320–330.

Boyatzis, R. E. (1982) *The Competent Manager: A Model for Effective Performance*. New York: Wiley.

Boyatzis, R. E. (1994) Rendering unto competence the things that are competent. *American Psychologist*, 49, 64–66.

Boyatzis, R. E., & Saatcioglu, A. (2008) A twenty-year view of trying to develop emotional, social and cognitive intelligence competencies in graduate management education. *Journal of Management Development*, 27(1), 92–108.

Burke, R. J. (2006) Why leaders fail: exploring the dark side. In R. J. Burke and C. L. Cooper (eds) *Inspiring Leaders*. Oxon, UK: Routledge. pp. 237–246.

Cable, D. M., & Judge, T. A. (1996) Person-organization fit, job choice decisions, and organizational entry. *Organizational Behavior and Decision Processes*, 67, 294–311.

Caligiuri, P. M., & Phillips, J. M. (2003) An application of self-assessment realistic job previews to expatriate assignments. *International Journal of Human Resource Management*, 14(7), 102–1116.

Callaghan, G., & Thompson, P. (2002) We recruit attitude: the selection and shaping of routine call centre labour. *Journal of Management Studies*, 39(2), 233–254.

Chan, D. (2005) Current directions in personnel selection research. *Current Directions in Psychological Science*, 3(4), 220–223.

CIPD (2011) *Learning and Talent Development: Survey Report*, London, CIPD.

Clarke, S., & Robertson, I. (2008) An examination of the role of personality in work accidents using meta-analysis. *Applied Psychology-an International Review-Psychologie Appliquee-Revue Internationale*, 57(1), 94–108.

Costa, P. T., & McCrae, R. R. (1985) *The NEO Personality Inventory Manual*. Odessa, FL: Psychological Assessment Resources.

Costa, P. T., & McCrae, R. R. (1992) *Revised NEO Personality Inventory (NEO-PI-R) and NEO Five-Factor Inventory (NEO-FFI) professional inventory*. Odessa, FL: Psychological Assessment Resources.

De Cooman, R., De Gieter, S., Pepermans R., & Jegers, M. (2011) A cross-sector comparison of motivation-related concepts in for-profit and not-for-profit service organizations. *Nonprofit and Voluntary Sector Quarterly*, 40(20), 296–317.

Digman, J. M. (1990) Personality structure: emergence of the five-factor model. *Annual Review of Psychology*, 41, 417–440.

Ekman, P., & Scherer, K. (1984) Questions about emotion: an introduction. In K. Scherer & P. Ekman (eds) *Approaches to Emotion*. Hillsdale New Jersey: Lawrence Erlbaum. 1–8.

Evers, W. J. G., Brouwers, A., & Tomic, W. (2006) A quasi-experimental study on management coaching effectiveness. *Consulting Psychology Journal: Practice and Research*, 58(3), 174–182.

Fein, E. C., & Klein, H. J. (2011) Personality predictors of behavioral self-regulation: linking behavioral self-regulation to five-factor model factors, facets, and a compound trait. *International Journal of Selection and Assessment*, 19(2), 132–144.

Flanagan, J. C. (1954) The critical incident technique. *Psychological Bulletin*, 51, 327–358.

Flint-Taylor, J. (2008) Too much of a good thing? Leadership strengths as risks to well-being and performance in the team, *Proceedings of the British Psychological Society Division of Occupational Psychology Annual Conference, Stratford*, January 2008, Leicester, BPS.

Flint-Taylor, J., Durose, J., & Wigley, C. (2011) Keeping pressure positive: improving well-being and performance in the NHS through innovative leadership development. In I. Robertson and C. Cooper (eds) *Well-Being; Productivity and Happiness at Work*, Basingstoke, Palgrave Macmillan.

Flint-Taylor, J., & Robertson, I. T. (2007) Leaders' impact on well-being and performance: an empirical test of a model, *Proceedings of the British Psychological Society, Division of Occupational Psychology, Annual Conference, Bristol*, January 2007. Leicester, BPS.

Flint-Taylor, J., Robertson, I., & Gray, J. (1999) The Five-Factor Model of personality: levels of measurement and the prediction of managerial performance and attitudes. *Proceedings of the British Psychological Society Occupational Psychology Conference, Blackpool*, January 1999. Leicester, BPS.

Fox, S., & Spector, P. (2000) Relations of emotional intelligence, practical intelligence, general intelligence, and trait affectivity with interview outcomes: it's not all just 'G'. *Journal of Organizational Behavior*, 21, 203–220.

Fredrickson, B. L., & Joiner, T. (2002) Positive emotions trigger upward spirals toward emotional well-being. *Psychological Science*, 13, 172–175.

Furnham, A. (2008) HR professionals' beliefs about, and knowledge of, assessment techniques and psychometric tests. *International Journal of Selection and Assessment*, 16, 300–305.

Ghiselli, E. E., & Barthol, R. P. (1953) The validity of personality inventories in the selection of employees. *Journal of Applied Psychology*, 37, 18–20.

Glasner-Edwards. S., & Rawson. R. (2010) Evidence-based practices in addiction treatment: review and recommendations for public policy. *Health Policy*, 97(2–3), 93–104.

Goleman, D. (1998) *Working with Emotional Intelligence*. London, Bloomsbury.

Goulet, L. R., & Frank, M. L. (2002) Organizational commitment across three sectors: Public, non-profit, and for-profit. *Public Personnel Management*, 31, 201–210.

Harter, J. K., Schmidt, F. L., & Keyes, C. L. M. (2003) Well-being in the workplace and its relationship to business outcomes. In C. L. M. Keyes and J. Haidt (eds) *Flourishing, Positive Psychology and the Life Well-lived*. Washington DC, USA: American Psychological Society. pp. 205–224.

Heinsman, H., De Hoogh, A. H. B., Koopman, P. L., & Van Muijen, J. J. (2007) Competencies through the eyes of psychologists: a closer look at assessing competencies. *International Journal of Selection and Assessment*, 15, 412–427.

Holbeche, L. (1996) Peer mentoring: the challenges and opportunities. *Career Development International*, 1(7), 24–27.

Huffcutt, A. I., Conway, J. M., Roth, P. L., & Klehe, U. (2004) The impact of job complexity and study design on situational and behavior description interview validity. *International Journal of Selection and Assessment*, 12(3), 262–273.

Jones, L., & Fletcher, C. (2002) Self-assessment in a selection situation: an evaluation of different measurement approaches. *Journal of Occupational and Organizational Psychology*, 75, 145–161.

Kaplan, B., & Kaiser, R. (2006) *The Versatile Leader: Make the Most of Your Strengths—Without Overdoing It.* San Francisco, CA: Pfeiffer.

Karl, K., Peluchette, J., Hall, L., & Harland, L. (2005) Attitudes toward workplace fun: a three sector comparison. *Journal of Leadership & Organizational Studies*, 12(2), 1–17.

Kobasa, S. C. (1979) Stressful life events, personality, and health: an inquiry into hardiness. *Journal of Personality and Social Psychology*, 37(1), 1–11.

Kristof-Brown, A. L., Zimmerman, R. D., & Johnson, E. C. (2005) Consequences of individuals' fit at work: a meta-analysis of person-job, person-organization, person-group, and person-supervisor fit. *Personnel Psychology*, 58, 281–342.

Latham, G. P., Saari, L. M., Pursell, Elliott D., & Campion, M. A. (1980) The situational interview. *Journal of Applied Psychology*, 65(4), 422–427.

Le, H., Oh, I.-S., Shaffer, J., & Schmidt, F. (2007) Implications of methodological advances for the practice of personnel selection: how practitioners benefit from meta-analysis. *Academy of Management Perspectives*, 21(3), 6–15.

Lightsey, O. R. Jr. (2006) Resilience, meaning, and well-being, *The Counseling Psychologist*, 34, 96.

MacLeod, D., & Clarke, N. (2009) *Engaging for Success: Enhancing Performance through Employee Engagement*. Department for Business Innovation and Skills, London.

McClelland, D. C. (1973) Testing for competence rather than for "intelligence". *American Psychologist*, 28, 1–14.

McClelland, D. C. (1993) Intelligence is not the best predictor of job performance. *Current Directions in Psychological Science*, 2(1), 5–6.

McClelland, D. C. (1998) Identifying competencies with behavioral-event interviews. *Psychological Science*, 9(5), 331–339.

McCulloch, M. C., & Turban, D. B. (2007) Using person-organization fit to select employees for high-turnover jobs. *International Journal of Selection and Assessment*, 15(1), 63–71.

McDaniel, M. A., Morgeson, F. P., Bruhn Finnegan, E., Campion, M. A., & Braverman, E. P. (2001) Use of situational judgment tests to predict job performance: a clarification of the literature. *Journal of Applied Psychology*, 86(4), 730–740.

Maslach, C., Schaufeli, W. B., & Leiter, M. P. (2001) Job burnout. *Annual Review of Psychology*, 52, 397–422.

Metzger, S. A., & Wu, M. (2008) Commercial teacher selection instruments: the validity of selecting teachers through beliefs, attitudes, and values. *Review of Educational Research*, 78(4), 921–940.

O'Connell, M. S., Hartman, N. S., McDaniel, M. A., Grubb, W. L., & Lawrence, A. (2007) incremental validity of situational judgment tests for task and contextual job performance. *International Journal of Selection and Assessment*, 15, 19–29.

Ones, D. S., Dilchert, S., Viswesvaran, C., & Judge, T. (2007) In support of personality assessments in organizational settings. *Personnel Psychology*, 60, 995–1027.

Ones, D. S., Viswesvaran, C., & Schmidt, F. L. (1993) Comprehensive meta-analysis of integrity test validities: findings and implications for personnel selection and theories of job performance. *Journal of Applied Psychology*, 78(4), 679–703.

Organ, D. W., & Ryan, K. (1995) A meta-analytic review of attitudinal and dispositional predictors of organizational citizenship behavior. *Personnel Psychology*, 48(4), 775–802.

Nowack, K. (1996) Is the Myers Briggs Type Indicator the Right Tool to Use? *Performance in Practice*, 6, American Society of Training and Development.

Palmer, S., Tubbs, I., & Whybrow, A. (2003) Health coaching to facilitate the promotion of healthy behaviour and achievement of health-related goals. *International Journal of Health Promotion and Education*, 41, 91–93.

Peterson, C., Semmel, A., Vonbaeyer, C., Abramson, L. Y., Metalsky, G. I., & Seligman, M. E. P. (1982). The attributional style questionnaire. *Cognitive Therapy and Research*, 6(3), 287–299.

Piotrowski, C., & Armstrong, T. (2006) Current recruitment and selection practices: a national survey of Fortune 1000 firms. *North American Journal of Psychology*, 8, 489–496.

Pittenger, D. J. (1993) Measuring the MBTI and coming up short. *Journal of Career Planning and Employment*, 54(1), 48–52.

Pittenger, D. (2005) Cautionary comments regarding the Myers-Briggs Type Indicator. *Consulting Psychology Journal: Practice and Research*, 57, 210–221.

Proudfoot, J. G., Corr, P. J., Guest, D. E., & Dunn, G. (2009) Cognitive-behavioural training to change attributional style improves employee well-being, job satisfaction, productivity, and turnover. *Personality and Individual Differences*, 46, 147–153.

Roberts, B. W., & Hogan, R. (eds) (2001) *Personality Psychology in the Workplace*. Washington, DC: American Psychological Association.

Robertson, I. T., & Cooper, C. L. (2010) Full engagement: the integration of employee engagement and psychological well-being. *Leadership & Organization Development Journal*, 31(4), 324–336.

Robertson, I., & Cooper, C. (2011) *Well-Being at Work*. London: Palgrave Macmillan.

Robertson, I. T., & Flint-Taylor, J. (2007) Leader personality and workforce performance: the role of psychological well-being. *EAWOP 2007, XIIIth European Congress of Work and Organizational Psychology*, May 2007, Stockholm.

Robertson I. T., & Flint-Taylor, J. (2009) Leadership, psychological well-being and organisational outcomes. In S. Cartwright and C. L. Cooper (eds), *Oxford Handbook on Organisational Well-being*. Oxford, Oxford University Press. pp. 159–179.

Robertson, I. T., & Smith, M. (2001) Personnel selection. *Journal of Occupational and Organizational Psychology*, 74, 441–472.

Rothstein, M. G., & Goffin, R. D. (2006) The use of personality measures in personnel selection: what does current research support? *Human Resource Management Review*, 16, 155–180.

Saari, L. M., & Judge, T. A. (2004) Employee attitudes and job satisfaction. *Human Resource Management*, 43, 395–407.

Schmidt, F. L., & Hunter J. E. (1998) The validity and utility of selection methods in personnel psychology: practical and theoretical implications of 85 years of research findings. *Psychological Bulletin*, 124, 262–274.

Seligman, M. (1990) *Learned Optimism: How to Change Your Mind and Your Life*. New York: Knopf.

Seligman, M. E. P., Abramson, L. Y., Semmel, A., & Baeyer, C. V. (1979) Depressive attributional style. *Journal of Abnormal Psychology*, 88(3), 242–247.

Seligman, M. E. P., & Csikszentmihalyi, M. (2000) Positive psychology: an introduction. *American Psychologist*, 55(1), 5–14.

Seligman, M. E. P., & Fowler, R. D. (2011) Comprehensive soldier fitness and the future of psychology. *American Psychologist*, 66(1), 82–86.

Sheldon, B. (2011) *Cognitive Behavioural Therapy: Research and Practice in Health and Social Care*. Abingdon: Routledge.

Smith, M. (1980) An analysis of three managerial jobs using repertory grids. *Journal of Management Studies*, 17, 205–213.

Spencer, L. M., McClelland, D. C., & Spencer, S. M. (1990) *Competency Assessment Methods: History and State of the Art*. Paper presented at the American Psychological Association Annual Conference, Boston, MA.

Sylva, H., & Mol, S. T. (2009) E-Recruitment: a study into applicant perceptions of an online application system. *International Journal of Selection and Assessment*, 17, 311–323.

Taylor, P. J., & Small, B. (2002) Asking applicants what they would do versus what they did; a meta-analytic comparison of situational and past behaviour employment interview questions. *Journal of Occupational and Organisational Psychology*, 75, 277–294.

Tett, R. P., & Christiansen, N. D. (2007) Personality tests at the crossroads: a response to Morgeson, Campion, Dipboye, Hollenbeck, Murphy, and Schmitt. *Personnel Psychology*, 60, 967–993.

Tett, R. P., & Christiansen, N. D. (2008) Personality assessment in organizations. In G. J. Boyle, G. Matthews, & D. H. Saklofske (eds) *The SAGE Handbook of Personality Theory and Assessment. Personality Theories and Models*. Thousand Oaks, CA: Sage Publications Inc. Vol. 1, pp. 720–742.

Tett, R. P., Jackson, D. N., & Rothstein, M. (1991) Personality measures as predictors of job performance: a meta-analytic review. *Personnel Psychology*, 44, 703–742.

Thomas, J. P., Whitman, D. S., & Viswesvaran, C. (2010) Employee proactivity in organizations: a comparative meta-analysis of emergent proactive constructs. *Journal of Occupational and Organizational Psychology*, 83, 275–300.

Viswesvaran, C., Deller, J., & Ones, D. S. (2007) Personality measures in personnel selection: some new contributions. *International Journal of Selection and Assessment*, 15, 354–358.

Waite, P. J. (2004) Determining the efficacy of resilience training in the work site. *Journal of Allied Health*, 33, 178–183.

Westerman, J. W., & Cyr, L. A. (2004) An integrative analysis of person–organization fit theories. *International Journal of Selection and Assessment*, 12(3), 252–261.

Yarker, J., Donaldson-Feilder, E., Lewis, R., & Flaxman, P.E. (2008) *Management Competencies for Preventing and Reducing Stress at Work: Identifying and Developing the Management Behaviours Necessary to Implement the HSE Management Standard: Phase 2*. London. HSE Books.

Yehuda, R., Flory, J.D., Southwick, S., & Charney, D. S. (2006) Developing an agenda for translational studies of resilience and vulnerability following trauma exposure. *Annals of the N.Y. Academy of Science*, 1071, 379–396

Zetterqvist, K., Maanmies, J., Ström, L., & Andersson, G. (2003) Randomized controlled trial of internet-based stress management. *Cognitive Behavior Therapy*. 32(3), 151–60.

Zibarras, L. D., & Woods, S. A. (2010) A survey of UK selection practices across different organization sizes and industry sectors. *Journal of Occupational and Organizational Psychology*, 83, 499–511.

10 *Meaningful Work is Healthy Work*

PAUL FAIRLIE

The last decade has seen a flurry of activity in academic and business circles on the topic of meaningful work. Several studies have explored the meaning of work (Ardichvili & Kuchinke, 2009; Flesher, 2009; Kuchinke, 2009). Both callings (Dik, Duffy & Eldridge, 2009) and sensemaking in the workplace (Wrzesniewski, Dutton & Debebe, 2003) have been explored. Forms of leadership (Lawler, 2005; Luthans & Avolio, 2003) and leadership communication (Ashman & Lawler, 2008) have been inspired by existential psychology and other meaning-based areas of inquiry. The growing interest in meaningful work has prompted several recent literature reviews on the topic (Rosso, Dekas & Wrzesniewski, 2010; Steger & Dik, 2005).

Themes of meaningful work have also appeared in best-selling books aimed at the general public (Crawford, 2009; Dyer, 2005; Leider, 2010; Waddington, 2007) and management (Pink, 2009; Sanders, 2008; Sinek, 2009; Ulrich, Ulrich & Goldsmith, 2010). Even stalwart business publications such as *Harvard Business Review* (Amabile & Kramer, 2010; Ashkanas, 2011; Erickson, 2011; Haque, 2012), *Ivey Business Journal* (Ulrich & Ulrich, 2010), *McKinsey Quarterly* (Amabile & Kramer, 2012) and *MIT Sloan Management Review* (Michaelson, 2010) have run features on meaningful work. At the time of writing, there were over five million hits for "meaningful work" on Google. com.

Despite the recent attention that it has garnered, meaningful work is in danger of becoming a passing fad. This would be regrettable, given the growing number of people that are reporting needs for interesting and socially-useful work on national surveys (Davis, Smith & Marsden, 2009). Perhaps because of unmet needs, a growing number of people may also be withdrawing from work as a meaningful life pursuit. Levels of work centrality (England, 1991; Twenge, Campbell, Hoffman & Lance, 2010) and work ethic (Highhouse, Zickar & Yankelevich, 2010; Weaver, 1997) have been slipping for decades.

What is needed to sustain interest in this area is more rigorous research on the nature and effects of meaningful work. First, meaningful work constructs must be clearly operationalized and informed by theories and models of psychological meaning (see Baumeister, 1991). Second, these variables should demonstrate criterion and incremental validity as predictors of important employee outcomes. Some research currently exists, with narrow features of meaningful work having been linked to work engagement (May, Gilson & Harter, 2004; Stringer, 2008), general employee attitudes (Chalofsky & Krishna, 2009; ter Doest, Maes & Gebhardt, 2006; Edwards & Cable, 2009) and performance (Duchon & Plowman, 2005; Grant, 2008). Some aspects of meaningful work have also been experimentally-linked to productivity (Ariely, Kamenica & Prelec, 2008).

The current chapter considers a multi-dimensional model of meaningful work in the context of employee well-being. Specifically, this chapter reviews three studies on observed relationships among meaningful work characteristics and depression, anxiety, stress, burnout, physical health, mental health and work engagement (Fairlie, 2010; 2011). These relationships were considered in the context in other, more well-known work characteristics. While many work characteristics have been connected to well-being (Karasek & Theorell, 1990; Siegrist, 2002; Warr, 1994), work characteristics that are aligned with dimensions of psychological meaning have received scant attention. It is hoped that the findings will support meaningful work as a neglected and under-utilized resource in the promotion and maintenance of employee well-being. This is a laudable aim, given the costs associated with employee mental health problems (Goetzel, Long, Ozminkowski, Hawkins, Wang & Lynch, 2004; Johnston, Westerfield, Momin, Phillipi & Naidoo, 2009; Kessler, Barber, Birnbaum, Frank, Greenberg, Rose & Wang, 1999).

What is Meaningful Work?

In psychology, discussions of meaning often entail issues of "life meaning, purpose, and coherence" (Ryff, 2000, p. 132). Additionally, "…having meaning is viewed as a feature of optimal human functioning, which involves having goals, being engaged, and possessing inner strength in the face of life's obstacles. But to live without meaning is to experience despair, alienation, and confusion" (Ryff, 2000, p. 132). Baumeister (1991) identified four main needs for meaning: purpose (including goals and fulfillments), values, efficacy and self-worth.

While there are individual differences in what people find meaningful, a number of researchers have identified several convergent themes (see Table 10.1). These include having purpose, values and goals, spirituality, relationships, service, autonomy, commitment, challenge, achievement, competence and self-realization (for example, Antonovsky, 1990; Baumeister, 1991; Ebersole, 1998; Emmons, 1999; Frankl, 1992; Kobasa, 1979; Maslow, 1970; Nakamura & Csikszentmihalyi, 2003; Ryan & Deci, 2000; Ryff & Keyes, 1995; Wong, 1998). Many of these themes are inherent in personal strivings (Emmons, 1991), current concerns (Klinger, 1998), personal projects (Little, 1983), life longings (Kotter-Grühn, Wiest, Zurek & Scheibe, 2009), self-determination (Ryan & Deci, 2000) and conceptions of the 'good life' (King & Napa, 1998).[1]

Meaningful work is subsequently defined as job and other workplace characteristics that facilitate the attainment or maintenance of one or more dimensions of meaning (see Fairlie, 2010). In other words, meaningful work pertains to work characteristics that would appear to foster one or more of the dimensions found in Table 10.1. The concept of meaningful work is not new. Both Maslow (1965) and Alderfer (1972) described work

---

1   Some of this research does not focus on meaning, per se. However, many of these constructs tend to overlap with dimensions found within models of meaning (for example, Ebersole, 1998; Wong, 1998).

characteristics that promote self-actualization. McGregor (1960) described work that allows the expression of imagination, ingenuity and creativity. "Motivator factors" in Herzberg's (1966) Motivator-Hygiene Theory have been identified elsewhere as meaningful work factors. Locke (1976) argued that job satisfaction is an outcome of doing what is personally valued. Finally, meaningfulness of work is a component of the Job Characteristics Model (Hackman & Oldham, 1975). Despite the long history of meaningful work concepts, few of these concepts are represented in models and measures of work characteristics (for example, Balzer, Kihm, Smith, Irwin, Bachiochi, Robie, Sinar & Parra, 2000; Campion & Thayer, 1985; Gay, Weiss, Hendel, Dawis & Lofquist, 1971; Parker & Wall, 1998; Moos, 1981; Spector, 1997).

The Rationale for Meaningful Work

There is a strong case for meaningful work as a condition for employee well-being. This rests on abundant research on the role of perceived meaning in well-being. For example, the fulfillment of basic needs has repeatedly been associated with well-being outcomes (for example, autonomy, competence and relatedness; Ryan & Deci, 2000, 2001; Tay & Diener, 2011). These same needs are similar to dimensions found in models of meaning (Ebersole, 1998; Emmons, 1999; Wong, 1998). Additionally, having a sense of life purpose (McKnight & Kashdan, 2009), goal pursuit (Diener, Suh, Lucas & Smith, 1999; Ryan & Deci, 2001), authentic goal pursuit (Brunstein, Schultheiss & Grässmann, 1998; Sheldon & Elliot, 1999) and autonomy (Fischer & Boer, 2011) have been related to positive well-being states.

Meaning has also been viewed as a component of well-being. The dimensions of psychological well-being forwarded by Ryff and Keyes (1995) are similar to commonly-found dimensions of meaning (for example, Crumbaugh & Maholick, 1964; Ebersole, 1998; Emmons, 1999; Wong, 1998). Well-being has also been described as both *hedonic* (that is, affective) and *eudaimonic* (that is, meaning-based; Lent, 2004; Ryan & Deci, 2001). The World Health Organization (2004) defines mental health, in part, by self-realization and service to one's community. These are common dimensions of meaning (Ebersole, 1998; Emmons, 1999; Maslow, 1970; Wong, 1998). Seligman (2011) views meaning and purpose as components of well-being. Finally, Keyes (2007) has shown that high levels of subjective well-being *and* meaning (that is, "flourishing") are associated with more positive mental health outcomes than high levels of subjective well-being alone. Thus, extent relationships among meaning and well-being states suggest that meaningful work may be a valuable resource for promoting and maintaining employee well-being.

Measuring Meaningful Work

The research in this chapter involved the Meaningful Work Inventory (MWI; Fairlie, 2010), which is a comprehensive employee survey of evidence-based work characteristics linked to employee outcomes, together with work characteristics that are aligned with models of psychological meaning. The MWI contains over 30 specific work characteristics scales and the following eight global work characteristics scales: Meaningful Work, Leadership and Organizational Features, Supervisory Relationships,

Coworker Relationships, Intrinsic Rewards, Extrinsic Rewards, Organizational Support, and Work Demands and Balance (see Table 10.2). Reliability and validity information is available elsewhere (Fairlie, 2010, 2011, 2012).

While each global scale contains varying amounts of meaningful work content, the Meaningful Work global scale is perhaps most aligned with dimensions of meaning. It contains four facets: Self-Actualizing Work (realizing one's full potential, purpose, values and goals through one's job and organization), Social Impact (having a positive impact on people and things through one's job and organization), Personal Accomplishment (feelings of personal accomplishment from one's job) and Career Advancement (belief that one can achieve one's highest career goals in one's current organization).

Meaningful Work and Well-Being: Current Research

What are the relationships among meaningful work characteristics and dimensions of well-being? What is the case for increasing levels of meaningful work as a way of promoting and maintaining healthy workplaces? The author conducted three studies to explore these relationships (Fairlie, 2010, 2011), two of which were undertaken to develop and validate the MWI (Fairlie, 2010). The following are capsule summaries from these studies.

DEPRESSION AND ANXIETY DAYS

Fairlie (2010) examined over 30 specific work characteristics as correlates of depression and anxiety days in a national sample of 1,477 full-time, working Americans.[2] The sample was mostly female (67 percent), non-management (59 percent), with one to less than ten years of tenure (57 percent) and educated at the university certificate or diploma level or higher (53 percent). The mean age was 48.30 (SD = 11.25). The participants were members of a paid, online panel. In addition to perceived work characteristics, participants were asked to report the number of days over the past month that they experienced symptoms of depression ("sad, blue, or depressed") and anxiety ("worried, tense, or anxious;")(Hennessy, Moriarty, Zack, Scherr & Brackbill, 1994; Moriarty, Zack & Kobau, 2003).

Some of the stronger correlates of depression and anxiety days were work characteristics aligned with one or more dimensions of meaning. This included most facets of the Meaningful Work global scale (that is, Self-Actualizing Work, Social Impact, Career Advancement). Met Job Expectations (that is, employers keep their pre-hire promises to employees) was the strongest correlate of anxiety days. It is also thematically-linked to authenticity (Harter, 2002). Work Enjoyment (that is, job tasks and activities are enjoyable) was the strongest correlate of depression days. This, along with Skill Utilization, relate to themes of being fully committed (Kobasa, 1979), engaged (Nakamura & Csikszentmihalyi, 2003) and challenged (Csikszentmihalyi, 1990; Kobasa, 1979). Job Autonomy relates to perceiving autonomy and control in one's life (for example, Ryan &

---

2   The eight MWI global work characteristics scales could not be computed in this study because several within-scale items were administered across different surveys to different participants.

Deci, 2000; Ryff & Keyes, 1995). Skill Utilization and Job Autonomy were also correlates of both outcomes.

Several of the strongest meaningful work correlates appeared to suggest the importance of self-transcendence through one's work. Big Picture Connection pertains to seeing one's job as connected to the greater goals and direction of the organization. This harks to being connected in broader relationships (Ebersole, 1998; Ryff & Keyes, 1995), generativity or service (Ebersole, 1998; Emmons, 1999) and perhaps attachment to some surrogate, higher power (for example, spirituality and religion; Emmons, 1999; Wong, 1998). Both Job-Induced Strengths (that is, job enables one to discover one's strengths) and Growth and Development are related to personal growth dimensions of meaning (Maslow, 1970; Ryff & Keyes, 1995). In short, perceptions of meaningful work characteristics in one's job and organization are associated with less frequent reports of mood problems.[3]

PHYSICAL AND MENTAL HEALTH DAYS

Global work characteristics were examined in the context of both physical and mental health days in a second national sample of 1,000 full-time, working Americans (Fairlie, 2010). The modal profile was female (56 percent), non-management (59 percent) and with one to less than five years of tenure (38 percent). The mean age was 42.60 (SD = 11.15). The participants were members of a paid, online panel. Participants were asked to report the number of days over the past month that their physical health (that is, physical illness, injury) and mental health (that is, stress, depression, emotional problems) were "not good" (Hennessy, Moriarty, Zack, Scherr & Brackbill, 1994).

In general, relationships among work characteristics and physical health days were not substantive. The temporal lags and distal gaps between perceived work characteristics and physical health outcomes are likely considerable. Work characteristics had stronger associations with mental health days, including Work Demands and Balance ($r = -.44$, $p < .001$) followed by Meaningful Work ($r = -.35$, $p < .001$). In a multiple regression analysis, the eight MWI global work characteristics accounted for 25 percent of the variance in mental health days ($F(8, 731) = 30.53$, $p < .001$). Both Meaningful Work, $\beta = -.24$, $t(731) = -4.61$, $p < .001$ and Work Demands and Balance, $\beta = -.41$, $t(731) = -9.04$, $p < .001$, remained significant in the equation. Thus, despite the sizable effect of Work Demands and Balance, Meaningful Work appears to have a unique role in the frequency of mental health complaints. In summary, perceptions of meaningful work characteristics were associated with less frequent reports of mental health problems.

WORK ENGAGEMENT, BURNOUT AND NEGATIVE MOOD

Fairlie (2011) also explored the role of meaningful work characteristics in the context of work engagement (Schaufeli, Bakker & Salanova, 2006), disengagement (Demerouti & Bakker, 2008), exhaustion (as a dimension of burnout; Demerouti & Bakker, 2008), and stress and depression symptoms (Lovibond & Lovibond, 1995). The participants were 574 American and Canadians who were at least part-time employed. They were mostly female (71 percent), full-time employed or self-employed (93 percent) and in a supervisory or management position (63 percent). The mean age was 46.42 (SD = 10.42). The participants

---

3   Work Demands and Work-Life Balance were also strong correlates of anxiety days.

were invited to complete a brief, web-based measure of emotional intelligence, followed by the survey battery for the current study in exchange for feedback scores on some measures.

Work engagement is not often construed as an employee well-being variable. Yet, the content of some work engagement variables overlaps with adjustment variables (Schaufeli, Bakker & Salanova, 2006). The vigor dimension of work engagement contains affective features. Additionally, (and conversely) circumplex models have identified engagement components within positive affect (Lucas, Diener & Larsen, 2003). Engagement concepts have also been included in emerging models of well-being (Seligman, 2011). Finally, the commitment dimension of hardiness, a personality variable linked to well-being, suggests a full engagement in one's situations and experiences (Kobasa, 1979).

All MWI global work characteristics significantly correlated with all of the well-being outcomes listed above (r's = $|.27|$ to $|.77|$, all $p < .001$). Meaningful Work had the strongest correlations of any global scale with work engagement ($r = .77$) and disengagement ($r = -.77$). It was tied with Intrinsic Rewards as the strongest correlate of depression symptoms ($r = -.46$). Next to Work Demands and Balance, Meaningful Work also had the second strongest correlation with Exhaustion ($r = -.52$). Meaningful Work had weaker relative relationships with stress symptoms. In select multiple regression analyses, global work characteristics accounted for substantive amounts of variance in work engagement [59 percent; $F(8, 398) = 71.60$, $p < .001$], exhaustion [43 percent; $F(8, 401) = 38.42$ $p < .001$] and depression symptoms [29 percent; $F(8, 406) = 20.30$, $p < .001$]. In each case, Meaningful Work had a significant effect while controlling for other global work characteristics. Meaningful Work was also the strongest unique predictor of engagement, $\beta = .64$, $t(398) = 12.64$, $p < .001$. Work Demands and Balance had a unique effect on exhaustion and depression symptoms, but not work engagement. Thus, perceptions of meaningful work appear to figure prominently in the levels of several well-being variables, particularly work engagement.

General Discussion

The results of three studies suggest that meaningful work plays a substantive role in employee well-being outcomes. For example, work characteristics that promote meaning appear more likely than other work characteristics, when absent, to be associated with more frequent, negative mood states (that is, depression and anxiety days). Meaningful work characteristics had the strongest relationships, compared to other work characteristics, with work engagement and disengagement. These same work characteristics also had substantive relationships with mental health days, exhaustion and depression symptoms. An absence of psychological meaning in life, in general, has long been tied to depression (Crumbaugh & Maholick, 1964; Mascaro & Rosen, 2008; Ryff, 1989). Moreover, regression results suggest that the effects of meaningful work on mental health days, work engagement, exhaustion, and depression symptoms are not accounted for by other, more well-known work characteristics. Thus, it would appear that when individuals occupy jobs with greater perceived opportunities for self-actualization (including purpose, values and goal alignment), social impact, personal accomplishment and career advancement, they experience higher levels of positive well-being and lower levels of negative well-being.

Meaningful work may play an exceptionally formative role in levels of work engagement. The strong link found between these variables echoes past findings, particularly those showing meaningful work characteristics as the strongest unique predictors of work engagement (May, Gilson & Harter, 2004; Stringer, 2008). A number of psychological mechanisms may account for this link. For example, individuals who see their jobs as enabling them to realize their full potential, purpose, values and goals, may be better aligned or "fitted" to their jobs. Work–role fit has been repeatedly linked to work engagement (Crawford, Lepine & Rich, 2010; May, Gilson & Harter, 2004). Grant and Sonnetag (2010) found that pro-social impacts buffer the effects of doing negative tasks on levels of work engagement. Given the long history of work engagement (Kahn, 1990) and the great deal of research that it has spawned (Bakker & Leiter, 2010; Christian, Garza & Slaughter, 2011; Shuck, 2011), it is ironic that meaningful work should only recently come to the fore as a prominent factor in this employee outcome.

GENERAL IMPLICATIONS

The reviewed studies suggest that the presence of meaningful work is related to several well-being outcomes. These results have implications not only for employee health, but also organizational performance. Work engagement, for example, has been repeatedly linked to employee performance (Christian, Garza & Slaughter, 2011; Rich, Lepine & Crawford, 2010) and organizational performance (Salanova, Agut & Peiro, 2005; Xanthopoulou, Bakker, Demerouti & Schaufeli, 2009). Burnout has been linked to poor employee health (Shirom, Melamed, Toker, Berliner & Shapira, 2005), absenteeism (Lee & Ashforth, 1996), lower work performance (Wright & Bonett, 1997) and turnover (Wright & Cropanzano, 1998), all of which affect organizational performance.

Additionally, there is a mounting need to understand sources of workplace depression. A growing body of research demonstrates a significant role for emotions (Ashkanasy & Ashton-James, 2005), and particularly positive affect (Ashkanasy & Ashton-James, 2007) in organizational behavior. Positive affect is related to work performance (Wright & Staw, 1994, 1999) and various forms of creativity and productivity (Fredrickson, 2001). A lack of positive affect is also a diagnostic feature of depression (American Psychiatric Association, 1994). Depression, itself, is associated with cognitive, motivational, and behavioral deficits (Austin, Mitchell & Goodwin, 2001) which can eventually affect work performance (Kessler, 2008). Depressed employees are costly, losing up to 3.2 more days per month than other workers, and leading to productivity losses of up to $395 per employee per month (Kessler, Barber, Birnbaum, Frank, Greenberg, Rose & Wang, 1999). Overall, the impact of depression on productivity is well-documented (Simon, Barber, Birnbaum, Frank, Greenberg, Rose, Wang & Kessler, 2001; Steffick, Fortney, Smith & Pyne, 2006).

In short, given the relationships that were found among meaningful work characteristics and well-being outcomes in the current studies, and among employee well-being outcomes and organizational performance found elsewhere, it would appear that employers could benefit in tangible ways from the promotion and maintenance of meaningful work in their organizations.

PRACTICAL IMPLICATIONS

The results have several practical implications for employers and organizational consultants. First, meaningful work characteristics should be measured on employee surveys (for example, self-actualizing work, social impact, personal accomplishment, career advancement). Additionally, relationships among these work characteristics and employee well-being outcomes should be examined in employee survey data to confirm the importance of these work characteristics within specific organizations.

Second, employees could be made aware of meaningful work characteristics that are already present in their jobs and organizations. Employee perceptions of the availability of meaningful work may be inaccurate (see Spector, 1992). For example, opportunities for meaningful work may exist 'unused' in formal job descriptions. Additionally, with respect to social impact, supervisors could assist direct reports in seeing the connections between their jobs and the mission and vision of the organization. In particular, programs could be developed to create deeper social relationships among employees and clients as a way of strengthening perceptions of social impact (that is, client testimonials, quality circles comprised of both employees and clients). Employees and clients could also be "twinned" on personal attributes and work together on product and service improvements.

Perceptions of meaningful work may partially stem from personality traits and cognitive styles. For example, an external locus of control may prompt employees to see less job autonomy (Wang, Bowling & Eschleman, 2010). Perceptions of low job autonomy could then lead to negative employee attitudes and behavior (Terry & Jimmieson, 1999; Theorell, 2003). Employees could be coached to examine their cognitive styles, including those associated with core self-evaluations (Judge & Bono, 2001), psychological capital (Luthans, Avey, Norman & Combs, 2006) and benefit-finding (Tennen & Affleck, 2002). For example, employees could be trained in mindfulness (that is, attention, awareness; Brown & Ryan, 2003) and work with supervisors to shift their perspectives on their jobs (for example, from "work" to "play;" Langer & Moldoveanu, 2000). Team assessments of personality traits and cognitive styles could inform these pursuits.

Third, organizational consultants could assist employers in their understanding of work motivation from the standpoint of meaning (for example, Wong, 1998). Models of meaning could be used as a "lens" for understanding how decisions may impact employee and organizational performance. Specifically, typical activities of managers (Borman & Brush, 1993) could be reviewed and modified to promote higher levels of meaningful work and well-being among employees. For example, developing and mentoring people is a common dimension of managerial work (Yukl, Wall & Lepsinger, 1990). Managers could use theories of self-actualization to inform employee development activities, and ensure that such efforts address employee-centered interests (that is, "human" development in addition to employee development).

Fourth, employers could revisit their career development programs to ensure that opportunities exist for employees to realize long-term career goals within the organization. Since this form of career advancement appears to be a facet of meaningful work, such long-term goals are likely aligned with employees' sense of self or identity. Career development programs could be better aligned with the life purposes, goals and values of employees. This idea is central to boundaryless (Arthur, 1994) and protean (Hall, 2002) concepts of career development. While the uniqueness of each employee would appear to make this cost-prohibitive, self-report inventories of goals, values and motives

(Hofstede, 1994; Reiss & Havercamp, 1998) and cluster analysis (Kaufman & Rousseeuw, 1990) could be employed to identify employee segments. A limited "suite" of program components could then be developed to address these segments.

Fifth, organizational consultants could assist managers and direct reports in their collaborative efforts to redesign jobs. Job crafting (Berg, Wrzesniewski & Dutton, 2010) could be undertaken to find ways of fulfilling roles and accountabilities while also satisfying employee needs for meaningful work. In terms of self-actualization, employees could be asked to imagine what they would do for the rest of their lives if they didn't have to work for money. Distilled themes from this exercise could be used to redesign jobs in ways that remain faithful to the needs of the organization. Employees could also be asked for ideas on how they could have a larger impact on clients, and the world in general.

Finally, employers could promote meaningfulness in employees' non-work lives. Studies show that less than 8 percent of individuals' life longings are work-related (Kotter-Grühn, Wiest, Zurek & Scheibe, 2009). Surveys could be used to identify the rest of employees' life longings, and inform initiatives to support them. These initiatives are not an employer's responsibility. Yet, studies show that contributing directly to employees' non-work lives can lead to higher organizational commitment (Cohen, 1997). While some supports could be monetary (for example, increased benefits), organizations may benefit more by sponsoring activities that directly address, for example, employee needs for social impact. For example, employees could engage in several paid days of community work per year. Non-work time created by compressed work weeks and sabbaticals could be used for continuing education. A suite of similar opportunities could be pre-developed in alignment with dimensions of meaning for the sake of cost and efficiency.

LIMITATIONS AND FUTURE DIRECTIONS FOR RESEARCH

The reviewed studies were not without limitations. First, they were based on convenience samples that were over-weighted by females and employees in supervisory positions. Future research should take advantage of probability sampling (Kidder & Judd, 1986). The results should also be replicated with other measures, as some work characteristics and well-being variables were measured with single items. The role of personality in both perceptions of meaningful work and well-being will also be considered in a future study.

The reviewed studies relied on self-report data, which could be associated with response sets (Crocker & Algina, 1986) and method variance effects (Spector & Brannick, 1995). Future studies should be conducted using other methods of data collection (for example, behavioral observation, ratings). The research was also cross-sectional in nature, which limits causal interpretations. Longitudinal and quasi-experimental methods could be employed to more accurately assess changes in the levels of employee well-being as a function of meaningful work.

Conclusions

In summary, three studies showed meaningful work characteristics to be strong correlates and unique predictors of several well-being variables among employed individuals. For most well-being variables, meaningful work characteristics were associated with the largest or second largest effects. The results were particularly compelling for a meaningful work composite consisting of self-actualizing work, social impact, personal accomplishment and career advancement. Yet, this meaningful work content is underrepresented in many models and measures of work characteristics (Campion & Thayer, 1985; Hackman & Oldham, 1975; Parker & Wall, 1998; Warr, 1994) and occupational health (Hurrell, Nelson & Simmons, 1998). This observation, together with the reviewed findings, suggest that meaningful work characteristics are an overlooked source of employee well-being, and a possible competitive advantage for employers. Employers may benefit from offering work that enables employees to realize their full potential, purpose, values and goals, to have significant social impacts, to feel a regular sense of accomplishment, and to achieve their highest career goals.

References

Alderfer, C. P. (1972) *Existence, Relatedness, and Growth: Human Needs in Organizational Settings*. New York: Free Press. Retrieved September 10, 2012.

Amabile, T. M., & Kramer, S. J. (2010) *The HBR list: breakthrough ideas for 2010*. Retrieved from http://hbr.org/2010/01/the-hbr-list-breakthrough-ideas-for-2010/ar/. Retrieved September 10, 2012.

Amabile, T. M., & Kramer, S. J. (2012) *How leaders kill meaning at work*. Available online at: http://www.mckinseyquarterly.com/How_leaders_kill_meaning_at_work_2910. Retrieved September 10, 2012.

American Psychiatric Association. (1994) *Diagnostic and Statistical Manual of Mental Disorders: DSM-IV* (4th Edition). Washington, DC: American Psychiatric Association.

Antonovsky, A, (1990) Personality and health: testing the sense of coherence model. In H.S. Friedman (ed.) *Personality and Disease, Wiley Series on Health Psychology/Behavioral Medicine*. Oxford: John Wiley & Sons. pp. 155–177.

Ardichvili, A., & Kuchinke, K. P. (2009) International perspectives on the meanings of work and working: Current research and theory. *Advances in Developing Human Resources*, 11, 155–167.

Ariely, D., Kamenica, E., & Prelec, D. (2008) Man's search for meaning: yhe case of Legos. *Journal of Economic Behavior & Organization*, 67, 671–677.

Arthur, M. B. (1994) The boundaryless career: a new perspective for organizational inquiry. *Journal of Organizational Behavior*, 15, 295–306.

Ashkanas, R. (2011) *Make the weekend last all week*. Retrieved from http://blogs.hbr.org/ashkenas/2011/02/make-the-weekend-last-all-week.html. Retrieved September 10, 2012.

Ashkanasy, N. A., & Ashton-James, C. E. (2005) Emotion in organizations: a neglected topic in i/o psychology, but with a bright future. In G. P. Hodgkinson & J. K. Ford (eds) *International Review of Industrial and Organizational Psychology*. New York: Wiley. Vol. 20, pp. 221–268.

Ashkanasy, N. A., & Ashton-James, C. E. (2007) Positive emotion in organizations: a multi-level framework. In D. L. Nelson & Cooper, C. L. (eds) Positive Organizational Behavior. London: Sage. pp. 57–73.

Ashman, I., & Lawler, J. (2008) Existential communication and leadership. *Leadership*, 4, 253–269.

Austin, M., Mitchell, P., & Goodwin, G. M. (2001) Cognitive deficits in depression: possible implications for functional neuropathology. *British Journal of Psychiatry*, 178, 200–206.

Bakker, A. B., & Leiter, M. P. (eds) (2010) *Work Engagement: A Handbook of Essential Theory and Research*. New York: Psychology Press.

Balzer, W. K., Kihm, J. A., Smith, P. C., Irwin, J. L., Bachiochi, P. D., Robie, C., Sinar. E. F., & Parra, L. F. (2000) *Users' Manual for the Job Descriptive Index (JDI; 1997 Revision) and Job in General (JIG) Scales*. Bowling Green, OH: Bowling Green State University.

Battista, J., & Almond, R. (1973). The development of meaning in life. *Psychiatry*, 36, 409–427.

Baumeister, R. (1991) *Meanings of Life*. New York: Guilford Press.

Berg, J. M., Wrzesniewski, A., & Dutton, J. E. (2010) Perceiving and responding to challenges in job crafting at different ranks: when proactivity requires adaptivity. *Journal of Organizational Behavior*, 31, 158–186.

Borman, W. C., & Brush, D. H. (1993) More progress toward a taxonomy of managerial performance requirements. *Human Performance*, 6, 1–21.

Brown, K. W., & Ryan, R. M. (2003) The benefits of being present: mindfulness and its role in psychological well-being. *Journal of Personality and Social Psychology*, 84, 822–848.

Brunstein, J. C., Schultheiss, O. C., & Grässmann, R. (1998) Personal goals and emotional well-being: the moderating role of motive dispositions. *Journal of Personality and Social Psychology*, 75, 494–508.

Campion, M. A., & Thayer, P. W. (1985) Development and field evaluation of an interdisciplinary measure of job design. *Journal of Applied Psychology*, 70, 29–43.

Chalofsky, N., & Krishna, V. (2009) Meaningfulness, commitment, and engagement: the intersection of a deeper level of intrinsic motivation. *Advances in Developing Human Resources*, 11, 189–203.

Christian, M. S., Garza, A. S., & Slaughter, J. E. (2011) Work engagement: a quantitative review and test of its relations with task and contextual performance. *Personnel Psychology*, 64, 89–136.

Cohen, A. (1997) Nonwork influences on withdrawal cognitions: an empirical examination of an overlooked issue. *Human Relations*, 50, 1511–1536.

Crawford, M. (2009) *Shop Class as Soulcraft: An Inquiry into the Value of Work*. New York: Penguin.

Crocker, L., & Algina, J. (1986) *Introduction to Classical and Modern Test Theory*. Fort Worth, TX: Harcourt, Brace & Jovanovich.

Crawford, E. R., Lepine, J. A., & Rich, B. L. (2010) Linking job demands and resources to employee engagement and burnout: a theoretical extension and meta-analytic test. *Journal of Applied Psychology*, 95, 834–848.

Crumbaugh, J. C., & Maholick, L. T. (1964) An experimental study in existentialism: the psychometric approach to Frankl's concept of noogenic neurosis. *Journal of Clinical Psychology*, 20, 200–207.

Csikszentmihalyi, M. (1990) *Flow: The Psychology of Optimal Experience*. New York: Harper & Row.

Davis, J. A., Smith, T. W., & Marsden, P. V. (2009) *General Social Surveys, 1972–2008: Cumulative Codebook*. Chicago, IL: National Opinion Research Center.

Debats, D. L. (1998). Measurement of Personal Meaning: The Psychometric Properties of the Life Regard Index. In P. T. P. Wong & P. S. Fry (eds) *The Human Quest for Meaning: A Handbook of Psychological Research and Clinical Applications*. Mahwah, NJ: Erlbaum. pp. 237–259.

Demerouti, E., & Bakker, A.B. (2008) The Oldenburg Burnout Inventory: A good alternative to measure burnout and engagement. In J. Halbesleben (ed.) *Stress and Burnout in Health Care*. Hauppage, NY: Nova Sciences. pp. 65–78.

Diener., E., Suh, E. M., Lucas, R. E., & Smith, H. L. (1999) Subjective well-being: three decades of progress. *Psychological Bulletin*, 125, 276–302.

Dik, B. J., Duffy, R. D., & Eldridge, B. M. (2009) Calling and vocation in career counseling: recommendations for promoting meaningful work. *Professional Psychology: Research and Practice*, 40, 625–632.

Duchon, D., & Plowman, D. A. (2005) Nurturing the spirit at work: impact on work unit performance. *The Leadership Quarterly*, 16, 807–833.

Dyer, F. (2005) *Why Do I Do This Every Day?: Finding Meaning in Your Work*. Oxford: Lion Publishing.

Ebersole, P. (1998) Types and depth of written life meanings. In P. T. P. Wong & P. S. Fry (eds) *The Human Quest for Meaning: A Handbook of Psychological Research and Clinical Applications*. Mahwah, NJ: Erlbaum. pp. 179–191.

Edwards, J. R., & Cable, D. M. (2009) The value of value congruence. *Journal of Applied Psychology*, 94, 654–677.

Emmons, R. A. (1991). Personal strivings, daily life events, and psychological and physical well-being. *Journal of Personality*, 59, 453–472.

Emmons, R. A. (1999) *The Psychology of Ultimate Concerns: Motivation and Spirituality in Personality*. New York: Guilford Press.

England, G. W. (1991) The meaning of working in the USA: recent changes. *European Work and Organizational Psychologist*, 1, 111–1124.

Erickson, T. (2011, March 23) *Meaning is the new money*. HBR Blog Network. Retrieved from http://blogs.hbr.org/erickson/2011/03/challenging_our_deeply_held_as.html. Retrieved 10 September, 2012.

Fairlie, P. (2010, August) *The Meaningful Work Inventory: Development and Initial Validation*. Paper presented at the 118th. Annual Convention of the American Psychological Association, San Diego, CA.

Fairlie, P. (2011) Meaningful work, employee engagement, and other key employee outcomes: implications for human resource development. *Advances in Developing Human Resources*, 13, 504–521.

Fairlie, P. (2012) *Meaningful Work Inventory Technical Monograph*. Toronto: Author.

Fischer, R., & Boer, D. (2011) What is more important for national well-being: money or autonomy? A meta-analysis of well-being, burnout, and anxiety across 63 societies. *Journal of Personality and Social Psychology*, 101, 164–184.

Flesher, J. (2009) The meaning of working: a perspective from practice. *Advances in Developing Human Resources*, 11, 253–260.

Frankl, V. (1992) *Man's Search for Meaning* (4th edition). Boston, MA: Beacon Press.

Fredrickson, B. L. (2001) The role of positive emotions in positive psychology: the broaden-and-build theory of positive emotions. *American Psychologist*, 56, 218–226.

Gay, E. G., Weiss, D. J., Hendel, D. D., Dawis, R. V., & Lofquist, L. H. (1971) *Manual for the Minnesota Importance Questionnaire*. Minneapolis, MN: Industrial Relations Center, University of Minnesota.

Goetzel, R. Z., Long, S. R., Ozminkowski, R. J., Hawkins, K., Wang, S., & Lynch, W. (2004) Health, absence, disability, and presenteeism cost estimates of certain physical and mental health conditions affecting US employers. *Journal of Occupational & Environmental Medicine*, 46, 398–412.

Grant, A. M. (2008) The significance of task significance: job performance effects, relational mechanisms, and boundary conditions. *Journal of Applied Psychology*, 93, 108–124.

Grant, A. M., & Sonnentag, S. (2010) Doing good buffers against feeling bad: prosocial impact compensates for negative task and self-evaluations. *Organizational Behavior and Human Decision Processes*, 111, 13–22.

Hackman, J. R., & Oldham, G. R. (1975) Development of the Job Diagnostic Survey. *Journal of Applied Psychology*, 60, 159–170.

Hall, D. T. (2002) *Protean Careers In and Out of Organizations*. Thousand Oaks, CA: Sage.

Haque, U. (2012) *Create a meaningful life through meaningful work*. Retrived from http://blogs.hbr.org/haque/2012/01/create_a_meaningful_life_throu.html. Retrieved 10 September, 2012.

Harter, S. (2002) Authenticity. In C. R. Snyder & S. J. Lopez (eds) Handbook of Positive Psychology Oxford: Oxford University Press. pp. 382–394.

Hennessy C. H., Moriarty, D. G., Zack, M. M., Scherr, P. A., & Brackbill, R. (1994) Measuring health-related quality of life for public health surveillance. *Public Health Reports*, 109, 665–672.

Herzberg, F. I. (1966) *Work and Nature of Man*. New York: Thomas Y. Crowell.

Highhouse, S., Zickar, M.J., & Yankelevich, M. (2010) Would you work if you won the lottery? tracking changes in the American work ethic. *Journal of Applied Psychology*, 95, 349–357.

Hofstede, G. (1994) *Values Survey Module 1994 Manual*. Maastricht, The Netherlands: University of Linberg.

Hogan, R., & Warremfeltz, R. (2003) Educating the modern manager. *Academy of Management Journal*, 2, 74–84.

Hurrell, J. J., Jr., Nelson, D. L., & Simmons, B. L. (1998) Measuring job stressors and strains: where we have been, where we are, and where we need to go. *Journal of Occupational Health Psychology*, 3, 368–389.

Johnston, K., Westerfield, W., Momin, S., Phillippi. R., & Naidoo, A. (2009) The direct and indirect costs of employee depression, anxiety, and emotional disorders: an employer case study. *Journal of Occupational and Environmental Medicine*, 51, 564–577.

Judge, T. A., & Bono, J. E. (2001) Relationship of core self-evaluations traits—self-esteem, generalized self-efficacy, locus of control, and emotional stability—with job satisfaction and job performance: a meta-analysis. *Journal of Applied Psychology*, 86, 80–92.

Kahn, W. A. (1990) Psychological conditions of personal engagement and disengagement at work. *Academy of Management Journal*, 33, 692–724.

Karasek, R., & Theorell, T. (1990) *Healthy Work: Stress, Productivity and the Reconstruction of Working Life*. New York: Basic Books.

Kaufman, L., & Rousseeuw, P. J. (1990) *Finding Groups in Data: An Introduction to Cluster Analysis*. New York: Wiley.

Kessler, R. C. (2008) Comparative and interactive effects of depression relative to other health problems on work performance in the workforce of a large employer. *Journal of Occupational Environmental Medicine*, 50, 809–816.

Kessler, R. C., Barber, C., Birnbaum, H. G., Frank, R. G., Greenberg, P. E., Rose, R. M., & Wang, P. (1999) Depression in the workplace: effects on short-term disability. *Health Affairs*, 18, 163–171.

Keyes, C. L. M. (2007) Promoting and protecting mental health as flourishing: a complementary strategy for improving national mental health. *American Psychologist*, 62, 95–108.

Kidder, L. H., & Judd, C. M. (1986) *Research Methods in Social Relations*. New York: Holt, Rinehart & Winston.

King, L. A., & Napa, C.K. (1998) What makes a life good? *Journal of Personality and Social Psychology*, 75, 156–165.

Klinger, E. (1998) The search for meaning in evolutionary perspective and its clinical implications. In P. T. P. Wong & P. S. Fry (eds), *Handbook of Personal Meaning: Theory, Research, and Application*. Mahwah, NJ: Erlbaum. pp. 27–50.

Kobasa, S. C. (1979) Stressful life events, personality, and health: an inquiry into hardiness. *Journal of Personality and Social Psychology*, 37, 1–11.

Kotter-Grühn, D., Wiest, M., Zurek, P. P., & Scheibe, S. (2009) What is it we are longing for? Psychological and demographic factors influencing the contents of Sehnsucht (life longings). *Journal of Research in Personality*, 43, 428–437.

Kuchinke, K. P. (2009) Changing meanings of work in Germany, Korea, and the United States in historical perspectives. *Advances in Developing Human Resources*, 11, 168–188.

Langer, E., & Moldoveanu, M. (2000) Mindfulness research and the future. *Journal of Social Issues*, 56, 129–139.

Lawler, J. (2005) The essence of leadership? Existentialism and leadership. *Leadership*, 1, 215–231.

Lee, R. T., & Ashforth, B. E. (1996) A meta-analytic examination of the correlates of the three dimensions of job burnout. *Journal of Applied Psychology*, 81, 123–133.

Leider, R. (2010) *The Power of Purpose: Find Meaning, Live Longer, Better*. San Francisco, CA: Berrett-Koehler.

Lent, R. W. (2004) Toward a unifying theoretical and practical perspective on well-being and psychosocial adjustment. *Journal of Counseling Psychology*, 51, 482–509.

Little, B. R. (1983) Personal projects: a rationale and method for investigation. *Environment and Behavior*, 15, 273–309.

Locke, E. A. (1976) The nature and causes of job satisfaction. In M. D. Dunnette (ed.) *Handbook of Industrial and Organizational Psychology*. Chicago, IL: Rand McNally. pp. 1297–1343.

Locke, E. A. (2002). Setting goals for life and happiness. In C. R. Snyder and S. J. Lopez (eds) *Handbook of Positive Psychology*. Oxford: Oxford University Press. pp. 299–312.

Lovibond, S. H., & Lovibond, P. F. (1995) *Manual for the Depression Anxiety Stress Scales* (2nd edition). Sydney: Psychology Foundation.

Lucas, R. E., Diener, E., & Larsen, R.J. (2003) Measuring positive emotions. In S. J. Lopez & C. R. Snyder (eds) *Positive Psychological Assessment: A Handbook of Models and Measures*. Washington: American Psychological Association. pp. 201–218.

Luthans, F., Avey, J. B., Norman, S. M., & Combs, G. J. (2006) Psychological capital development: toward micro-intervention. *Journal of Organizational Behavior*, 27, 387–393.

Luthans, F., & Avolio, B. J. (2003) Authentic leadership: a positive developmental approach. In K. S. Cameron, J. E. Dutton, & R. E. Quinn (eds) *Positive Organizational Scholarship: Foundations of a New Discipline*. San Francisco: Berrett-Koehler. pp. 241–258.

Mascaro, N., & Rosen, D. H. (2008) Assessment of existential meaning and its longitudinal relations with depressive symptoms. *Journal of Social and Clinical Psychology*, 27, 576–599.

Maslow, A. H. (1965) *Eupsychian Management*. Chicago, IL: Irwin-Dorsey.

Maslow, A. H. (1970) *Motivation and Personality* (2nd edition). New York: Harper and Row.

May, D. R., Gilson, R. L., & Harter, L. M. (2004) The psychological conditions of meaningfulness, safety and availability and the engagement of the human spirit at work. *Journal of Occupational and Organizational Psychology*, 77, 11–37.

McGregor, D. (1960) *The Human Side of Enterprise*. New York: McGraw-Hill.

McKnight, P. E., & Kashdan, T. B. (2009) Purpose in life as a system that creates and sustains health and well-being: an integrative, testable theory. *Review of General Psychology*, 13, 242–251.

Michaelson, C. (2010) *The importance of meaningful work*. MIT Sloan Management Review. Retrieved from http://sloanreview.mit.edu/the-magazine/2010-winter/51202/the-importance-of-meaningful-work/. Retrieved September 10, 2012.

Moos, R. H. (1981) *Work Environment Scale Manual*. Palo Alto, CA: Consulting Psychologists Press.

Moriarty, D. G., Zack, M. M., & Kobau, R. (2003) The Centers for Disease Control and Prevention's healthy days measures: population tracking of perceived physical and mental health over time. *Health and Quality of Life Outcomes*, 1, 1–8.

Nakamura, J., & Csikszentmihalyi, M. (2003) The construction of meaning through vital engagement. In C. L. M. Keyes & J. Haidt (eds) *Flourishing: Positive Psychology and the Life Well-lived*. Washington: American Psychological Association. pp. 83–104.

Parker, S., & Wall, T. (1998) *Job and Work Design: Organizing Work to Promote Well-being and Effectiveness*. Thousand Oaks, CA: Sage Publications.

Pink, D.H. (2009) *Drive: The Surprising Truth about What Motivates Us*. New York: Putnam.

Reiss, S., & Havercamp, S. M. (1998) Toward a comprehensive assessment of fundamental motivation: factor structure of the Reiss Profiles. *Psychological Assessment*, 10, 97–106.

Reker, G. T., & Peacock, E. J. (1981). The Life Attitude Profile (LAP): A multidimensional instrument for assessing attitudes toward life. *Canadian Journal of Behavioural Science*, 13, 264–273.

Rich, B. L., Lepine, J. A., & Crawford, E. R. (2010) Job engagement: antecedents and effects on job performance. *Academy of Management Journal*, 53, 617–635.

Rogers, C. R. (1961). *On Becoming a Person*. Boston, MA: Houghton Mifflin.

Rosso, B. D., Dekas, K. H., & Wrzesniewski, A. (2010) On the meaning of work: a theoretical integration and review. In A. Brief & B. M. Staw (eds) *Research in Organizational Behavior*, 30, 91–127.

Ryan, R. M., & Deci, E. L. (2000) Self-determination theory and the facilitation of intrinsic motivation, social development, and well-being. *American Psychologist*, 55, 68–78.

Ryan, R. M., & Deci, E. L. (2001) On happiness and human potentials: a review of research on hedonic and eudaimonic well-being. *Annual Review of Psychology*, 52, 141–66.

Ryff, C. D. (1989) Happiness is everything, or is it? Explorations on the meaning of psychological well-being. *Journal of Personality and Social Psychology*, 57, 1069–1081.

Ryff, C. D. (2000) Meaning of life. In A. E. Kazdin (ed) *Encyclopedia of Psychology*. Oxford: Oxford University Press. pp. 132–135.

Ryff, C. D., & Keyes, C. L. M. (1995) The structure of psychological well-being revisited. *Journal of Personality and Social Psychology*, 69, 719–727.

Salanova, M., Agut, S., & Peiro, J. M. (2005) Linking organizational resources and work engagement to employee performance and customer loyalty: the mediation of service climate. *Journal of Applied Psychology*, 90, 1217–1227.

Sanders, T. (2008) *Saving the World at Work: What Companies and Individuals Can Do to go Beyond Making a Profit to Making a Difference*. New York: Doubleday.

Schaufeli, W. B., Bakker, A. B., & Salanova, M. (2006) The measurement of work engagement with a short questionnaire—a cross national study. *Educational and Psychological Measurement*, 66, 701–716.

Seligman, M. E. P. (2011) *Flourish: A Visionary New Understanding of Happiness and Well-being*. New York: Free Press.

Sheldon, K. M., & Elliot, A. J. (1999) Goal striving, need satisfaction, and longitudinal wellbeing: the self-concordance model. *Journal of Personality and Social Psychology*, 76, 482–497.

Shirom, A., Melamed, S., Toker, S., Berliner, S., & Shapira, I. (2005) Burnout and health review: current knowledge and future research directions. In G. P. Hodgkinson & J. K. Ford (eds) *International Review of Industrial and Organizational Psychology*. New York: Wiley. Vol. 20, pp. 269–308.

Shuck, B. (2011) Four emerging perspectives of employee engagement: an integrative literature review. *Human Resource Development Review*, 10, 304–328.

Siegrist J. (2002) Effort-reward imbalance at work and health. In P. Perrewe & D. Ganster (eds) *Research in Occupational Stress and Well being* New York: JAI Elsevier. pp. 261–291.

Simon, G. E., Barber, C., Birnbaum, H. G., Frank, R. G., Greenberg, P. E., Rose, R. M., Wang, P. S., & Kessler, R. C. (2001) Depression and work productivity: the comparative costs of treatment versus nontreatment. *Journal of Occupational and Environmental Medicine*, 4, 2–9.

Sinek, S. (2009) *Start with Why: How Great Leaders Inspire Everyone to Take Action*. New York: Portfolio.

Spector, P. E. (1992) A consideration of the validity and meaning of self-report measures of job conditions. In C. L. Cooper and I. T. Roberston (eds) *International Review of Industrial and Organizational Psychology*. New York: Wiley. Vol. 7, pp. 123–151.

Spector, P. E. (1997) *Job Satisfaction: Applicatisons, Assessment, Causes, and Consequences*. Thousand Oaks, CA: Sage.

Spector, P. E., & Brannick, M. T. (1995) The nature and effects of method variance in organizational research. In C. L. Cooper & I. T. Robertson (eds) *International Review of Industrial and Organizational Psychology*. West Sussex, England: Wiley. pp. 249–274.

Steffick, D. E., Fortney, J. C., Smith, J. L., & Pyne, J. M. (2006) Worksite disease management programs for depression: potential employer benefits. *Disability Management Health Outcomes*, 14, 13–26.

Steger, M. F., & Dik, B. J. (2005) Work as meaning: individual and organizational benefits of engaging in meaningful work. In P. A. Linley, S. Harrington, & N. Garcea (eds) Oxford Handbook of Positive Psychology and Work. Oxford: Oxford University Press. pp. 131–142.

Stringer, C. (2008) The relationship between strategic alignment, meaningful work, and employee engagement. *Dissertation Abstracts International Section A: Humanities and Social Sciences*, 68(7–A), 3034.

Tay, L., & Diener, E. (2011) Needs and subjective well-being around the world. *Journal of Personality and Social Psychology*, 101, 354–365.

Tennen, H., & Affleck, G. (2002) Benefit-finding and benefit-reminding. In C. R. Snyder & S. J. Lopez (eds) *Handbook of Positive Psychology*. New York: Oxford University Press. pp. 584–597.

ter Doest, L., Maes, S., & Gebhardt, W. A. (2006) Personal goal facilitation through work: implications for employee satisfaction and well-being. *Applied Psychology: An International Journal*, 55, 192–219.

Terry, D. J., & Jimmieson, N. L. (1999) Work control and employee well-being: a decade review. In C. L. Cooper and I. T. Roberston (eds) *International Review of Industrial and Organizational Psychology*. New York: Wiley. Vol. 14, pp. 95–148.

Theorell, T. (2003) To be able to exert control over one's own situation: a necessary condition for coping with stressors. In J. C. Quick and L. E. Tetrick (eds) Handbook of Occupational Health Psychology. Washington: American Psychological Association. pp. 201–219.

Twenge, J. M., Campbell, S. M., Hoffman, B. J., & Lance, C. E. (2010) Generational differences in work values: leisure and extrinsic values increasing, social and intrinsic values decreasing. *Journal of Management*, 36, 1117–1142.

Ulrich, D., & Ulrich, W. (2010, July/August) Leaders who make meaning meaningful. *Ivey Business Journal*. Available online at: http://www.iveybusinessjournal.com/topics/leadership/leaders-who-make-meaning-meaningful. Retrieved September 10, 2012.

Ulrich, D., Ulrich, W., & Goldsmith, M. (2010) *The Why of Work: How Great Leaders Build Abundant Organizations That Win*. New York: McGraw-Hill.

Waddington, T. (2007) *Lasting Contribution: How to Think, Plan, and Act to Accomplish Meaningful Work*. Evanston, IL: Agate Publishing.

Wang, Q., Bowling, N. A., & Eschleman, K. J. (2010) A meta-analytic examination of work and general locus of control. *Journal of Applied Psychology*, 95, 761–768.

Warr, P. (1994) A conceptual framework for the study of work and mental health. *Work and Stress*, 8, 84–97.

Weaver, C. N. (1997) Has the work ethic in the USA declined? Evidence from nationwide surveys. *Psychological Reports*, 81, 491–495.

Wong, P. T. P. (1998) Implicit theories of meaningful life and the development of the Personal Meaning Profile. In P. T. P. Wong & P. S. Fry (eds) *The Human Quest for Meaning: A Handbook of Psychological Research and Clinical Applications*. Mahwah, NJ: Erlbaum. pp. 111–140.

World Health Organization. (2004) *Promoting Mental Health: Concepts, Emerging Evidence, Practice* (Summary report) Geneva: Author.

Wright, T. A., & Bonett, D. G. (1997) The contribution of burnout to work performance. *Journal of Organizational Behavior*, 18, 491–499.

Wright, T. A., & Cropanzano, R. (1998) Emotional exhaustion as a predictor of job performance and voluntary turnover. *Journal of Applied Psychology*, 83, 486–493.

Wright, T. A., & Staw, B. M. (1994) In search of the happy/productive worker: a longitudinal study of affect and performance. *Proceedings of the National Academy of Management*, 54, 274–278.

Wright, T. A., & Staw, B. M. (1999). Affect and favorable work outcomes: two longitudinal tests of the happy-productive worker thesis. *Journal of Organizational Behavior*, 20, 1–23.

Wrzesniewski, A., Dutton, J. E., & Debebe, G. (2003) Interpersonal sensemaking and the meaning of work. In B. M Staw and R. I. Sutton (eds) *Research in Organizational Behavior*. Greenwich, CT: JAI Press. Vol. 25, pp. 93–135.

Xanthopoulou, D., Bakker, A. B., Demerouti, E., & Schaufeli, W. B. (2009) Work engagement and financial returns: a diary study on the role of job and personal resources. *Journal of Occupational and Organizational Psychology*, 82, 183–200.

Yukl, G. A., Wall, S., & Lepsinger R. (1990) Preliminary report on the validation of the management practices survey. In K. E. Clark & M. B. Clark (eds) *Measures of Leadership*. West Orange, NJ: Leadership Library of America. pp. 223–238.

Appendix

Table 10.1 Commonly-found dimensions of psychological meaning

Theme	Reference
Purpose in life	• Battista & Almond (1973) • Baumeister (1991) • Crumbaugh and Maholick (1964) • Debats (1998) • Reker & Peacock (1981) • Ryff and Keyes (1995)
Living according to one's purpose, values, and goals	• Baumeister (1991) • Ebersole (1998) • Frankl (1992) • Locke (2002) • Sheldon and Elliot (1999)
Authenticity	• Harter (2002)
Spirituality and religion	• Ebersole (1998) • Emmons (1999) • Wong (1998)
Relationships	• Ebersole (1998) • Emmons (1999) • Hogan and Warremfeltz (2003) • Ryan and Deci (2000) • Ryff and Keyes (1995) • Wong (1998)
Generativity, service, and self-transcendence	• Ebersole (1998) • Emmons (1999) • Wong (1998)
Autonomy and control	• Antonovsky (1990) • Csikszentmihalyi (1990) • Kobasa (1979) • Ryan and Deci (2000) • Ryff and Keyes (1995)
Commitment and engagement	• Antonovsky (1990) • Kobasa (1979) • Nakamura & Csikszentmihalyi (2003)

Table 10.1 Commonly-found dimensions of psychological meaning *continued*

Theme	Reference
Challenge	• Csikszentmihalyi (1990) • Kobasa (1979)
Achievement, competence, and mastery	• Emmons (1999) • Hogan and Warremfeltz (2003) • Ryan and Deci (2000) • Ryff and Keyes (1995) • Wong (1998)
Self-realization, growth, and fulfillment	• Baumeister (1991) • Ebersole (1998) • Maslow (1970) • Rogers (1961) • Ryff and Keyes (1995) • Wong (1998)
Self-acceptance	• Ryff and Keyes (1995) • Wong (1998)
Making sense of one's life	• Antonovsky (1990) • Hogan and Warremfeltz (2003)

Table 10.2 Meaningful Work Inventory (MWI) global work characteristics scales

Scale	Facets
Meaningful Work	• Self-actualizing work (e.g., job enables one to fulfill one's potential and become a fully-functioning person) • Social impact (i.e., legacy, generativity, "mattering") • Job enables one to fulfill one's life purpose, goals, and values • Feelings of personal accomplishment • Belief in achieving one's highest career goals in one's organization
Leadership & Organizational Features	• Integrity (i.e., fair, honest, trustworthy, respectful, democratic) • Authenticity (i.e., consistent words and actions) • Clear communication of goals and direction • Corporate social responsibility (i.e., protects and maintains human rights and the environment)
Supervisory Relationships	• Integrity (i.e., fair, honest, trustworthy, respectful, accountable, democratic) • Social support (i.e., emotional, appraisal) • Feedback • Recognition • Communicates the importance of one's job
Co-Worker Relationships	• Integrity (i.e., trustworthy, respectful) • Social support (i.e., emotional, instrumental)
Intrinsic Rewards	• Autonomy • Skill utilization • Task variety • Task identity • Creative freedom • Involvement and participation • Job-induced self-efficacy (e.g., job enables one to discover one's strengths) • General opportunities for growth and development
Extrinsic Rewards	• Fair pay • Perks • Other rewards for one's efforts
Organizational Support	• Efficient operations (i.e., policies, procedures) • Resources (i.e., people, things, training) • Communications • Role clarity
Work Demands & Balance	• Work demands (i.e., realistic) • Work–life balance

11 Discrimination in the Workplace and Employee Health

ROBERT L. DIPBOYE, BARBARA A. FRITZSCHE AND
LINDSAY DHANANI

Members of disadvantaged, historically oppressed and minority groups must often deal with the negative feelings, beliefs and actions of those belonging to dominant groups. Discrimination frequently occurs in the work organizations in which adults spend much of their waking lives, and the costs to the individual employees, organizations and society are too large to ignore. The present chapter addresses the consequences that experienced discrimination can have on physical and mental health, and offers possible solutions to create healthier work environments that embrace diversity, tolerance and inclusion.

The stress of discrimination can make people physically and mentally ill. Some sense of what victims experience comes from the vivid testimony of plaintiffs in recent discrimination lawsuits in the US and Great Britain.

> ... there was some days I go home and I just think about it, there was a lot of pain. ... My stomach, I would have pain. It was really—sometimes I used to ... just pull over for half an hour, just pull over because I don't want to have an accident, you know, after they call you camel, camel jockeys. (Kamil Issa and Edgar Rizkallah v. Roadway Package System, Inc., dba RPS, INC, et al, 2002, p. 626)

> ... That was probably the worst part. Being home with a new baby and being scared about how I was going to support her and my son and my husband and how the house payment was going to get made and how we're going to pay for this car that we had to buy. ... it's like when you think you're safe and secure and then all of a sudden the rug is like ripped out from under you. (Velez v. Novartis Corp., 04-cv-09194, U.S. District Court, Southern District of New York (Manhattan). (Amy Velez et al, v. Novartis Pharmaceuticals Corp., 2010, p. 2568)

> I had never been pushed to the brinks that I had been pushed to ... what happened, continually, on a daily and weekly basis for that long a period of time, created such an enormous amount of stress that I continually got sick, for like several years after the event, just from the high amount of stress and anxiety. I don't know if anybody could ever, ever understand what I went through. (Amy Valez et al, v. Novartis Pharmaceuticals Corp., 2010, p. 1732)

> The whole experience has been emotionally draining ...What happened sucked the life out of me and (now) I'm tired, emotional and always crying. (Sims, 2009)

In all four of these cases, substantial awards were given to the plaintiffs. Although the expense of litigation is one reason to avoid discrimination, the risk of monetary loss is exaggerated and should not be the primary motivation for creating nondiscriminatory workplaces. In the US, and possibly other countries, employers have the upper hand in that courts usually decide in favor of the defendant (Seiner, 2008). A very small percentage of those who perceive they have been discriminated against in the workplace file an internal or external complaint, and a tiny percentage of those succeed in their complaint (Neilson & Nelson, 2008; Ottinger, 2011).

Rather than focusing on the monetary costs associated with lawsuits and United States Equal Employment Opportunity Commission (EEOC) complaints, a less visible but far more pernicious cost of discrimination is the damage that discrimination can inflict on the health and well-being of employees. These costs deserve more attention and are a more important reason than avoiding lawsuits for organizations to create non-discriminatory work environments. In this chapter we will explore the impact of discrimination on the health and well-being of employees and consider approaches to creating a non-discriminatory work environment that eliminates these effects.

Perceived Discrimination as a Source of Health Disparities

Ethnic minorities and other historically marginalized groups are more likely to suffer mental and physical illnesses relative to those who are afforded higher status (Herek, Gillis & Cogan, 2009; Huebner & Davis, 2007; Landry & Mercurio, 2009; Mays, Cochran & Barnes, 2007; Meyer, 2003). Although several variables are entangled in these differences (Williams & Mohammed, 2009), the perception that one is the victim of unfair discrimination is a source of health disparities (Kessler, Mickelson & Williams, 1999).

Self-reports of discrimination in everyday life have been shown related to indicators of health and well-being. Studies have linked health outcomes to perceived discrimination on the basis of gender (for example, Goldenhar, Swanson, Hurrell, Ruder & Deddens, 1998), race (Clark, Anderson, Clark & Williams, 1999) and sexual orientation (for example, Waldo, 1999). Pascoe and Richman (2009) reported a recent meta-analysis of over 100 studies conducted between 1987 and 2007. They found that self-reports of being discriminated against were related to (1) heightened physiological and psychological stress responses; (2) more unhealthy behaviors (alcohol use, smoking and missed doctor appointments); (3) less healthy behaviors (such as getting enough sleep and exercise, and eating a healthy diet); (4) poorer physical health (for example, blood pressure, diabetes, pelvic inflammatory disease, cardiovascular disease, nausea, pain, headaches); and (5) poorer mental health (for example, reports of depression). Included in the meta-analysis were experiments in which perceptions of discrimination against others were manipulated. Short-term experimental manipulations of perceived discrimination against others were found to significantly impact stress responses of passive observers of discrimination.

DISCRIMINATION DOES NOT HAVE TO BE BLATANT TO WREAK HAVOC ON HEALTH

As social attitudes shift, so too does the nature of discrimination, making less overt forms of discrimination increasingly more common (Bobo, 1998; Sellers & Shelton, 2003).

Subtle forms of discrimination, which have also been termed microaggressions, are pervasive, everyday events that convey denigrating messages to members of minority groups (Sólorzano, Ceja & Yosso, 2000). Microaggressions include behaviors such as avoidance, unfriendly verbal and non-verbal communication, a lack of eye contact and unwillingness to provide assistance (Pettigrew & Martin, 1987). Subtle forms of discrimination are typically experienced far more frequently than overt forms of discrimination (Kessler, Mickelson & Williams, 1999) and can have a cumulative effect on the individual's well-being, leading to feelings of hopelessness, discouragement, self-doubt, isolation and resignation (Solórzano, Ceja & Yosso, 2000). Some evidence suggests that subtle discrimination may have a greater negative impact on health status than blatant forms of discrimination (Guyll, Matthews & Bromberger, 2001; Williams, Yu & Jackson, 1997). A person responding to blatant discrimination will be more likely to perceive social support and the perpetrator may be more likely to be blamed for the act, allowing the individual who perceived discrimination to better cope with the event (Guyll, Matthews & Bromberger, 2001).

Relation of Perceived Work Discrimination to Health and Well-being

The experience of subtle and overt discrimination, chronic stress, poorer health habits, and a lack of coping skills and access to coping resources all combine to create unhealthy environments for socially disadvantaged individuals (Taylor, Repetti & Seeman, 1997). Much of the previous research has focused on everyday discrimination in non-work settings, but a growing body of research indicates that the perception of workplace discrimination is a particularly important correlate of health and well-being. Perceived discrimination is related to poorer health and well-being regardless of whether the discrimination is based on gender, race or sexual orientation.

THE RELATION OF GENDER DISCRIMINATION AND SEXUAL HARASSMENT WITH WOMEN'S HEALTH AND WELL-BEING

Several researchers have focused specifically on gender discrimination. Female employees who reported more incidents of gender harassment and/or discrimination, also report more physical symptoms of poor health (Pavalko, Mossakowski & Hamilton, 2003; Raver & Nishii, 2010; Goldenhar, Swanson, Hurrell, Ruder & Deddens, 1998), lower mental health and higher psychological distress (Ajrouch, Reisine, Lim, Sohn & Ismail, 2010; Flores, Tschann, Dimas, Pasch & deGroat, 2010; Goldenhar, Swanson, Hurrell, Ruder & Deddens, 1998; Hatzenbuehler, 2009; Roberts, Swanson & Murphy, 2004), and lower job satisfaction, organizational commitment and well-being (Bond, Punnett, Pyle, Cazeca & Cooperman, 2004; Buchanan & Fitzgerald, 2008; Burke, 2004; Jick & Mitz, 1985; Nelson & Quick, 1985; Ryan, Haslam, Hersby, Kulich & Wilson-Kovacs, 2009). Using a more objective measure of health, another study found that reports of sexual harassment were positively related to elevated systolic blood pressure among women workers (Krieger, Chen, Waterman, Hartman, Stoddard, Quinn, Sorensen & Barbeau, 2008). In a study that used a large representative sample of working adults, and controlled for demographics, life stressors and job pressure reports, women who reported discrimination and harassment at work due to gender over the previous year were more likely to report problem drinking

(Rospenda, Richman & Shannon, 2009). Interestingly, in this same study, men who reported sexual harassment over the previous year were also more likely to report problem drinking.

THE RELATION OF PERCEIVED RACIAL DISCRIMINATION WITH HEALTH AND WELL-BEING

To the extent that employees perceive that they are discriminated against on the basis of race and ethnicity, they tend to report more physical symptoms of poor health (DeCastro, Gee & Takeuchi, 2008; Fujishiro, 2009; Raver & Nishii, 2010; Schneider, Hitlan & Radhakrishnan, 2000), more job stress and tension (Buchanan & Fitzgerald, 2008; Wated & Sanchez, 2006), higher blood pressure (Din-Dzietham, Nembhard, Collins & Davis, 2004; James, 1994; Richman, Pek, Pascoe & Bauer, 2010), more negative attitudes toward their work situation (Buchanan & Fitzgerald, 2008; Deitch, Barsky, Butz, Chan, Brief & Bradley, 2003; Ensher, Grant-Vallone & Donaldson, 2001), and lower mental health (Buchanan & Fitzgerald, 2008). Interestingly, one study found that receiving benefits because of discrimination against other groups was associated with negative health outcomes (Fujishiro, 2009). The researcher in this case analyzed data from a large national survey in which respondents were asked whether they were treated at work worse than, the same as, or better than people of other races over the last 12 months. No matter what the race of the respondent, self-reported negative treatment was positively related to self-reports of poorer health and more days of lost work due to poor health. Among white respondents, reports of being treated better than others on the basis of race was also related to poorer health and more days of work lost due to illness.

THE RELATION OF PERCEIVED DISCRIMINATION ON THE BASIS OF SEXUAL ORIENTATION WITH HEALTH AND WELL-BEING

Lesbian, bisexual and transgendered employees who report physical symptoms of illness and less satisfaction with their health also tend to report that they have been discriminated against on the basis of sexual orientation over the previous year (Waldo, 1999). Structural modeling suggested that the relation of perceived heterosexism and health conditions is mediated by psychological distress. In other surveys of gay and lesbian employees, perceived discrimination has been found to be associated with negative work attitudes and more negative job and career attitudes (James, Lovato & Cropanzano, 1994; Ragins & Cornwell, 2001).

Stress Mediates the Impact of Perceived Discrimination on Health and Well-being

An increasing amount of research and theory suggests that perceptions of discrimination harm health and well-being as the result of creating stress (for example, Goldenhar, Swanson, Hurrell, Ruder & Deddens, 1998; Hatzenbuehler, 2009; Meyer, 2003; Rusch, Corrigan, Wassel, Michaels, Olschewski, Wilkniss & Batia, 2009; Waldo, 1999). Discrimination is a stressor that elicits physiological responses as the victim prepares physically and mentally react to what they perceive as a threat, harm, or challenge (Richman, Bennett, Pek, Siegler &

Williams, 2007). A negative impact on health and well-being is most likely when individuals experience a sense that they lack the resources to deal with the discrimination and the associated physiological and psychological responses are sustained over time. In examining the role of stress as a mediator of the impact of discrimination on health outcomes and considering how an organization can create healthy work environments, it is useful to first explore each step in the process by which perceived discrimination creates stress that adversely affects health, starting with stressors in the form discrimination, the primary and secondary appraisal, and then coping.

DISCRIMINATION AS A STRESSOR

Discrimination is usually defined as the behavior of perpetrators toward the victim in which they treat the victim unfairly on the basis of group membership (for example, race, sex, sexual orientation, age). We would propose that prejudice, the negative feelings held toward persons on the basis of group membership, and stereotypes, the beliefs about persons belonging to a category, can also cause stress, independent of how members of the category are actually treated. On the one hand, a person may experience discrimination in the sense of an unfair allocation of resources (for example, promotions, salary increases, job assignments) in a work environment that appears quite tolerant and free of prejudice and stereotyping. On the other hand, members of an outgroup may not perceive discrimination in the way they are treated or the allocation of resources, but may still sense that their supervisors and peers are prejudiced and stereotype them. For instance, racial minority persons may not feel that they are discriminated against with regard to wages, job assignments, promotions and evaluations, but may still feel that supervisors and other employees hold prejudicial attitudes and stereotypes. Although discrimination, prejudice and stereotypes are independent stressors, in the interest of simplicity we will simply refer to discrimination to describe all three.

THE PERCEPTIONS OF DISCRIMINATION AS APPRAISAL

In transactional models of stress, an objective discriminatory event would be considered the stressor and the perception is an outcome of the appraisal of the stressor (Lazarus & Folkman, 1984). The primary appraisal of discrimination can be viewed as a process of prototype matching (Harris, Lievens & Van Hoye, 2004). People hold expectations or prototypes of what constitutes discrimination and then judge events that they observe against these prototypes in inferring whether they are the targets of unfair discrimination. Numerous scales have been used to measure perceptions of workplace discrimination (Burkard, Boticki & Madson, 2002), and there is some evidence that such measures are reliable and valid accounts of discriminatory events (Krieger, Smith, Naishadham, Hartman & Barbeau, 2005). From the perspective of stress theory, if members of a group perceive that they are the targets of unfair treatment, this perception is sufficient to indicate that there is a problem that needs to be addressed regardless of the veridicality of the report.

COPING WITH DISCRIMINATORY EVENTS

How individuals cope with discrimination reflects the emotions that result from the appraisal of the event such as anxiety, fear, disgust, anger, sadness as well as physiological responses associated with appraisal (Perrewe & Zellars, 1999). Although numerous alternative modes of coping exist, four strategies that have been distinguished are withdrawal (for example, avoiding the people who are the source of discrimination), reducing the emotions experienced (for example, drinking to reduce the anxiety), solving the problem (for example, filing a complaint) and seeking social support (for example, validating one's feelings and perceptions with others or banding together with others who are targets of discrimination). The effects on psychological and physical health occur as a consequence of long-term exposure to stressful events and the inability to successfully cope with these events.

Adaptive coping reduces the harmful physiological and psychological responses to discrimination whereas maladaptive coping fails in this regard. In general, active or problem-solving coping mechanisms, such as talking with friends about the event, are among the more adaptive coping responses (McNeilly, Anderson, McManus, Armstead, Clark, Pieper, Simons & Saulter, 1996). Another coping approach considered adaptive is attempting to solve the problem of discrimination through changing the situation or through self-improvement (Mallett & Swim, 2009). By comparison, more passive or avoidant coping mechanisms, such as substance use or keeping quiet have been found to be maladaptive, especially when used in response to chronic racism (Clark, Anderson, Clark & Williams, 1999; Pascoe & Richman, 2009; Utsey, Ponterotto, Reynolds & Cancelli, 2000). Another coping response that is often considered maladaptive is acting out or expressing hostility and anger (Armstead, Lawler, Gorden, Cross & Gibbons, 1989). Although proactive efforts to change oneself are generally adaptive, they can become maladaptive when targets of discrimination overcompensate in the belief that they must prove themselves. In so-called John-Henryism, the victims of discrimination attempt to compensate for perceptions that they are lazy or incompetent by exerting excessive amounts of effort that damage their health (James, Hartnett & Kalsbeek, 1983).

The act of acknowledging or denying discrimination can reflect a means of coping. Perceiving discrimination as the cause of a negative outcome can protect the self-esteem of members of the group that is discriminated against relative to denying discrimination (Crocker & Major, 1989). Several studies have reported a U-shaped relationship between reports of workplace discrimination and blood pressure in which those with the highest blood pressure were those who reported no discrimination and those who reported a high level of discrimination (Krieger, 1990; Krieger & Sidney, 1996; Huebner & Davis, 2007). Along similar lines, being able to attribute social exclusion at work to racism has been shown to buffer the negative effects of the exclusion on health (Schneider, Hitlan & Radhakrishnan, 2000).

Mediators and Moderators of the Stressful Consequences of Discrimination

Williams and Mohammed (2009) observe that not all stressful events have adverse impacts on health even when they are appraised as threats. Four particularly important variables influencing the impact of workplace discrimination on health and well-being are control over the stressors, identification with the group, social support and organizational climate.

CONTROL OVER THE STRESSORS

Those stressors that are perceived as less controllable are the ones that have the greater potential damage on health (Christie & Barling, 2009; Landry & Mercurio, 2009; Moradi & Hasan, 2004; Williams & Mohammed, 2009). Several researchers have extended these results to suggest that a sense of personal control mediates the adverse effects of perceived discrimination on mental health and well-being (Branscombe & Ellemers, 1998; Jang, Chiriboga, Kim & Rhew, 2010; Landry & Mercurio; 2009; Moradi & Hasan, 2004).

GROUP IDENTIFICATION

Consistent with Rejection-Identification model (Branscombe, Schmitt & Harvey, 1991), persons who perceive that they are discriminated against on the basis of their group membership identify more strongly with the group that is the source of the devaluation. This relation has been found for Jews, women, African Americans, lesbians, gay men and college students belonging to fringe groups such as punks and nerds (Armenta & Hunt, 2009). Moreover, employees strongly identifying with their race tend to interpret workplace incivility as discrimination (Kern & Grandey, 2009).

At the same time that identification with a group may enhance interpretation of adverse events as discrimination against that group, group identity also has been found to ameliorate the adverse effect of perceived discrimination on health. Sellers and Shelton (2003) found that respondents who emphasized the uniqueness of being African American evidenced less of a relation between perceptions of racial discrimination and psychological distress. The role of group identification as a buffer appears quite complex, however, and varies with the nature of the discrimination (Quinn & Chaudoir, 2009).

SOCIAL SUPPORT

The extent to which people perceive that they have social support has been shown to be an important correlate of how they experience and cope with stress (Thorsteinsson & James, 1999; Viswesvaran, Sanchez & Fisher, 1999). Ajrouch, Reisine, Lim, Sohn and Ismail (2010) found that African American women who reported that they were the targets of discrimination were less likely to report psychological distress if they also reported instrumental support from others than if they reported less support. As in the case of group identity, the relationship appears to differ as a function of the type of discrimination. In one study lesbian, gay and bisexual respondents reported more isolation and poorer quality social support in response to discrimination, whereas African Americans reported more social support and less isolation (Hatzenbuehler, 2009).

ORGANIZATIONAL CLIMATE

Organizations vary on the extent to which they are perceived as placing a high priority on supporting diversity and opposing discrimination (Buchanan & Fitzgerald, 2008; Buttner, Lowe & Billings-Harris, 2010; Pugh, Dietz, Brief & Wiley, 2008; Hanover & Cellar, 1998; Kunze, Boehm & Bruch, 2011; Merritt, Ryan, Mack, Leeds & Schmitt, 2010; Stewart, 2011). Employees who perceive discrimination on the basis of race, age, religion and disability tend to report more stress and lower job satisfaction than those who perceive a more tolerant organizational climate (Walsh, Matthews, Tuller, Parks & McDonald, 2010).

Creating Healthy Work Environments through Non-discrimination

The process by which stress mediates the impact of perceived discrimination on health and the research on the factors influencing this process suggest possible strategies that organizations can use to deal with the problem. The alternatives can be distinguished on the basis of the focus of the intervention.

INTERVENTIONS THAT FOCUS ON THOSE WHO ARE THE PERPETRATORS

One approach is to focus on the individuals and groups who are likely to engage in discrimination against members of stigmatized, disadvantaged and minority groups. By far the most prevalent intervention is diversity training. Such training typically attempts to improve the appreciation and management of diversity and almost always includes a component in which participants are made aware of their own biases and instructed in how to deal with these biases (Chrobot-Mason & Quiñones, 2002). Along these lines, diversity programs often include training in how to comply with civil rights laws and regulations and enhancement of skills in how to interact effectively with persons from other cultures and groups. Diversity training has evolved over the years from a primary focus on legal compliance to a greater focus on effective interaction and teamwork.

Such training has become widespread in organizations with 65 percent of large US employers using this training according to one survey (Esen, 2005). Diversity training appears to be effective in changing the knowledge and attitudes of participants in the direction of greater appreciation of diversity (Kulik & Roberson, 2008). There is also some evidence that increasing manager sensitivity to diversity and awareness of legal issues can lower employee grievances. However, the training may be less effective in improving interpersonal skills involved in managing diversity (Kulik & Roberson, 2008) and with participants from collectivistic as opposed to individualistic cultures (Holladay & Quiñones, 2005).

A problem with diversity training is that trainees often seem to resist and resent diversity training (Chrobot-Mason, Hays-Thomas & Wishik, 2008). One suggestion is to make the training more palpable by framing programs in a way that avoids the negative connotations of diversity (Holladay, Knight, Paige & Quiñones, 2003). Also, training should convey the business case for diversity and nondiscrimination by communicating in the language of management (Kormanik & Rajan, 2010), supporting the transfer of what is learned to the workplace (Roberson, Kulik & Pepper, 2009) and coaching managerial participants (Kormanik & Rajan, 2010). Having trainees empathize with the victims of discrimination may be more effective than teaching them to accurately identify discriminatory behavior (Dovidio, Vergert, Stewart, Gaertner, Johnson, Esses, Riek & Pearson, 2004).

FOCUSING ON THOSE WHO ARE THE VICTIMS OF DISCRIMINATION

Focusing attention on the persons and groups who are the potential targets of discrimination is another approach. Given that it is the sustained psychological and physiological responses to stress that eventually causes health problems, one approach is to train targets of discrimination to effectively manage their emotional responses. For instance, potential targets could be trained in stress management techniques such as relaxation, cognitive restructuring, meditation and the like. We would argue that such training runs the risk of encouraging perpetrators and victims to accept discrimination as the status quo. Helping potential victims reduce the negative emotions resulting from discrimination may be useful but it should never be the sole focus.

A more effective alternative is to teach potential targets how to take control of the situation and solve the problem of discrimination. Hirsh and Kmec (2009) evaluated one approach in which organizations trained employees who were potential targets of discrimination to be aware of civil rights laws and regulations, to recognize violations and how to submit complaints to the proper authorities. They found that hospitals in which this type of training was provided were more likely to receive complaints of discrimination than hospitals that did not. Is this a good thing? One can understand how managers might be uncomfortable with an approach that informs employees in how they can complain about discrimination. However, from a stress perspective, efforts to bolster employees' sense of control over discrimination may be crucial to eliminating the threat to health that perceived discrimination poses (Jang, Chiriboga, Kim & Rhew, 2010).

The targets of discrimination also could be helped in their efforts to eliminate prejudice by instructing them in how to manage impressions so as to contradict stereotypes (King, Shapiro, Hebl, Singletary & Turner, 2006). For instance, they could be instructed in how to exhibit non-verbal and verbal behaviors that are likely to convey positive impressions or how to effectively disclose stigma. Employees who were more politically skilled were found in one study to be less likely to experience job tension as a consequence of perceiving that others in the organization receive undeserved advantages (Hochwarter, Summers, Thompson, Perrewe & Ferris, 2010). One implication is to train potential targets of discrimination in political tactics and strategies that could be used to counteract discrimination.

Based on research showing that a positive identification with the group may be an effective buffer against the stress of discrimination, another strategy is to support devalued group identities. Branscombe, Schmitt and Harvey (1999) suggested that "celebrating multiculturalism could be an important means of increasing minority group identification and enhancing well-being. A multicultural society provides opportunities for people to identify with the devalued group, especially in comparison to an assimilationist society, which encourages people to think of themselves as individuals, not as group members." Examples of celebrating minority group identity would include the use of affinity groups, allowing employees to wear attire associated with their group identity, and holding events honoring holidays associated with the group.

Consistent with the research showing the importance of organizational climate, visible efforts should be made to signal to employees that diversity and non-discrimination is a high priority (Triana & Garcia, 2009; Triana, Garcia & Colella, 2010). It is not enough to simply do the right thing. Organizations should attempt to mold a shared perception of the organization as non-discriminatory and open to diversity by bringing attention to and celebrating efforts to improve tolerance. Also needed are organizational structures that support efforts to eliminate discrimination (Kalev, Kelly & Dobbin, 2006). Supportive structures include affirmative action plans, oversight and advocacy committees, and positions and departments responsible for implementing and monitoring the plans.

Although caution should be observed in reporting the results of rankings of organizations on their diversity friendliness, lessons can be learned from what appear to be strategies used by firms that appear to be among the best in promoting diversity and reducing discrimination. The top 50 US firms in their diversity efforts according to Diversity Inc magazine's yearly rankings are characterized by minorities and women in visible managerial positions, policies that go beyond what is legally required, organizational structures to promote and enforce these policies, flexible work arrangements, accountability for nondiscrimination, and the formation of groups to support ethnic and other minority identities (Diversity Inc, 2011).

1. *Diversity at the managerial ranks*. Firms are likely to reduce perceptions of discrimination by being proactive and assertive in their attempts to create a diverse workforce at all levels, including managerial levels. Hewlett-Packard, Palo Alto, CA, USA, has four Black women as vice-presidents. IBM, Armonk, NY has increased by 121 percent the number of black executives since 1995 with substantial representation at the highest levels of the executive leadership team. In Kaiser-Permanente in California, USA, Black, Latino and Asians constitute 50 percent of the board of directors and 38 percent of top management. Women make up 36 percent of the board of directors and 25 percent of the top management team.

2. *Organizational diversity policies*. The existence of no tolerance, formal policies that forbid discrimination, seems especially important to reducing minority stress (Ragins & Cornwell, 2001). All of the firms in the Diversity Inc top diversity-friendly corporations appear to have such policies. Unlike firms that restrict their policies to only those categories of discrimination forbidden by law, diversity friendly corporations extend their nondiscrimination policies to sexual orientation, which has yet to be covered under US Federal laws. Merrill Lynch, New York, allows individuality in dress and hairstyles (for example, women with buzz cuts, twists and braids, ethnic themes in business attire).

3. *Flexible work arrangements*. Since much of the stress associated with gender discrimination is associated with work–family conflict, it is not surprising that some of the most diversity-friendly firms encourage flexibility in work schedules and settings. An example is General Electric Co., Fairfield, Connecticut, which makes available to all workers a variety of flexible options including job sharing and compressed workweeks. Such arrangements not only help the potential targets of discrimination but also yield benefits for all workers, as seen by the fact that about half of GE employees take advantage of these options.

4. *Holding employees accountable for non-discrimination*. Sodexo cites diversity and inclusion as one of six strategic corporate imperatives. Twenty-five percent of executive bonuses are based on showing gains on metrics aimed at measuring executive performance on these dimensions. Interestingly, bonuses are paid for gains independent of the overall financial performance of the firm. Moreover, non-discrimination policies are visibly enforced at all levels of the organization.

5. *High-level positions with responsibility for diversity and non-discrimination with authority to implement policy*. Firms that are best on diversity and non-discrimination have official positions and occupants of these positions are given the authority to aggressively pursue initiatives. Sodexo has a senior vice president who oversees what appears to be a highly successful cross-divisional and cross-functional mentoring program,

diversity training at all levels, affinity groups and leadership development programs aimed at fostering management talent among diverse groups of employees.

6. *Groups to support networking and support among employees with common attributes or heritage.* There are numerous affinity groups at Sodexo including the *African American Leadership Forum, Honoring Our Nation's Finest with Opportunity and Respect* (a military network group), *Diversity and Equality* (a gay, lesbian, bisexual and transgender employee group), and *Sodexo Organization for Disabilities Resources.* Eli Lilly and Company currently has eight affinity groups including the Lilly's Chinese Culture Network, the women's Network, the India Club and deaf-employee networks. Over 25 percent of employees at Johnson & Johnson participate in one or more of ten affinity groups.

Conclusion

As described in this chapter, perceived discrimination is a psychosocial stressor that contributes to the development of unhealthy work environments for women, minorities and stigmatized persons who are the targets of discrimination. Research is mounting that shows the devastating effects of an unhealthy work environment on the physical and mental health of employees, especially those who deal with other social, family and economic environments that are unhealthy (Krieger, 1999; Taylor et al., 1997). When discrimination results in underemployment or lack of employment, the health risks are even greater (Blustein, 2008). Moreover, the health of non-minorities and other socially advantaged individuals is also impacted. Over 60 percent of employees report experiencing day-to-day workplace discrimination (Kessler, Mickelson & Williams, 1999), and studies show negative effects on the health of bystanders who observe discrimination against others (Pascoe & Richman, 2009). Clearly, perceived discrimination is a serious health problem affecting large segments of the working population. Reducing discrimination, using some of the ideas presented here, should be a key focus of workplace initiatives to create environments characterized by psychological safety, control, fairness, and where individuals can form positive social ties, so that employees can thrive and have healthy, satisfying work lives.

References

Ajrouch, K. J., Reisine, S., Lim, S., Sohn, W., & Ismail, A. (2010) Perceived everyday discrimination and psychological distress: does social support matter? *Ethnicity & Health*, 15(4), 417–434.

Armenta, B. E., & Hunt, J. S. (2009) Responding to societal devaluation: effects of perceived personal and group discrimination on the ethnic group identification and personal self-esteem of Latino/ Latina adolescents. *Group Processes & Intergroup Relations*, 12(1), 23–39.

Armstead, C. A., Lawler, K. A., Gorden, G., Cross, J., & Gibbons, J. (1989) Relationship of racial stressors to blood pressure responses and anger expression in Black college students. Health Psychology, 8(5), 541–556.

Amy Valez et al v. Novartis Pharmaceutical Corporation p4-cv-09194 pp. 2524–2677. (US District Court, Southern District of New York 2010).

Blustein, D. L. (2008) The role of work in psychological health and well-being: A conceptual, historical, and public policy perspective. *American Psychologist*, 63, 228–240.

Bobo, L. (1998) Race, interests, and beliefs about affirmative action: unanswered questions and new directions. *American Behavioral Scientist*, 41, 985–1003.

Bond, M. A., Punnett, L., Pyle, J. L., Cazeca, D., & Cooperman, M. (2004) Gendered work conditions, health, and work outcomes. *Journal of Occupational Healthy Psychology*, 9, 28–45.

Branscombe, N. R., & Ellemars, N. (1998) Coping with group-based discrimination: Individualistic versus group-level strategies. In J. K. Swim & C. Strangor (eds) *Prejudice: The Target's Perspective*. San Diego, CA: Academic Press. pp. 243–266.

Branscombe, N. R., Schmitt, M. T., & Harvey, R. D. (1999) Perceiving pervasive discrimination among African Americans: implications for group identification and well-being. *Journal of Personality and Social Psychology*, 77, 135–149.

Buchanan, N. T., & Fitzgerald, L. F. (2008) Effects of racial and sexual harassment on work and the psychological well-being of African American women. *Journal of Occupational Health Psychology*, 13, 137–151.

Burkard, A. W., Boticki, M. A., & Madson, M. B. (2002) Workplace discrimination, prejudice, and diversity measurement: a review of instrumentation. *Journal of Career Assessment*, 10(3), 343–361.

Burke, R. J. (2004). Work experiences, stress and health among managerial women: Research and practice. In M. J. Schabracq, J. A. M. Winnubst, & C. L. Cooper (eds) *The Handbook of Work and Health Psychology* (2nd ed.). Chichester, England: Wiley. pp. 259–278.

Buttner, E., Lowe, K. B., & Billings-Harris, L. (2010) Diversity climate impact on employee of color outcomes: does justice matter? *The Career Development International*, 15(3), 239–258.

Christie, A. M., & Barling, J. (2009) Disentangling the indirect links between socioeconomic status and health: the dynamic roles of work stressors and personal control. *Journal of Applied Psychology*, 94, 1466–1478.

Chrobot-Mason, D., Hays-Thomas, R., & Wishik, H. (2008) Understanding and defusing resistance to diversity training and learning. In K. M. Thomas & K. M. Thomas (eds) *Diversity Resistance in Organizations*. New York, NY: Taylor & Francis Group/Lawrence Erlbaum Associates. pp. 23–54.

Chrobot-Mason, D., & Quiñones, M. A. (2002) Training for a diverse workplace. In K. Kraiger (ed.) *Creating, Implementing and Managing Effective Training and Development*. San Francisco, CA: Jossey-Bass.

Clark, R., Anderson, N. B., Clark, V. R., & Williams, D. R. (1999) Racism as a stressor for African Americans: a biopsychosocial model. *American Psychologist*, 54, 805–816.

Crocker, J., & Major, B. (1989) Social stigma and self-esteem: the self-protective properties of stigma. *Psychological Review*, 96(4), 608–630.

De Castro, A. B., Gee, G. C., & Takeuchi, D. T. (2008) Workplace discrimination and health among Filipinos in the United States. *American Journal of Public Health*, 98, 520–526.

Deitch, E. A., Barsky, A., Butz, R. M., Chan, S., Brief, A. P., & Bradley, J. C. (2003) Subtle yet significant: the existence and impact of everyday racial discrimination in the workplace. *Human Relations*, 56, 1299–1324.

Din-Dzietham, R., Nembhard, W. N., Collins, R., & Davis, S. K. (2004) Perceived stress following race-based discrimination at work is associated with hypertension in African-Americans. The metro Atlanta heart disease study, 1999–2001. *Social Science & Medicine*, 58 (3), 449–461.

DiversityInc. The DiversityInc Top 50 Companies for Diversity®. Available at: http://www.diversityinc.com/pages/DI_50_2011.shtml. Retrieved August 17, 2011.

Dovidio, J. F., Vergert, M. T., Stewart, T. L., Gaertner, S. L., Johnson, J. D., Esses, V. M., Riek, B. M., & Pearson, A. R. (2004) Perspective and prejudice: antecedents and mediating mechanisms. *Personality and Social Psychology Bulletin*, 30, 1537–1549.

Ensher, E. A., Grant-Vallone, E. J., & Donaldson, S. I. (2001) Effects of perceived discrimination on job satisfaction, organizational commitment, organizational citizenship behavior, and grievances. *Human Resource Development Quarterly*, 12(1), 53–72.

Esen, E. (2005) *2005 Workplace Diversity Practices Survey Report*. Alexandria, VA: Society for Human Resource Management.

Flores, E., Tschann, J. M., Dimas, J. M., Pasch, L. A., & deGroat, C. L. (2010) Perceived racial/ethnic discrimination, posttraumatic stress symptoms, and health risk behaviors among Mexican American adolescents. *Journal of Counseling Psychology*, 57, 264–273.

Fujishiro, K. (2009) Is perceived racial privilege associated with health? Findings from the behavioral risk factor surveillance system. *Social Science and Medicine*, 68, 840–844.

Goldenhar, L. M., Swanson, N. G., Hurrell, J. J., Ruder, A., & Deddens, J. (1998) Stressors and adverse outcomes for female construction workers. *Journal of Occupational Health Psychology*, 3, 19–32.

Guyll, M., Matthews, K. A., & Bromberger, J. T. (2001) Discrimination and unfair treatment: relationship to cardiovascular reactivity among African American and European American women. *Health Psychology*, 20, 315–325.

Hanover, J. B., & Cellar, D. F. (1998) Environmental factors and the effectiveness of workforce diversity training. *Human Resource Development Quarterly*, 9(2), 105–124.

Harrell, J. P., Hall, S., & Taliaferro, J. (2003) Physiological responses to racism and discrimination: an assessment of the evidence. *American Journal of Public Health*, 93(2), 243–248.

Harris, M. M., Lievens, F., & Van Hoye, G. (2004) "I think they discriminated against me": using prototype theory and organizational justice theory for understanding perceived discrimination in selection and promotion situations. *International Journal of Selection and Assessment*, 12, 54–65.

Hatzenbuehler, M. L. (2009) How does sexual minority stigma "get under the skin"? A psychological mediation framework. *Psychological Bulletin*, 135, 707–730.

Herek, G. M., Gillis, J. R., & Cogan, J. C. (2009) Internalized stigma among sexual minority adults: Insights from a social psychological perspective. *Journal of Counseling Psychology*, 56, 32–43.

Hirsh, E., & Kmec, J. A. (2009) Human resource structures: reducing discrimination or raising rights awareness? *Industrial Relations*, 48, 512–532.

Hochwarter, W. A., Summers, J. K., Thompson, K. W., Perrewe, P. L., & Ferris, G. R. (2010) Strain reactions to perceived entitlement behavior by others as a contextual stressor: moderating role of political skill in three samples. *Journal of Organizational Health Psychology*, 15, 388–398.

Holladay, C. L., Knight, J. L., Paige, D. L., & Quiñones, M. A. (2003) The influence of framing on attitudes toward diversity training. *Human Resource Development Quarterly*, 14(3), 245–263.

Holladay, C. L., & Quinones, M. A. (2005) Reactions to diversity training: an international comparison. *Human Resource Development Quarterly*, 16, 529–545.

Huebner, D. M., & Davis, M. C. (2007) Perceived antigay discrimination and physical health outcomes. *Health Psychology*, 26, 627–634.

James, K. (1994) Social identity, work stress, and minority workers' health. In G. Keita, J.r. Hurrell, G. Keita, J.r. Hurrell (eds) *Job Stress in a Changing Workforce: Investigating Gender, Diversity, and Family Issues*. American Psychological Association. pp. 127–145.

James, S. A., Hartnett, S. A., & Kalsbeek, W. D. (1983) John Henryism and blood pressure differences among Black men. *Journal of Behavioral Medicine*, 6(3), 259–278.

Jang, Y., Chiriboga, D. A., Kim, G., & Rhew, S. (2010) Perceived discrimination, sense of control, and depressive symptoms among Korean American Older Adults. *Asian American Journal of Psychology*, 1, 129–135.

Jick, T. D., & Mitz, L. F. (1985) Sex differences in work stress. *Academy of Management Review*, 10(3), 408–420.

Kalev, A., Kelly, E., & Dobbin, F. (2006) Best practices or best guesses? Assessing the efficacy of corporate affirmative action and diversity policies. *American Sociological Review*, 71, 589–617.

Kamil Issa and Edgar Rizkallah v. Roadway Package System, Inc., dba RPS, Inc, et al. Volume III CSR No. 7913, pp. 420–646 (Superior Court of California 2002).

Kern, J. H., & Grandey, A. A. (2009) Customer incivility as a social stressor: the role of race and racial identity for service employees. *Journal of Occupational Health Psychology*, 14, 46–57.

Kessler, R. C., Mickelson, K. D., & Williams, D. R. (1999) The prevalence, distribution, and mental health correlates of perceived discrimination in the United States. *Journal of Health and Social Behavior*, 4, 208–230.

King, E. B., Shapiro, J. R., Hebl, M. R., Singletary, S. L., & Turner, S. (2006) The stigma of obesity in customer service: a mechanism for remediation and bottom-line consequences of interpersonal discrimination. *Journal of Applied Psychology*, 91, 579–593.

Krieger, N. (1999) Embodying inequality: A review of concepts, measures, and methods for studying health consequences of discrimination. *International Journal of Health Services*, 29, 295–352.

Kormanik, M. B., & Rajan, H. C. (2010) Implications for diversity in the HRD curriculum drawn from current organizational practices in addressing workforce diversity in management training. *Advances in Developing Human Resources*, 12, 367–384.

Kossek, E. E., & Zonia, S. C. (1993) Assessing diversity climate: a field study of reactions to employer efforts to promote diversity. *Journal of Organizational Behavior*, 14, 61–81.

Krieger, N. (1990) Racial and gender discrimination: risk factors for high blood pressure? *Social Science & Medicine*, 30, 1273–1281.

Krieger, N., Chen, J. T., Waterman, P. D., Hartman, C., Stoddard, A. M., Quinn, M. M., Sorensen, G., & Barbeau, E. M. (2008) The inverse hazard law: blood pressure, sexual harassment, racial discrimination, workplace abuse and occupational exposures in US low-income black, white, and Latino workers. *Social Science and Medicine*, 67, 1970–1981.

Krieger, N., & Sidney, S. (1996) Racial discrimination and blood pressure: the CARDIA study of young black and white adults. *American Journal of Public Health*, 86(10), 1370–1378.

Krieger, N., Smith, K., Naishadham, D., Hartman, C., & Barbeau, E. M. (2005) Experiences of discrimination: validity and reliability of a self-report measure for population health research on racism and health. *Social Science & Medicine*, 61, 1576–1596.

Kulik, C. T., & Roberson, L. (2008) Common goals and golden opportunities: evaluations of diversity education in academic and organizational settings. *Academy of Management Learning and Education*, 7(3), 309–331.

Kunze, F., Boehm, S. A., & Bruch, H. (2011) Age diversity, age discrimination climate and performance consequences—a cross organizational study. *Journal of Organizational Behavior*, 32, 264–290.

Landry, L. J., & Mercurio, A. E. (2009) Discrimination and women's mental health: the mediating role of control. *Sex Roles*, 61, 192–203.

Lazarus, R. S., & Folkman, S. (1984) *Stress, Appraisal, and Coping*. New York: Springer Publishing Company.

James, K., Lovato, C., & Cropanzano, R. (1994) Correlational and known-group comparison validation of a workplace prejudice/discrimination inventory. *Journal Of Applied Social Psychology*, 24(17), 1573–1592.

Mallett, R. K., & Swim, J. K. (2009) Making the best of a bad situation: proactive coping with racial discrimination. *Basic and Applied Social Psychology*, 31(4), 304–316.

Mays, V. M., Cochran, S. D., & Barnes, N. W. (2007) Race, race-based discrimination and health outcomes among African Americans. *Annual Review of Psychology*, 58, 201–225.

McNeilly, M., Anderson, N. B., Robinson, E. F., McManus, C. F., Armstead, C. A., Clark, R., Pieper, C. F., Simons, C., & Saulter, T. D. (1996) The convergent, discriminant, and concurrent criterion validity of the perceived racism scale: A multidimensional assessment of White racism among African Americans. In R. L. Jones (ed.) *Handbook of Tests and Measurements for Black Populations*. Hampton, VA: Cobb and Henry. Vol. 2, pp. 359–374.

Merritt, S. M., Ryan, A. M., Mack, M. J., Leeds, J. P., & Schmitt, N. (2010) Perceived ingroup and outgroup preference: a longitudinal causal investigation. *Personnel Psychology*, 63, 845–879.

Meyer, I. H. (2003) Prejudice, social stress, and mental health in lesbian, gay, and bisexual populations: conceptual issues and research evidence. *Psychological Bulletin*, 129, 674–697.

Moradi, B., & Hasan, N. T. (2004) Arab American persons' reported experiences of discrimination and mental health: the mediating role of personal control. *Journal of Counseling Psychology*, 4, 418–428.

Nelson, D. L., & Quick, J. C. (1985) Professional women: are distress and disease inevitable?. *Academy of Management Review*, 10(2), 206–218.

Nielsen, L. B., & Nelson, R. L. (2008) Scaling the pyramid: a sociolegal model of employment discrimination. In L. B. Neilson & R. L. Nelson (eds) *Handbook of Employment Discrimination Research: Rights and Realities*. New York London: Springer. pp. 3–32.

Ottinger, R. (2011) Employment discrimination verdicts often get reduced on appeal. *Wall Street Journal*. Available online at: http://www.newyorkemploymentlawyerblog.com/2011/06/employment_discrimination_verd.html, accessed July 29, 2011.

Pascoe, E. A., & Richman, L. S. (2009) Perceived discrimination and health: a meta-analytic review. *Psychological Bulletin*, 135, 531–554.

Pavalko, E. K., Mossakowski, K. N., & Hamilton, V. J. (2003) Does perceived discrimination affect health? Longitudinal relationships between work discrimination and women's physical and emotional health. *Journal of Health and Social Behavior*, 4, 18–33.

Perrewe, P. L., & Zellars, K. L. (1999) An examination of attributions and emotions in the transactional approach to the organizational stress process. *Journal of Organizational Behavior*, 20, 739–752.

Pettigrew, T. F., & Martin, J. (1987) Shaping the organizational context for Black American inclusion. *Journal of Social Issues*, 43, 41–78.

Pugh, S., Dietz, J., Brief, A. P., & Wiley, J. W. (2008) Looking inside and out: the impact of employee and community demographic composition on organizational diversity climate. *Journal of Applied Psychology*, 93(6), 1422–1428.

Quinn, D. M., & Chaudoir, S. R. (2009) Living with a concealable stigmatized identity: the impact of anticipated stigma, centrality, salience, and cultural stigma on psychological distress and health. *Journal of Personality and Social Psychology*, 97, 634–651.

Ragins, B. R., & Cornwell, J. M. (2001) Pink triangles: antecedents and consequences of perceived workplace discrimination against gay and lesbian employees. *Journal of Applied Psychology*, 86, 1244–1261.

Raver, J. L., & Nishii, L. H. (2010) Once, twice, or three times as harmful? Ethnic harassment, gender harassment, and generalized workplace harassment. *Journal of Applied Psychology*, 95, 236–254.

Richman, L. S., Bennett, G. G., Pek, J., Siegler, I., & Williams, R. B. (2007) Discrimination, dispositions, and cardiovascular responses to stress. *Health Psychology*, 26, 675–683.

Richman, L. S., Pek, J., Pascoe, E., & Bauer, D. J. (2010) The effects of perceived discrimination on ambulatory blood pressure and affective responses to interpersonal stress modeled over 24 hours. *Health Psychology*, 29, 403–411.

Roberson, L., Kulik, C. T., & Pepper, M. B. (2009) Individual and environmental factors influencing the use of transfer strategies after diversity training. *Group & Organization Management*, 34(1), 67–89.

Roberts, R. K., Swanson, N. G., & Murphy, L. R. (2004) Discrimination and occupational mental health. *Journal of Mental Health*, 13, 129–142.

Rospenda, K. M., Richman, J. A., & Shannon, C. A. (2009) Prevalence and mental health correlates of harassment and discrimination in the workplace: results from a national study. *Journal of Interpersonal Violence*, 24, 819–843.

Rusch, N., Corrigan, P. W., Wassel, A., Michaels, P., Olschewski, M., Wilkniss, S., & Batia, K. (2009) A stress-coping model of mental illness stigma: predictors of cognitive stress appraisal. *Schizophrenia Research*, 110, 59–64.

Ryan, M. K., Haslam, S., Hersby, M. D., Kulich, C., & Wilson-Kovacs, M. (2009) The stress of working on the edge: implications of glass cliffs for both women and organizations. In M. Barreto, M. K. Ryan, M. T. Schmitt, M. Barreto, M. K. Ryan & M. T. Schmitt (eds) *The Glass Ceiling in the 21st Century: Understanding Barriers to Gender Equality*. American Psychological Association. pp. 153–169.

Schneider, K. T., Hitlan, R. T., & Radhakrishnan, P. (2000) An examination of the nature and correlates of ethnic harassment: experiences in multiple contexts. *Journal of Applied Psychology*, 85, 3–12.

Seiner, J. A. (2008) The failure of punitive damages in employment discrimination cases: a call for change. *William & Mary Law Review*, 50, 735–796.

Sellers, R. M., & Shelton, J. N. (2003) The role of racial identity in perceived racial discrimination. *Journal of Personality and Social Psychology*, 84, 1079–1092.

Sims, P. (April 6, 2009) Asian council officer told to eat alone because she did not 'fit in' wins £112,000 race case payout. MailOnline. Available online at: http://www.dailymail.co.uk/news/article-1167984/Asian-council-officer-told-eat-did-fit-wins-112-000-race-case-payout.html. Accessed July 30, 2011.

Solórzano, D., Ceja, M., & Yosso, T. (2000) Critical race theory, racial microaggressions and campus racial climate: the experiences of African-American college students, *Journal of Negro Education*, 69(1/2), 60–73.

Stewart, R. W. (2011) You support diversity, but are you ethical? Examining the interactive effects of diversity and ethical climate perceptions on turnover intentions. *Journal of Business Ethics*, 99(3), 453–465.

Taylor, S. E., Repetti, R. L., & Seeman, T. (1997). Health psychology: What is an unhealthy environment and how does it get under the skin? *Annual Review of Psychology*, 48, 411–447.

Thorsteinsson, E. B., & James, J. E. (1999) A meta-analysis of the effects of experimental manipulations of social support during laboratory stress. *Psychology & Health*, 14(5), 869–886.

Triana, M. D. C., & Garcia, M. F. (2009) Valuing diversity: a group-value approach to understanding the importance of organizational efforts to support diversity. *Journal of Organizational Behavior*, 30, 941–962.

Triana, M. D. C., Garcia, M. F., & Colella, A. (2010) Managing diversity: how organizational efforts to support diversity moderate the effects of perceived racial discrimination on affective commitment. *Personnel Psychology*, 63, 817–843.

Utsey, S. O., Ponterotto, J. G., Reynolds, A. L., & Cancelli, A. A. (2000) Racial discrimination, coping, life satisfaction, and self-esteem among African Americans. *Journal of Counseling & Development*, 78, 72–80.

Visweswaran, C., Sanchez, J. I., & Fisher, J. (1999) The role of social support in the process of work stress: a meta-analysis. *Journal of Vocational Behavior*, 54, 314–334.

Waldo, C. R. (1999) Working in a majority context: a structural model of heterosexism as minority stress in the workplace. *Journal of Counseling Psychology*, 46, 218–232.

Walsch, B. M., Matthews, R. A., Tuller, M. D., Parks, K. M., & McDonald, D. P. (2010) A multilevel model of the effects of equal opportunity climate on job satisfaction in the military. *Journal of Occupational Health Psychology*, 15(2), 191–207.

Wated, G., & Sanchez, J. I. (2006) The role of accent as a work stressor on attitudinal and health-related work outcomes. *International Journal of Stress Management*, 13, 329–350.

Williams, D. R., & Mohammed, S. A. (2009) Discrimination and racial disparities in health: evidence and needed research. *Journal of Behavioral Medicine*, 32(1), 20–47.

Williams, D. R., Yu, Y., & Jackson, J. S. (1997) Racial differences in physical and mental health: socioeconomic status, stress, and discrimination. *Journal of Health Psychology, 2*, 335–351.

12 Changing Sexual Harassment within Organizations via Training Interventions: Suggestions and Empirical Data[1]

VICKI J. MAGLEY,[2] LOUISE F. FITZGERALD, JAN SALISBURY,
FRITZ DRASGOW AND MICHAEL J. ZICKAR

Just as no organization can ever be free of job stress, no organization can be entirely free of sexual harassment. In this chapter, we present an overview of using training to reduce the incidence of sexual harassment, from which employee well-being is protected. Although organizational training programs designed to sensitize employees to the seriousness of sexual harassment and increase their knowledge of organizational procedures and policies have become common, evaluation of the effectiveness of such programs has been almost non-existent (Fitzgerald & Shullman, 1993; Goldberg, 2011; Grundmann, O'Donohue & Peterson, 1997; Perry, Kulik & Field, 2009). Although stated over 15 years ago, Pryor and McKinney's (1995, p. 609) assertion, "perhaps the most alarming gap in the literature on sexual harassment is in the area of evaluation research," remains all too current. The reason for this lack of evaluation is very head-in-the-sand: if the organization does not ask whether its training was effective, it does not have to be accountable for continued corrective actions. We argue here that not all sexual harassment training is equal in possible positive organizational change and provide suggestions for Best Practice components. Additionally, we present empirical data from two organizations that delivered sexual harassment awareness training that meets many of these components. Before doing so, however, a review of the existing underlying rationale for such training and existing empirical evaluations is in order.

1   The authors would like to thank Charles L. Hulin, Kimberly Schneider and members of the SexHarass research lab for their assistance in data collection and thoughtful comments. Portions of this manuscript were presented at the annual meeting of the Society for Industrial and Organizational Psychology, St. Louis, MO, April 1997. The research reported here was supported by a Shannon Award and by grant number 1 R01 MH50791-01A2 from the National Institute of Mental Health.

2   Correspondence concerning this article should be addressed to Vicki J. Magley, Department of Psychology, University of Connecticut, 406 Babbidge Road, Unit 1020, Storrs, CT 06269-1020. Electronic mail may be sent to vicki.magley@uconn.edu.

Why Companies Implement Sexual Harassment Training

Organizations' interest in conducting sexual harassment awareness training is multi-faceted. Although organizational research has increased awareness of the negative impact of sexual harassment on individuals and organizations (for example, Coles, 1986; Dansky & Kilpatrick, 1997; Schneider, Swan & Fitzgerald, 1997), high-profile incidents, such as the Tailhook scandal and the Mitsubishi $34 million class action settlement, have certainly heightened organizational sensitivity to the issue. Perhaps most motivating is the possibility of reduced legal liability by implementing training as alluded to in the Supreme Court's jointly-decided 1998 sexual harassment cases of *Burlington Industries, Inc. v. Ellerth* and *Faragher v. City of Boca Raton* and more blatantly stated in the Equal Employment Opportunity Commission's (EEOC updated 1999 Guidelines regarding supervisory harassment (Bell, Cycyota & Quick, 2002; Bell, Quick & Cycyota, 2002; Bisom-Rapp, 2001; Grossman, 2003). If not voluntarily undertaken, numerous organizations also conduct sexual harassment training as a result of legal settlements or, as is the case in Connecticut, Maine and California, mandates from state legislatures (Martucci & Lu, 2005).

The implementation of such training programs is not foolproof, however, in satisfying such mandates or liability protection efforts. As even very early case law grappled with interpreting the Supreme Court decisions (c.f., Baty v. Willamette Industry, 1999; Bremiller v. Cleveland Psychiatric Institute, 2000; Gauthier v. New Hampshire Department of Corrections, 2000; Ogden v. Wax Works, Inc., 1999; Powell v. Morris and Ohio Department of Rehabilitation and Correction, 1999; Williams v. Spartan Communication, Inc., 2000), it was clear that organizational liability hinges on *effective* rather than *mere presence* of training. Additionally, training follow-up, as well as serious efforts to reduce any retaliatory actions, are equally important in documenting that the organization does not tolerate sexual harassment. Given such importance within a legal framework, evidence of the effectiveness of training programs in reducing sexual harassment incidence rates, changing attitudes about sexual harassment, and increasing knowledge of organizational policy and procedures would be beneficial to both organizations and the courts.

Unfortunately, sexual harassment training programs often lack well-articulated theoretical or empirical foundations (Grundmann, O'Donohue & Peterson, 1997), thus rendering any evaluation quite difficult. Varying along many dimensions (for example, length, formality, amount of integration with other training and/or employees' normal work routine), such programs lack consistent rationales, goals or procedures and little research exists to guide their development or to assess their effectiveness.

GOALS OF HARASSMENT PREVENTION PROGRAMS

Although the overarching goal of sexual harassment prevention programs is just that, such programs accomplish this goal in a variety of ways. For example, one of the primary functions of these interventions is to train supervisors and employees to recognize sexual harassment and to understand the organization's policies and procedures for responding to potential incidents (Aalberts & Seidman, 1996). Thus, such *communicative training programs* communicate the mechanisms of the organization's policies to both employees and management. Such efforts—if carried out appropriately—would presumably alter the organization's climate toward sexual harassment, where climate can be conceptualized as shared values, beliefs and principles that employees perceive are held within their organization (Schneider, 1975).

A second aspect of training programs is to sensitize employees to the seriousness of sexual harassment. These *sensitivity programs* may include role-play activities in which employees take on the parts of victims and harassers (Thacker, 1994), video-tape presentations of harassment scenarios, and discussions among male and female employees about the degree of offensiveness of sexual harassment. Thus, the goal of sensitivity programs is to reduce the incidence of sexual harassment by altering individual-level attitudes about sexual harassment, as well as individual-level understanding of how and why sexual harassment has deleterious effects on their workplace. For example, men who might have previously told crude jokes about women without understanding the impact of such behavior may subsequently refrain from doing so.

Outside of the sexual harassment literature, there has been extensive research on the effectiveness of sensitivity training in improving empathy toward co-workers. In a meta-analysis across 63 studies, Faith, Wong and Carpenter (1995) found a mean effect size of $d = .62$, indicating that sensitivity training had a moderate effect on outcomes. However, their research failed to identify which types of organizational outcomes were changed as an effect of this training. It is also unclear whether or how general sensitivity relates to sensitivity toward sexual harassment. Thus, Faith, Wong and Carpenter's (1995) research is encouraging but leaves many questions unanswered.

Although important, the distinction between communicative and sensitization programs is largely theoretical. In practice, most training programs incorporate both types of material and aim to change both knowledge of organizational policies and individual attitudes. Participants in a well-designed prevention program should demonstrate both increased knowledge of sexual harassment in general, as well as the policies of the organization and increased sensitivity regarding the seriousness of sexual harassment.

Previous Research on Sexual Harassment Prevention

Few studies exist that empirically evaluate programs designed to prevent sexual harassment. As one example of such research, Maurizio and Rogers (1992) evaluated an educational program designed to increase the knowledge of sexual harassment and to change the attitudes toward sexual harassment in a sample of community care workers. This two and a half hour training program used handouts, discussion and role playing in groups of 60 employees. Attitudes toward sexual harassment and knowledge of sexual harassment were assessed prior to training for half of the participants and immediately after training for the other half. Participants who completed the post-training surveys were more likely to correctly define sexual harassment, understand its legal ramifications, evaluate it as more of a problem at work than previously thought and report less victim-blaming attitudes. Unfortunately, these results are seriously weakened by not assessing pre-training attitudes on the same group of employees who took the post-training assessment. Also problematic is the immediacy of the post-training assessment; it is unclear whether the change due to training would be sustained over longer periods of time. Finally, 95 percent of the sample was female; as previous research has shown that attitudes and cognitions about sexual harassment differ vastly for men and women (Berdahl, Magley & Waldo, 1996; Frazier, Cochran & Olson, 1995; Rotundo, Nguyen & Sackett, 2001), differential effects of training programs on men and women should be more carefully considered.

It is inaccurate to say that there has not been any research conducted on sexual harassment training programs. Because Goldberg (2011) very recently reviewed the existing studies, it would be redundant to repeat that detailed of an account here. (To benefit the reader, though, we do provide a listing of the studies that we have found to date: Antecol & Cobb-Clark, 2003; Barak, 1994; Beauvais, 1986; Bingham & Scherer, 2001; Blakely, Blakely & Moorman, 1998; Blaxall, Parsonson & Robertson, 1993; Bonate & Jessell, 1996; Goldberg, 2007; Jacobs, Bergen & Korn, 2000; Kearney, Rochlen & King, 2004; Moyer & Nath, 1998; Perry, Kulik & Schmidtke, 1998; Preusser, Bartels & Nordstrom, 2011; Robb & Doverspike, 2001; Roscoe, Strouse, Goodwin, Taracks & Henderson, 1994; York, Barclay & Zajack, 1997.) Despite the growing body of research, we have to admit a certain level of dissatisfaction with the bulk of it. Without going into the details, suffice it to say that the literature generally suffers from studies that have questionable or non-existent comparison groups, post-training-only designs, short (occasionally immediate) post-training time lags and small, student-only samples. Perhaps the most curious aspect of the sexual harassment training evaluation literature is that it almost exclusively evaluates researcher-designed training, not training that is actually implemented in the workplace. Given this, one of the gaps in this literature is an understanding of the nature and content of sexual harassment research within real-world organizational settings.

Importance of Research Design and Realistic Goals

As suggested by the previous review, the design of an evaluative effort is critical to the utility of the findings. The most powerful design to detect training effects is the Solomon Four-Group design (Campbell & Stanley, 1963), which allows the potential threats to internal validity, specifically those of history, maturation and testing, to be controlled or explicitly tested. The design contains two crossed factors: the survey observations and the training itself. Groups 1 and 2 complete pre- and post-training surveys; as only Group 2 receives training, however, the comparison between these two groups allows the threat of historical effects to be controlled. Group 3 completes only the post-training survey, whereas Group 4 receives training and completes the post-training survey. Comparing post-training means across the four groups allows the effects of testing to be evaluated to ensure that such efforts are not sensitizing participants and, hence, interfering with the impact of the training. See Table 12.1 for a depiction of the design, where the four groups described above are represented in the Time 2 cells.

Table 12.1 Sample sizes for women (W) and men (M) within Solomon Four-Group design

Sample 1: Time 1

Not Scheduled to be Trained	Scheduled to be Trained
W: 28 M: 66	W: 431 M: 631

Time 2

	Not Trained	Trained
Previously Surveyed	1 W: 22 M: 62	2 W: 124 M: 164
Not Previously Surveyed	3 W: 12 M: 32	4 W: 54 M: 126

Sample 2: Time 1

Not Scheduled to be Trained	Scheduled to be Trained
W: 221 M: 230	W: 198 M: 194

Time 2

	Not Trained	Trained
Previously Surveyed	W: 82 M: 99	W: 90 M: 107
Not Previously Surveyed	W: 99 M: 107	W: 91 M: 95

Note: Solomon Four-Group cell references appear in the upper left-hand corner of the Time 2 cells for Sample 1.

The second crucial component of any training evaluation is the choice of variables to be included in the pre- and post-training assessment. It is important to recognize that organizations may have inappropriate expectations for the results of sexual harassment training programs. For example, they may expect frequency rates and thus complaints to decrease immediately and dramatically; when familiarity with the procedures and resources stimulates an *increase* in complaints, organizations may react quite negatively.

In conceptualizing the possible effects of training programs, it seems unlikely that such programs will have an immediate effect on behavioral outcomes. Specifically, it is unreasonable to expect such programs to have the immediate effect of reducing frequency rates of sexual harassment. However, employees' knowledge about sexual harassment, as well as their perceptions of the organization's tolerance of such behavior, could feasibly be affected by such training efforts. Additionally, increased individual sensitivity toward sexual harassment—perhaps as indicated by either attitudes toward sexual harassment or propensity to label experiences *as* sexual harassment—have often been suggested to be the target of change efforts with training programs (for example, Perry, Kulik & Schmidke, 1998). Realistically, though, such well-formed attitudes could prove extremely difficult to change (McGuire, 1968), particularly attitudes about what constitutes appropriate and inappropriate behavior between sexes because these might be based on gender roles learned during early childhood. Therefore, prevention programs that purport to reduce incidents of sexual harassment in a training session that lasts one day or less are probably unrealistically optimistic; individual attitudes, let alone interpersonal behaviors, are not that malleable.

In conclusion, we posit that a realistic goal for organizations to have in evaluating their sexual harassment training is to recognize that the training is more likely to have an immediate effect on knowledge than on attitudes. Additionally, training programs may have a direct, immediate result on women's identifying their experiences as harassment. Women who receive sexual harassment training may also be more likely to take organizational actions in response to a harassment incident, especially if they perceive the organization as being intolerant of sexual harassment. The incidence of harassment itself, however, is unlikely to decrease within the time frame of any particular study. We turn now to the description of the evaluation of two organizationally-based sexual harassment training programs.

Empirical Evidence from Two Organizations' Sexual Harassment Training Programs

THE ORGANIZATIONS AND THEIR TRAINING

Sample 1

As a result of a previous sexual harassment incident that settled out of court, the first organization (a large, regulated utility organization in the Northwest, referred to as Sample 1 hereafter) wanted to follow up on a ten-years-prior sexual harassment training program. As a stimulus for applying concepts concerning gender differences and causes of sexual harassment, the organization implemented a half-day experiential training session, entitled "Plays That Work." The primary goal of this program was to sensitize employees to the seriousness of sexual harassment and other unacceptable harassing or discriminatory behavior. This "play" consisted primarily of two 30-minute, one-act scenes portrayed by professional actors and was created by a combination of professional playwrights, legal and psychological experts in sexual harassment. Structured to portray realistic and meaningful dialogue and content, these scenes were designed to experientially stimulate the audience. In addition to the play, there were short lectures defining legal aspects of harassment, group discussions facilitated by extensively trained employees from the organization and exercises. These lectures fulfilled the communicative aspects of training previously discussed; the play itself was designed to address the sensitivity goal of training. Although some of the training did focus on other forms of workplace disrespect and abuse—paralleling the organization's harassment-free policy prohibiting harassment of any of the protected classes—approximately 70 percent of the training focused specifically on sexual harassment. Employees and supervisors were trained together in groups of approximately 100.

Pre-training (Time 1) survey data were collected from 459 female and 697 male employees. To obtain a sample with a significant number of women in non-traditional occupations, a systematic stratified sample was drawn at this initial data collection based on work site (oversampling field sites) and department (oversampling departments with job classifications that are non-traditional for women); all women within selected department/work site combinations were encouraged, but not required, by the organization's Human Resources Department to participate in the study. Ninety-one percent of the women and

84 percent of the men who were selected did participate, with absences primarily due to work absence or scheduling conflicts. These men and women ranged in age from early twenties to late fifties with their mean age between 40 to 44. The overall sample was nearly 90 percent Caucasian; 80 percent of the men and 66 percent of the women were married and approximately one-third were college graduates. Twenty percent of the women and 4 percent of the men were in non-traditional jobs and indicated that they were one of the first of their sex to hold their job. Sixty-eight percent of the women and 88 percent of the men worked for male supervisors; 43 percent of the women were employed in a job environment where women were in the minority, whereas only 8 percent of the men reported that they worked in an environment where men were in the minority. Participants' job classifications varied considerably, with approximately 31 percent of the women and 46 percent of the men employed in the field (for example, line crew, technician), 30 percent of the men and women as professionals (for example, engineering, management) and 19 percent of the women and 1 percent of the men as clerical workers.

Ten months after the initial data collection (and within approximately six months of the completion of the training of the employees), the post-training data were collected from 218 female and 400 male employees. The numbers of men and women within each of the four cells of the Solomon Four-Group design as well as the numbers scheduled to be trained or not at Time 1 are displayed in Table 12.1. Note that the frequencies are not balanced within the cells of the design; this was due to organizational difficulty in co-ordinating the training with the follow-up assessment.

Sample 2

We also evaluated the sexual harassment training program from a second organization (Sample 2), an agribusiness organization in the intermountain region of the US, which was more sensitive to the research needs of the follow-up sampling (to strengthen the ability to detect training effects) and had greater racial diversity. As part of a gender discrimination settlement, this company was under a consent decree to provide management training to prevent sexual harassment and discrimination. As a result, all managers and supervisors of the work locations in the study received two days of training that was designed to prevent and resolve discrimination and reduce sexual harassment. Although the employee training was not required by the consent decree, the company decided that it was appropriate and more effective to train all employees and used a training program entitled "Respectful Workplace Training." This training was conducted in groups of 15–25 employees by a two-person extensively trained male/female team and lasted approximately three hours. Role playing between the trainers, short lectures on the organization's policies and procedures, video examples, group discussions and various group exercises provided the stimuli for application of the concepts and information learned during the training; thus, this program also satisfied the functions of communication and sensitization. Nearly half of the workforce at this organization was Hispanic. For Spanish-speaking participants, materials were translated into Spanish and some of the session facilitators were Spanish-speaking to ensure comprehension of and comfort with the material. Additionally, bilingual peers were seated at tables as translators in case there were other problems.

Pre-training data were collected from 419 women and 424 men from three plant locations of the organization. Participants were selected based on a stratified sampling plan based on plant, gender, job category and ethnicity (Caucasian White vs. Minority); participation rate was 82 percent for the women and 79 percent for the men. These men and women ranged in age from late teens to late fifties with their mean age in the 40 to 44 interval; over 69 percent of these women and 74 percent of these men were married. This sample was considerably more gender segregated and ethnically diverse than the first organization. Only 11 percent of these women and 9 percent of these men reported that they were one of the first of their sex to do their job. For the women, only 16 percent worked primarily with men and 50 percent had female supervisors. Similarly, the men worked with few women; only 15 percent worked primarily with women and 23 percent had a female supervisor. Overall, 36 percent of the sample were Hispanic and 58 percent were Non-Hispanic. This second sample also differed from the first in that only slightly more than 3 percent of the women and 7 percent of the men were college graduates. Participants' jobs were also more homogeneous; 88 percent of the men and 76 percent of the women worked in some facet of production.

We collected the follow-up data six months following the initial data collection (and within approximately three months of the completion of the training). The follow-up sample consisted of 379 female and 423 male employees; the number of men and women within each of the Solomon Four-Group design cells is displayed in Table 12.1. Additionally, the organization provided data on the complaints filed with each of the three plants at both the plant and corporate Human Resource levels for a period of five months prior to and five months after the training.

THE TRAINING EVALUATION PROTOCOL

The general procedures were the same for both organizations; that is, some participants were assessed prior to training to establish a baseline against which to compare the effects of the training as well as to establish any effects due solely to the elapse of time. Employees from both organizations completed a "Workplace Environment Survey," were assured that their answers would be kept private, and were given opportunity to refuse to participate or to complete only the part(s) of the survey they felt appropriate. With the exception of those employees working in corporate headquarters who completed their survey in large groups in the company training auditorium, most Sample 1 participants completed their survey in groups with an average size of approximately 20. Sample 2 participants chose to complete either an English or Spanish version of a paper-and-pencil Workplace Environment Survey in groups that varied from one to approximately 50 in size. The Spanish version of the questionnaire was constructed by using two two-person (male and female) native Spanish-speaking teams, with one team translating the survey and the other back-translating it. Additionally, lower reading-level employees were assigned to the smaller groups where researchers or locally-hired translators could assist them in completing a shortened version of the survey. The shortened surveys were created based on item analyses from previous data collections; reliability indices indicated that the shorter scales were psychometrically sound. Evaluation analyses were conducted only for those items that were identical to all participants at both data administrations.

The Workplace Environment Survey was designed to tap into Kirkpatrick's (1977) widely known training criteria of reactions, learning and behavioral change. Qualitative, open-ended questions were included in the post-training data collections to assess *reactions*, that is, participants' immediate liking and perceived value of the training. Both samples answered knowledge-based questions as one part of assessing *learning*. Questions for Sample 1 were taken from the US Merit Systems Protection Board studies (USMSPB, 1981; 1987) and tapped into employees' knowledge of organizational programs (for example, Has your organization provided awareness training for managers and EEO officials?) and practices (for example, Has your organization enforced penalties against sexual harassers?), as well as separate evaluations of both of their effectiveness. The awareness items used a 3-point response scale (*Yes, No, Don't Know*) and were recoded to represent dichotomous ratings of the existence of such programs or actions taken by the organization. If respondents knew for certain that the organization had indeed taken such steps (that is, the respondent marked *yes* to the awareness item), they were asked to rate how effective that measure had been on a 5-point scale ranging from 1 (*not at all effective*) to 5 (*very effective*). A different measure of knowledge about facets of sexual harassment was developed for Sample 2 and was based more explicitly on the content of the training program. Ten items were administered using both multiple choice and true/false response scales and were scored as correct or incorrect; thus, the participant's score on this measure was the number of items s/he answered correctly.

Two additional *learning* indicators were assessed: organizational climate for and individual attitudes toward sexual harassment. The Organizational Tolerance for Sexual Harassment Inventory (OTSHI) was included to assess employees' perceptions of the degree to which an organization tolerates sexual harassment of female employees by other organizational members (either a co-worker or supervisor; Hulin, Fitzgerald & Drasgow, 1996; Zickar, 1994). The measure consists of brief scenarios depicting sexual harassment followed by three questions about (1) the *risk to the victim* for reporting the incident; (2) the likelihood that a *complaint would be taken seriously*; and (3) the likelihood that the *harasser would receive meaningful sanctions* by the organization. Each item is scored on a 5-point scale and higher scores on the scale indicate higher organizational tolerance of sexual harassment. Organizational tolerance for sexual harassment has been shown to predict frequency of harassment; in other words, employees in work groups that reported high levels of perceived tolerance of sexual harassment were more likely to be sexually harassed than employees in work groups that reported low levels of perceived tolerance (Fitzgerald, Drasgow, Hulin, Gelfand & Magley, 1997; Zickar, 1994). Employees' personal attitudes about the seriousness of sexual harassment in organizations were assessed with items based on the Tolerance for Sexual Harassment Inventory (TSHI; Lott, Reilly & Howard, 1982). Each item utilizes a 7-point Likert scale, with higher scores indicating stronger belief that sexual harassment is "a big deal."

Assessing *behavioral change* with respect to sexual harassment raises some interesting challenges. Obviously, the best approach would be to examine individual's tendency to perpetrate harassment. Given problems with social desirability, however, we chose to examine whether self-reported sexual harassment frequency changed as a result of training and whether individuals were more likely to label their experiences as sexual harassment. Female participants in both samples completed the Sexual Experiences Questionnaire—Revised (SEQ-R), a 20-item measure developed by Fitzgerald and her colleagues (Fitzgerald, Shullman, Bailey, Richards, Swecker, Gold, Ormerod & Weitzman, 1988; Fitzgerald, Gelfand & Drasgow, 1995) to assess the frequency of sexual harassment. All items of the SEQ-R are written in behavioral terms, and the words "sexual harassment" do not appear until the end of the inventory to avoid biasing participants and to improve reliability. Participants respond on a 5-point scale, which ranges from 1 (*never*) to 5 (*most of the time*), and were asked to report only situations they had experienced in the target organization in the past two years. Because the pre-audit demonstrated that very few female employees had experienced sexual coercion, these items were dropped from the follow up. The final item in the scale asked women if they had ever been sexually harassed, indicating if she labeled her experiences as sexual harassment.

In constructing scale composites, data were first discarded for participants with more than 50 percent missing data. For participants with missing data, we substituted item means (rounded to their integer value) for missing responses if a respondent omitted one item on a short scale (ten items or less) and up to two items on longer scales (more than ten items); more missing data resulted in participants being dropped from analyses involving these scales. Missing data were not imputed for program/practice effectiveness ratings given the probability of larger quantities of missing data because respondents only rated those factors they knew existed. Instead, composites were created by taking the mean of all existing data. The means, standard deviations and internal consistency reliabilities of all quantitative variables for both samples are presented in Table 12.2.

ANALYSES AND RESULTS

One of the strengths of the Solomon Four-Group Design is its capability to discern effects from the intervention from effects from the initial surveying efforts (Campbell & Stanley, 1963). Hence, analyses were conducted in two phases, which first considered pre-test sensitization and second examined the effects of the training. For Sample 1, three 2 (Pre-surveyed: yes vs. no) x 2 (Trained: yes vs. no) MANOVAs were conducted using only the Time 2 data with the following sets of dependent variables: (1) OTSHI, attitudes toward sexual harassment and knowledge; (2) effectiveness evaluation scales (analyzed separately as they were only asked as follow-up items, thus restricting the sample size available for analysis); and (3) for the women only, sexual harassment frequency and self-labeling as having been sexually harassed. Similar analyses were conducted with Sample 2 data, omitting the second block. Pre-test sensitization did not occur for either sample, as evidenced by non-significant multivariate interactions and pre-survey main effects (Braver & Braver, 1984).[3]

The second phase of the analyses was conducted to partial out the effects of training. The ideal analysis at this point would be a 2 (Trained: yes vs. no) x 2 (Time: pre-training vs. post-training) repeated measures MANOVA.[4] However, because we were unable to collect individual identifiers to link the Time 1 and 2 data, we were unable to assess change over time, but could still compare data between those who had and had not participated in the training. Additionally, because we know that men and women perceive sexual harassment differently (Rotundo, Nguyen & Sackett, 2001), we examined the possibility that the training affected men and women differently; for Sample 2, we extended the possibility of the training differentially affecting diverse groups to including minority status in the analysis. Hence, we conducted a series of 2 (Trained: yes vs. no) x 2 (Gender: male vs. female) MANOVAs using the same sets of dependent variables as detailed above; we also examined the same dependent variables in a 2 (Trained: yes vs. no) x 2 (Ethnicity: Non-Hispanic vs. Hispanic) MANOVA for Sample 2. Training effect statistics are presented in Table 12.3; design cell means and standard deviations are in Table 12.4.

---

3   Detailed results are available from the first author upon request.

4   See Braver and Braver (1988) for an interesting alternative meta-analytic approach to analyzing Solomon Four-Group data, which also assumes individual identifiers to link data across the evaluation timepoints.

Table 12.2 Descriptive statistics

		Sample 1						Sample 2					
		Time 1 Administration			Time 2 Administration				Time 1 Administration			Time 2 Administration		
Construct	# Items	M	SD	α	M	SD	α	# Items	M	SD	α	M	SD	α
Organizational Tolerance for Sexual Harassment	18	36.13	14.21	.96	34.30	13.60	.96	12	26.66	10.74	.92	26.60	11.55	.93
Attitudes toward Sexual Harassment	12	60.64	11.95	.81	60.38	11.83	.82	9	43.68	8.35	.67	43.50	8.17	.62
Knowledge about Sexual Harassment	—							10	6.18	2.11	.62	6.21	2.26	.66
Knowledge of Harassment Programs	5	3.34	1.34	.64	3.64	1.23	.62	—						
Knowledge of Harassment Practices	3	1.62	1.26	.80	1.68	1.21	.74	—						
Evaluation of Harassment Programs	5	4.00	.81	.88	3.80	.84	.90	—						
Evaluation of Harassment Practices	3	4.38	.72	.86	4.03	.78	.86	—						
Sexual Harassment	12	15.81	5.45	.88	15.42	4.58	.83	16	21.20	6.79	.87	20.44	7.85	.92
Labeling Sexual Harassment	1	1.42	.70	—	1.52	.73	—	1	1.24	.43	—	1.09	.29	—

Note: Means for sexual harassment and labeling are for women only.

Table 12.3 Training effect statistics

Sample 1

	Trained*Sex	Sex	Trained
1) MANOVA	Wilks' λ = .994, F = .85	Wilks' λ = .907, F = 13.56***	Wilks' λ = .936, F = 9.07***
Org'l Tol. for SH	F = 1.25	F = 24.55***, η^2 = .044	F = 2.63
Attitudes toward SH	F = .23	F = 28.85***, η^2 = .051	F = 3.87*, η^2 = .007
Knowledge—Program	F = .02	F = .43	F = 2.56
Knowledge—Practices	F = .71	F = 1.42	F = 20.17***, η^2 = .037
2) MANOVA	Wilks' λ = .997, F = .52	Wilks' λ = .991, F = 1.80	Wilks' λ = .967, F = 6.71***
Evaluation—Program	F = .84	F = 2.97	F = 3.98*, η^2 = .010
Evaluation—Practices	F = .12	F = 3.22	F = 12.80***, η^2 = .032
3) MANOVA			Wilks' λ = .994, F = .57
Sexual Harassment			F = .97
Labeling SH			F = .01

Sample 2

	Trained*Ethnicity	Ethnicity	Trained
1) MANOVA	Wilks' λ = .977, F = 4.32**	Wilks' λ = .818, F = 39.95***	Wilks' λ = .997, F = .59
Org'l Tol. for SH	F = .43	F = 10.07**, η^2 = .018	F = .18
Attitudes toward SH	F = 2.42	F = .82	F = 1.02
Knowledge about SH	F = 10.33***, η^2 = .019	F = 115.55***, η^2 = .176	F = 1.18

	Trained*Sex	Sex	Trained
1) MANOVA	Wilks' λ = .994, F = 1.24	Wilks' λ = .899, F = 21.81***	Wilks' λ = .982, F = 3.66**
Org'l Tol. for SH	F = .42	F = 13.56***, η^2 = .023	F = .10
Attitudes toward SH	F = 2.46	F = 44.59***, η^2 = .071	F = 3.76*, η^2 = .006
Knowledge about SH	F = .11	F = .38	F = 9.41**, η^2 = .016
2) MANOVA			Wilks' λ = .996, F = .69
Sexual Harassment			F = .40
Labeling SH			F = .13

Note: Degrees of freedom. Sample 1: Block 1 multivariate $F_{(4, 529)}$, univariate $F_{(1, 532)}$; Block 2 multivariate $F_{(2, 390)}$, univariate $F_{(1, 391)}$; Block 3 women's multivariate $F_{(2, 213)}$, univariate $F_{(1, 214)}$. Sample 2: Trained*Ethnicity Block 1 multivariate $F_{(3, 539)}$, univariate $F_{(1, 541)}$; Trained*Sex Block 1 multivariate $F_{(3, 584)}$, univariate $F_{(1, 586)}$; Block 2 women's multivariate $F_{(2, 359)}$, univariate $F_{(1, 360)}$.

* $p < .05$

** $p < .01$

*** $p < .001$

Table 12.4 Training effect means (standard deviations)

Construct	Sample 1 Main Effects				Sample 2 Main Effects				Sample 2 Ethnicity* Trained Interaction			
	Sex		Trained		Sex		Ethnicity		Non-Hispanic		Hispanic	
	Men	Women	Not Trained	Trained	Men	Women	Non-Hispanic	Hispanic	Not Trained	Trained	Not Trained	Trained
Organizational Tolerance for SH	31.95 (12.59)	38.50 (14.34)	30.72 (12.02)	35.24 (13.85)	25.00 (10.67)	28.50 (12.27)	25.01 (11.24)	28.43 (11.14)	24.84 (11.38)	25.18 (11.12)	28.66 (11.40)	28.12 (10.84)
Attitudes toward SH	57.66 (11.39)	65.53 (10.92)	57.41 (12.36)	61.20 (11.56)	41.40 (7.86)	45.77 (7.89)	43.96 (8.35)	43.32 (7.66)	42.84 (8.57)	45.12 (7.96)	43.03 (7.52)	43.66 (7.86)
Knowledge about SH					6.33 (2.32)	6.08 (2.18)	7.00 (2.04)	4.95 (2.00)	6.61 (2.04)	7.38 (1.97)	5.15 (1.96)	4.72 (2.02)
Knowledge—Program	3.61 (1.29)	3.68 (1.12)	3.41 (1.54)	3.70 (1.13)								
Knowledge—Practices	1.79 (1.21)	1.47 (1.18)	2.16 (1.12)	1.55 (1.21)								
Evaluation—Program	3.87 (.82)	3.66 (.86)	4.05 (.83)	3.73 (.83)								
Evaluation—Practices	4.08 (.75)	3.91 (.83)	4.31 (.73)	3.93 (.77)								
Sexual Harassment			14.71 (3.73)	15.55 (4.72)		20.44 (7.85)						
Labeling SH			1.53 (.75)	1.52 (.73)		1.08 (.27)						

Note: SH = sexual harassment. Means for sexual harassment and labeling are for women only.

Consistent with previous gender differences research, women from both organizations did perceive their organizations to be considerably more tolerant of sexual harassment than did the men; further, they also believed that sexual harassment is a more serious issue than did the men. Similarly, for Sample 2, Hispanic employees believed that their organization was more tolerant of sexual harassment than did Non-Hispanic employees. In general, training did somewhat sensitize employees to sexual harassment with respect to individual-level attitudes; this was true for both organizations, after controlling for participant gender. (This attitudinal effect was nonsignificant, though, for Sample 2 when controlling for participant ethnicity.) Unexpectedly, trained employees in Sample 1 indicated decreased knowledge about organizational practices surrounding sexual harassment and decreased evaluations of both organizational programs *and* practices. (Although not explicitly examined, it could be that the increased attitudinal sensitivity influenced these harsher appraisals of the organization's efforts.) Training did not affect participants' perceptions of the extent to which the organizations tolerated sexual harassment. For Sample 2, trained Non-Hispanic employees answered more of the knowledge questions correctly than did untrained Non-Hispanic employees; training did not improve Hispanic employees' knowledge about sexual harassment. Neither training programs differentially affected men and women. When considering only the women's data from both organizations, training did not affect the frequency with which they experienced sexual harassment or how they labeled it.

Responses to the open-ended question asking for participants' reactions to the training program were coded for the perceived effectiveness of the program. Fifty-one percent of the women and 41 percent of the men in Sample 1 felt that the program increased awareness of sexual harassment and was helpful in identifying what constitutes sexual harassment as well as its consequences; however, only 4 percent of the women and 7 percent of the men felt that the program would actually result in behavioral change and/or reduce sexual harassment. Further, 6 percent of the women and 9 percent of the men felt that the training program was a waste of money and was designed so that the company could protect itself from lawsuits. Thus, although there were many positive comments, some employees were skeptical about the eventual effects of the program as well as the motivation underlying its implementation.

Similarly, when Sample 2 participants were prompted to describe what they liked least and best about the training program, these employees primarily made comments regarding (1) the information presented in the training or the training in general or (2) the organization's efforts in providing the training. Of the 117 employees who commented about the informational aspects of the training and/or the training overall, the vast majority (84 percent) reported comments that were very positive in nature; a typical example read, "It was good, informative, and educational. It changed my way of thinking." Thus, the vast majority of employees who wrote comments indicated that the training was useful and informative. Despite these reactions to the training itself, 64 percent of those who commented on the organization's efforts to follow through with the training were fairly negative and cynical. One person wrote, "It seemed they went through a pre-set informational meeting to comply with a ruling that was required." Several people commented on how things had not really changed, paralleling the lack of change in the employees' perceptions of organizational tolerance for sexual harassment. Although the absolute number of such comments was small, compared to the many hundreds of employees who were surveyed, they do underscore the importance of consistency and follow-up of organizational commitment to change.

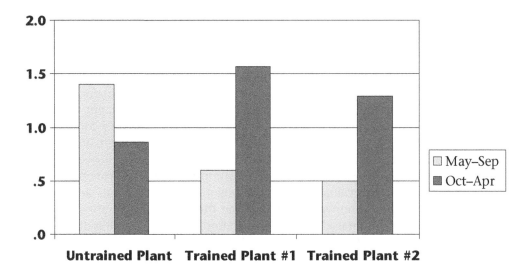

Figure 12.1 Complaints filed per month with individual plant HR in Sample 2

Finally, there was some evidence suggesting that actual complaints to Human Resources increased following the intervention. As can be seen in Figure 12.1, the average number of complaints filed per month at the individual plants increased following the training. (Significance tests were not conducted due to the small numbers overall.)

There was an increase in the number of complaints filed per month at the trained plants in contrast to an apparent decrease at the untrained plant. Average number of complaints filed per month at the corporate level increased over time for all plants; however, this increase was slightly greater for the trained plants than for the untrained plant (Figure 12.2).

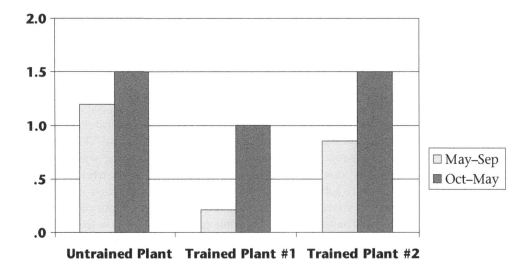

Figure 12.2 Complaints filed per month with corporate plant HR in Sample 2

These effects most likely reflect the multi-faceted approach that the organizational took in preventing sexual harassment. Prior to the training at the individual plants, corporate Human Resources began improving their procedures for complaint follow-up as well as providing employees with a number of additional resources (for example, hotlines). Thus, the training and the other overall corporate efforts show promise for encouraging targets to report their unwanted experiences to their respective plant as well as at the corporate level.

Insights, Future Needs and Concluding Thoughts

The previous results represent some of the first empirical data from evaluating large-scale, intact organizations' sexual harassment training programs and, as such, are illuminative. Although employees from both organizations generally agreed that the training programs were useful first steps in addressing sexual harassment in their workplace, they were also fairly skeptical as to the intent and effectiveness of this program. Factual understanding of sexual harassment was improved for at least some of the employees whereas personal attitudes toward sexual harassment and perceptions of the organization's tolerance for sexual harassment were minimally changed or completely unchanged. Training did not affect the frequency of sexual harassment experienced by the women nor how they perceived their experiences in relation to definitions of sexual harassment. Although trained women were more likely to file complaints with Human Resources at various levels within Sample 2, their labeling of experiences with sexual harassment *as* sexual harassment did not increase. This latter non-significant effect is important as it suggests that training does not *over-sensitize* women to think that everything is sexual harassment. Finally, the results suggested that the training program did not increase the Hispanic employees' knowledge of organizational procedures and policies of sexual harassment; further research and practice should be sensitive to creating culturally appropriate training programs and evaluation tools.

Despite what can be learned from these data, we believe that the sexual harassment training literature is likely one of the last open areas of inquiry within the larger sexual harassment literature. We turn next to thoughts toward improving that venture.

IT'S REALLY ONLY MINIMALLY ABOUT THE TRAINING PER SE

Effective training does not occur within a vacuum. Bell, Quick and Cycyota (2002) and Perry, Kulik and Field (2009) both provide very thoughtful guidance to the creation of harassment-free and supportive work environments. Both highlight the extensive role of non-training factors in creating such an environment. Additionally, Licata and Popovich (1987) argued—quite some time ago, at this point—that establishing a proactive approach to reducing sexual harassment is far superior than a reactive one. Specifically, beginning with a careful needs analysis that includes an evaluation of both the system-wide readiness for harassment intervention and the general perceptions of organizational tolerance of harassment are crucial first steps toward developing a healthier environment for all employees.

Part of this general readiness for change is understanding the extent to which employees are cynical toward organizational change efforts. Is there a belief system within the organization that what is talked about and written about is actually what is carried out? What trust issues are already in place, both positively and negatively? This pre-existing belief system is already in place based on previous organizational issues and has to be considered when preparing for sexual harassment training.

Additionally, prior to the implementation of the sexual harassment training, considerable time and effort needs to be invested in assessing how the organization is set up to respond to complaints. For instance, are the policies and procedures defining the parameters of what will and will not be tolerated with respect to sexual harassment clear? Are they appropriately distributed among the employees? How are HR staff trained to investigate complaints? Are there adequate numbers of trained staff so that immediate responses *can* actually occur? All of this indicates an organization's ability to effectively prevent and respond to complaints of sexual harassment.

Only after these contextual parameters are clearly understood is it time to begin specifying clear training objectives from which both the training *and its evaluation* will be based. Related to the development of explicit training objectives is a consideration of the modality of the training itself. Recently, web-based instruction has become increasingly common (Sitzmann, Kraiger, Steward & Wisher, 2006), both in general and for sexual harassment programs. Based on a meta-analytic review of the general training literature, Sitzmann, Kraiger, Steward and Wisher (2006) found that web-based instruction was slightly superior to classroom instruction in terms of teaching declarative knowledge and that the two media approaches were equally effective for teaching procedural knowledge. Similar results were found by Preusser, Bartels and Nordstrom (2011) when comparing a computer-based sexual harassment program to an instructor-led program with 70 university employees. With the limited sample size of the Preusser, Bartels and Nordstrom piece and the lack of explicitly considering the moderating role of social-skills training compared to more skill-based training in the Sitzmann, Kraiger, Steward and Wisher piece, we strongly believe that the jury is still out on the comparative efficacy of web-based instruction for sexual harassment programs. We strongly encourage researchers to consider this more carefully and strongly caution practitioners to take care when selecting unvalidated web-based training programs.

Earlier we presented a fair bit of detail regarding the objectives and goals of the training itself, as well as the importance of developing an evaluation plan. As we found when evaluating the two organizations' training programs, employees expressed concern whether management was truly serious about the issue of sexual harassment. Such results suggest that organizations should expect a period of sensitization following their training efforts and be prepared to be proactive by (1) initiating prompt investigations and fair, consistent corrective actions to the very likely increase in complaints about sexual harassment filed with the organization and (2) communicating with their employees that sexual harassment is a serious issue and will not be tolerated. Employees will be very attentive to such organizational actions; it is crucial that they witness the training lessons be reinforced by the organizational culture.

Obviously, the evaluation process itself can send a very positive message to employees that the organization is serious about discovering the breadth and depth of the change that has taken place. If organizations expect training programs similar to the two reviewed earlier to fully remedy existing sexual harassment problems, they will likely be disappointed. Evaluations, though, are so desperately needed in the sexual harassment training literature. Considerably more effort needs to be devoted to evaluating the many different types of sexual harassment training so that organizations can make their training decisions based on empirically-demonstrated results. For example, evaluations of training programs can highlight the areas where training can make a difference (for example, knowledge of existing programs and policies) so that other types of interventions can be designed to address areas where training has been shown to be ineffective.

VIEWING SEXUAL HARASSMENT TRAINING AS A NECESSARY, BUT INSUFFICIENT ACTIVITY

Organizational culture change is a complex process that evolves slowly over time (for example, Kotter & Heskett, 1992). Viewing sexual harassment interventions as one component of a long-term effort—that is, not simply one week of an organization's life—is crucial to the success of the program. In fact, without such a perspective, organizations risk nullifying the training efforts by not providing appropriate post-training follow-through. Although training is only one piece of a solid prevention plan, it is an important basis as, with clear presentation of appropriate organizational boundaries around sexual harassment, the organization can hold employees accountable for their behaviors. However, if training programs continue to be considered the panacea for all ills, and are developed and marketed with no theoretical analysis or empirical evaluation, organizations will continue to make irrational decisions that may lead to serious consequences.

References

Aalberts, R. J., & Seidman, L. H. (1996) Sexual-harassment policies for the workplace: a tale of two companies. *Cornell Hotel and Restaurant Administration Quarterly*, 37, 78–85.

Antecol, H., & Cobb-Clark, D. (2003) Does sexual harassment training change attitudes? A view from the federal level. *Social Science Quarterly*, 84, 826–842.

Barak, A. (1994) A cognitive-behavioral educational workshop to combat sexual harassment in the workplace. *Journal of Counseling and Development*, 72, 595–602.

Baty v. Willamette Industry (1999) 172 F.3d 1232.

Beauvais, K. (1986) Workshops to combat sexual harassment: a case study of changing attitudes. *Signs*, 12, 130–145.

Bell, M. P., Cycyota, C. S., & Quick, J. C. (2002) An affirmative defense: the preventive management of sexual harassment. In D. L. Nelson & R. J. Burke (eds) *Gender, Work Stress and Health*. Washington, DC: American Psychological Association. pp. 191–210.

Bell, M. P., Quick, J. C., & Cycyota, C. S. (2002) Assessment and prevention of sexual harassment of employees: an applied guide to creating healthy organizations. *International Journal of Selection and Assessment*, 10, 160–167.

Berdahl, J. L., Magley, V. J., & Waldo, C. R. (1996) The sexual harassment of men? Exploring the concept with theory and data. *Psychology of Women Quarterly*, 20, 527–547.

Bingham, S. G., & Scherer, L. L. (2001) The unexpected effects of a sexual harassment educational program. *Journal of Applied Behavioral Science*, 37, 125–153.

Bisom-Rapp, S. (2001) Fixing watches with sledgehammers: the questionable embrace of employee sexual harassment training by the legal profession. *University of Arkansas at Little Rock Law Review*, 24, 147–161.

Blakely, G. L., Blakely, E. H., & Moorman, R. H. (1998) The effects of training on perceptions of sexual harassment allegations. *Journal of Applied Social Psychology*, 28, 71–83.

Blaxall, M. C. D., Parsonson, B. S., & Robertson, N. R. (1993) The development and evaluation of a sexual harassment contact person training package. *Behavior Modification*, 17, 148–163.

Bonate, D. L., & Jessell, J. C. (1996) The effects of educational intervention on perceptions of sexual harassment. *Sex Roles*, 35, 751–764.

Braver, M. C. W., & Braver, S.L. (1988) Statistical treatment of the Solomon four-group design: a meta-analytic approach. *Psychological Bulletin*, 104, 150–154.

Bremiller v. Cleveland Psychiatric Institute (2000) 195 F.R.D. 1.

Burlington Industries, Inc. v. Ellerth (1998) 524 U.S. 742.

Campbell, D. T., & Stanley, J. C. (1963) *Experimental and Quasi-experimental Designs for Research.* Chicago, IL: Rand McNally.

Coles, F. S. (1986) Forced to quit: sexual harassment complaints and agency response. *Sex Roles*, 14, 81–95.

Dansky, B. S., & Kilpatrick, D. G. (1997) Effects of sexual harassment. In W. O'Donohue (ed.) *Sexual Harassment: Theory, Research, and Treatment.* Boston: Allyn & Bacon, pp. 152–174.

Faith, M. S., Wong, F. Y., & Carpenter, K. M. (1995) Group sensitivity training: update, meta-analysis, and recommendations. *Journal of Counseling Psychology*, 42, 390–399.

Faragher v. City of Boca Raton (1998) 524 U.S. 775.

Fitzgerald, L. F. (March, 1990) *Assessing Strategies for Coping with Sexual Harassment: A Theoretical/ Empirical Approach.* Paper presented at the annual meeting of the Association for Women in Psychology, Tempe, AZ.

Fitzgerald, L. F., Drasgow, F., Hulin, C. L., Gelfand, M. J., & Magley, V. J. (1997) The antecedents and consequences of sexual harassment in organizations: a test of an integrated model. *Journal of Applied Psychology*, 82, 578–589.

Fitzgerald, L. F., Gelfand, M. J., and Drasgow, F. (1995) Measuring sexual harassment: theoretical and psychometric advances. *Basic and Applied Social Psychology*, 17, 425–445.

Fitzgerald, L. F., & Shullman, S. L. (1993) Sexual harassment: a research analysis and agenda for the 1990s. *Journal of Vocational Behavior*, 42, 5–27.

Fitzgerald, L. F., Shullman, S., Bailey, N., Richards, M., Swecker, J., Gold, A., Ormerod, A. J., & Weitzman, L. (1988) The incidence and dimensions of sexual harassment in academia and the workplace. *Journal of Vocational Behavior*, 32, 152–175.

Frazier, P. A., Cochran, C. C., & Olson, A. M. (1995) Social science research on lay definitions of sexual harassment. *Journal of Social Issues*, 51, 21–37.

Gauthier v. New Hampshire Department of Corrections (2000) 2000 WL 1513705 (D.N.H.).

Goldberg, C. B. (2007) The impact of training and conflict avoidance on responses to sexual harassment. *Psychology of Women Quarterly*, 31, 62–72.

Goldberg, C. B. (2011) What do we really know about sexual harassment training effectiveness? In M. A. Paludi, C. A. Paludi, & E. R. DeSouza (eds) *Praeger Handbook on Understanding and Preventing Workplace Discrimination*. Santa Barbara, CA: Praeger. Vols 1 & 2, pp. 45–48.

Grossman, J. L. (2003) The culture of compliance: rhe final triumph of form over substance in sexual harassment law. *Harvard Women's Law Journal*, 26, 3–75.

Grundmann, E. O., O'Donohue, W., & Peterson, S. H. (1997) The prevention of sexual harassment. In W. O'Donohue (ed.) *Sexual Harassment: Theory, Research, and Treatment*. Boston, MA: Allyn & Bacon. pp. 175–184.

Hulin, C. L., Fitzgerald, L. F., & Drasgow, F. (1996) Organizational influences on sexual harassment. In M. Stockdale (ed.) *Sexual Harassment in the Workplace*. Thousand Oaks, CA: Sage. Vol. 5, pp. 127–150.

Jacobs, C. D., Bergen, M. R., & Korn, D. (2000) Impact of a program to diminish gender insensitivity and sexual harassment at a medical school. *Academic Medicine*, 75, 464–469.

Kearney, L. K., Rochlen, A. B., & King, E. B. (2004) Male gender role conflict, sexual harassment tolerance, and the efficacy of a psychoeducative training program. *Psychology of Men and Masculinity*, 5, 72–82.

Kirkpatrick, D. L. (1977) Evaluating training programs: evidence vs. proof. *Training and Development*, 31, 9–12.

Kotter, J. P., & Heskett, J. L. (1992) *Corporate Culture and Performance.* New York: Free Press.

Lazarus, R. S., & Folkman, S. (1984) *Stress, Appraisal, and Coping.* New York: Springer.

Licata, B. J., & Popovich, P .M. (1987) Preventing sexual harassment: a proactive approach. *Training and Development Journal*, 41, 34–38.

Lott, B., Reilly, M. E., & Howard, D. (1982) Sexual assault and harassment: a campus community case study. *Signs*, 8, 296–319.

Martucci, W. C., & Lu, Z. (2005) Sexual-harassment training: yhe wave of the future in state legislative efforts. *Employment Relations Today*, 32, 87–95.

Maurizio, S. J., & Rogers, J. L. (1992) Sexual harassment and attitudes in rural community care workers. *Health Values*, 16, 40–45.

McGuire, W. J. (1968) Attitudes and attitude change. In G. Lindzey & E. Aronson (eds) *Handbook of Social Psychology* (3rd Edition) New York: Random House. Vol. 5, pp. 127–150.

Moyer, R. S., & Nath, A. (1998) Some effects of brief training interventions on perceptions of sexual harassment. *Journal of Applied Social Psychology*, 28, 333–356.

Ogden v. Wax Works, Inc. (1999) 214 F.3d 999.

Perry, E., Kulik, C., & Field, M. (2009) Sexual harassment training: recommendations to address gaps between the practitioner and research literatures. *Human Resource Management*, 48, 817–837.

Perry, E. L., Kulik, C. T., & Schmidtke, J. M. (1998) Individual differences in the effectiveness of sexual harassment awareness training. *Journal of Applied Social Psychology*, 28, 698–723.

Powell v. Morris and Ohio Department of Rehabilitation and Correction (1999) 37 F. Supp.2d 1011.

Preusser, M. K., Bartels, L. K., & Nordstrom, C. R. (2011) Sexual harassment training: person vs. machine. *Public Personnel Management*, 40, 47–62.

Pryor, J. B., & McKinney, K. (1995) Research on sexual harassment: lingering issues and future directions. *Basic and Applied Social Psychology*, 17, 605–611.

Robb, L. A., & Doverspike, D. (2001) Self-reported proclivity to harass as a moderator of the effectiveness of sexual harassment-prevention training. *Psychological Reports*, 88, 85–88.

Roscoe, B., Strouse, J. S., Goodwin, M. P., Taracks, L., & Henderson, D. (1994) Sexual harassment: an educational program for middle school students. *Elementary School Guidance and Counseling*, 29, 110–120.

Rotundo, M., Nguyen, D-H., & Sackett, P.R. (2001) A meta-analytic review of gender differences in perceptions of sexual harassment. *Journal of Applied Psychology*, 86, 914–922.

Schneider, B. (1975) Organizational climates: an essay. *Personnel Psychology*, 28, 447–479.

Schneider, K. T., Swan, S., & Fitzgerald, L. F. (1997) Job-related and psychological effects of sexual harassment in the workplace: empirical evidence from two organizations. *Journal of Applied Psychology*, 82, 401–415.

Sitzmann, T., Kraiger, K., Stewart, D., & Wisher, R. (2006) The comparative effectiveness of web-based and classroom instruction: a meta-analysis. *Personnel Psychology*, 59, 623–664.

Thacker, R. A. (1994) Innovative steps to take in sexual harassment prevention. *Business Horizons*, 37, 29–32.

US Merit Systems Protection Board (1981) *Sexual Harassment of Federal Workers: Is It a Problem?* Washington, DC: US Government Printing Office.

US Merit Systems Protection Board (1987) *Sexual Harassment of Federal Workers: An Update.* Washington, DC: United States Government Printing Office.

Williams v. Spartan Communication, Inc. (2000) 210 F.3d 364, 2000 WL 331605 (4th Cir. (S.C.))

York, K. M., Barclay, L. A., & Zajack, A. B. (1997) Preventing sexual harassment: the effect of multiple training methods. *Employee Responsibilities and Rights Journal*, 10, 277–289.

Zickar, M. (April, 1994) *Antecedents of Sexual Harassment.* Paper presented at a Symposium on Sexual Harassment at the Society for Industrial and Organizational Psychology, Nashville.

13 *The Relationship between Work Design and Retirement: Implications for Organizational Policy*

AMANDA GRIFFITHS, ALEC KNIGHT AND
NOR DIANA MOHD MAHUDIN

Introduction

In most developed countries the population is ageing. A combination of factors is responsible, although increasing life expectancy and declining birth rates are the primary drivers. National-level initiatives, such as increasing the age at which people can access their pensions, are encouraging later retirement. The upshot of this is that many people, largely for financial reasons, currently find themselves needing to extend their working lives, and to postpone their previously planned retirement. For many people, continuing to work will be an economic necessity; others may wish to continue to work even if not financially compelled to do so. For some, work contributes to a sense of purpose, self-esteem and provides opportunities for engagement; for others it can be tedious, unpleasant and stressful. Some may choose to continue to work not because in itself it provides meaningful activity, but because it funds other activities that hold purpose and enjoyment. Yet others may prefer to work part time in a job that does not hold much excitement, because it affords time to engage in more interesting activities outside work. But the general result will be that over the next few decades, many organizations will see changes in the profile of their workforces, with more workers approaching the transitional phase leading toward retirement.

Traditionally, retirement has been conceptualized as an event, at a certain point in time, when paid employment ceases. For reasons which this chapter endeavors to set out, retirement may be better regarded as a process that takes place over many years, facilitated by supportive organizational policies. Such an approach fits well the latest evidence on the nature of retirement, on working in later life and on health from mid-life onwards. For many people, the period when paid employment has ceased may be a long one, and it is important to explore all the factors that will contribute to making it as healthy and fulfilling as possible.

The recent public debate and media coverage has focussed largely on the economic drivers of later retirement. However, there are other factors involved in individuals' complex decision-making processes about how long to remain in the labor force. Much of the relevant research concerns the impact of work and work-related stress on health, well-being and performance. Until recently, this has largely produced "age-free" models. More recently, however, these topics are being explored from an age perspective. Evidence is emerging, for example, to suggest that the quality of work can impact on health and well-being not just during working life, but also after retirement (Council of Civil Services Unions/Cabinet Office, 2004; Ilmarinen, 2009). Such findings would suggest that investments in the length and quality of people's active period in retirement should be made *during* working life, not just afterwards. When brought together this research gives us an insight into the better design of work for tomorrow's older workers. This is the aim of this chapter.

Retirement

Two key themes in the relevant literature on retirement relate to (i) the causal link between stressful work and workforce exit and (ii) whether or not work ceases voluntarily. People may move from employment to retirement as a result of involuntary (push) factors such as poor health, disability or redundancy, or voluntary (pull) factors such as elected early retirement or a healthy financial situation (Banks & Smith, 2006; Phillipson & Smith, 2005; Shultz, Morton & Weckerle, 1998; Taylor & Shore, 1995). Retirement may reflect a gradual transition or, more commonly, an abrupt termination of work. Overall, there is strong evidence that work-related stress and associated precursors such as low job autonomy, poor quality of work, long and inflexible working hours, and effort–reward imbalance, are consistently related to all forms of workforce exit, including retirement and intention to retire (Alavinia & Burdorf, 2008; Andrews, Manthorpe & Watson, 2005; Blekesaune & Solem, 2005; Doshi, Cen & Polsky, 2008; Harkonmäki, Lahelma, Martikainen, Rahkonen & Silventoinen, 2006; Karpansalo, Kauhanen, Lakka, Manninen, Kaplan & Salonen, 2005; Phillipson, 2002; Phillipson & Smith, 2005; Pransky, Benjamin & Savageau, 2005; Rambur, Palumbo, McIntosh & Thomas, 2008; Salonen, Arola, Nygård, Huhtala & Koivisto, 2003; Siegrist, Wahrendorf, von dem Knesebeck, Jurges & Borsch-Supan, 2007; Siegrist, Wahrendorf, von dem Knesebeck, Jürges & Börsch-Supan, 2006). Whether an individual's mental health will improve, decrease or remain the same in the immediate period after retirement is dependent on access to finances, personal health and relationships (van Solinge & Henkens, 2008), whether he or she would prefer to be employed (Falba, 2008; Warr, Butcher, Robertson & Callinan, 2004), and whether retirement was voluntarily or was imposed as a result of ill-health or organizational factors such as downsizing (Calvo, Haverstick & Sass, 2009; Isaksson & Johansson, 2000; Sharpley & Layton, 1998). Overall, most research has concluded that voluntary retirement or retirement at normal retirement age is associated with an improvement in mental health (Costa, 2005; Drentea, 2002; Fernandez, Mutran & Reitzes, 1998; Fernandez, Mutran, Reitzes & Sudha, 1998; Mein, Martikainen, Hemingway, Stansfeld & Marmot, 2003; Melzer, Buxton & Villamil, 2004).

The Older Worker

There are no agreed criteria used by researchers as to what constitutes an "older worker." Much of the lack of agreement reflects the different employment and social welfare practices between countries. However, the scientific literature on work stress excludes significant groups of older workers. There is a notable lack of information on workers who are over 65 as most research has focused on those aged 45–65 years. Further, the vast majority of participants in research studies on work are in paid employment in medium and large-sized organizations; but the vast majority of workers are either self-employed or employed in small or micro companies (1–49 employees) and a substantial proportion of these are older workers (European Foundation for the Improvement of Living and Working Conditions, 2008). In addition, as workers become older they are more likely to take ill-health retirement. This may be related or unrelated to the nature of their work. Thus older workers in research studies may largely be "healthy survivors."

It should also be noted that research tends to refer "older workers" as if they are a homogenous group, based on chronological age. Chronological age on its own may not be a reliable indicator of a person's ability to perform certain types of work task. Although it might be generally true that older workers are less able to do certain tasks than younger workers (Tuomi, Ilmarinen, Seitsamo, Huuhtanen, Martikainen, Nygård & Klockars, 1997), the scientific literature notes an *increase* in variability with age in both health and in performance (Costa, Goedhard & Ilmarinen, 2005a, 2005c; Rabbitt, 1993). A 55-year old may be functionally similar to a 35-year-old. Legislation and policy about retirement ages may not reflect this increased diversity, although history would suggest that such decisions are often political and economic, rather than based on the evidence relating to health and performance.

Work-related Stress

There is strong evidence that a major reason for older workers exiting the labor force is the experience of work-related stress and related psychological ill-health (Alavinia & Burdorf, 2008; Andrews, Manthorpe & Watson, 2005; Cox, Griffiths & Rial-Gonzalez, 2000; Doshi, Cen & Polsky, 2008; Harkonmäki, Lahelma, Martikainen, Rahkonen & Silventoinen, 2006; Karpansalo, Kauhanen, Lakka, Manninen, Kaplan & Salonen, 2005; Pransky, Benjamin & Savageau, 2005; Rambur, Palumbo, McIntosh & Thomas, 2008; Salonen, Arola, Nygård, Huhtala & Kovisto, 2003), alongside dissatisfaction with work, long working hours and concerns that stress may exacerbate existing health conditions (Barnes & Taylor, 2004; Phillipson, 2002; Phillipson & Smith, 2005; Shultz, Morton & Weckerle, 1998). Several stress-related work characteristics are known to be associated with early exit from the workforce: low job autonomy, poor quality of work, long and inflexible working hours, and effort–reward imbalance, among others (Blekesaune & Solem, 2005; Phillipson, 2002; Siegrist, Wahrendorf, von dem Knesebeck, Jürges & Börsch-Supan, 2006). Work-related stress is a significant cause of illness, disease and underperformance. In the UK, for example, it is thought to be responsible for more lost working days than any other single cause (Health and Safety Executive, 2009b). Stress is currently defined by the British Government's Health & Safety Executive (also known as HSE) as "an adverse reaction" and "the process that arises where work demands of various types and combinations exceed the person's capacity and capability to cope" (Health and Safety Executive, 2009b). Further, ill-health resulting from stress may not occur instantaneously; there are suggestions that it may appear years later (Clays, Bacquer, Eynen, Kornitzer, Kittel & De Backer, 2007; Ohman, Bergdahl, Nyberg & Nilsson, 2007).

Employee reports of stress are traditionally associated with difficulties concerning the way work is designed and managed. Problems with workload, working hours, organizational culture and change, control, career development, relationships and support all appear influential (Cooper & Marshall, 1976; Cox, Griffiths & Rial-Gonzalez, 2000; Health and Safety Executive, 2009b). The literature uses many terms to refer to stress and its associated precursors, psychological states or consequences: for example, stressors, psychosocial hazards, stress, anxiety, depression, depressive mood, distress, strain, psychological ill-health, mental ill-health, emotional exhaustion, burnout or minor psychiatric morbidity. Some literature does not use the term "stress" at all, preferring to refer to direct associations between a limited set of broad work characteristics (such as demands, control, support or reward) and established diagnoses such as depression or heart disease. There is considerable overlap in terminology, as well as occasional lack of clarity as to causes, processes or outcomes. Many studies of the association between work characteristics and health are cross-sectional; on the basis of such evidence it is difficult to ascertain how much work characteristics influence health, or, vice versa, poor health influences the positioning of people with respect to such aspects of work. Poor psychological health, for example, could predispose people to self-select into poorly designed and managed jobs, and might negatively influence their ability to maintain healthy working relationships or maintain acceptable performance. A combination of such mechanisms might drive this relationship. Nonetheless, where longitudinal evidence exists it does point in the direction of certain aspects of work having detrimental effects on psychological and physical health. However, by and large, the focus of all this work is on groups of workers rarely distinguished by age. If we want to unpack the likely aspects of work implicated in the early ill-health retirement, it would be useful to establish whether certain aspects of work are more stressful for older workers than for the whole age-range. But first, is stress any more or less of a problem for older workers than it is for younger workers?

Work-related Stress and Age

Taken at face value, much of the current evidence suggests that older people in general, and older workers specifically, report less stress and better psychological health than their younger counterparts (Griffiths, Knight & Mohd Mahudin, 2009). However, several substantive studies, such as the surveys carried out periodically by the UK's Health and Safety Executive, suggest that the relationship between age and the report of stress is actually curvilinear (Birdi, Warr & Oswald, 1995; Health and Safety Executive, 2009a; Kenney, 2000). Data have been made available by the Health and Safety Executive that combine information on age and work-related stress and associated psychological ill-health (anxiety and depression) from the Self-reported Work-related Illness Surveys of 2004/2005 through to 2007/2008. There is a flat inverted U-shaped relationship between age and the self-report of work-related stress, anxiety and depression. Younger workers, aged 34 years and less, and older workers, aged 55 and over, report less stress, anxiety and depression than workers aged between 35 and 54. The lower levels of report in the group aged 55 years and over are largely due to levels of report for those aged 60 and older (Griffiths, Knight & Mohd Mahudin, 2009). Data from the Whitehall study of British civil servants also reveal an inverse-U relationship between mental health and age, with the oldest workers reporting better mental health (Chandola, Ferrie, Sacker & Marmot, 2007). Both surveys also suggest that workers' psychological health improves after retirement.

The Self-reported Work-related Illness Surveys in the UK also reveal that women aged 45–54 (Health and Safety Executive, 2009a) report more stress than men of the same age (and more stress than any other group of workers). Many factors may combine to explain this finding. Women may be more prepared to report stress, but it also represents a time of life that coincides with potentially significant personal changes such as the menopause which can cause some women problems at work (British Occupational Health Research Foundation, 2010) as well as a high probability of shouldering considerable domestic and caring responsibilities for both children and parents.

Several processes may contribute to the fact that research studies reveal older workers to report less stress and psychological ill-health than mid-life workers, including the "healthy worker" and related effects, and the "frame of reference" effect. Few studies make allowance for these. The healthy worker effect refers to the possibility that workers leave jobs they find stressful and move into those they find more congenial before reaching an older working age (Eskelinen, Toikkanen, Tuomi, Mauno, Nygård, Klockers & Ilmarinen, 1991), or that they voluntarily leave the work force altogether before normal retirement age, or that they take early ill-health retirement. It is thus possible that the older workers who participate in research studies are largely "survivors." It is conceivable that these survivors have more adaptive personality traits or coping strategies (Garrosa, Moreno-Jiménez, Liang & González, 2006; Heyink, 1993; Kenney, 2000; Landa, Lopez-Zafra, Martos & Aguilar-Luzon, 2008), or may have made their way into a more senior position where they are more in control of their working life and are better supported (Jorm, Windsor, Dear, Anstey, Christensen & Rodgers, 2005). These older workers may also benefit from better intrinsic rewards than younger, less senior workers (Birdi, Warr & Oswald, 1995). Research does show that, in general, workers who are more satisfied with their job are less likely report stress (Hendel & Horn, 2008) and this also holds true for older workers (Abramson, Gofin, Habib, Noam & Kark, 1994; Abramson, Ritter, Gofin & Kark, 1992; Blythe, Baumann, Zeytinoglu, Denton, Akhtar-Danesh, Davies & Kolotylo, 2008). Exploring the relationship between age and job satisfaction reveals a curvilinear relationship (U-shaped). Large-scale studies found that high stress, low job satisfaction and poor psychological health all peaked in mid-life workers (Birdi, Warr & Oswald, 1995; Clark, Oswald & Warr, 1996). Older workers tended to report higher job satisfaction, lower stress and better psychological health. These studies reveal that such relationships may not simply increase or decrease with age, but rise and fall over working life. The implications for our current concern are that in addition to an exploration of stressful work characteristics, we should also investigate the constituents of job satisfaction and motivation for workers approaching retirement age: a topic which we will address below. In addition to the healthy worker effect, a "frame of reference" effect might contribute to the apparent report of less stress and related psychological health problems by older workers. There is evidence from studies where health is measured both objectively and subjectively that older people report more positively about their health than do younger people (Ferraro, 1980; Idler, 1993; Lindeboom & van Doorslaer, 2004; Shmueli, 2003).

This has been explained in terms of peer-referenced decision making on one's state of health: a process whereby ratings of health are contextualized with regard to age (Maddox, 1962; Shanas & Maddox, 1976).

With regard to physical ill-health, although increasing age is associated with a greater likelihood of physical illness, it is agreed that work can make a significant and independent contribution. Strong evidence exists that work-related stress is associated with increased likelihood of developing cardiovascular or musculoskeletal disorders. And both are common reasons for early ill-health retirement (Pattani, Constantinovici & Williams, 2001; Poole, 1997). Some evidence exists for the role of stress (both work-related and non-work-related) in the development of other conditions. Various mechanisms might be operative since stress is known to affect neural, endocrine and immune systems and inflammatory processes (Chandola, Britton, Brunner, Hemingway, Malik, Kumari, Badrick, Kivimaki & Marmot, 2008; Cohen, Janicki-Deverts & Miller, 2007). In addition, several studies have demonstrated that stress has a negative effect on older workers' sleeping patterns, and a greater impact on their ability to recover from fatigue than it does for younger workers (Akerstedt, Knutsson, Westerholm, Theorell, Alfredsson & Kecklund, 2002; Jansson-Frojmark, Lundqvist, Lundqvist & Linton, 2007). Disturbed sleep and inability to recover from fatigue may lead to adverse health outcomes for older workers and may exacerbate other ailments (Costa, Goedhard & Ilmarinen, 2005b; Kiss, De Meester & Braeckman, 2008; Winwood, Winefield & Lushington, 2006).

Overall, the current evidence suggests that older workers report less stress and psychological ill-heath than mid-life workers but that this finding is not as straightforward as it might appear since older workers may represent "healthy survivors" who also frame their expectations and perceptions about health more positively. And it is established that stress is associated with early retirement. The extent of the problem stress presents for older workers may be underestimated by various biases in the available data. The next question is, from the array of work characteristics known to cause stress at work, are there any that are particularly problematic for older workers?

Risk Factors for Stress in Older Workers

Evidence emerging from recent research suggests that three broad groups of "stressful" factors for older workers: (i) physical aspects of work; (ii) time pressures, shift work, and lack of autonomy and flexibility in working arrangements; and (iii) inappropriate line management and organizational culture.

First, older workers often find high physical demands and adverse physical work environments (for example, temperature extremes) stressful (Ilmarinen, 1994; Ilmarinen, Tuomi Eskelinen, Nygård, Huuhtanen & Klockars, 1991). Thus, any jobs defined by such characteristics may be more easily managed by younger (or fitter) workers. However, as discussed above, there is a widening variability in ability with age, so it may be safer to deal with such matters on an individual basis rather than select people on the basis of chronological age alone.

Second, time pressures, being on call and extended working hours are particularly demanding for older workers, and have a negative impact on their health, well-being and efficiency (Reijula, Räsänen, Hämäläinen, Juntunen, Lindbohm, Taskinen, Bergbom & Rinta-Jouppi, 2003; Volkoff & Pueyo, 2005). Good work–rest schedules and adequate rest breaks may be beneficial (Ritvanen, Louhevaara, Helin, Vaisanen & Hanninen, 2006; Volkoff & Pueyo, 2005). Most researchers concur on the detrimental effect of non-standard working patterns (particularly night shifts) on older workers. It seems likely that it is the cumulative effect of the number of years spent shift working that is important in predicting ill-health effects (Brugere, Barrit, Butat, Cosset & Volkoff, 1997; Costa, 2005; Härmä & Kandolin, 2001; Keran & Duchon, 1999), some say even more powerfully than chronological age (De Zwart & Meijman, 1994). Some evidence suggests that older workers are more likely to report themselves as "morning types" (Keran & Duchon, 1999). Shift work experts tend to recommend, as age appropriate, systems which involve flexibility, rapid forward rotation and earlier start and end times (Härmä, Hakola, Kandolin, Sallinen, Virkkala, Bonnefond, & Mutanen, 2006; Härmä & Kandolin, 2001). Flexibility in work arrangements can beneficially affect the functional capacity and reduce the experience of stress in older workers. This is particularly true of those with chronic illnesses (Eskelinen, Toikkanen, Tuomi, Mauno, Nygård, Klockars & Ilmarinen, 1991) and carers. Combining work and caring often results in stress, tiredness, lack of personal leisure time and ill-health (Hirsch, 2003; Phillips, Bernard & Chittenden, 2002; Pinquart & Sörensen, 2003; Yeandle, Bennett, Buckner, Fry & Price, 2007). Many carers find they have to leave work entirely in order to accommodate their caring responsibilities, even though many would prefer to work part time or more flexibly. In the UK, one in three people are grandparents by the age of 50, and may also give up work to care for grandchildren (Ford, 2005). These roles are commonly part of normal life after the age of 50, and workers may be as equally committed to them as they are to their work roles. Such roles are not often recognized in organizational policy.

The third characteristic of work known to be particularly difficult for older workers is poor line management and organizational culture: the devaluing behaviors of supervisors, lack of feedback and a dearth of opportunities for professional development are examples (Kloimuller, Karazman & Geissler, 1997). Older workers are more alert to organizational politics than younger workers and this can impact negatively on job satisfaction (Miller, Rutherford & Kolodinsky, 2008). Where older workers report good relationships with their supervisors or line managers, where those managers are knowledgeable about ageing, and where workers are managed in an age appropriate manner, the evidence suggests that those workers are less likely to suffer poor health and are less likely to retire early (Ilmarinen, Tuomi Eskelinen, Nygård, Huuhtanen & Klockars, 1991; Tuomi, Ilmarinen, Klockars, Nygård, Seitsamo, Huuhtanen, Martikainen, & Aalto, 1997). Continued good health is also more likely among older workers if provided with choice to engage with the level and type of work that they prefer (Herzog, House & Morgan, 1991). Several studies have suggested that social support is particularly beneficial for older workers (Freeborn, 2001; Robson & Hansson, 2007; Tuomi, Ilmarinen, Klockars, Nygård, Seitsamo, Huuhtanen, Martikainen, & Aalto, 1997). Arguably, the most impressive series of longitudinal studies has been carried out in Finland, where management style and behavior has consistently emerged as the strongest predictor of continued and successful working, followed by leisure time physical activity (Kilbom, Westerholm, Hallsten & Furåke, 1996). Evidence for the important role of exercise in maintaining physical and psychological health and cognition in later life is becoming increasing strong (Hamer, Stamatakis & Steptoe, 2009; Hillman, Erickson & Kramer, 2008).

It is clear from the evidence presented above that work holds particular risks for mid-life and older workers. And that exposure to these working conditions may herald illness and premature retirement. However, it is also clear from another stream of research that focuses more on the positive aspects of work, that there are counterbalancing factors which will draw older workers to remain in work.

Work Motivation

Kanfer and Ackerman, in their framework for understanding adult development and motivation, proposed that as people enter mid-life, extrinsic rewards "lose their lustre" (2004, p.453) in favor of affirming identity, protecting self-concept and experiencing emotionally positive transactions. These transformations may be underpinned by changes in abilities (which may require additional effort or compensatory strategies to overcome), phases of the life cycle (for example, having child or eldercare responsibilities), or adjustments in life goals (for example, a wish to "give something back"). Recent evidence supports such shifts in the nature of work motivation. Evidence from a study with over 10,000 individuals suggested a shift from extrinsically to intrinsically rewarding job features with age (Inceoglu, Segers & Bartram, 2011). Various studies have similarly suggested that factors like pay, career progression and status may become less important, whereas the feeling of doing a worthwhile job, a desire to act as mentor and coach, may become progressively more important. The Royal College of Nursing in the UK has highlighted that many nurses want or need to work past normal retirement ages. They report wanting their skills and experience to be valued by their employers, to enjoy good relationships and a friendly culture at work. The importance of a congenial working atmosphere and social support as motivating factors has been highlighted in other studies of older workers (Chartered Insitute of Personal Development, 2008; Feldt, Mäkikangas, Kinnunen & Kokko, 2009; Robson & Hansson, 2007).

One of the most important motivators for older workers, and one that is reported in virtually all studies, is that of autonomy and flexibility in working hours and location (Smeaton, Vegeris & Sahin-Dikmen, 2009). It may even make the difference in decisions about when to retire. For example, among workers who did not plan to remain in work after the age of 65, nearly a third said they would change their mind if their employer allowed them to work flexibly (Chartered Insitute of Personal Development, 2008). A survey of working conditions across Europe concluded that work autonomy was positively associated with higher employment rates among older workers (European Foundation for the Improvement of Living and Working Conditions, 2008). Motivating factors for older workers might also be suitable holiday and special leave entitlements, time off in lieu, opportunities for part-time work or job shares. Career breaks, transfers to a less demanding job, horizontal mobility or job enrichment may be welcome alternatives to upward career progression. Many of these, as we have seen above, may also serve to protect health. Flexible retirement and pension arrangements are often quoted as being desirable, as are better professional development opportunities for older workers (Chartered Insitute of Personal Development, 2008).

Although surveys show that workers tend not to move jobs in a recession, once labor market conditions become more favorable, many intend to move (Chartered Insitute of Personal Development, 2011). Retaining highly valued employees will involve a consideration of age-diverse employee reward packages, organizational culture and working conditions. It is likely that few organizations consider the changing motivations of an age-diverse workforce and thus few have explored the various rewards that might maximize engagement. There are some organizations where age appropriate policies are well established: in the UK, BT is one of them.

BT CASE STUDY

BT is the largest communications service provider in the UK and one of the largest communication companies in the world. It provides service to customers in more than 170 countries with an IP network that connects over 1,270 cities. It helps customers make the most of the convergence of networks and services; mobile and fixed products; media and communications. It is currently the employer of over 90,000 people in 65 countries across a wide range of job types. Diversity is at the heart of its business and the company has a long history of actively ensuring that its employees are treated fairly and equally regardless of their background. It has also long been a pioneer in the area of flexible working and sees this as an enabler for people to balance their responsibilities at work with those in their personal lives, be that managing illness or disability, caring or childcare responsibilities. It considers this a strong motivator, an effective way of achieving a better work–life balance and a key component in attracting and retaining key talent within its organization.

BT is at the forefront of flexible working: selling flexible working solutions to its customers and for its own employees. They believe that most jobs offer possibilities for flexibility that will suit employees, their customers and the company alike. They have developed a number of flexible working solutions for employees at various stages of their career, some of which may be particularly attractive for older workers as they move towards retirement. These options include: wind down (part-time working and job sharing); step down (moving to a lower grade); time out (phased sabbaticals); helping hands (full-time or part-time secondments); and ease down (gradual reduction in hours or responsibilities).

BT advocates the use of conferencing services both as a means of reducing the necessity to travel, but also to facilitate homeworking. They believe that alternative working arrangements help them get the best out of everyone, and hang on to their best people. Their experience has led them to conclude that flexible working makes the business more productive, cost effective and energized.

BT acknowledges statistics that that one in seven people in the workplace will have caring responsibilities for a disabled, chronically ill or elderly friend or relative. This equates to nearly 13,000 of their workforce. With an ageing population this figure is likely to grow. It is in recognition of these commitments and responsibilities borne by a large proportion of its employees that they have developed a policy for carers, so these individuals can make adjustments to attendance, balance their time, for example by making up time and using annual leave at short notice and work flexibly. A practical solution is agreed between the individual and line manager. Equally, it is recognized that employees will themselves experience increasing ill-health and disability with age. BT aims to create an inclusive, respectful and barrier-free environment at work. It provides online advice and support for individuals and their line managers about managing changing capabilities, how to make simple adjustments, and how to maintain personal development. In more complex cases, a specialist service will advise. Master classes on many health-related topics (for example, stroke, pain management, hearing impairment) are available on its intranet. BT has worked with its Trades Unions to produce a 'disability passport'. Its network for people with disabilities portrays a positive image, highlighting the achievements of notable role models both within and outside the company.

The company offers a series of "Planning for Retirement" seminars for all its employees on the principles of personal finance. These are run by independent experts. As well as making sure that employees are well informed on their BT Pensions, they are given information on the principles of capital investment, tax efficiency, state benefits and other related topics. Employees aged 45 plus are also offered seminars on longer-term planning for retirement, focusing on helping them think about what they want from their retirement and how best to achieve it.

Conclusions

Reviews concur that despite declines in various abilities, older workers' overall performance is rarely affected, probably because they compensate for such declines with greater experience and job knowledge (Griffiths, 2007). Older workers may still make valuable contributions late in life, but that contribution may be different from that undertaken earlier (Rabbitt, 1993). The key is to foster work characteristics known to herald both an enjoyable and productive final stage of working life, as well as a healthy and voluntary retirement process. Recognizing that each case is unique, and that individuals may be proactive, reactive or reluctant decision-makers, line managers might begin to involve workers in conversations about their needs and motivations in their progression towards retirement, from at least the age of 50 (Strebler & Baldwin, 2010). This will require an organisational culture where talking about later life planning is legitimate and retirement is not stigmatised. Such conversations would move from "flagging up" issues to fact-finding and finally to decision making. This will require a willingness to accommodate people's changing needs and abilities. Such an approach will increase the likelihood of (i) reducing the risk of exposure to stressful work characteristics; (ii) making work intrinsically more motivating and rewarding; and (iii) easing the transition toward retirement.

Drawing these largely disparate streams of research together produces similar implications for work design. The following suggestions are offered as a tentative summary of what mid-life and older workers need:

- adaptable routes into retirement;
- early advice on pensions and financial planning;
- flexible and transparent options on working hours and location;
- entitlement to time off in lieu, special leave, career breaks and job transfers;
- adequate recovery time (rest breaks and holiday entitlements);
- cutting back long working hours, late night, shift and on call work;
- reduction in physically demanding work;
- opportunities for home working;

- choice in the level and type of work, accommodating age-related changes;
- well-designed tools, equipment and technology;
- an age-aware and age-tolerant organizational culture;
- appreciation of their experience, skills and contribution;
- continued opportunities for professional development;
- information on the importance of physical activity and lifestyle;
- a congenial and respectful social environment.

A few notes of caution are in order. As we move into the twenty-first century, we are witnessing increases in state pension age, sometimes adjusted automatically to increased life expectancy. The resulting extension to working life may disadvantage lower socio-economic groups more than the financially better off, for two reasons: (i) wealth is linked to life expectancy, so the former tend to die younger and (ii) the jobs in which they are typically employed are characterized by physical demands and working conditions known to be associated with stress and related ill-health outcomes. Older blue collar workers are more likely to exhibit negative health outcomes than older white collar workers (Christ, Lee, Fleming, LeBlanc, Arheart, Chung-Bridges, Caban & McCollister, 2007; Eskelinen, Toikkanen, Tuomi, Mauno, Nygård & Ilmarinen, 1991; Fors, Lennartsson & Lundberg, 2007; Petersen & Zwerling, 1998). For them, later retirement may mean longer exposure to adverse working conditions. Recent evidence suggests that retirement may have a particularly beneficial effect on the health and cognitive function of blue collar workers (Coe, von Gaudecker, Lindeboom & Maurer, 2011; Westerlund, Kivimaki, Singh-Manoux, Melchior, Ferrie, Pentti, Jokela, Leineweber, Goldberg, Zins & Vahtera, 2009) suggesting the stronger negative impact of their work. This increased vulnerably of blue collar workers and the possible widening of health inequalities has been subject to little public debate. These workers are also under-represented in studies on ageing and motivation; most research is carried out with people in administrative and managerial jobs.

Further, much research on working conditions has involved limited measures of the working environment. It might be argued that the rapidly changing world of work requires us to be aware of the possibilities of new risk factors: lack of feedback, inadequate appraisal mechanisms, not feeling "valued," poor communication with senior management, inappropriate target-setting, a lack of dignity, perceived inequality or injustice, lack of resources and work–life imbalance. These may reflect more contemporary concerns.

Of course, the general arguments presented here about the need for healthy work and for work–life balance are not new. The nineteenth-century English essayist and critic John Ruskin famously noted: "In order that people may be happy in their work, these three things are needed: they must be fit for it; they must not do too much of it; and they must have a sense of success in it" (1851, p. 7). What is new is that we now understand better the mechanisms linking the quality and quantity of work to a rounded and fulfilling life. Further, it is now clear that the nature of working life has important implications for the quality of life and health both whilst in work and in retirement. As we age, different things become important. Many, as they move toward retirement, experience a desire for a more healthy balance between work and leisure. Enlightened employers recognize this and it is reflected in their policies. Where employers wish to retain the skills and experience of older workers, to promote their productivity, and to protect their health at work and in their future retirement, an evidence-based argument is building for the better design of tomorrow's jobs.

References

Abramson, J. H., Gofin, J., Habib, J., Noam, G., & Kark, J. D. (1994) Work satisfaction and health in the middle-aged and elderly. *International Journal of Epidemiology*, 23(1), 98–106.

Abramson, J. H., Ritter, M., Gofin, J., & Kark, J. D. (1992) Work health relationships in middle-aged and elderly residents of a Jerusalem community. *Social Science & Medicine*, 34(7), 747–755.

Akerstedt, T., Knutsson, A., Westerholm, P., Theorell, T., Alfredsson, L., & Kecklund, G. (2002) Sleep disturbances, work stress and work hours: a cross-sectional study. *Journal of Psychosomatic Research*, 53(3), 741–748.

Alavinia, S. M., & Burdorf, A. (2008) Unemployment and retirement and ill-health: a cross-sectional analysis across European countries. *International Archives of Occupational and Environmental Health*, 82(1), 39–45.

Andrews, J., Manthorpe, J., & Watson, R. (2005) Employment transitions for older nurses: a qualitative study. *Journal of Advanced Nursing*, 51(3), 298–306.

Banks, J., & Smith, S. (2006) Retirement in the UK. *Oxford Review of Economic Policy*, 22(1), 40–56.

Barnes, H., J., P., & Taylor, R. (2004) *Working after State Pension Age: Qualitative Research*. London: DWP.

Birdi, K., Warr, P., & Oswald, A. (1995) Age differences in three components of employee well-being. *Applied Psychology—An International Review*, 44(4), 345–373.

Blekesaune, M., & Solem, P. E. (2005) Working conditions and early retirement: a prospective study of retirement behavior. *Research on Aging*, 27(1), 3–30.

Blythe, J., Baumann, A., Zeytinoglu, I. U., Denton, M., Akhtar-Danesh, N., Davies, S., & Kolotylo, C. (2008) Nursing generations in the contemporary workplace. *Public Personnel Management*, 37(2), 137–159.

British Occupational Health Research Foundation. (2010) Women's experience of working through the menopause. BOHRF London. Available online at: http://www.bohrf.org.uk/downloads/Womens_Experience_of_Working_through_the_Menopause-Dec_2010.pdf, accessed 10 October, 2012.

Brugere, D., Barrit, J., Butat, C., Cosset, M., & Volkoff, S. (1997) Shift work, age and health: an epidemiologic investigation. *International Journal of Occupational and Environmental Health*, 3, S15–19.

Calvo, E., Haverstick, K., & Sass, S. A. (2009) Gradual retirement, sense of control, and retirees' happiness. *Research on Aging*, 31(1), 112–135.

Chandola, T., Britton, A., Brunner, E., Hemingway, H., Malik, M., Kumari, M., Badrick, E., Kivimaki, M., & Marmot, M. (2008) Work stress and coronary heart disease: what are the mechanisms? *European Heart Journal*, 29, 640–648.

Chandola, T., Ferrie, J., Sacker, A., & Marmot, M. (2007) Social inequalities in self reported health in early old age: follow-up of prospective cohort study. *British Medical Journal*, 334 (7601), 990–993B.

Christ, S. L., Lee, D. J., Fleming, L. E., LeBlanc, W. G., Arheart, K. L., Chung-Bridges, K., Caban, A. J., & McCollister, K. E. (2007) Employment and occupation effects on depressive symptoms in older Americans: does working past age 65 protect against depression? *Journals of Gerontology Series B: Psychological Sciences & Social Sciences*, 62B(6), S399–403.

Chartered Institute of Personal Development. (2008) *Managing an Ageing Workforce: The Role of Total Reward*. London: Chartered Institute of Personnel Development.

Chartered Institute of Personal Development. (2011) *Employee Turnover and Retention*. London: Chartered Institute of Personnel Development.

Clark, A., Oswald, A., & Warr, P. (1996) Is job satisfaction U-shaped in age? *Journal of Occupational & Organizational Psychology*, 69(1), 57–81.

Clays, E., De Bacquer, D., Eynen, F. L., Kornitzer, M., Kittel, F., & De Backer, G. (2007) Job stress and depression symptoms in middle-aged workers—prospective results from the Belstress study. *Scandinavian Journal of Work, Environment & Health*, 33(4), 252–259.

Coe, N. B., von Gaudecker, H.-M., Lindeboom, M., & Maurer, J. (2011) The effect of retirement on cognitive functioning. *Health Economics*, 21(8), 913–927.

Cohen, S., Janicki-Deverts, D., & Miller, G. (2007) Psychological stress and disease. *Journal of the American Medical Association*, 298(14), 1685–1687.

Cooper, C. L., & Marshall, J. (1976) Occupational sources of stress: a review of the literature relating to coronary heart disease and mental health. *Journal of Occupational Psychology*, 49, 11–28.

Costa, G. (2005) *Some Considerations about Aging, Shift Work and Work Ability*. Paper presented at the Assessment and Promotion of Work Ability, Health and Well-being of Ageing Workers, Verona, Italy.

Costa, G., Goedhard, W. J. A., & Ilmarinen, J. (2005a) *Assessment of Work Ability and Vitality—A Study of Teachers of Different Age Groups*. Paper presented at the Assessment and Promotion of Work Ability, Health and Well-being of Ageing Workers.

Costa, G., Goedhard, W. J. A., & Ilmarinen, J. (2005b) *Need for Recovery in Ageing Workers*. Paper presented at the Assessment and Promotion of Work Ability, Health and Well-being of Ageing Workers.

Costa, G., Goedhard, W. J. A., & Ilmarinen, J. (2005c) *Work Ability and Perceived Work Stress*. Paper presented at the Assessment and Promotion of Work Ability, Health and Well-being of Ageing Workers.

Council of Civil Services Unions/Cabinet Office. (2004) Work, Stress and Health: The Whitehall II study.

Cox, T., Griffiths, A., & Rial-Gonzalez, E. (2000) *Work-related Stress* (No. 92-828-9255-7). Luxembourg: Office for Official Publications of the European Communities.

De Zwart, B. C. H., & Meijman, T. F. (1994) The aging shiftworker: adjustment or selection. A review of the combined effects of aging and shiftwork. In J. Snel & R. Cremer (eds) *Work and Aging: A European Perspective*. London: Taylor & Francis. pp. 107–120.

Doshi, J. A., Cen, L., & Polsky, D. (2008) Depression and retirement in late middle-aged US workers. *Health Services Research*, 43(2), 693–713.

Drentea, P. (2002) Retirement and mental health. *Journal of Aging & Health*, 14 (2), 167–194.

Eskelinen, L., Toikkanen, J., Tuomi, K., Mauno, I., Nygård, C. H., & Ilmarinen, J. (1991) Symptoms of mental and physical stress in different categories of municipal work. *Scandinavian Journal of Work, Environment & Health*, 17(S1), 82–86.

Eskelinen, L., Toikkanen, J., Tuomi, K., Mauno, I., Nygård, C. H., Klockars, M., & Ilmarinen, J. (1991) Work-related stress symptoms of aging employees in municipal occupations. *Scandinavian Journal of Work, Environment & Health*, 17(S1), 87–93.

European Foundation for the Improvement of Living and Working Conditions. (2008) *Working Conditions of an Ageing Workforce*. Luxembourg: Office for Official Publications of the European Communities.

Falba, T. A. (2008) *Work Expectations, Realizations and Depression in Older Workers*. Cambridge, MA: National Bureau of Economic Research.

Feldt T., H., K., Mäkikangas, A., Kinnunen, U., & Kokko, K. (2009) Development trajectories of Finnish manager's work ability over a 10-year period. *Scandinavian Journal of Work Environment & Health*, 35 (1), 37–47.

Fernandez, M. E., Mutran, E. J., & Reitzes, D. C. (1998) Moderating the effects of stress on depressive symptoms. *Research on Aging,* 20 (2), 163–182.

Fernandez, M. E., Mutran, E. J., Reitzes, D. C., & Sudha, S. (1998) Ethnicity, gender, and depressive symptoms in older workers. *Gerontologist,* 38(1), 71–79.

Ferraro, K. F. (1980) Self-ratings of health among the old and the old-old. *Journal of Health and Social Behavior,* 20, 45–51.

Ford, G. (2005) *Am I Still Needed? Guidance and Learning for Older Adults.* Derby, UK: Centre for Guidance Studies, University of Derby.

Fors, S., Lennartsson, C., & Lundberg, O. (2007) Health inequalities among older adults in Sweden 1991–2002. *European Journal of Public Health,* 18(2), 138–143.

Freeborn, D. K. (2001) Satisfaction, commitment, and psychological well-being among HMO physicians. *Western Journal Of Medicine,* 174(1), 13–18.

Garrosa, E., Moreno-Jiménez, B., Liang, Y., & González, J. L. (2006) The relationship between socio-demographic variables, job stressors, burnout, and hardy personality in nurses: an exploratory study. *International Journal of Nursing Studies,* 45(3), 418–427.

Griffiths, A. (2007) Healthy work for older workers: work design and management factors. In W. Loretto, Vickerstaff, S, White, P. (ed.) *The Future for Older Workers: New Perspectives.* Bristol: Policy Press. pp. 121–137.

Griffiths, A., Knight, A., & Mohd Mahudin, D. (2009) *Ageing, Work-related Stress and Health.* London: The Age and Employment Network, Age Concern and Help the Aged (Age UK).

Hamer, M., Stamatakis, E., & Steptoe, A. (2009) Dose response relationship between physical activity and mental health: the Scottish Health Survey. *British Journal of Sports Medicine,* 43(14), 1111–1114.

Harkonmäki, K., Lahelma, E., Martikainen, P., Rahkonen, O., & Silventoinen, K. (2006) Mental health functioning (SF–36) and intentions to retire early among ageing municipal employees: the Helsinki Health Study. *Scandinavian Journal of Public Health,* 34(2), 190–198.

Härmä, M., Hakola, T., Kandolin, I., Sallinen, M., Virkkala, J., Bonnefond, A., & Mutanen, P. (2006) A controlled intervention study on the effects of a very rapidly forward rotating shift system on sleep-wakefulness and well-being among young and elderly shift workers. *International Journal of Psychophysiology,* 59(1), 70–79.

Härmä, M., & Kandolin, I. (2001) Shift work, age and well-being: recent developments and future perspectives. *Japanese Journal of Ergology,* 30, 287–293.

Health and Safety Executive. (2009a) Self-reported work-related illness (SWI) and workplace injuries (LFS). Available online at: http://www.hse.gov.uk/statistics/publications/swi.htm, accessed 1 April, 2009.

Health and Safety Executive. (2009b) Work-related stress—health and safety in the workplace. Available online at: http://www.hse.gov.uk/stress/index.htm. Accessed 1 April, 2009.

Hendel, D. D., & Horn, A. S. (2008) The relationship between academic life conditions and perceived sources of faculty stress over time. *Journal of Human Behavior in the Social Environment,* 17(1–2), 61–88.

Herzog, A. R., House, J. S., & Morgan, J. N. (1991) Relation of work and retirement to health and well-being in older age. *Psychology and Aging,* 6(2), 202–211.

Heyink, J. (1993) Adaptation and wellbeing. *Psychological Reports,* 73, 1331–1342.

Hillman, C. H., Erickson, K. I., & Kramer, A. F. (2008) Be smart, exercise your heart: exercise effects on brain and cognition. *Nature Reviews Neuroscience,* 9(1), 58–65.

Hirsch, D. (2003) *Crossroads after 50: Improving Choices in Work and Retirement.* York, UK: Joseph Rowntree Foundation.

Idler, E. L. (1993) Age differences in self-assessments of health: age changes, cohort differences, or survivorship. *Journal of Gerontology,* 48, S289–300.

Ilmarinen, J. (1994) Promoting the health and well-being of the older worker: the Finnish experience. In A. Widdecombe & Baroness Cumberlege (eds) Investing in Older People at Work. Contributions, Case Studies and Recommendations; A Symposium for Employers, Policy Makers and Health Professionals from Europe 11–13 October, 1993. London: Health Education Authority. pp. 90–104.

Ilmarinen, J. (2009) Work ability: a comprehensive concept for occupational health research and prevention. *Scandinavian Journal of Work Environment & Health*, 35(1), 1–5.

Ilmarinen, J., Tuomi, K., Eskelinen, L., Nygård, C. H., Huuhtanen, P., & Klockars, M. (1991) Summary and recommendations of a project involving cross-sectional and follow-up studies on the aging worker in Finnish municipal occupations (1981–1985). *Scandinavian Journal of Work, Environment & Health*, 17(S1), 135–141.

Inceoglu, I., Segers, J., & Bartram, D. (2011) Age-related differences in work motivation. *Journal of Occupational and Organisational Psychology*, 85(2), 300–329.

Isaksson, K., & Johansson, G. (2000) Adaptation to continued work and early retirement following downsizing: long-term effects and gender differences. *Journal of Occupational & Organizational Psychology*, 73(2), 241–256.

Jansson-Frojmark, M., Lundqvist, D., Lundqvist, N., & Linton, S. J. (2007) Psychosocial work stressors for insomnia: a prospective study on 50–60-year-old adults in the working population. *International Journal of Behavioral Medicine*, 14(4), 222–228.

Jorm, A. F., Windsor, T. D., Dear, K. B., Anstey, K. J., Christensen, H., & Rodgers, B. (2005) Age group differences in psychological distress: the role of psychosocial risk factors that vary with age. *Psychological Medicine*, 35(9), 1253–1263.

Kanfer, R., & Ackerman, P. L. (2004) Aging, adult development, and work motivation. *Academy of Management Review*, 29(3), 440–458.

Karpansalo, M., Kauhanen, J., Lakka, T. A., Manninen, P., Kaplan, G. A., & Salonen, J. T. (2005) Depression and early retirement: prospective population based study in middle aged men. *Journal of Epidemiology & Community Health*, 59(1), 70–74.

Kenney, J. W. (2000) Women's 'inner-balance': a comparison of stressors, personality traits and health problems by age groups. *Journal of Advanced Nursing*, 31(3), 639–650.

Keran, C., & Duchon, J. C. (1999) *Age Differences in the Adjustment to Shift Work*. In Proceedings of Human Factors and Ergonomics Society Annual Meeting. New York: Human Factors and Ergonomics Society. pp. 182–185.

Kilbom, Å., Westerholm, P., Hallsten, L., & Furåke, B. (1996) *Work after 45?* Proceedings from a scientific conference held in Stockholm 22–25 September 199. Paper presented at the Work after 45?, Stockholm.

Kiss, P., De Meester, M., & Braeckman, L. (2008) Differences between younger and older workers in the need for recovery after work. *International Archives of Occupational and Environmental Health*, 81(3), 311–320.

Kloimuller, I., Karazman, R., & Geissler, H. (1997) How do stress impacts change with aging in the profession of bus drivers? Results from a questionnaire survey on 'health and competition' among bus drivers in a public transport system in 1996. In P. Seppala, T. Luopajarvi, C.-H. Nygård & M. Mattila (eds) *From Experience to Innovation: Volume V*. Helsinki, Finland: Finnish Institute of Occupational Health. pp. 454–456.

Landa, J. M. A., Lopez-Zafra, E., Martos, M. P. B., & Aguilar-Luzon, M. D. C. (2008) The relationship between emotional intelligence, occupational stress and health in nurses: a questionnaire survey. *International Journal of Nursing Studies*, 45(6), 888–901.

Lindeboom, M., & van Doorslaer, E. (2004) Cut-point shift and index shift in self-reported health. *Journal of Health Economics*, 23, 1083–1099.

Maddox, G. L. (1962) Some correlates of differences in self-assessment of health status among the elderly. *Journal of Gerontology*, 17, 180–185.

Mein, G., Martikainen, P., Hemingway, H., Stansfeld, S., & Marmot, M. (2003) Is retirement good or bad for mental and physical health functioning? Whitehall II longitudinal study of civil servants. *Journal of Epidemiology & Community Health*, 57(1), 46–49.

Melzer, D., Buxton, J., & Villamil, E. (2004) Decline in common mental disorder prevalence in men during the sixth decade of life—evidence from the National Psychiatric Morbidity Survey. *Social Psychiatry and Psychiatric Epidemiology*, 39(1), 33–38.

Miller, B. K., Rutherford, M. A., & Kolodinsky, R. W. (2008) Perceptions of organizational politics: a meta-analysis of outcomes. *Journal of Business and Psychology*, 22(3), 209–222.

Ohman, L., Bergdahl, J., Nyberg, L., & Nilsson, L. G. (2007) Longitudinal analysis of the relation between moderate long-term stress and health. *Stress and Health*, 23(2), 131–138.

Pattani, S., Constantinovici, N., & Williams, S. (2001) Who retires early from the NHS because of ill health and what does it cost? A national cross sectional study. *British Medical Journal*, 332, 208–209.

Petersen, J. S., & Zwerling, C. (1998) Comparison of health outcomes among older construction and blue-collar employees in the United States. *American Journal of Industrial Medicine*, 34(3), 280–287.

Phillips, J., Bernard, M., & Chittenden, M. (2002) *Juggling Work and Care: The Experiences of Working Carers of Older Adults*. Bristol, UK: The Policy Press.

Phillipson, C. (2002) *Transitions from Work to Retirement: Developing a New Social Contract*. York, UK: Joseph Rowntree Foundation.

Phillipson, C., & Smith, A. (2005) *Extending Working Life: A Review of the Research Literature* (No. 299). London, UK: Department for Work and Pensions.

Pinquart, M., & Sörensen, S. (2003) Differences between caregivers and noncaregivers in psychological health and physical health: a meta-analysis. *Psychology and Aging*, 18(2), 250–267.

Poole, C. (1997) Retirement on grounds of ill-health: cross sectional survey in six organisations in United Kingdom. *British Medical Journal*, 314, 929–932.

Pransky, G. S., Benjamin, K. L., & Savageau, J. A. (2005) Early retirement due to occupational injury: who is at risk? *American Journal of Industrial Medicine*, 47(4), 285–295.

Rabbitt, P. (1993) Management of the working population. *Ergonomics*, 34, 775–790.

Rambur, B., Palumbo, M. V., McIntosh, B., & Thomas, C. (2008) A cross-disciplinary statewide healthcare workforce analysis. *Journal of Allied Health*, 37(2), 105–109.

Reijula, K., Räsänen, K., Hämäläinen, M., Juntunen, K., Lindbohm, M. L., Taskinen, H., Bergbom, B., & Rinta-Jouppi, M.. (2003) Work environment and occupational health of Finnish veterinarians. *American Journal of Industrial Medicine*, 44(1), 46–57.

Ritvanen, T., Louhevaara, V., Helin, P., Vaisanen, S., & Hanninen, O. (2006) Responses of the autonomic nervous system during periods of perceived high and low work stress in younger and older female teachers. *Applied Ergonomics*, 37(3), 311–318.

Robson, S. M., & Hansson, R. O. (2007) Strategic self development for successful aging at work. *International Journal of Aging & Human Development*, 64(4), 331–359.

Ruskin, J. (1851) *Pre-Raphaelitism*. New York: John Wiley.

Salonen, P., Arola, H., Nygård, C. H., Huhtala, H., & Koivisto, A. M. (2003) Factors associated with premature departure from working life among ageing food industry employees. *Occupational Medicine*, 53(1), 65–68.

Shanas, E., & Maddox, G. L. (1976) Aging, health and the organization of health resources. In R. Binstook & E. Shanas (eds) *Handbook of Aging and the Social Sciences*. New York: Van Nostrand Reinhold. pp. 592–618.

Sharpley, C. F., & Layton, R. (1998) Effects of age of retirement, reason for retirement, and pre-retirement training on psychological and physical health during retirement. *Australian Psychologist*, 33(2), 119–124.

Shmueli, A. (2003) Socio-economic and demographic variation in health and in its measures: the issue of reporting heterogeneity. *Social Science & Medicine*, 57, 125–134.

Shultz, K., Morton, K., Weckerle, J. (1998) The influence of push and pull factors on voluntary and involuntary early retirees' retirement decision and adjustment. *Journal of Vocational Behaviour*, 53, 45–57.

Siegrist, J., Wahrendorf, M., von dem Knesebeck, O., Jurges, H., & Borsch-Supan, A. (2007) Quality of work, well-being, and intended early retirement of older employees—baseline results from the SHARE Study. *European Journal of Public Health*, 17(1), 62–68.

Siegrist, J., Wahrendorf, M., von dem Knesebeck, O., Jürges, H., & Börsch-Supan, A. (2006) Quality of work, well-being, and intended early retirement of older employees—baseline results from the share study. *European Journal of Public Health*, 17(1), 62–68.

Smeaton, D., Vegeris, S., & Sahin-Dikmen, M. (2009) *Older Workers: Employment Preferences, Barriers and Solutions*. Manchester: Equality and Human Rights Commission.

Strebler, M., & Baldwin, S. (2010) *Should I Stay, or Should I Go? Older Employees' Later Life Planning in a Business Context*. Brighton: Institute for Employment Studies.

Taylor, M., & Shore, L. (1995) Predictors of planned retirement age: an application of Beehr's model. *Psychology and Aging*, 10(1), 76–83.

Tuomi, K., Ilmarinen, J., Klockars, M., Nygård, C.-H., Seitsamo, J., Huuhtanen, P., Martikainen, R., & Aalto, L. (1997) Finnish research project on aging workers in 1981–1992. *Scandinavian Journal of Work, Environment & Health*, 23(S1), 7–11.

Tuomi, K., Ilmarinen, J., Seitsamo, J., Huuhtanen, P., Martikainen, R., Nygård, C. H., & Klockars, M. (1997) Summary of the Finnish research project (1981–1992) to promote the health and work ability of aging workers. *Scandinavian Journal of Work Environment & Health*, 23(S1), 66–71.

van Solinge, H., & Henkens, K. (2008) Adjustment to and satisfaction with retirement: two of a kind? *Psychology & Aging*, 23(2), 422–434.

Volkoff, S., & Pueyo, V. (2005) How do elderly workers face tight time constraints? *International Congress Series*, 1280, 17–22.

Warr, P., Butcher, V., Robertson, I., & Callinan, M. (2004) Older people's well-being as a function of employment, retirement, environmental characteristics and role preference. *British Journal of Psychology*, 95(297–324).

Westerlund, H., Kivimaki, M., Singh-Manoux, A., Melchior, M., Ferrie, J. E., Pentti, J., Jokela, M., Leineweber, C., Goldberg, M., Zins, M., & Vahtera, J. (2009) Self-related health before and after retirement in France (GAZEL): a cohort study. *The Lancet*, 374(9705), 1889–1896.

Winwood, P. C., Winefield, A. H., & Lushington, K. (2006) Work-related fatigue and recovery: the contribution of age, domestic responsibilities and shiftwork. *Journal of Advanced Nursing*, 56(4), 438–449.

Yeandle, S., Bennett, C., Buckner, L., Fry, G., & Price, C. (2007) *Managing Caring and Employment*. London, UK: Carers UK.

14 Creating a Safe and Healthy Work Environment: The Latest Thinking and Research Evidence

SHARON CLARKE, SARA GUEDIRI AND ELINOR O'CONNOR

The responsibility of organizations to protect their workforce from injuries and ill-health has long been enshrined in the health and safety legislation of many countries; for example, in the UK the Health and Safety at Work Act (1974) and in the US, the Occupational Safety and Health Act (1970). There is little doubt that the effective management of health and safety has significant financial benefits for organizations, in terms of avoiding the substantial costs associated with occupational injuries and ill-health. In 2008/09, workplace injuries in the UK led to 4.7 million lost work days, with considerable financial cost to employers and the economy (Health and Safety Executive, 2010). Furthermore, there is growing evidence that effective management of health and safety is positively associated with the bottom-line profitability of organizations (for example, Fernández-Muñiz, Montes-Peón & Vázquez-Ordás, 2009; Huang, Leamon, Courtney, Chen & DeArmond, 2007; Kaminski, 2001; Maudgalya, Genaidy & Shell, 2008). Given the increased emphasis on organizations to integrate social responsibility into their corporate mission, the provision of positive and healthy working conditions may be viewed as a competitive advantage, as well as a moral and legal obligation. In relation to corporate social responsibility, organizations should understand that poor workplace health and safety will have repercussions for corporate reputation, as well as causing financial and human losses (Hart, 2010). These are significant issues, especially in hard economic times, when there is often a tendency to see a squeeze on organizations' investment in health and safety.

Although from an organizational perspective, health and safety issues have tended to be viewed as a single domain, researchers have focused on either safety or health, with relatively little attention devoted to the crossover between them. Broadly speaking, occupational psychologists have focused their attention on two main research strands. The first is concerned with psychological well-being at work, with a particular focus on occupational stress, including the causes of stress, its consequences for the individual and the organization, and interventions for stress risk management. The second area of interest is focused on psychological aspects of physical safety at work, such as psychological factors in managing risks to physical health (for example, exposure to hazards, such as loud noise) and human factors in accident causation and prevention. More recently, researchers have begun to explore possible mechanisms linking well-being and safety. Applied implications include: the development of targeted interventions for improving safety in the workplace, as well as the potential for stress management interventions to be of benefit to organizational safety, in addition to the reduction of workplace stress.

In terms of accident reduction, organizations have made significant progress through the implementation of strategies aimed at the risk assessment and control of physical hazards, technological advances in machinery and equipment, and safety management systems. However, the diminishing return of such investment signals the need for increased effort to understand the human contribution to accidents, and the cultural and social context within which they occur. This has led to the rise in popularity of the concept of "safety climate" (for example, Cox & Flin, 1998; Glendon, 2008). Safety climate refers to employees' shared perceptions about safety procedures, practices and the priority that is assigned to safety in an organization in relation to other company goals (Neal & Griffin, 2006). There is substantial evidence to link a positive safety climate with lower workplace accident rates (Clarke, 2006). Recent research has focused on identifying the antecedents of safety climate and their relative influence on safety outcomes (Clarke, 2010). This research can be implemented in the design of interventions to improve safety climate and so lead to accident reduction. Increasingly emphasis has moved away from interventions at the "coal-face" (for example, behavioral safety) toward the managerial and organizational level (for example, leadership interventions).

This chapter will review the latest thinking and research in these areas. The conclusions will focus on the implications for the design and implementation of safety interventions and recommendations for organizations seeking to provide a safe and healthy working environment.

Enhancing Workplace Safety and Health: The Role of Safety Climate

Safety climate developed as a specific construct out of the theoretical background of universal organizational climate, which describes employee attitudes and perceptions about a wide range of aspects within their work environment (Reichers & Schneider, 1990). Schneider (1975) stressed that organizational policies and practices relate to specific aspects of a company such as ethics, service quality or safety, and that these can often stand in relative contention with each other. Safety in the workplace tends to be rewarded and supported to varying degrees depending on situational conditions (Zohar, 2010). For instance, under time pressure or when costs are rising, safety might be less emphasized than if a project is on schedule or within budget. Thus, the formally espoused value of safety and the concrete realization of safety may differ and change depending on competing organizational demands (Zohar, 2010; Shannon & Norman, 2009). The definition and operationalization of safety climate needs to focus on the true priority of safety as it is this actual practice of safety, as opposed to formally advocated policies, that guides employees' behavior in equivocal situations where safety conflicts with other targets (Zohar, 2008, 2010).

A substantial body of research has linked safety climate to different safety-related outcomes including compliance with safety rules and participation in safety activities (Neal & Griffin, 2006; Neal, Griffin & Hart, 2000), injury frequency rates (Hofmann & Stetzer, 1996; Zohar, 2000), injury severity (Johnson, 2007) and accident under-reporting (Probst, Brubaker & Barsotti, 2008; Probst & Estrada, 2010). It is theorized that employees use their shared safety climate perceptions as guidance to infer organizational standards as to which behaviors are desired, appropriate and rewarded with regards to safety (Zohar, 2000). In a meta-analytic study including 35 studies across different industries, Clarke (2006) found that safety climate acts as a predictor of safety performance. Further, studies were found to differ in their design as to whether safety outcomes were assessed prior, or subsequent, to measuring safety climate (that is, studies either had a retrospective or a prospective design). It was found that research design moderated the relationship between safety climate and accident involvement; that is, under a prospective study design, safety climate functioned as a significant predictor of accident involvement, but not when safety climate was used to indicate past safety outcomes (retrospective design). Beus, Payne, Bergman and Arthur (2010) extended this research and tested safety climate as a leading and a lagging indicator of injuries. The results from their meta-analysis demonstrated that safety climate is linked to future injury rates and that safety climate perceptions at the individual- and organizational-level are affected by past injuries that occurred in an organization. Thus, past injuries can have a detrimental impact on employees' safety climate perceptions, which in turn increases the likelihood of future injuries. To avoid the impetus of this vicious circle, it is important to demonstrate the steps that have been taken in response to an injury to employees, in order to prevent a deterioration of safety climate perceptions and avert future injuries (Beus, Payne, Bergman & Arthur, 2010). Christian, Bradley, Wallace and Burke (2009) meta-analytically tested the underlying pathways through which safety climate impacts upon employees' safety performance. The findings indicated that a favorable safety climate increases employees' safety knowledge and safety motivation, which in turn lowered accident and injury rates. Clarke (2010) investigated how safety climate affects safety outcomes and provided meta-analytical evidence that the relationship between safety climate and accidents is partially mediated through employee health and well-being. In line with this, Nahrgang, Morgeson and Hofmann (2011) found that safety climate had an indirect effect on adverse safety events (that is, near misses, errors) through alleviating employee "burnout" (an extreme form of psychological strain). Thus, a positive safety climate is associated with reduced stress and anxiety levels, which in turn are related to fewer adverse safety events. This demonstrates that a positive safety climate improves workplace safety not only through motivational processes, as Christian, Bradley, Wallace and Burke (2009) argued, but also through creating a more positive work environment where workers are shielded against mental and physical job demands (Clarke, 2010; Nahrgang, Morgeson & Hofmann, 2011).

Evidence for an Association between Occupational Stress and Workplace Safety

Although recent research has highlighted possible associations between safety climate and psychological well-being, there is a body of research dating back to the 1980s which has examined links between workplace safety and occupational stress. An early review by Murphy, Dubois and Hurrell (1986) reported that although few studies had been conducted, empirical evidence indicated the existence of an association between stress and workplace accidents. Murphy, Dubois and Hurrell suggested that stress-related factors, such as anxiety, fatigue, reduced motivation and increased alcohol consumption, might compromise employee performance, increasing the risk of human error and accidents at work. Almost a decade later, a comprehensive literature review by Johnston (1995) identified just 20 papers that reported quantitative data on the relationship between stress and workplace injuries and accidents. Johnston's review supported the existence of an association between stress and workplace safety, although she noted that methodological limitations in research, particularly with regard to the definition and measurement of stress, necessitated that more rigorous investigation of the link be conducted. Later research has focused on specific workplace stressors and their links with safety at work (see Clarke & Cooper, 2004, for a review), with a particular emphasis on the mediating role of psychological strain.

Research studies have drawn on transactional theories of workplace stress (for example, Lazarus & Folkman, 1984) to explain significant associations between occupational stressors (sources of pressure, such as job insecurity), stress symptoms (such as psychological strain) and safety outcomes. Cognitive, emotional and motivational pathways would be expected to mediate the influence of psychological strain on safety outcomes (such as accidents). Murphy, Dubois and Hurrell (1986) suggested cognitive pathways whereby the relationship between occupational stress and accidents might reflect an increased risk of human error in stressed workers. A number of studies have investigated the link between occupational stress and human error (for example, Elfering, Semmer & Grebner, 2006), including cognitive failure (for example, Wadsworth, Simpson, Moss & Smith, 2003). Cognitive failure refers to a category of commonplace errors involving problems with concentration (for example, starting a task and getting distracted into doing something else); memory (for example, forgetting where an object has been placed); or the execution of an action (for example, selecting the wrong object when carrying out an action, such as pouring from a carton of juice, rather than a carton of milk, into a cup of coffee). The unifying feature of these diverse events is that they involve "absentmindedness:" a failure in executive control of attention. Although cognitive failures are an everyday occurrence and are frequently of trivial consequence, they can result in accidents, particularly in safety-critical work settings (for example, Chappelow, O'Connor, Johnson & Blair, 1999). A number of studies have provided evidence of a relationship between occupational stressors, psychological strain and violation of workplace procedures (for example, Cullen & Hammer, 2007; Greiner, Krause, Ragland & Fisher, 1998). For example, Fogarty and McKeon (2006) found that individual distress had a significant influence on nurses' failure to follow regulations, which in turn increased the likelihood of medication errors. Given the nature of violations, pathways are more likely to be motivational, rather than cognitive (Reason, Manstead, Stradling & Baxter, 1990).

Particular attention has been focused on the role of "burnout," an extreme form of psychological strain, which is characterized by feelings of exhaustion, negative and cynical attitudes to work, and a sense of reduced professional efficacy (Maslach & Schaufeli, 2001). Using the Conservation of Resources (COR) stress model (Hobfoll, 1989), Halbesleben (2010) proposed that people affected by emotional exhaustion (a dimension of burnout) lack the personal resources to follow time-consuming or complicated procedures at work, including procedures that are designed to protect safety. Halbesleben argued that exhausted workers might husband their depleted personal resources by circumventing demanding safety procedures, increasing the risk of injury and accidents. In a cross-lagged study of healthcare staff, Halbesleben found support for the mediating role of violations in the relationship between exhaustion and injury, with exhaustion related to self-reported violations of safety procedures, which was in turn associated with a greater incidence of subsequent self-reported injuries. There is also evidence that burnout increases the likelihood of errors, especially cognitive failure. Shanafelt, Balch, Bechamps, Russell, Dyrbye, Satele, Collicot, Novotny, Sloan & Freischlag (2010) found a positive association between surgeons' scores on the Maslach Burnout Inventory and self-reported clinical errors occurring in the previous three months. Although the underlying model hypothesizes that burnout leads to greater frequency of errors, in this study self-reported errors were associated with a subsequent measure of burnout. Given that burnout is characterized by a sense of reduced professional efficacy, greater frequency of errors might reflect a negative appraisal of their own performance by those experiencing burnout, rather than a causal relationship in either direction between strain and error. Evidence for this argument is provided by a study conducted by Fahrenkopf, Sectish, Barger, Sharek, Lewin, Chiang, Edwards, Wiedermann & Landrigan (2008). They found that hospital doctors affected by burnout reported committing both a greater number of drug errors and more frequent "significant" drug errors in the previous month than those with low burnout scores. However, objectively-measured drug error rates between the two groups did not differ. In addition to the effects on self-perceived performance, there is evidence that burnout has a significant effect on attentional control. A study by Van der Linden, Keijsers, Eling and van Schaijk (2005) investigated the relationships of self-reported cognitive failures and two objective measures of attentional control with a measure of burnout. Three groups participated in the study: a group affected by "clinical" burnout, who had high scores on the Maslach Burnout Inventory and had taken leave of absence from work; a group with elevated, but not extreme, burnout scores, who remained at work; and a control group of workers with low burnout scores. Higher burnout scores were associated with greater frequency of self-reported cognitive failure. The clinical burnout group demonstrated poorer control of attention in the objective performance tasks than the control group. It is notable that the clinical burnout group did not show poorer performance on all elements of the tasks; only those aspects that reflected attentional control were impaired. A recent study by Willert, Thulstrup, Hertz and Bonde (2010) provides further evidence of an association between strain and impairment of attentional control: they reported a significant reduction in cognitive failure as one of several outcomes in an evaluation of a cognitive–behavioral intervention for work-related stress.

Most recently, research on the interactions between occupational stress and workplace safety has used the Job Demands–Resources (JD–R) framework (Bakker & Demerouti, 2007) to investigate whether job-related characteristics that are associated with well-being are also related to safety outcomes at work. The JD–R model proposes that job demands (for example, role conflict) are aspects of work that consume the individual's personal resources and potentially impair well-being. In contrast, job resources (for example, job control and social support) foster employee motivation and engagement, and can also counter the negative impact of job demands. Hansez and Chmiel (2010) found that the job demands of work overload and role ambiguity were associated with greater frequency of "routine" violations of work procedures (that is, regular use of less-effortful, non-standard means of completing tasks). The relationship between demands and violations was mediated by lower well-being. Conversely, the job resources of autonomy, support from colleagues, and job quality were associated with lower frequency of both routine and "situational" violations (that is, deviations fostered by specific circumstances), with the relationship mediated by engagement. Turner, Chmiel, Hershcovis and Walls (2010) used the JD–R model to investigate the relationship between well-being and safety in railway maintenance work. They proposed that perceived support for safety from colleagues could be considered as a job resource with the potential to moderate the association between job demands (role overload) and poor safety outcomes. Turner, Chmiel, Hershcovis and Walls found that role overload was positively associated with self-reported exposure to hazardous events at work in the previous year. Support for safety on the part of managers, supervisors and co-workers was associated with fewer reports of hazardous experiences. Co-worker support alone moderated the association between overload and hazardous events: when role overload was high, fewer incidences of exposure to danger were reported by those who perceived that they had high levels of co-worker support. Turner, Chmiel, Hershcovis and Walls suggested that the contribution of co-worker support (but not supervisor or manager support) to reducing risk when overload was high was due to track maintenance workers having relatively more interaction with their co-workers than with supervisors or managers.

Therefore, there is evidence to suggest that the JD–R framework can be usefully extended to understanding the role of occupational stress in workplace safety (Hansez & Chmiel, 2010; Turner, Chmiel, Hershcovis & Walls, 2010). Nahrgang, Morgeson and Hofmann (2011) also applied the JD–R model in a comprehensive meta-analytic review of the relationship between psychological well-being and safety outcomes in four industry sectors: health care, construction, transportation and manufacturing/processing. The study focused on job demands and resources that are characteristic of safety-critical work settings. The job demands assessed included the presence of hazards, physical demand, task complexity and task ambiguity; these were identified by the authors as "hindrance" rather than "challenge" demands. Hindrance demands are those that impede performance, and are negatively related to engagement, whereas challenge demands have the potential to promote a sense of mastery, and are positively associated with engagement (Crawford, LePine & Rich, 2010). The job resources assessed included safety knowledge, general and safety-specific support from colleagues, leadership and safety climate. Both the presence of hazards in the workplace and task complexity were associated with poorer well-being, which in turn was related to more frequent injuries and accidents. Greater safety knowledge and supportive colleagues were related to greater well-being and engagement; the latter was linked in turn to safer behavior and fewer adverse events in the workplace, but was unrelated to injuries and accidents. A valuable contribution of Nahrgang, Morgeson and Hofmann's study was its identification of differences across work sectors in the relative importance of different job demands and resources to well-being and engagement, and in turn, workplace safety. For example, the presence of hazards made the largest contribution to variation in well-being in the construction and transportation sectors, whereas in the health care and manufacturing sectors, task complexity was most important for variation in well-being.

To date the primary mechanism that has been investigated is the mediating role of psychological strain and burnout. There has been less investigation of other possible mechanisms. However, Clarke (2011) has looked at the effects of hindrance and challenge stressors on safety behaviors mediated by cognitive, affective and motivational pathways, which are not the effects of strain or burnout. The meta-analytic review found that the hypothesized adverse effects of hindrance stressors on safety outcomes were supported, as hindrance stressors were associated with lower safety compliance and safety participation, and subsequently greater near-misses and injuries. However, challenge stressors (which are appraised as challenging but manageable and so may be viewed as opportunities for personal growth) were hypothesized to have positive cognitive, affective and motivational effects on behavior, leading to greater compliance and participation, and subsequently fewer near-misses and injuries. Although these safety benefits were not supported, challenge stressors were found to have zero effects on both compliance and injuries. These findings suggest that different types of stressor will have differential effects on safety outcomes. Safety climate is likely to act as a significant moderator in the relationship between occupational stressors and safety outcomes. When the safety climate is positive, employees are more likely to expend the extra effort required to maintain both safety and production-related behavior: as rewards for complying with safety rules and procedures are most likely to be given in a positive safety climate. In a negative safety climate, however, rewards are not associated with safety performance, and safety is not prioritized over production goals. Therefore, employees are less likely to maintain compliance with safety procedures or help co-workers, when short-cuts and violations may speed production and lead to rewards for meeting production targets (Wallace & Chen, 2006).

Antecedents of Safety Climate

Given the significant role of safety climate—both as a mediator and a moderator—in relation to safety outcomes, it is crucial to understand its antecedents, that is, those factors which shape employees' safety perceptions. Safety climate has been defined as reflecting management commitment to safety. Whilst this is reflected in policies, procedures and practices, daily interactions with managers and supervisors will determine employees' perceptions of the "real" priority given to safety (Zohar, 2008, 2010). Understanding the factors that influence employees' safety perceptions will provide important information about the points at which organizations may most successfully intervene to improve safety climate.

Leadership Style as a Predictor of Safety Climate

Leaders are a crucial source of influence for employee behaviors and attitudes (Podsakoff, MacKenzie & Bommer, 1996; Walumbwa, Avolio & Zhu, 2008). This contention is supported by a long tradition of leadership research stretching back to the early work of Lewin (1951). Transferred to the domain of safety this suggests that leaders shape employee perceptions about the value of safety in their organization (that is, safety climate), which in turn influences employees' individual safety performance (Clarke & Ward, 2006; Zacharatos, Barling & Iverson, 2005). Based on social learning theory (Bandura, 1977) and the concept of social-sense-making (Blumer, 1969; Weick, 1995), it is postulated that leaders' influence on employee climate perceptions is the product of a social learning process (Zohar, 2010). Employees extract interpretations about organizational-level practices and procedures (that is, climate) from their repeated observations and interactions with their leader (Dragoni, 2005; Richardson & Vandenberg, 2005). As safety often competes with other organizational targets such as productivity, it creates ambiguous situations for employees as to what behavior is desired and appropriate (Zohar, 2010). To make sense of such an ambiguous work environment, employees draw upon their leader's verbal accounts and behavior. By rewarding and disciplining certain behaviors, leaders affect employees' motivation to display some behavior and refrain from others, which in turn fosters a shared sense of values and higher-order goals among employees. Thus, leaders convey the organizational value of safety through their interactions and communications with their subordinates and hence shape perceptions of safety climate and affect safety performance (Zohar, 2010).

Empirical research investigating leadership as a determinant of safety climate and employee safety behavior has focused on transformational leadership style (Bass, 1985, 1990). Transformational leaders are described as fostering close relationships, concerned about employee well-being, with their behavior transmitting a sense of purpose, shared goals and mutual understanding (Avolio, Bass & Jung, 1999). Empirical studies have demonstrated that transformational leadership is associated with positive safety outcomes (for example, Barling, Loughlin & Kelloway, 2002; Kelloway, Mullen & Francis, 2006; Zacharatos, Barling & Iverson, 2005; Zohar, 2002a). Barling, Loughlin and Kelloway (2002) showed that safety-specific transformational leadership influences safety climate perceptions, which in turn links to safety-related events and occupational injuries. In a longitudinal study, Clarke and Flitcroft (2008) provided empirical evidence for a lagged effect of transformational leadership on employees' safety perceptions. Their findings in particular identified inspirational motivation as an effective leader tactic to enhance the perceived value of safety. Kelloway, Mullen and Francis (2006) demonstrated that transformational leadership has a positive effect on safety, and that passive leadership does not have a neutral effect on safety, but instead a detrimental influence on safety outcomes. Passive or laissez-faire leadership describes the absence of leadership where leaders are uninvolved, unavailable and avoid making decisions or taking responsibility (Avolio, Bass & Jung, 1999; Hartog, Muijen & Koopman, 1997). Kelloway, Mullen and Francis's (2006) finding underlines that a leader does not have to explicitly endorse unsafe behavior for a detrimental impact on safety to occur, but that the sheer lack of safety leadership has a negative effect on safety (even if a leader does not necessarily approve unsafe behavior or compromises safety). Thus, to positively influence employees' safety attitudes and behavior, leaders need to proactively engage in the importance of safety.

The importance of front-line supervisors for workplace safety was demonstrated by Zohar and Luria (2010). They showed that supervisory leaders can compensate for a poor safety climate at the organizational level and are essential for implementing management safety policies. Supervisors who are characterized as highly transformational create a positive safety climate within their work team, even if senior management policies and strategies do not actively promote the priority of safety. Thus, transformational supervisors can safeguard their work team against managerial choices that compromise the priority of safety. If a favorable safety climate does exist at the higher organizational level, transformational supervisors are more effective in implementing this higher-level organizational support of safety within their group, in comparison to leaders who are less transformational. This research places front-line supervisors in a focal point where they function as "gatekeepers" who are critical in implementing organizational policies that recognize the importance of safety as well as protecting their team members against organizational strategies that devalue safety (Zohar & Luria, 2010).

Mullen, Kelloway and Teed (2011) note that in real-life situations, leaders are likely to display a range of leadership tactics and do not usually rely to just one type of leadership. They tested the effect on safety of leaders who are not consistent in their style of leadership, but sometimes use transformational tactics and at other times rely on passive leadership. The findings indicate that leaders, who use both transformational and passive leadership, counteract or weaken the positive effects on safety of transformational leadership with their passive leadership behavior. Hence, inconsistent leaders mixing poor and competent leadership styles are less effective in promoting workplace safety.

While passive leadership is generally regarded as a non-effective leadership style, with the exception of transformational leadership, there is little research on the influence of other positive forms of leadership on safety. General organizational research highlights that the active components of transactional leadership have a positive impact on organizational outcomes (Judge & Piccolo, 2004). In the context of safety, Clarke and Ward (2006) showed that transactional leader behavior has beneficial effects on safety. They included transformational as well as transactional leadership characteristics when testing the effect of different behavioral leader tactics on employees' safety climate perceptions and safety participation. The leadership tactics that emerged as significant predictors of increased safety were rational persuasion, inspirational appeals and consultation. Rational persuasion, which emerged as the most powerful influence tactic of safety behavior in their study, is associated with transactional leadership style. Coalition as an influence tactic, which also is related to transactional leadership, showed a direct positive effect on safety behavior. Thus, these findings lend support for more directive leader behaviors to be important variables in increasing workplace safety. Safety performance distinguishes itself from other aspects of job performance, as a substantial part of it involves refraining from certain behavior, abiding by instructions, rules and regulations, and to relinquish short-term goals such as comfort or production speed. A leader may provide an initial argument for safety rules and regulations through active monitoring of safety performance and offering incentives for safety obedience (transactional leadership) and then further enhance the importance of safety by creating enthusiasm for it through inspirational appeals and intellectual stimulation, which are tactics associated with transformational leadership style. Thus, a leader may have to decide in which situations transactional leadership may be more appropriate than transformational leadership and vice versa. Zohar (2002a) provides empirical evidence that both contingent reward, which is a component of transactional leadership, and transformational leadership predict injury rates through safety climate. Hence, the combination of transformational and transactional techniques may be effective to maximize a leader's influence on workers' safety attitudes and behavior, although little research has empirically tested this suggestion.

Quality of Leader–Employee Relationships as a Source of Safety

In addition to adapting certain types of leadership, the quality of the relationship between managers and their subordinates is important in order to positively influence employee safety behavior and attitudes. Leader–member exchange (LMX) theory characterizes high-quality interactions between leaders and members through loyalty, trust, mutual concern and openness (Graen & Uhl-Bien, 1995; Yukl, 2010). Leaders who display these values in their social exchanges with employees are being perceived as concerned and committed to their workforce, which is reciprocated by employees through displaying desirable behaviors, such as working safely (Hofmann & Morgeson, 1999; Hofmann, Morgeson & Gerras, 2003; Zohar, 2002a). Empirical research shows that high LMX induces open safety communication and the expression of safety concerns by employees (Hofmann & Morgeson, 1999) and positively influences safety citizenship behavior (Hofmann, Morgeson & Gerras, 2003). Thus, managers can promote safety and reduce the likelihood of accidents by fostering close, high-quality relations with their employees.

Trust in the leader–employee relationship has emerged as a particularly important relational characteristic for enhancing safety. Conchie and Donald (2009) showed that the extent to which employees trust their leaders with regards to safety, contributes to the effect of leadership on safety; that is, under high levels of trust in a leader, leadership is more likely to result in enhanced safety behavior, while under low trust conditions, leaders' actions have a weaker effect on employee safety behavior. This can be explained in the way that if a leader is trusted by his/her subordinates, employees are more likely to interpret the leader's actions in a positive way and react favorably, but under low trust levels the same action is likely to be interpreted more negatively by employees (Dirks & Ferrin, 2002). Hence, if workers trust that their supervisor or manager is competent and knowledgeable in safety concerns, they are more likely to take communicated safety information on board and translate it into behavioral actions. Luria (2010) related trust between leaders and their subordinates to actual injury rates through a positive safety climate. It should be noted that the link between trust and safety has been attributed to an effect of trust on employees' as well as leaders' behavior (Luria, 2010; Conchie, Taylor & Charlton, 2011). Employees that trust their leaders are more receptive to management's safety information and feel a stronger sense of obligation to put this into practice, and simultaneously leaders that are trusted by their workforce are more committed to their workers' welfare and therefore make greater efforts to create a safe work environment.

The findings on trust in the leader–subordinate relationship underline that in order for leaders' efforts to enhance safety to be effective, managers and supervisors need to gain their employees' trust as well as engage in positive leadership styles. It follows from this that intervention efforts should include strategies on building trusting, high LMX relationships with employees. This is in line with empirical qualitative and quantitative research, which has identified trust in management as an important facet for the success of safety initiatives (De Pasquale & Geller, 1999; Cox, Jones & Rycraft, 2004). Integrity and ability have been identified as the most important managerial characteristics to develop employees' trust in safety leadership, and lack of integrity and lack of benevolence are linked to distrust in safety leadership (Conchie, Taylor & Charlton, 2011), providing guidance on the qualities that leaders ought to develop in order to promote trust within their employee relations.

Co-worker Relationships as a Source of Safety

Research has shown that while hierarchical relationships with supervisors and management are important for workplace safety, a growing body shows that lateral relations with co-workers can function as sources of influence to promote safety. Earlier research on co-workers and safety suggested that if co-workers care about their colleagues' welfare and safety, they actively engage in behavior that promotes a safer work environment to prevent each other from harm (Geller, 1991; Geller, Roberts & Gilmore, 1996). More recently, studies have demonstrated that co-workers function as behavioral models for each other that enhance safety performance. Jiang, Yu, Li and Li (2009) showed that employees' perceptions about their co-workers' safety behavior and knowledge influenced their own safety behavior; this suggests that providing employees with the opportunity to observe their co-workers' safety practices and encourage sharing of safety knowledge between co-workers can increase employees' engagement in safe behavior. Parallel to the influence of leaders, employees utilize perceptions and observations of their fellow workers as information cues to verify the relative value of safety within an organization and clarify behavioral norms (Ashforth, 1985; Bommer, Miles & Grover, 2003). If an employee observes his/her co-workers as committed to safety, then he or she is also more likely to engage in safe behavior. However, the findings by Jiang, Yu, Li and Li (2009) showed that employee safety behavior was highest if positive perceptions about peers' safety performance were coupled with a high safety climate, and the effect of peer perceptions on safety behavior was weakened under low safety climate. This would suggest that management efforts to develop a positive safety climate remain crucial in order to capitalize on the role of co-workers as behavioral safety models. However, research by Yagil and Luria (2010) found that if safety climate is low, high-quality relationships among co-workers can provide a buffer against a detrimental effect on safety behavior. Such findings indicate that co-worker support can, in some circumstances, substitute for poor safety climate. High-quality social interactions between work colleagues are characterized through genuine, mutual concern for each other, which is not dependent on management's priority of safety and thus has a positive influence on workplace safety outcomes, even under conditions of poor safety climate (Yagil & Luria, 2010). Empirical evidence shows that interpersonal support for safety between co-workers is associated with better safety communication (Tucker, Chmiel, Turner, Hershcovis & Stride, 2008) and fewer hazardous safety events (Turner, Chmiel, Hershcovis & Wallis, 2010). Although there is evidence that co-workers can promote safety within teams, there is inconsistent evidence to date regarding the extent to which this can substitute for weak safety leadership.

Overall, empirical findings emphasize that peers can function as agents of support and guidance, which positively affects safety outcomes. Moreover research signifies that co-workers influence safety through two pathways: employees use their peers' safety behavior as a source of guidance and direction (for example, Jiang, Yu, Li & Li, 2009) and the second pathway refers to interpersonal concern and caring, where employees remind each other of hazards or risks to avoid that one of their colleagues gets injured (for example, Geller 1991; Yagil & Luria, 2010).

The Relative Importance of Leaders and Co-Workers for Workplace Safety

Organizational research (not safety-specific) has shown that co-workers exert mutual influence on each other, which is effective over and above the impact of single leadership (Bowers & Seashore, 1966; Ensley, Hmieleski & Pearce, 2006; Pearce & Sims, 2002). Formal leaders are not always available and co-workers often have greater proximity to each other than supervisor–employee relationships (Ensley, Hmieleski &

Pearce, 2006; Yukl, 2010). In other words, co-workers by definition have the same hierarchical status, which entails greater presence to each other relative to vertical leaders, so that interactions among co-workers occur more frequently and are less restricted than leader–employee interactions (Ferris & Mitchell, 1987). This highlights co-workers as a more available source to interpret organizational policies and clarify the true priority of safety (Lingard, Cooke & Blismas, 2009; Turner, Chmiel, Hershcovis & Wallis, 2010). Support for this comes from Turner, Chmiel, Hershcovis and Wallis (2010) who showed that under demanding work conditions, co-workers are the most important resource to alleviate a detrimental effect of high job demands on safety. In this study, role overload (as a measure of job demands) was associated with increased hazardous events. However, if co-workers were experiencing high levels of role overload, but also felt supported by their co-workers in safety matters, then this resulted in fewer hazardous events. Supervisor and organizational support as potential alternative resources for employees to draw on when faced with high job demands were not as strongly related to fewer hazardous events compared to co-worker support. Yet, under less demanding working conditions, co-worker safety support was no longer associated with reduced rates safety hazardous events. The authors concluded that in situations of high job demands, employees are more likely to rely on their co-workers as a source of safety support than on supervisors or senior management, while in other, less stressful conditions, co-workers are not as relevant a resource for promoting safety. Therefore, it is important that research does not only focus on one source that offers safety support for employees (that is, the supervisor, their co-workers, their manager), but instead explores the effect of several sources of influence in the work environment (Turner, Chmiel, Hershcovis & Wallis, 2010). Luria (2008) tested the combined influence of formal leadership and group cohesion on safety climate. Results from the study showed that under poor leadership conditions, a strong safety climate can still be achieved if group cohesion is high. The strongest safety climate was found under conditions of high transformational leadership and high group cohesion. Luria (2008) concluded that leadership and co-worker cohesion exert an additive, concomitant effect on safety climate, with social co-worker interactions augmenting the effect of positive formal leadership and countervailing the effect of poor leadership. Nahrgang, Morgeson and Hofmann (2011) compared the relative importance of different antecedents, including co-worker social support and leadership for safety outcomes in a meta-analytic study using primary studies from a range of industries. Social support among co-workers explained the largest amount of variance in accident and injury rate as well as adverse safety events. However, leadership explained a larger amount of variance in unsafe behavior compared to co-worker social support, although the greatest amount of variance in unsafe behavior was accounted for by safety climate. They suggest that workplace safety is best achieved if companies develop a supportive environment that integrates all sources of support rather than focusing on individual agents of support. For instance, leadership training to managers and supervisors should not only concentrate on leaders' behavior and their dyadic relationship with employees, but should also offer information on how to encourage and facilitate social support among co-workers.

In sum, a growing body of research on the relationship between co-workers' social interactions and workplace safety indicates that co-workers offer an important source of influence that can supplement good leadership to maximize safety, and compensate poor leadership to avoid deterioration of safety.

Integration of the Research Work on Safety Climate and Safety Outcomes

In a meta-analytic study, Clarke (2010) integrated the different antecedents of workplace safety that research has identified into a dynamic net of influence and support. In the model, employee perceptions about the different aspects in their work environment (that is, perceptions about leadership, job, work group, organization) were combined into the higher-order construct of psychological climate. The results showed that employees' psychological climate perceptions affected safety climate, which had an effect on safety behavior through organizational commitment and job satisfaction. Ultimately, safety behavior was linked to accident and injury rates. With regards to the different dimensions of psychological climate, perceptions about organizational attributes (for example, openness, awareness, innovation) had the strongest effect on safety climate, followed by perceptions about leadership (for example, trust, support, interaction), work group (for example, co-operation, friendliness) and job characteristics (for example, control, autonomy). Overall, the study underlines that a wide range of influence sources form a mesh that shapes workplace safety. It highlights that in addition to narrow safety-specific initiatives, organizations can efficiently enhance employees' perceptions about the value of safety by adopting an approach that addresses wider aspects of psychological climate. Leadership and co-workers have so far emerged as the most salient determinants of workplace safety, but in response to calls that a work environment consists of a wider, dynamic web of influence sources, research has attributed attention to other psychosocial factors.

Drawing on findings from global organizational research, Ford and Tetrick (2011) explored the link between empowerment, organizational identification and safety. They point out that a sense of self-control and a feeling of belonging to one's organization have been identified as core predictors of organizational outcomes. However, in high-risk, hazardous work environments, it may be more difficult to promote these employee attitudes due to the often more restrictive and regulated nature of safety-critical work contexts (Ford & Tetrick, 2011). In their study, Ford and Tetrick (2011) compared empowerment perceptions and organizational identification of hospital employees who work across different job roles, but all on the same worksite. The results highlighted that occupational hazards were negatively associated with empowerment and organizational identification. In job roles that were more hazardous, employees were more likely to feel a lack of control and identified less with their organizations. Consistent with this, earlier research has signified that employees' perceptions of high risk in their jobs are related to lower levels of job satisfaction (McLain, 1995). Yet, at the same time, empirical findings indicate that such job orientations and attitudes are important for safe behavior, that is, empowerment has been positively linked with safety participation (Ford & Tetrick, 2011), unsafe behavior and accident rates (Hechanaova-Alampay & Beehr, 2001). Similarly, autonomy has been positively associated with safe working behavior (Parker, Axtell & Turner, 2001), fewer adverse safety events (Nahrgang, Morgeson & Hofmann, 2011) and less occupational injuries (Barling, Kelloway & Iverson, 2003). These studies indicate that the psychological state of having control over one's work, and a self-sense of competence and meaningfulness lead employees to engage in and take responsibility for the promotion of safety. Similarly, research has demonstrated a positive link between employees' job attitudes and safety. High levels of job satisfaction have been related to better safety behavior (Clarke, 2010; Barling, Kelloway & Iverson, 2003) and organizational identification was associated with safety participation in Ford and Tetrick's (2011) study. Barling, Kelloway and Iverson (2003) suggested that positive attitudes toward one's job and company (for example, job satisfaction and organizational identification) and a sense of control and competence (for example, empowerment and autonomy) positively affect safety through propelling a feeling of ownership, meaning and better application of skill and knowledge. Thus, while positive role perceptions and a sense of self-determination of one's work actions are important for workplace safety, these appear to be more difficult to establish for employees who work in hazardous environments. This implies that management needs to dedicate particular attention to the development of a sense of satisfaction, belonging and self-determination for employees who work in hazardous job roles. For instance, McLain (1995) demonstrated that it is employees' subjective interpretation of risk that is linked to job satisfaction. If employees work in an occupation or work environment that is inherently hazardous, organizations should make efforts to reduce employees' subjective risk perception and hence increase job attitudes by demonstrating commitment to safety.

Overview on Interventions and Recommendations for Organizations

Overall, there is substantial evidence that a strong, positive safety climate is a pivotal variable in maximizing safe behavior and reducing the likelihood of accidents and injuries. These findings caption safety climate as a viable preventive measure for managers to assess and monitor a company's safety levels before an accident occurs. Although some efforts have been made to design interventions to directly enhance safety climate, evidence of their success is lacking (Glendon, Clarke & McKenna, 2006). However, identifying key antecedents of safety climate may offer more accessible points for intervention.

Leadership and leadership style have been discussed as important predictors of safety climate and safety outcomes. Although various styles of active leadership may be effective in promoting safety, there is consistent research support for the importance of a transformational leadership style. There is evidence that transformational leadership style can be taught to managers (Barling, Weber & Kelloway, 1996) and longitudinal research provides empirical support that companies can train their managers and supervisors to engage in types of leadership that promotes safe behavior and safety attitudes (Zohar, 2002b). In a study by Mullen and Kelloway (2009) managers in health care organizations were randomly assigned to one of three groups: (1) an intervention group that received safety-specific transformational leadership training; (2) an intervention group that received general (non safety-specific) transformational leadership training; and (3) a control group that did not receive leadership training. The leadership interventions were half-day, group workshops aimed at providing participating managers with an understanding of transformational leadership theory and equip them with practical strategies on how to use transformational leader tactics in their day-to-day work. The safety-specific and the generic leadership training intervention were analogous to each other with a former focusing on safety-related goals of leadership. The post-training assessment showed that managers who participated in the safety-specific leadership training had higher perceptions about their self-efficacy as a leader and more positive safety attitudes compared to the group that received generic leadership training and the control group. Also, intentions to promote safety were higher in the safety-specific training group than in the control group, but did not significantly differ from the group that received the generic leadership intervention. Moreover, employees who had managers that participated in the safety-specific leadership training rated their leaders as higher in transformational safety-specific leadership and had more positive safety climate perceptions than the control group. The effect of leadership training on employees' safety climate perceptions shows that training a small number of key individuals (that is, managers in the company) can have positive downward effects on a wider number of employees, thus identifying leadership safety training as an efficient way to improve workplace safety.

A comparison of the pre-training and the post-training ratings in Mullen and Kelloway's (2009) study showed that these did not increase but were in fact slightly lower than after the training workshops across all three training conditions. This highlights the importance of other organizational factors than leadership as antecedents of workplace safety. For instance, Luria, Zohar and Erev (2008) demonstrated that the effectiveness of safety leadership interventions is dependent on employees' visibility in the work environment. Visibility referred to the extent that the physical work environment in the department made it easy for the managers to observe their employees' working behavior. Managers at five different manufacturing factories participated in a leadership intervention program that aimed to increase safety-related interactions between leaders and their subordinate. While all managers received feedback and guidance on how to improve their safety-related exchanges with employees, managers who worked in high visibility work environments (for example, a single, open work space) showed a stronger increase in their safety interactions with subordinates over time than managers who worked in low visibility work environments (that is, employees work in different rooms, spread out across the plant site). The study is an example of how the engineering approach and the behavioral approach to safety can be combined to maximize safe working. Thus, implementing supervisor-based as opposed to front-line individual-based safety interventions, offers the economic advantage that through the actions of a few key individuals site-wise safety behavior change can be achieved (Mullen & Kelloway, 2009; Zohar, 2002a); however, work contextual factors need to be taken into consideration in order to ensure effectiveness of such training factors. Previous discussion has also highlighted the importance of other contextual factors in the success of leadership interventions, including the existing level of trust and LMX between managers and employees. Leadership interventions may be less successful when applied in an unfavorable climate of low trust and poor relations with employees.

Evidence regarding the relationship between occupational stress and safety has important implications for new approaches to developing and implementing workplace safety interventions. Research has shown that safety outcomes are affected by psychological strain and employees' general health and well-being. There is substantial research evidence to highlight the deleterious effects of burnout on safety; therefore, organizations would be recommended to carefully monitor their workforce to identify and remediate cases of employee burnout. As a preventive measure, interventions should be focused on stress management, prior to stressors leading to such debilitating conditions for employees as burnout. Stress management interventions have been found to have positive effects not only on psychological well-being, but also on variables associated with accidents. For example, Willert, Thulstrup, Hertz and Bonde (2010) demonstrated that a cognitive–behavioral intervention for work-related stress was effective in reducing levels of cognitive failure (which can lead to accidents). Mearns, Hope, Ford and Tetrick (2010) found that corporate workforce health investment (that is, degree of investment in health promotion activities and occupational health training) was significantly related to safety climate, employee commitment and safety compliance. Such findings support the safety-related benefits that may be gained from investment in stress management activities. Although there is a small body of research evidence at present, there is positive indication that investment in both health and safety interventions can have a significant impact on the promotion of a safe and healthy work environment.

References

Ashforth, B. E. (1985) Climate formation: issues and extension. *Academy of Management Review*, 10(4), 837–847.

Avolio, B. J., Bass, B. M., & Jung, D. (1999) Re-examining the components of transformational and transactional leadership using the Multifactor Leadership Questionnaire. *Journal of Occupational and Organizational Psychology*, 72(4), 441–462.

Bakker, A. B., & Demerouti, E. (2007) The job demands–resources model: state of the art. *Journal of Managerial Psychology*, 22, 309–328.

Bandura, A. (1977) *Social Learning Theory*. Englewood Cliffs, NJ: Prentice-Hall.

Barling, J., Loughlin, C., & Kelloway, E. K. (2002) Development and test of a model linking safety-specific transformational leadership and occupational safety. *Journal of Applied Psychology*, 87(3), 488–496.

Barling, J., Kelloway, E. K., & Iverson, R. D. (2003) High-quality work, job satisfaction, and occupational injuries. *Journal of Applied Psychology*, 88(2), 276–283.

Barling, J., Weber, T., & Kelloway, E. K. (1996) Effects of transformational leadership training on attitudinal and financial outcomes: a field experiment. *Journal of Applied Psychology*, 81(6), 827–832.

Bass, B. M. (1985) *Leadership and Performance Beyond Expectations*. London: Free Press, Collier Macmillan.

Bass, B. M. (1990) From transactional to transformational leadership: learning to share the vision. *Organizational Dynamics*, 18(3), 19–31.

Beus, J. M., Payne, S. C., Bergman, M. E., & Arthur, W. (2010) Safety climate and injuries: an examination of theoretical and empirical relationships. *Journal of Applied Psychology*, 95(4), 713–27.

Blumer, H. (1969) *Symbolic Interactionism: Perspective and Method*. Englewood-Cliffs, NJ: Prentice-Hall.

Bommer, W. H., Miles, E. W., & Grover, S. L. (2003) Does one good turn deserve another? Coworker influences on employee citizenship. *Journal of Organizational Behavior*, 24(2), 181–196.

Bowers, D. G., & Seashore, S. E. (1966) Predicting organizational effectiveness with a four-factor theory of leadership. *Administrative Science Quarterly*, 11(2), 238–263.

Chappelow, J. W., O'Connor, E. M., Johnson, C., & Blair, R. C. (1999) *Causal Factors in Military Aircraft Accidents*. DERA CHS Report CR990245, DERA Centre for Human Sciences, Farnborough, UK.

Christian, M. S., Bradley, J. C., Wallace, J. C., & Burke, M. J. (2009) Workplace safety: a meta-analysis of the roles of person and situation factors. *Journal of Applied Psychology*, 94(5), 1103–1127.

Clarke, S. (2006) The relationship between safety climate and safety performance: a meta-analytic review. *Journal of Occupational Health Psychology*, 11(4), 315–327

Clarke, S. (2010) An integrative model of safety climate: linking psychological climate and work attitudes to individual safety outcomes using meta-analysis. *Journal of Occupational and Organizational Psychology*, 83(3), 553–578.

Clarke, S. (2011) *The Effects of Occupational Stressors on Work Accidents and Safety Behaviour: A Meta-analytic Review*. Annual Meeting of the Academy of Management, San Antonio TX, USA, August 2011.

Clarke, S., & Cooper, C. L. (2004) *Managing the Risk of Workplace Stress: Health and Safety Hazards*. London: Routledge.

Clarke, S., & Flitcroft, C. (2008) The effects of transformational leadership on perceived safety climate—a longitudinal study. *Journal of Occupational Health and Safety—Australia and New Zealand*, 24(3), 237–247.

Clarke, S., & Ward, K. (2006) The role of leader influence tactics and safety climate in engaging employees' safety participation. *Risk Analysis*, 26(5), 1175–1185.

Conchie, S. M., & Donald, I. J. (2009) The moderating role of safety-specific trust on the relation between safety-specific leadership and safety citizenship behaviors. *Journal of Occupational Health Psychology*, 14 (2), 137–147.

Conchie, S. M., Taylor, P. J., & Charlton, A. (2011) Trust and distrust in safety leadership: mirror reflections? *Safety Science*, 49(8–9), 1208–1214.

Cox, S., & Flin, R. (1998) Safety culture: philosopher's stone or man of straw? *Work and Stress*, 12(3), 189–201.

Cox, S., Jones, B., & Rycraft, H. (2004) Behavioural approaches to safety management within UK reactor plants. *Safety Science*, 42(9), 825–839.

Crawford, E. R., LePine, J. A., & Rich, B. L. (2010) Linking job demands and resources to employee engagement and burnout: a theoretical extension and meta-analytic test. *Journal of Applied Psychology*, 95, 834–848.

Cullen, J. C., & Hammer, L. B. (2007) Developing and testing a theoretical model linking work-family conflict to employee safety. *Journal of Occupational Health Psychology*, 12(3), 266–278.

DePasquale, J., & Geller, E. S. (1999) Critical success factors for behavior-based safety: a study of twenty industry-wide applications. *Journal of Safety Research*, 30(4), 237–249.

Dirks, K. T., & Ferrin, D. L. (2002) Trust in leadership: meta-analytic findings and implications for research and practice. *Journal of Applied Psychology*, 87(4), 611– 628.

Dragoni, L. (2005) Understanding the emergence of state goal-orientation in organizational work groups: the role of leadership and multilevel climate perceptions. *Journal of Applied Psychology*, 90(6), 1084–1095.

Elfering, A., Semmer, N. K., & Grebner, S. (2006) Work stress and patient safety: observer-rated work stressors as predictors of characteristics of safety-related events reported by young nurses. *Ergonomics*, 49, 457–469.

Ensley, M. D., Hmieleski, K. M., & Pearce, C. L. (2006) The importance of vertical and shared leadership within new venture top management teams: implications for the performance of startups. *Leadership Quarterly*, 17(3), 217–231.

Fahrenkopf, A. M., Sectish, T. C., Barger, L. K., Sharek, P. J., Lewin, D., Chiang, V. W., Edwards, S., Wiedermann, B. L., & Landrigan, C. P. (2008) Rates of medication errors among depressed and burnt out residents: prospective cohort study. *British Medical Journal*, 336(7642), 488–491.

Fernández-Muñiz, B., Montes-Peón, J. M., & Vázquez-Ordás, C. J. (2009) Relation between occupational safety management and firm performance. *Safety Science*, 47, 980–991.

Ferris, G. R., & Mitchell, T. R. (1987) The components of social influence and their importance for human resources research. In K. M Rowland & G. R Ferris (eds) *Research in Personnel and Human Resources Management*. Greenwich, CT: JAI Press. pp. 103–128.

Fogarty, G. J., & McKeon, C. M. (2006) Patient safety during medication administration: the influence of organizational and individual variables on unsafe work practices and medication errors. *Ergonomics*, 49, 444–456.

Ford, M. T., & Tetrick, L. E. (2011) Relations among occupational hazards, attitudes, and safety performance. *Journal of Occupational Health Psychology*, 16(1), 48–66.

Geller, E. S. (1991) If only more would actively care. *Journal of Applied Behavior Analysis*, 24(4), 607–612.

Geller, E. S., Roberts, D. S., & Gilmore, M. R. (1996) Predicting propensity to actively care for occupational safety. *Journal of Safety Research*, 27(1), 1–8.

Glendon, I. (2008) Editorial—Safety culture: snapshot of a developing concept. *Journal of Occupational Health and Safety—Australia and New Zealand*, 24(3), 179–189.

Glendon, A. I., Clarke, S. G., & McKenna, E. (2006) *Human Safety and Risk Management* (2nd Edition). Boca Raton, Florida: CRC Press.

Graen, G. B., & Uhl-Bien, M. (1995) Relationship-based approach to leadership: development of leader–member exchange (LMX) theory of leadership over 25 years: applying a multi-level multi-domain perspective. *Leadership Quarterly*, 6(2), 219–247.

Greiner, B. A., Krause, N., Ragland, D. R., & Fisher, J. M. (1998) Objective stress factors, accidents and absenteeism in transit operators: a theoretical framework and empirical evidence. *Journal of Occupational Health Psychology*, 3(2), 130–146.

Halbesleben, J. R. B. (2010) The role of exhaustion and workarounds in predicting occupational injuries: a cross-lagged panel study of health care professionals. *Journal of Occupational Health Psychology*, 15(1), 1–16.

Hansez, I., & Chmiel, N. (2010) Safety behavior: job demands, job resources, and perceived management commitment to safety. *Journal of Occupational Health Psychology*, 15(3), 267–278.

Hart, S. M. (2010) Self-regulation, corporate social responsibility, and the business case: do they work in achieving workplace equality and safety? *Journal of Business Ethics*, 92(4), 585–600.

Hartog, D. N., Muijen, J. J., & Koopman, P. L. (1997) Transactional versus transformational leadership: an analysis of the MLQ. *Journal of Occupational and Organizational Psychology*, 70(1), 19–34.

Health and Safety Executive. (2010) *Self-reported Work-related Illness and Workplace Injuries in 2008/09: Results from the Labour Force Survey*. Available online at: http://www.hse.gov.uk/statistics/lfs/lfs0809.pdf. Accessed September 2010.

Hechanova-Alampay, R., & Beehr, T. A. (2001) Empowerment, span of control, and safety performance in work teams after workforce reduction. *Journal of Occupational Health Psychology*, 6(4), 275–282.

Hobfoll, S. E. (1989) Conservation of resources: a new attempt at conceptualizing stress. *American Psychologist*, 44(3), 513–524.

Hofmann, D. A., & Morgeson, F. P. (1999) Safety-related behavior as a social exchange: the role of perceived organizational support and leader-member-exchange. *Journal of Applied Psychology*, 84(2), 286–296.

Hofmann, D. A., Morgeson, F. P., & Gerras, S. (2003) Climate as a moderator of the relationship between LMX and content specific citizenship: safety climate as an exemplar. *Journal of Applied Psychology*, 88(1), 170–178.

Hofmann, D. A., & Stetzer, A. (1996) A cross-level investigation of factors influencing unsafe behaviours and accidents. *Personnel Psychology*, 49(2), 307–339.

Huang, H-Y, Leamon, T. B., Courtney, T. K., Chen, P. Y., & DeArmond, S. (2007) Corporate financial decision-makers' perceptions of workplace safety. *Accident Analysis and Prevention*, 39, 767–775.

Jiang, L., Yu, G., Li, Y., & Li, F. (2010) Perceived colleagues safety knowledge/behavior and safety performance: safety climate as a moderator in a multilevel study. *Accident Analysis and Prevention*, 42(5), 1468–1476.

Johnson, S. E. (2007) The predictive validity of safety climate. *Journal of Safety Research*, 38(5), 511–521.

Johnston, J. J. (1995) Occupational injury and stress. *Journal of Occupational Health and Environmental Medicine*, 37(10), 1199–1203.

Judge, T. A., & Piccolo, R. F. (2004) Transformational and transactional leadership: a meta-analytic test of their relative validity. *Journal of Applied Psychology*, 89(5), 755–768.

Kaminski, M. (2001) Unintended consequences: organizational practices and their impact on workplace safety and productivity. *Journal of Occupational Health Psychology*, 6(2), 127–138.

Kelloway, E. K., Mullen, J., & Francis, L. (2006) Divergent effects of transformational and passive leadership on employee safety. *Journal of Occupational Health Psychology*, 11(1), 76–86.

Lazarus, R. S., & Folkman, S. (1984) *Stress, Appraisal, and Coping*. New York: Springer.

Lingard, H. C., Cooke, T., & Blismas, N. (2009) Group-level safety climate in the Australian construction industry: within-group homogeneity and between-group differences in road construction and maintenance. *Construction Management and Economics*, 27(4), 419–432.

Lewin, K. (1951) *Field Theory in Social Science* (2nd edition). New York: Harper.

Luria, G. (2008) Climate strength: how leaders form consensus. *Leadership Quarterly*, 19(1), 42–53.

Luria, G. (2010) The social aspects of safety management: trust and safety climate. *Accident Analysis and Prevention*, 42(4), 1288–1295.

Luria, G., Zohar, D., & Erev, I. (2008) The effect of workers visibility on effectiveness of intervention programs: supervisory-based safety interventions. *Journal of Safety Research*, 39(3), 273–280.

Maslach, C., and Schaufeli, W. (2001) Job burnout. *Annual Review of Psychology*, 52(1), 397–422.

Maudgalya, T., Genaidy, A., & Shell, R. (2008) Productivity–quality–costs–safety: a sustained approach to competitive advantage: a systematic review of the National Safety Council's case studies in safety and productivity. *Human Factors and Ergonomics in Manufacturing*, 18(2), 152–179.

McLain, D. L. (1995) Responses to health and safety risk in the work environment. *Academy of Management Journal*, 38(6), 1726–1743.

Mearns, K., Hope, L., Ford, M. T., & Tetrick, L. E. (2010) Investment in workforce health: exploring the implications for workforce safety climate and commitment. *Accident Analysis and Prevention*, 42, 1445–1454.

Mullen, J. E., & Kelloway, E. K. (2009) Safety leadership: a longitudinal study of the effects of transformational leadership on safety outcomes. *Journal of Occupational and Organizational Psychology*, 82(2), 253–272.

Mullen, J. E., Kelloway, E. K., & Teed, M. (2011) Inconsistent style of leadership as a predictor of safety behaviour. *Work & Stress*, 25(1), 41–54.

Murphy, L. R., DuBois, D., & Hurrell, J. J. (1986) Accident reduction through stress management. *Journal of Business and Psychology*, 1(1), 5–18.

Nahrgang, J. D., Morgeson, F. P., & Hofmann, D. A. (2011) Safety at work: a meta-analytic investigation of the link between job demands, job resources, burnout, engagement, and safety outcomes. *Journal of Applied Psychology*, 96(1), 71–94.

Neal, A., & Griffin, M. A. (2006) A study of the lagged relationships among safety climate, safety motivation, safety behaviour, and accidents at the individual and group levels. *Journal of Applied Psychology*, 91(4), 946–953.

Neal, A., Griffin, M. A., & Hart, P. M. (2000) The impact of organizational climate on safety climate and individual behavior. *Safety Science*, 34(1–3), 99–109.

Parker, S. K., Axtell, C. M., & Turner, N. (2001) Designing a safer workplace: importance of job autonomy, communication quality, and supportive supervisors. *Journal of Occupational Health Psychology*, 6(3), 211–228.

Pearce, C. L., & Sims, H. P. (2002) The relative influence of vertical vs. shared leadership on the longitudinal effectiveness of change management teams. *Group Dynamics: Theory, Research and Practice*, 6(2), 172–197.

Podsakoff, P. M., MacKenzie, S. B., & Bommer, W. H. (1996) Transformational leader behaviors and substitutes for leadership as determinants of employee satisfaction, commitment, trust, and organizational citizenship behaviors. *Journal of Management*, 22(2), 259–298.

Probst, T. M., & Estrada, A. X. (2010) Accident under-reporting among employees: testing the moderating influence of psychological safety climate and supervisor enforcement of safety practices. *Accident Analysis and Prevention*, 42(5), 1438–1444.

Probst, T. M., Brubaker, T. L., & Barsotti, A. (2008) Organizational under-reporting of injury rates: an examination of the moderating effect of organizational safety climate. *Journal of Applied Psychology*, 93(5), 1147–1154

Reason, J. T., Manstead, A., Stradling, S., & Baxter, J. S (1990) Errors and violations on the roads: a real distinction? *Ergonomics*, 33(10–11), 1315–1332.

Reichers, A. E., & Schneider, B. (1990) Climate and culture: an evolution of constructs. In B. Schneider (ed.) *Organizational Climate and Culture*. San Francisco, CA: Jossey-Bass. pp. 5–39.

Richardson, H. A., & Vandenberg, R. J. (2005) Integrating managerial perceptions and transformational leadership into a work-unit level model of employee involvement. *Journal of Organizational Behavior*, 26(5), 561–589.

Schneider, B. (1975) Organizational climates: an essay. *Personnel Psychology*, 28(4), 447–479.

Shanafelt, T. D., Balch, C. M., Bechamps, G., Russell, T., Dyrbye, L., Satele, D., Collicott, P., Novotny, P. J., Sloan, J., & Freischlag, J. (2010) Burnout and medical errors among American surgeons. *Annals of Surgery*, 251(6), 995–1000.

Shannon, H., & Norman, G. (2009) Deriving the factor structure of safety climate scales. *Safety Science*, 47(3), 327–329.

Tucker, S., Chmiel, N., Turner, N., Hershcovis, M. S., & Stride, C. B. (2008) Perceived organizational support for safety and employee safety voice: the mediating role of coworker support for safety. *Journal of Occupational Health Psychology*, 13(4), 319–330.

Turner, N., Chmiel, N., Hershcovis, M. S., & Walls, M. (2010) Life on the line: job demands, perceived co-worker support for safety, and hazardous work events. *Journal of Occupational Health Psychology*, 15(4), 482–493.

Van der Linden, D., Keijsers, G. P., Eling, P., & Van Schaijk, R. (2005) Work stress and attentional difficulties: an initial study on burnout and cognitive failures. *Work and Stress*, 19(1), 23–36.

Wadsworth, E. J. K., Simpson, S. A., Moss, S. C., & Smith, A. P. (2003) The Bristol stress and health study: accidents, minor injuries and cognitive failures at work. *Occupational Medicine*, 53(6), 392–397.

Wallace, C., & Chen, G. (2006) A multilevel integration of personality, climate, self-regulation, and performance. *Personnel Psychology*, 59, 529–557.

Walumbwa, F. O., Avolio, B., & Zhu, W. (2008) How transformational leadership weaves its influence on individual job performance: the role of identification and efficacy beliefs. *Personnel Psychology*, 61(4), 791–825.

Willert, M. V., Thulstrup, A. M., Hertz, J., & Bonde, J. P. (2010) Sleep and cognitive failures improved by a three-month stress management intervention. *International Journal of Stress Management*, 17(3), 193–213.

Weick, K. E. (1995) *Sensemaking in Organizations*. Thousand Oaks, CA: Sage.

Yagil, D., & Luria, G. (2010) Friends in need: the protective effect of social relationships under low-safety climate. *Group & Organization Management*, 35(6), 727–750.

Yukl, G. (2010) *Leadership in Organizations* (7th edition). Upper Saddle River, NJ: Pearson Prentice Hall.

Zacharatos, A., Barling, J., & Iverson, R. D. (2005) High-performance work systems and occupational safety. *The Journal of Applied Psychology*, 90(1), 77–93.

Zohar, D. (2000) A group-level model of safety climate: testing the effect of group climate on microaccidents in manufacturing jobs. *Journal of Applied Psychology*, 85(4), 587–596.

Zohar, D. (2002a) The effects of leadership dimensions, safety climate, and assigned priorities on minor injuries in work groups. *Journal of Organizational Behavior*, 23(1), 75–92.

Zohar D. (2002b) Modifying supervisory practices to improve sub-unit safety: a leadership-based intervention model. *Journal of Applied Psychology*, 34(5), 567–577.

Zohar, D. (2008) Safety climate and beyond: a multi-level multi-climate framework. *Safety Science*, 46(3), 376–387.

Zohar, D. (2010) Thirty years of safety climate research: reflections and future directions. *Accident Analysis and Prevention*, 42(5), 1517–1522.

Zohar, D., & Luria, G. (2010) Group leaders as gatekeepers: testing safety climate variations across levels of analysis. *Applied Psychology*, 59(4), 647–673.

15 Inculcating Values-based Leadership: One Canadian Firm's Attempted Effort

MARK S. SCHWARTZ

Ethics and leadership go hand-in hand.

(Hitt, 1990, p. 1)

When it comes to the establishment of an ethical corporate culture, there appears to be at least two inter-related foundational requirements: (1) the existence of an explicit set of core ethical values; and (2) the presence of ethical leadership, that is, an ethical "tone at the top." Some companies appear however to have been more successful than others when it comes to establishing an appropriate "tone at the top," that is, leaders that behave according to an explicit set of core ethical values. Building on previous values-based leadership research, this study examines the process of one Canadian-based firm's initial efforts, following a series of embarrassing scandals and negative publicity, to inculcate values-based leadership via a set of core ethical values.

Ethical Corporate Culture

However, before one can define an "ethical" corporate culture, one must start with a definition of the broader concept of corporate culture found in organizational theory literature (see Geertz, 1973; Pettigrew, 1979; Schein, 1985). For example, corporate culture has been defined as: "...a property of an organization constituted by (1) its members' taken-for granted beliefs regarding the nature of reality, called assumptions; (2) a set of normative, moral, and functional guidelines or criteria for making decisions, called values; and (3) the practices or ways of working together that follow from the aforementioned assumptions and values, called artifacts" (Jones, Felps & Bigley, 2007, p. 142). For the purposes of this study however, corporate culture might be considered more simply as representing "... the shared assumptions, values, and beliefs and is the social glue that holds the organization together" (Treviño & Nelson, 2007, p. 259).

Building on this general definition, Treviño and Nelson (2011, p. 153) suggest that an "ethical" corporate culture represents a "slice" or "sub-set" of the organization's broader culture and is "...maintained through a complex interplay [and alignment] of formal [that is, policies, leadership, authority structures, reward systems, training programs] and informal organizational systems [that is, peer behavior and ethical norms]." In terms of how an ethical corporate culture can lead to expected ethical behavior, Treviño and Nelson (2011) argue that employees can act consistently in accordance with the firm's ethical norms either through a socialization process (that is, employees feel they are expected to behave accordingly) or an internalization process (that is, employees adopt the ethical norms as their own). The goal then is for firms to possess a "strong" ethical corporate culture (rather than a "weak" one) which increases the probability that employees will conform to desired ethical norms.

Ethical culture, however, overlaps to a large degree with the notion of "ethical climate," which can be considered a sub-set of the organizational climate literature (Treviño, Butterfield & McCabe, 1998). Ethical climate has been defined as "the prevailing perceptions of typical organizational practices and procedures that have ethical content" (Victor & Cullen, 1988, p. 101). Collectively, both the dimensions of "ethical corporate culture" and "ethical climate" establish a firm's "ethical context" or "ethical environment" for managers and employees (Treviño, Butterfield & McCabe, 1998). For the purposes of this study, however, the concept of "ethical corporate culture" will be referred to as being considered more pertinent from a normative perspective when it comes to guiding and shaping ethical behavior, as opposed to "ethical climate" which appears to be more associated with a descriptive characterization of the attitudes held at a firm (Treviño, Butterfield & McCabe, 1998). Many continue to stress the importance of additional research on organizational ethical context (that is, including ethical culture and ethical climate) in relation to ethical decision making and behavior (Dean, Beggs & Keane, 2010; Martin & Cullen, 2006; Pimentel, Kuntz & Elenkov, 2010).

When it comes to discussing the importance of ethical corporate culture, however, it is important to consider whether its existence (however defined) will actually make a difference with respect to all employees and managers. For the purposes of this chapter, this position is rejected as being clearly unrealistic, since illegal and unethical activity will always continue despite the existence of even an "ideal" ethical corporate culture. For example, there are many in the fraud prevention field who accept a "20-60-20" rule (see Brooks & Dunn, 2010, p. 256)—in other words, 20 percent of a given workforce will always do the right thing (for example, act legally or ethically) regardless of one's circumstances or work environment. Another 20 percent will always engage in illegal or unethical behavior when the opportunity exists, the rewards are sufficient and there is a perceived low likelihood of getting caught. The remaining 60 percent of the workforce however, while basically honest, may decide to engage in illegal or unethical behavior, depending on the environment in which they work, based on such factors as managerial pressure, peer pressure or reward systems (see O'Fallon & Butterfield, 2005), or in the belief that they are acting in the best interests of their firm (Schwartz, 2001). Such employees have been referred to as "fence sitters" (Goldmann, 2009, p. 11). This position is supported by Treviño and Nelson (2011, p. 153) who state: "...unfortunately, most employees can be socialized into behaving unethically." Turning this fact into a potential positive, it is this 60 percent that arguably can be most influenced to do the "right thing" when they work within an ethical corporate culture, and thus these "fence sitters" are the target group of this study. In other words, the goal is to identify those measures that can help mitigate or minimize (as oppose to completely eliminate) the extent to which illegal or unethical activity is taking place within or on behalf of business firms.

If a majority of employees are in fact influenced by their work environments with respect to their behavior, it potentially becomes extremely important for board members, executives and managers to understand how to best develop and sustain an ethical corporate culture. While recognizing that there may not be a "one size fits all" solution for all business organizations (see Treviño & Nelson, 2007, p. 257), one can certainly postulate in general that certain core elements should be in place at a minimum if one is to have the greatest chance of developing and maintaining an ethical corporate culture.

So what then are the critical elements of an ethical corporate culture, and is there a relationship between an ethical corporate culture and financial performance? The following will argue that while there are many elements leading to an ethical corporate culture to choose from, the two most critical or necessary include: (1) core ethical values; and (2) ethical leadership.

Core Values and Corporate Culture

The existence of a set of core values appears to be critical in establishing an ethical corporate culture. For example, "Corporate values have long been referred to as the central dimension of an organization's culture..." (Hunt, Wood & Chonko, 1989, p. 79). An ethical corporate culture has in turn been recognized as important to ethical decision making. O'Fallon and Butterfield (2005: 397), as part of their extensive literature review on ethical decision making, state: "The research generally supports the notion that ethical climates and cultures have a positive influence on ethical decision making." Despite the recognized importance of core ethical values however, research suggests that many employees perceive their firms as lacking ethical values. For example, in a survey of 23,000 US employees, only 15 percent felt they worked in a high-*trust* environment; only 13 percent have highly *co-operative* working relationships with other groups or departments; and only 10 percent felt that their organization holds people *accountable* for results (Covey, 2004).

Ethical Leadership and Corporate Culture

It has also been argued that in order to successfully embed values within an organization's culture, an ethical "tone at the top" must exist (Schwartz, Dunfee & Dunfee, 2005; Sheeder, 2005; Weaver & Treviño, 1999). In fact, many suggest that an ethical corporate culture is contingent upon ethical leadership. For example: "...the moral tone of an organization is set best by top management (Laczniak, 1983) and ... workers generally get their ethical cues by observing what their bosses do ... Leaders are clearly viewed as key to the development and maintenance of a strong ethical climate in their organizations" (Treviño, 1990, p. 203). According to Brown, Treviño & Harrison (2005, p. 117): "Leaders should be the key source of ethical guidance for employees." According to Northouse (2001, p. 255), a relationship exists between ethical leaders and the presence of values within an organization: "Ethics is central to leadership because of the ... impact leaders have on establishing the organization's values."

The relationship between ethical leadership and ethical behavior has also been observed. According to Hitt: "The results of research studies demonstrate that the ethical conduct of individuals in organizations is influenced greatly by their leaders" (1990, p. 3). Perceptions among employees that their supervisors and managers possess a set of core ethical values and act upon them has been shown to have a significant impact on the ethical corporate culture of the firm. According to Trevino, Weaver, Gibson &Toffler (1999), based on a survey of over 10,000 US employees: "When employees perceived that supervisors and executives regularly pay attention to ethics, take ethics seriously, and care about ethics and values as much as the bottom line, all of the outcomes [that is, less unethical/illegal behavior, greater awareness of ethical/legal issues, employees more likely to look for advice within the firm, willing to deliver bad news to management, report ethical violations and more committed to the organization] were significantly more positive" [emphasis added].

Despite the recognized importance of ethical leadership within business, there appears to be a perception that such leadership is lacking. For example, a 2010 Gallup survey found that only 15 percent of over 1,000 US adults perceived business executives as having "very high" or "high" honesty and ethical standards, even lower than auto mechanics (28 percent) and TV reporters (23 percent) (Gallup, 2010). Canadian's perceptions of ethical business leaders were similar. In a 2003 Ipsos-Reid survey, 1,007 Canadian adults were asked "Whom do you trust?" CEOs were only trusted by 21 percent of respondents, significantly below auto mechanics (33 percent), journalists (31 percent) and lawyers (29 percent), while only placing above car salespeople (10 percent) and national politicians (9 percent). The research suggests that there is significant room for improvement in society's perception of the ethical values of business leaders.

Core Values, Ethical Leadership and Financial Performance

Not only are core values and an ethical tone at the top considered to be foundational elements of an ethical corporate culture, several studies have examined the long-term financial impact of having a core set of explicit values (Paine, 2003). In one study, Collins and Porras in their 1997 best-seller *Built to Last*, conclude the following (based on a sample of 36 companies): "*Visionary companies* [that is, companies with superior returns over many decades] pursue a cluster of objectives, of which making money is only one—and not necessarily the primary one. Yes, they seek profits, but they're equally guided by a core ideology—*core values and sense of purpose beyond just making money*. Yet, paradoxically, the visionary companies make more money than the more purely profit-driven comparison companies" [emphasis added]. Many of the core values emphasized by visionary companies can be considered to be "ethical" values, such as respect, honesty and integrity.

Several researchers have commented on the process by which a set of core values translates, either directly or indirectly, into enhanced bottom-line performance. "For an organization, values serve to convey a sense of identity to its members, enhance the stability of its social system, direct managers' attention to important issues, guide subsequent decisions by managers, and ... facilitate commitment to something larger than self" (Hunt, Wood & Chonko, 1989, p. 80). The types of benefits attained by firms with the "right values" include being able to: avoid penalties, fines, lawsuits and criminal penalties; build employee loyalty; reduce hiring and training costs; reduce theft and other anti-company activity; drive sales and build customer loyalty; create community good will; attract quality applicants with minimum investment in recruitment; and maintain loyal vendor relationships, reducing loss of suppliers and unexpected increases (Devero, 2003).

A relationship has also been identified between perceptions of values-based leadership and financial performance: "The impact of ... ethical leadership on organizational effectiveness has been frequently noted and supported in past literature" (Parry & Proctor-Thomson, 2002). The reasoning is as follows: "... ethically led organizations are ... more effective due to strengthened organizational culture; lower levels of staff turnover, and increased employee effort" (Storr, 2004, p. 422).

Unfortunately there are too many examples of companies that failed to establish an ethical "tone at the top" leading to significant scandals, which have occasionally led to their downfall (Gini, 2004). For example, firms (and their former CEOs) such as WorldCom (Bernie Ebbers), Hollinger (Conrad Black), Tyco International (Dennis Kozlowski) and Adelphia (John Rigas), clearly appear to have been lacking an appropriate tone at the top. Even Enron, despite possessing a comprehensive compliance or ethics program, collapsed at least partly due to an inappropriate tone at the top led by former CEO Jeffrey Skilling, who emphasized bottom-line results as opposed to ethical values (Watkins, 2003). On the other hand, firms such as Johnson & Johnson, following extensive efforts by former CEO James Burke to embed its corporate Credo throughout the organization including among its most senior leadership, was able to not only withstand the 1982 Tylenol tampering crisis, but to derive a competitive advantage from it years later. The firm did so by relying on its Credo's values which placed safety ahead of financial considerations (Treviño & Nelson, 2004). Other examples of ethical leadership setting the tone for their organizations include Arthur Andersen (Toffler & Reingold, 2003) and Bill George, the former CEO of Medtronic (Treviño & Brown, 2004, p. 75). Clearly, some companies appear to have been more successful than others when it comes to establishing an appropriate "tone at the top" through accepting and behaving according to a set of explicit core ethical values.

Figure 15.1 summarizes the proposed relationship between core ethical values, ethical leadership (that is, "tone"), ethical corporate culture, ethical behavior and financial performance.

Figure 15.1 Relationship between values, leadership, culture and performance

Building on previous values-based leadership research, this study examines and evaluates the perceptions of senior executives of one Canadian firm during its effort to inculcate values-based leadership. The discussion among executive participants focused on two general topics: (1) corporate values and decision making; and (2) corporate values and ethical leadership (or "tone at the top").

With respect to the first topic, values and decision making, the following issues were examined: (a) How can values assist in resolving ethical dilemmas?; (b) How important are the values relative to other factors in making important personnel decisions?; and (c) How important are the values when working through a crisis situation?

In terms of the second topic, values and ethical leadership, the following issues were discussed by participants: (d) How important are values with respect to effective leadership?; (e) How do senior executives perceive the "value" of corporate values?; (f) What do senior executives need to do in relation to the values?; (g) What can be learned from clients with respect to the firm living the values?; and (h) What statements from the CEO demonstrate the importance of the values?

Background to "Leadership Development Workshop"

The study involved one large Canadian financial firm that employs approximately 40,000 employees. While the vast majority of employees work in offices across Canada, there are also offices in the US, Europe, Asia and Australia. The firm's revenues are in the billions of dollars (US), and it is has consistently been one of the more profitable companies in Canada since coming into existence over 100 years ago. Following a series of embarrassing scandals, negative publicity and a settlement with US government regulators (all leading to a significant drop in share price), a decision was made by the Canadian firm's most senior leadership in 2002 to adopt a new set of core values in addition to a new mission and vision, and to attempt to embed the core values throughout the various levels of the organization.

The firm utilized an outside consultant to verify through a company-wide survey which core values were currently in existence at the firm, which values were lacking, and which values were desired by employees. After a lengthy process, the senior leadership team (SLT) (that is, top 60 executives) came to a consensus on which three values would become the firm's core values: (1) trust; (2) teamwork; and (3) accountability. While the firm could have selected a lengthier list of core values, the SLT felt comfortable with having only three values, believing that it would be easier for employees to remember and focus on only three.

Once the vision, mission and the three core values were established, a training process commenced at the very top of the firm. A "Leadership Workshop Seminar" was conducted involving over 600 of the firm's most senior executives (that is, vice-president level or higher up to and including the CEO). The content of the seminar was dictated by several factors, including the desire to only have two days spent on the program, as well as trying to make it interactive and interesting. The desire was not to have any sort of organizational "transformation" process take place in the corporate culture or to highly publicize or "glamorize" the values with posters, table tents, wallet cards or pens, but to provide senior executives with an opportunity to become familiar with the values and their importance to the firm through reflection, discussion and analysis.

The content and format of the two-day workshop consisted of the following. In addition to an introduction and closing by the CEO (or on occasion another member of the senior executive team), the participants discussed several issues during the workshop related to corporate values. The two-day seminar included a number of different modules, including a keynote lecture/discussion on the "value" of corporate values, a customized case involving a difficult hiring decision for a senior executive position (whereby strong financial performance potentially conflicted with the values), a customized crisis management simulation based on an actual incident previously faced by the firm, a series of ethical dilemmas and a presentation by a client. Beginning with the senior executive team's pilot session, over 30 two-day sessions were conducted in Toronto, New York, London and Montreal during 2005.

The actual content of the workshop, although ultimately confirmed by a committee made up of the firm's SLT, was primarily developed and delivered by the researcher. A decision was also made to focus the workshop on the three core values, as opposed to the newly established vision and mission.

Findings: Values and Decision-Making

(A) HOW CAN VALUES ASSIST IN RESOLVING ETHICAL DILEMMAS?

Similar to the ethics training taking place at many firms, several ethical dilemmas were used (approximately four to six) in an attempt to put the values into a concrete real-life setting. The following is just one example of an ethical dilemma discussed by participants:

> While taking an executive training course at a top business school, you remember how your manager, a star performer at the firm, had once mentioned to you that he had received his MBA degree from the school. Out of interest, you drop in on the alumni office to check out what year your manager graduated, only to hear that your manager, at least according to the name you give to the office, apparently never graduated from the school. How do you handle this? How do the core values relate?

Some of the lessons from the dilemmas raised or identified by participants with respect to the values include the following:
  Information/Implications

- get as much information as possible before making decisions;
- get different perspectives;
- make sure facts are accurate, investigate;
- don't be afraid to get help, use hotline if necessary;
- think about the big implications from what might initially be considered small issues;
- look at people involved and the effect on the company;
- there is a message you send to others based on values application.

Decision making

- nothing is typically clear cut, there are often shades of grey;
- although not necessarily a right answer, values can help get to a better decision, faster and more effectively;
- although one always wants more information, at some point there is a need to "pull the trigger" and make a decision;
- the risk of doing nothing is often greater than taking action;
- values and the bottom line do not necessarily have to be in conflict;
- the values should apply to everyone.

(B) HOW IMPORTANT ARE THE VALUES RELATIVE TO OTHER FACTORS IN MAKING IMPORTANT PERSONNEL DECISIONS?

One of the key components of the workshop involved the "Difficult Hiring Decision" case. Participants were asked to rank order three final candidates for a VP–regional sales position for a poorly performing region which required a turnaround specialist. They had to choose between: (1) Charlotte, the internal candidate (a solid performer with a strong set of values but lacking some experience); (2) Scott, an external candidate (a very strong performer and turnaround specialist with some more questionable values); and (3) Jim, another external candidate (with both experience and a strong set of values). The case attempted to highlight the issue of performance versus values (when such a conflict might arise), and the extent to which values should dominate the hiring decision process itself.

For most of the firm's employees, the primary learning objective of understanding the importance of values relative to mere performance became clear in making the hiring decision. Concerns over one of Scott's values, despite his excellent performance and capabilities, led many participants to reject him for the VP position. Values became a "filter" or "gate" in the hiring decision for many, rather than merely an additional criterion to be applied. In other words, if the candidate did not make it through the gate due to their values, then their experience, capabilities and performance, even if outstanding, became completely irrelevant to the hiring decision. Of possible interest however, significantly different rankings of the three final candidates took place in London vis-à-vis Toronto, with the London office preferring Jim, based on his experience, and Scott, due to his financial performance, rather than Charlotte. In addition, many participants originally ranked Scott first or second, only to drop him following their small group discussions. The group discussion seemed to lead to greater emphasis over the importance of values in making the hiring decision.

(C) HOW IMPORTANT ARE THE VALUES WHEN WORKING THROUGH A CRISIS SITUATION?

In addition to the "Difficult Hiring Decision" case, a second case was developed that actually involved the firm during the previous year, which had led to significant negative publicity. The incident involved a series of transmissions containing personal and confidential client information that were unfortunately misdirected and sent to a non-customer. Despite the non-customer's complaints, the firm failed to adequately respond and address the problem, and the misdirected transmissions continued, leading the non-customer to contact the media. Over a three-hour session, participants were asked to assume they were part of a crisis management team and to prepare for a mock media conference simulation. New information was delivered throughout the session that the participants would have to react to.

The case simulation led many participants to the realization that it is often easy to forget the values (even during a values-based training seminar) when facing (even a simulated) stressful and time-constrained situation. Applying the values during the crisis appeared however to assist many other participants in helping guide the firm through both the short-term containment and the long-term recovery strategy.

Findings: Values and Leadership

(D) HOW IMPORTANT ARE VALUES WITH RESPECT TO EFFECTIVE LEADERSHIP?

One of the first questions seminar participants were asked was: "What makes a leader?" Many different traits were mentioned, the most prominent ones including: ability to motivate; inspirational; decisive; passionate; vision; and humility. But what stood out (albeit possibly due to the focus of the seminar) were the ethical traits or values of integrity, honesty and trustworthiness. In other words, for the firm's executives, *ethical values* appear to be what are considered to be most important with respect to leadership.

(E) HOW DO SENIOR EXECUTIVES PERCEIVE THE "VALUE" OF CORPORATE VALUES?

One of the key components of the workshop involved a discussion, prior to the keynote lecture, of the value (if any) of having a set of corporate values. This sort of question could be raised by several different constituents, including a member of the firm's Board of Directors, executive team, managers, employees, clients or investors. Certain themes emerged from the participants' responses in terms of the "value" of having a set of corporate values. The dominant (and inter-related) themes included the following: (i) setting a framework; (ii) establishing an identity; (iii) performance; (iv) employees; (v) clients; and (vi) regulators.

i) *Framework*: According to participants, values have "value" by acting as a possible framework for managers and employees in many different respects, in terms of decision making, behaviour and even policy formulation. Although "framework" was the dominant construct, participants referred to other similar terms including: alignment; balancing interests; benchmark for evaluating employees or executives; clarity of grey areas; common belief system; common culture; commonality instilled; compass for organization; consistency; corporate constitution; create boundaries and parameters for acceptable actions; foundation; guide; guideposts; guiding light; higher standards; level playing field; overarching direction; permeate everything we do; principles versus rule-based; roadmap; screening mechanism; setting expectations; shared mission; signposts; tool; uniformity; and yardstick.

ii) *Identity*: Participants also raised the notion that values have value in the sense that they help establish the identity of a firm. Several other concepts related to identity were suggested such as: branding; reputation; differentiation; external perceptions; and defining what you are (for both internal and external audiences).

iii) *Performance*: Participants also viewed values as leading directly to better performance for the firm, and hence a better bottom line. Other concepts similar to performance included the following: better decisions; competitive advantage; create clarity and focus; efficiency; guides policy formation; less litigation; performance management; productivity; reduces conflict; simplifies decisions; supporting vision; supports business units' interdependence; sustainability; sustains results/talent; and underpins strategic direction.

iv) *Employees*: Values were clearly seen as having a value in relation to both retaining and attracting employees, that is, people who share similar values. Other suggestions that relate to the benefit of values with respect to employees include: helping to improve morale; creating a positive internal environment; establishing trust; developing a sense of loyalty; developing a greater emotional connection with the firm; enhancing equity and fairness; developing a sense of community and family; and leading to less personal risk for employees.

v) *Clients*: Participants also reflected on the importance of a set of values if one is to become the "leader" with respect to clients. Without a perception that the firm operates according to a set of values, clients will lose confidence in the firm and business will be lost as a result.

vi) *Regulators*: With a strong set of values, participants suggested that there may be less of a need for oversight and compliance. In addition, values require "thinking" as opposed to merely ticking off boxes, and facilitate holding people accountable for their actions. Values also help manage risk and the potential downside of decisions, and by doing so, may help keep the firm out of trouble in the future, especially in terms of regulators.

What was very clear however is that virtually all the firm's executives appeared to accept that there is a value, whether tangible or intangible, to having a set of corporate values. One of the important issues discussed with participants is that if values are only undertaken because they are believed to be good for the bottom line, they will most likely immediately be forgotten when there is a potential conflict with the bottom line. In addition, one can't always attach a "value" to values, as it is often difficult to know what scandal might have been avoided due to the impact of values in decision-making or behavior.

(F) WHAT DO SENIOR EXECUTIVES NEED TO DO IN RELATION TO THE VALUES?

When participants were asked the question: "What does the senior executive team need to do with respect to values?" several dominant themes emerged including the following: (i) actions/accountability; (ii) reward system/compensation; (iii) firm structure; (iv) communication; and (v) sustained emphasis.

i) *Actions/accountability*: One of the greatest risks to the success of a values-based initiative is that executives, managers and employees will perceive that the firm's most senior leaders do not support the values. This view was supported by seminar participants when asked the question: "What does the Senior Executive Team (SET) (that is, the ten most senior executives of the firm) need to do with respect to values?" The most dominant request was that words be backed by consistent actions and behavior. This was reflected in comments such as: walk the talk; see actions to backup statements; get rid of bad behaviors; deal with those who are not living up to values; don't want to hear a lot more, do something; need for evidence, stories, legends; delivering consequences; haven't seen the SET deliver the behavior; need to see proof of progress; and values must be consistently applied.

ii) *Reward system/compensation*: Several participants raised the notion that they wanted the SET to bring compensation (that is, "change the compensation system") at the firm into alignment with the values. One example was to "align pay [to the values] so it's not just bottom line created" or to simply celebrate those who exemplify the values.

iii) *Firm structure*: Participants also raised concerns regarding the firm's structure. Many of these comments related to the perception of silos at the firm, such as the need to "get rid of 'warring factions'", "get rid of the silo mentality," or to "attack limiting values to break down silos." Firm structure was also reflected in comments such as "define how teams and business units work together, perhaps redesign them."

iv) *Communication*: Others raised concerns over how communication takes place with respect to the values, in terms of decision making. For example, participants noted the importance of "top down communication to the non-executive population," especially any significant organizational changes and "how they relate to the vision, mission and values."

v) *Sustained emphasis*: Other concerns related to whether the new CEO (who was recently appointed) would sufficiently endorse the initiative, so that it would not be perceived as the former CEO's initiative. Some were concerned that this could be seen as the "flavor of the week," and were not convinced that it would be sustainable during a period of downsizing.

There was a very clear recognition among executives that for the values to permeate throughout the organization, it was not just the responsibility of the senior executive team, but the responsibility of the entire senior leadership team (that is, 600 most senior managers) of the firm. As a result, "walking the talk" was an expectation not merely of the SET, but of the entire firm's senior leadership. This was demonstrated by comments that all executives reflect upon, use and communicate the values in all decision making.

In addition to seeing consistent action among all executives, participants also commented on the need to hold the SET and other senior leaders accountable for action: be prepared to stand up and be counted when things go wrong; push up and escalate issues as they arise; have the courage to push back at one's bosses when things are done that are not aligned; and call one another on behaviors, regardless of role or level. Other comments included the need for each of the leaders to communicate with their own teams regarding the importance of the values, being adamant about doing the right thing, and assessing how each one's team is performing in relation to the values.

(G) WHAT CAN BE LEARNED FROM CLIENTS REGARDING THE VALUES?

One component of the program which appeared to yield some interesting feedback involved the clients' presentations. Clients of the firm were invited to speak to the participants regarding their perceptions of the values of the firm. A number of clients were quite candid in their assessment of the firm's performance, suggesting that the firm might have room for improvement with respect to listening to its clients.

As just one example, a long-standing and wealthy client indicated that a letter was sent to him starting off with "Dear Valued Customer...," at which point he considered leaving the firm. Another long-standing and valued client received a letter demanding immediate payment of a loan from the firm's lawyers when a simple phone call would have quickly rectified the issue. What appeared to come out of the client sessions is that the presence of values does not necessarily win you the business, but a lack of values can quickly lose your business. On the positive side, one client indicated that what impressed him most about the firm was that the firm appeared to be more concerned about the client's interests and well-being than the fees that were to be paid, unlike many of the firm's competitors.

(H) WHAT STATEMENTS FROM THE CEO DEMONSTRATE THE IMPORTANCE OF THE VALUES?

Many important statements were made by the CEO including that: (i) values "trump" economics; (ii) legal, compliance and industry practice are necessary but insufficient tests with respect to decision making; (iii) the values should be applied early in the process rather than after the fact; and (iv) values should be applied to all business decisions such as new products, hiring, firing, promotion and compensation. The statements appeared to have an important influence over later discussion during the seminar by participants, in particular, the CEO's statement that "values trump economics" was referred to in many instances during other components of the seminar.

Discussion and Conclusion

Although cynicism still appeared to exist among several executives, the workshop appeared to be considered a valuable start to the journey of embedding the values throughout the firm's policies, practices and processes. As part of the process for establishing an appropriate tone at the top, the two-day workshop clearly demonstrated the importance of executives actually spending quality time discussing the values and their importance, as well as having an opportunity to apply them in various hypothetical contexts.

Although the study only examined a single firm, and did not focus on the actual effectiveness of the training, several observations are noteworthy. The major findings include the following:

- values were viewed by the participants as being clearly important with respect to establishing an ethical corporate culture;
- values serve an important purpose with respect to ethical decision making;
- values are clearly of value to the firm in many respects, including leading to better financial performance;
- the existence of values is necessary but insufficient in order to establish an ethical corporate culture, ethical leadership (that is, tone at the top) is also necessary.

Finally, the study appears to reinforce the proposition that there is a relationship between values, leadership and an ethical corporate culture: "Many argue that ethical behavior stems from an ethical corporate culture ... the strong approach [to managing culture to improve ethics in organizations] is characterized by the creation of a unitary culture in which *values* and norms are shared by all employees. The support and *leadership of top management* is crucial to create an organizational culture that evokes a uniform response to ethical issues" (Chen, Sawyers & Williams, 1997, pp. 857–858) [emphasis added]. Whether the new core values will actually become firmly embedded into the firm's corporate culture and be sustained into the future however now depends to a great extent on the firm's executive leadership.

References

Brooks, L. J., & Dunn, P. (2010) *Business and Professional Ethics* (5th edition). Mason, OH: South Western Cengage Learning.

Brown, M. E., Treviño, L. K., & Harrison, D. A. (2005) Ethical leadership: a social learning perspective for construct development and testing. *Organizational Behavior and Human Decision Processes*, 97(2), 117–134.

Chen, A. Y. S., Sawyers, R. B., & Williams, P. F. (1997) Reinforcing ethical decision making through corporate culture. *Journal of Business Ethics*, 16(8), 855–865.

Collins, J., & Porras, J. I. (1997) *Built to Last: Successful Habits of Visionary Companies*. New York: HarperCollins Publishers.

Covey, S. (2004) *The 8th Habit*. New York: Free Press.

Dean, K. L., Beggs, J. M., & Keane, T. P. (2010) Mid-level managers, organizational context, and (un) ethical encounters. *Journal of Business Ethics*, 97, 51–69.

Devero, A. (2004) Corporate values aren't just wall posters – They're strategic tools. In J. Richardson. *Annual Editions, Business Ethics* (16th edition) 04/05. New York: McGraw Hill, pp. 19–21.

Gallup. (2010) Honesty/ethics in professions. Available online at http://www.gallup.com/poll/1654/honesty-ethics-professions.aspx. Accessed on September 12, 2012.

Geertz, C. (1973) *The Interpretation of Cultures: Selected Essays*. New York: Basic Books.

Gini, A. (2004) Business, ethics, and leadership in a post enron era. *Journal of Leadership & Organizational Studies*, 11(1), 9–16.

Goldmann, P. (2009) *Anti-Fraud Risk and Control Workbook*. Hoboken, NJ: Wiley & Sons.

Hitt, W. D. (1990) *Ethics and Leadership: Putting Theory into Practice*. Columbus, OH: Battelle Press.

Hunt, S. D., Wood, V. R., & Chonko, L. B. (1989) Corporate ethical values and organizational commitment in marketing. *Journal of Marketing*, 53(3), 79–90.

Ipsos-Reid. (2003) So, whom do we trust? Reader's digest trust survey finds that pharmacists, doctors and airline pilots top the list as Canada's most trusted professions. Available online at: http://www.ipsos-na.com/news/pressrelease.cfm?id=1716. Accessed on September 12, 2012.

James, H. S. Jr. (2000) Reinforcing ethical decision making through organizational structure. *Journal of Business Ethics*, 28(1), 43–58.

Jones, T. M., Felps, W., & Bigley, G. A. (2007) Ethical theory and stakeholder-related decisions: the role of stakeholder. *The Academy of Management Review*, 32(1), 137–155.

Laczniak, G. R. (1983) Framework for analyzing marketing ethics. *Journal of Macromarketing*, 3, 7–18.

Martin, K. D., & Cullen, J. B. (2006) Continuities and extensions of ethical climate theory, a meta-analytic review. *Journal of Business Ethics*, 69(2), 175–194.

Northouse, P. G. (2001) *Leadership Theory and Practice* (2nd edition). London: Sage Publications.

O'Fallon, M. J., & Butterfield, K. D. (2005) A review of the empirical ethical decision-making literature: 1996–2003. *Journal of Business Ethics*, 59(4), 375–413.

Paine, L.S. (2003) *Value Shift*. New York: McGraw Hill.

Parry, K. W., & Proctor-Thomas, S. B. (2002) Perceived integrity of transformational leaders in organisational settings. *Journal of Business Ethics*, 35(2), 75–96.

Pettigrew, A. M. (1979) On studying organizational cultures. *Administrative Science Quarterly*, 24, 570–581.

Pimentel, J. R. C., Kuntz, J. R., & Elenkov, D. S. (2010) Ethical decision-making: an integrative model for business practice. *European Business Review*, 22(4), 359.

Schein, E. H. (1985) *Organizational Culture and Leadership*. San Francisco: Jossey-Bass.

Schwartz, M. S. (2001) The nature of the relationship between corporate codes of ethics and behaviour. *Journal of Business Ethics*, 32(3), 247–262.

Schwartz, M. S., Dunfee, T. W., & Kline, M. J. (2005) Tone at the top: an ethics code for directors? *Journal of Business Ethics*, 58(1), 79–100.

Sheeder, F. (2005) What exactly is "tone at the top" and is it really that big of a deal? *Journal of Health Care Compliance*, 7(3), 35–38.

Storr, L. (2004) Leading with integrity: a qualitative research study. *Journal of Health Organization and Management*, 18(6), 415–434.

Toffler, B.L., & Reingold, J. (2003) *Final Accounting: Ambition, Greed, and the Fall of Arthur Andersen*. New York: Broadway Books.

Treviño, L. K. (1990) A cultural perspective on changing and developing organizational ethics. *Research in Organizational Change and Development*, 4, 195–230.

Treviño, L. K., & Brown, M. E. (2004) Managing to be ethical: debunking five business ethics myths. *The Academy of Management Executive*, 18(2), 69–81.

Treviño, L. K., Butterfield, K. D., & McCabe, D. (1998) The ethical context in organizations: influences on employee attitudes and behaviors. *Business Ethics Quarterly*, 8(3), 447–476.

Treviño, L. K., & Nelson, K. A. (2004) *Managing Business Ethics: Straight Talk about How to Do It Right* (3rd edition). Hobeken, NJ: John Wiley, pp. 202–203.

Treviño, L. K., & Nelson, K. A. (2007) *Managing Business Ethics* (4th edition). New York: John Wiley.

Treviño, L. K., & Nelson, K. A. (2011) *Managing Business Ethics* (5th edition). New York: John Wiley.

Treviño, L., Weaver, G. R., Gibson, D. G., & Toffler, B. L. (1999) Managing ethics and legal compliance: what works and what hurts. *California Management Review*, 41(2), 131–151.

Victor, B., & Cullen, J. B. (1988) The organizational bases of ethical work climates. *Administrative Science Quarterly*, 33(1), 101–125.

Watkins, S. (2003) Pristine ethics: who do you trust? *Vital Speeches of the Day*, 69(14), 435–440.

Weaver, G. R., & Treviño, L. K. (1999) Compliance and values oriented ethics programs: influences on employees' attitudes and behavior. *Business Ethics Quarterly*, 9(2), 315–336.

16 Corporate Wellness Programs: Why Investing in Employee Health and Well-being is an Investment in the Health of the Company

FIKRY W. ISAAC AND SCOTT C. RATZAN

At Johnson & Johnson, our corporate health and wellness program more than pays for itself. In fact, for every dollar we invest in wellness, we see a return of nearly $4 in reduced health care costs, lower absenteeism and improved productivity.

It's no surprise that we invest in "keeping the well well"—that is, disease prevention. But "wellness" encompasses more than disease, so we also invest in a variety of programs that help employees and their families experience a greater sense of —including an exciting initiative we call "Energy for Performance in Life."

Let's start by looking briefly at what we've learned about what it means to run a "successful" health and wellness program. Then we'll delve into the big picture of where corporate wellness programs and "personal fulfillment" intersect.

Four Essential Leadership Beliefs That Lead to Health and Wellness Success

A DEFINITION OF "HEALTH" THAT INCLUDES "WELL-BEING"

In 1947, the World Health Organization (WHO) defined "health" as "a state of complete physical, mental and social well being and not merely the absence of disease or infirmity." It's easier for corporations to measure absolutes such as health care costs or days lost to absenteeism than it is to measure intangibles like well-being or fulfillment, but successful health and wellness programs don't lose sight of their importance. In fact, successful health and wellness programs take a *holistic* view of "health" that includes physical, occupational, intellectual, social/spiritual and emotional components because there's a clear connection between wellness, productivity and competitiveness.

A 2010 National Business Group on Health report, for instance, concludes that the successful execution of health and wellness programs translates to a significant financial and human capital advantage (Towers Watson, 2009/2010). Not only do companies with successful health and wellness programs experience lower health care costs, they experience higher workforce *effectiveness* in the form of lower presenteeism (workers who are present but are not effective due to illness, stress or another focus-diverting cause), fewer lost days due to illness or disability and lower levels of employee turnover. Plus, in a world where knowledge, creativity and the ability to solve complex problems in innovative new ways are key to business success, companies increasingly need fully engaged employees.

"Full engagement" is a tough nut to crack, but employees are more capable of being fully engaged if they're physically healthy, sufficiently rewarded, able to achieve work–life balance and not over-burdened by sustained stress. Corporations can increase the degree to which their employees are able to be fully engaged in many ways:

- One of the most important is by improving "health literacy." This term refers to more than merely improving health education; it includes *empowering* employees with resources and opportunities to improve their knowledge and skills so that they can take more control of their lives and make better decisions for themselves. At Johnson & Johnson, our health literacy efforts go beyond traditional topics such as stress reduction, blood pressure, cholesterol, diabetes and cardiovascular disease to identifying and dealing with workplace bullies, improving driving skills and appreciating workplace diversity.
- Corporations can also improve full engagement through benefits design that provides peace of mind. Johnson & Johnson US benefits, for instance, are built on four cornerstones: (i) employees are protected financially in the event of serious illness or injury; (ii) employees have access to a wide range of materials, classes, workshops and health/mental health professionals who support them as they seek to live healthier, happier and more fulfilled lives; (iii) employees have access to quality care; and (iv) employees always have choices about how they spend their health care dollars and who they receive care from.
- Reducing worry and providing access to expertise that employees can't be expected to have on their own is still another way that corporations can free employees' minds to focus on the interests of the corporation. One of our partners, for instance, not only helps employees resolve health insurance claims, it helps employees understand and resolve Medicare-related issues for their parents and parents-in-law. We also have partners that help employees better plan for their retirement, better protect their family through insurance products and much more.

DEDICATION TO PREVENTION AND ENGAGEMENT IN HEALTH DIPLOMACY

In 1886, Robert Wood Johnson heard a speech by the antiseptic-surgery pioneer Joseph Lister that inspired Johnson to join his brothers in creating and marketing a line of ready-to-use sterile dressings to prevent infection. That was over 125 years ago and we've been focused on preventing illness ever since—not just in the products and devices we manufacture and the services we offer, but within our employee population *and* in our capacity as a thought-leader respected by government and non-government organizations around the world.

- We're a leading voice, for example, at the APEC (Asia-Pacific Economic Cooperation) Life Science Innovation Forum. One of their goals is to address the rapid rise of chronic and lifestyle diseases in the region, which are an increasing burden on their economies.
- We were one of the first companies to achieve Gold Standard accreditation with The CEO Cancer Gold Standard™. This is an initiative that challenges CEOs to be "bold and venturesome" in the fight against cancer in American workplaces through prevention, early detection and access to quality care—including cancer clinical trials.
- During the national debate on health care reform in the US, we were a strong voice in favor of disease prevention programs that focus on nurturing healthy behaviors.
- In 2011, Johnson & Johnson shared the stage at the Clinton Global Initiative with the US Department of Health and Human Services, Mayo Clinic, American Cancer Society, Campaign for Tobacco-Free Kids and GBCHealth in announcing a Global Smoke-Free Worksite Challenge. This partnership strives to advance healthier lifestyles and outcomes via smoke-free policies and leadership at the worksites, supply chain locations and communities in which we work.
- And we (the authors) have personally held leadership roles with the US Partnership for Prevention, World Economic Forum (WEF) Workplace Wellness Alliance and the WEF Global Agenda Council on Health and Wellbeing. Plus, we've helped to advance workplace well-being at the global level, such as through participation in the WHO's Non-communicable Disease (NCD) and led industry efforts at the United Nations High Level Meeting on NCDs, including raising standards with an evidence base on health and wellness.

But why are we telling you all this? Given our history and vast base of knowledge, we're in a unique position to share the story of what corporate wellness programs can bring both to the companies that offer them and the individuals whose lives are enriched by them. Plus, we've had excellent results. In addition to reversing the trend on key population health risks (NCD), we've saved $565 per employee per year on health care expenditures between 2001 and 2009. This success is due in large part to prevention programs that fall into three categories: (i) prevention-focused education; (ii) rewards for healthy behavior; and (iii) creating environments in which it's natural for employees to engage in healthy behaviors.

i) Education

Our prevention education efforts take *many* forms because different people are receptive to different forms of information. A few of our various education programs include:

- Every employee has an opportunity to take a voluntary health risk assessment. When risks are identified, health professionals contact each employee one-on-one to ensure that s/he is aware of the numerous ways our programs can help them reduce or reverse their risk.

- We post health news on walls, on doors, in elevators and TV monitors throughout our buildings—and change the news and tips frequently to keep it fresh. We provide e-mailed daily health tips to all of our employees who have *opted* to receive them. And we create and disseminate a variety of health and benefits publications. In short, clear, easy-to-understand health-enhancing information is everywhere.
- We also maintain websites, including HealthMedia® Digital Health Coaching, that allow employees to privately choose individualized and tailored online tools for addressing a myriad of issues such as stress reduction, work–life balance, inactivity, nutrition needs, binge eating and other unhealthy eating behaviors, smoking and more.

ii) Financial rewards

Over 15 years ago, we were one of the first companies to link wellness to benefit design (US) by providing financial incentives to employees who take active steps toward understanding and improving their health. When employees take the voluntary health risk assessment described above, they receive a $500 credit toward their health plan contribution; if a health risk is identified, the employee is expected to participate in a health advising session in order to retain the $500 credit.

We started offering this financial incentive as a way to increase health risk assessment participation, which increased from around 26 percent participation in 1995 to around 90 percent between 1995 and 1999, and an average over 80 percent in the past ten years. This success led us to expand our financial incentives to other health-promoting behaviors. For instance, we now offer financial rewards to at-risk employees for participation in a chronic disease management program, a maternity program and a healthy-weight program in which employees with a Body Mass Index over 30 receive a credit toward their health plan contribution for losing 10 percent of their weight in a year. Plus, all employees over age 50 are eligible for a financial incentive for undergoing a preventive colonoscopy consistent with current preventive screening guidelines. And we've recently announced a financial incentive designed to reduce the level of hospital-acquired infections.

iii) Healthful environment

A healthful environment not only makes it easier for employees to engage in healthy behaviors, it gives the impression that *everyone* is living more healthfully—healthful behaviors become the default, not the exception. This is important because many people naturally engage in the behaviors exemplified by their peers and managers.

- Our cafeterias, vending machines and catered events, for instance, have increased the healthy food options they offer through a program we call *eatcomplete* that has rolled out to over 80 percent of our US operating companies. This is especially important when you consider that the average employee eats one to two meals during the workday. The program focuses not only on providing nutritionally dense whole foods but on communicating the importance of healthy portion sizes and education about where salt, sugars and fats are hidden in foods. We recently extended our efforts to reach out to the "master chef of the employee's household" with healthful cooking tips.

- We offer exercise reimbursement programs and many of our company locations have onsite fitness centers with fitness/wellness professionals, including occupational health nurses. We've created walking and running trails. We host exercise, yoga, meditation and other classes. Where onsite facilities are not feasible, we support the creation of "energy and recovery spaces"—spare rooms that contain stretching and movement—encouraging tools, as well as electronic health and sports gaming devices.
- We make pedometers available and challenge employees to reach 10,000 steps a day (a recognized measure of a good activity level). At last count, over 30,000 pedometers have been distributed. And thousands of employees have reached one million steps a year.
- To support employees who seek to achieve optimal weight, we make it affordable and easy to participate in WeightWatchers® or undergo nutritional counseling.
- We create health-focused company events that many employees participate in. Small groups of employees, for instance, challenge other small groups to lose a healthy amount of weight over a healthful period of time in "Lose To Win" competitions.
- And more than 98 percent of Johnson & Johnson workplaces *worldwide* are tobacco-free. That includes buildings, company vehicles and company-sponsored meetings.

Note that our preventative efforts take a *wide* variety of forms. You can narrowly define the behaviors you want to change, but success comes from offering a broad, non-stop range of materials, programs and events—so that employees *always* have an opportunity to become engaged whenever they're receptive. Our policy is to "reach people wherever they are now, rather than where we want them to be." We continuously develop, test and measure new ways to engage employees (and their families). This is important because the single biggest challenge to changing unhealthy behaviors is lack of employee engagement (Towers Watson Survey Report, 2010).

The other lesson here is that effective prevention programs must reach out to the *individual*. In other words, financial incentives will motivate many individuals, but it's also important to find ways to strike a chord with what is intrinsically important to the human beings who comprise our workforce—human beings who have different motivations and concerns. That's why some of our educational materials and health events seek to help people envision the consequences of their unhealthful decisions on their ultimate purpose in life. Other materials frame personal health risks as "true health age." And other materials appeal to people's desires to feel better, look better, sleep better, have more energy, or be more fully engaged with their families, their jobs and other aspects of their lives. Plus, we engage with employees one-on-one through a variety of programs, which allows us to understand what's really at the heart of an individual's obesity: Is it depression? Is there an underlying health condition? Is it lack of education? Is the danger of high body weight unreal to the employee? Are there workplace or family issues for which the individual is compensating by engaging in poor eating habits?

COMMITMENT TO A CULTURE OF HEALTH

In the 1940s, long before "social responsibility" was a buzzword, our Credo was put into words: it's the moral compass Johnson & Johnson lives by today and it clearly states that our company has a profound responsibility toward our employees. As Johnson &

Johnson's former CEO William C. Weldon has said, "An important part of our Credo responsibility to our employees is providing them with resources to lead healthier lives."

Given the number of hours that people spend at work, companies are in a unique position to play a positive role in employees' lives. But this isn't pure altruism. Companies that are committed to health as a business imperative achieve significantly better financial outcomes and lower employee turnover as noted above (Towers Watson 2009/2010).

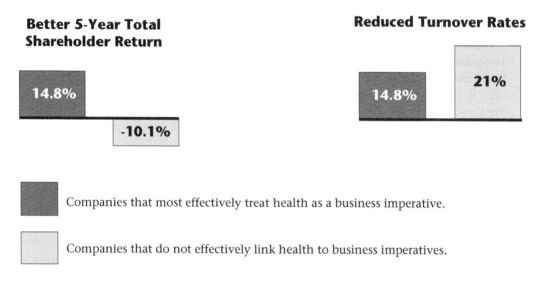

Better 5-Year Total Shareholder Return

14.8%

-10.1%

Reduced Turnover Rates

14.8%

21%

Companies that most effectively treat health as a business imperative.

Companies that do not effectively link health to business imperatives.

Figure 16.1 2009/2010 Staying @ Work Report (Towers Watson)

Our Wellness and Prevention Inc. studies also show that an employer's commitment to employee well-being is as critical to employees as opportunity for advancement, and more important than competitiveness of pay and benefits to overall job satisfaction (Wellness & Prevention, Inc. Landmark Study, 2009).

In short, the health of the employee is inseparable from the health of the business. But what exactly is a "culture of health"? We describe it in many ways. A culture of health is everything it takes to have the healthiest, most engaged workforce allowing for full and productive lives. A culture of health means providing the leadership and resources to enable the well-being, full engagement and productivity of our employees worldwide.

We've identified five factors that contribute to culture-of-health success.

i) Demonstrate continuous leadership and commitment

Outside the company, we advocate for healthy, innovative workplaces. Inside the company, we not only encourage but *partake in* healthy behavior throughout the business day—for instance, by eating healthfully in the cafeteria, holding walking meetings and using the fitness center. We call this talking the talk and walking the walk.

Our executives and front-line managers are taught about the connection between good health and business success. And they're taught that a culture of health can't send mixed signals: we cannot, for instance, maintain onsite fitness centers and encourage workers to be more active, then be critical if an employee uses the facility during working hours.

Our senior managers regularly communicate the importance of living a healthy lifestyle. They personally champion and participate in health initiatives. *And* they provide budgets that support those initiatives.

> *It's an investment, not a cost. Spending money before people get sick, to help keep them well, makes sense. (Alex Gorsky, Johnson & Johnson CEO)*

ii) Deliver enterprise programs

Delivering a culture of health means offering a wide variety of integrated programs that are holistic in the sense that they address all the health-related needs an employee may have—from mental health support, to healthy behavior support, to benefits that protect employees and their families from the devastating cost of serious illness or injury. Many of the programs discussed above fit this category, but here are a few more:

- We provide 24-hour access to counseling by telephone, plus no-cost access to employee assistance professionals who are able to address a wide range of issues that keep people from being the best they can be—from stress management, to financial counseling, parenting support, elder-care support and many more.
- Our CareConnect chronic condition management program is available for US employees and their family members who suffer from conditions that are most likely to negatively impact the individual's life and result in high medical costs, absenteeism or lost productivity for the company. These conditions include diabetes, chronic back pain, hypertension and several others.
- Because navigating the health care and health insurance system can be complicated for everyone, we provide an advocacy service that helps US employees appeal insurance claims, get appointments with specialists, and find facilities and practitioners that are best suited to their needs. As mentioned earlier, this service even advises them on health care issues for their *parents*, since understanding and arranging for elders' services can be stressful and time-consuming.

iii) Establish policies and procedures

While we believe it's important for our decentralized operating companies to have the autonomy to implement programs in a way that fits with their cultures, it's imperative that all Johnson & Johnson locations meet certain standards. For instance, we've identified core programs that we believe are required in order for a culture of health to exist:

- employee assistance services;
- opportunities for physical activity;
- medical surveillance;
- general health promotion programs;
- stress management/resiliency training;
- cancer awareness and promotion programs;
- modified/alternate or light duty return to work after illness or injury;

- access to travel health resources;
- and implementation of the following: a tobacco-free workplace policy, an HIV/AIDS policy, a personal health risk assessment program and a healthy eating/healthy cafeteria effort.

To speed implantation and share learning, we develop standardized procedures (tool kits) that help companies hit the ground running when these and other new initiatives and programs are adopted.

iv) Improve engagement and participation through marketing

Marketing professionals understand that communicating key messages clearly isn't enough. *Marketing* involves understanding your target audience's motivations, interests and vulnerabilities then devising multiple messages—delivered via various media—over time. Results are measured (quantitatively and qualitatively), then messaging, media and strategies are tweaked.

To be measurable, communications need a clear quantifiable goal and pre-established reporting and accountability protocols.

And to be effective, good marketing needs consistent branding. We at Johnson & Johnson have developed "HealthyPeople" branding for employee communications, which includes memorable, impactful and consistent design elements and messages.

v) Measure outcomes, not effort

A big step in the development of our culture of health came in 1978 when we introduced a program called "Live for Life." It was then that we first gave voice to the goal of having the healthiest employees in the world. We—like many companies—were also faced with an astounding, unsustainable increase in health care costs. We started by (a) giving employees information about their individual health risk factors and easy access to behavior modification programs designed to reduce those risks, and (b) setting goals for bringing down the company's cost of health.

We focused on the risks that were responsible at the time for the largest share of the company's health care costs: smoking, overeating, alcohol abuse, emotional stress, hypertension and unsafe driving. We started the process of asking employees to voluntarily complete a health assessment questionnaire, and we made it as convenient as possible for employees to assess their risks and overcome them. For instance, we set up convenient onsite clinics to perform medical evaluations, advise on nutrition and weight management, provide vaccinations and manage smoking cessation programs. We also set up one of the first-ever Employee Assistance Programs to provide counseling. And the first onsite gyms were created.

Then as now, Johnson & Johnson was a decentralized company. It was left to the leaders of our autonomous operating companies to decide whether—and to what degree—to implement Live for Life. Implementation varied. Management support, budget and the availability and expertise of onsite health care professionals differed from company to company and from site to site within companies. The uneven implementation, however, provided an opportunity to study how the various approaches were meeting the established goals.

There are several important messages in this story.

First, we identify the greatest risks in our employee population and focus resources on them. They change over time. And they're different in different companies and different parts of the world. But the bottom line is that we measure the effectiveness of our efforts in terms of the *outcomes*. In other words, we measure how many people reach or maintain a healthy weight rather than how many brochures or newsletters we've published. We measure what percentage of our employee population can be characterized as low risk (for instance, zero to two health risks) rather than how many new wellness programs we've introduced.

Second, we implement pilot programs first, and phase in new program features after we've studied their effectiveness. To speed post-pilot program success, we develop tool kits and other policies and procedures—measuring the success of outcomes along the way.

And third, our programs are scalable and sustainable. For a culture of health to succeed, it can't be a flash in the pan. Its goals must become ever-more ambitious and its measurable outcomes must improve over time.

We also believe there's value in publicizing our goals and results, and sharing our best practices, because human cost and the financial cost of poor health are global concerns.

WORLDWIDE, OUR HEALTH SUSTAINABILITY GOALS FOR 2015 INCLUDE

- Increasing the number of employees who have access to the essential culture of health programs identified above to at least 90 percent.
- Increasing the number of employees who complete a health risk assessment so they know their key health indicators to at least 80 percent.
- And increasing the percentage of our population whose health risks are categorized as "low" to 80 percent.

We define "health risks" as conditions or behaviors measured in a health risk assessment that are modifiable and proven to have a significant impact on health. Risks include unhealthy eating, inactivity, obesity, high blood pressure, high blood sugar, high cholesterol, excessive alcohol use, significant depression, stress, safety belt use and tobacco use. We define "low risk" as having zero to two of these risks.

But Why is a Culture of Health so Important?

Committing to a culture of health is important because in companies where there is a strong culture of health, employees are three times more likely to report taking action on their health (Wellness & Prevention, Inc. Landmark Study, 2009). Plus employees who work for companies that foster a strong culture of health rate all aspects of their performance higher than employees who employers do not have a strong culture of health. In other words, employees who work for companies with a strong culture of health rate their overall personal life, their overall work life, their job performance, their career path, and their ability to fulfill their potential at work more positively than employees whose companies don't exemplify a strong culture of health (Wellness & Prevention, Inc. Landmark Study, 2009).

The next logical question is, how successful has our culture of health been? We've been successful, but part of our culture of health is a recognition that we can *always* do better. At this point in time, the Johnson & Johnson population is healthier than the general US population. Our rate of heart disease is 41 percent below national standards and high blood pressure is 75 percent below. As a group, our employees are more active and smoke less. Better still, between 2006 and 2011 there was an increase in the "low risk" population from 78 percent to 87 percent. And there was a corresponding decline in the percentage of our population categorized as "high risk."

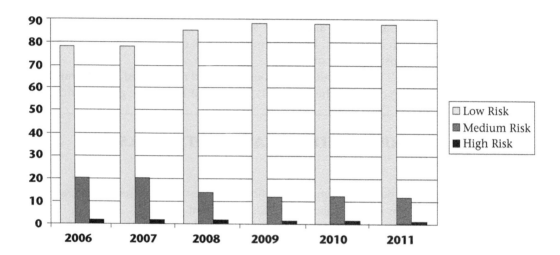

Figure 16.2 How successful our culture of health has been 2006–2011(Johnson & Johnson)

RECOGNITION THAT PEOPLE INVEST EMOTIONALLY IN THEIR JOBS AS WE INVEST IN THEM

As we've seen above, a culture of health can lead to healthier employees, which leads to more engaged, more energized employees who perform better at work, better at home and better everywhere. When companies improve employee health, they have an opportunity to turn the accelerating dual burden of health care costs and diminished productivity into a competitive advantage. Here's where corporate initiatives that support employees in their efforts to become not only healthier but *happier and more personally fulfilled* come into play.

Notice that we said "support employees in their effort." We can't force changes. But we can implement programs and institute policies that help employees understand that they are *accountable* for their health and responsible for their own lives. In fact, one way of looking at our culture of health is to see it as a plethora of tools people can use to recognize their health risks, accept personal responsibility for them, take control of their actions and attitudes, and sustain their good behaviors for life.

But this is easier said than done—for employees of all ages and education levels, from entry-level workers to C-level executives.

One exciting—and fairly new—way we're supporting employees as they seek to take more control of every aspect of their lives is called "Energy for Performance in Life." It's a partnership effort between Johnson & Johnson Global Health Services and Wellness & Prevention, Inc. The initiative has been built on the energy management principles of the Human Performance Institute, which was acquired in 2008 by Johnson & Johnson and is now part of our Wellness & Prevention, Inc. business.

Let's set the scene. Regardless of the position an employee holds in any of our operating companies, there is a pervasive sense that we all have impossible demands to fulfill. Our jobs and our lives require so much of us that it can be challenging to stay healthy, to succeed at work, to enjoy relationships, to feel fulfilled, or to grow personally and professionally.

To get everything done and done *well*, we need energy. But many of us have a "personal energy crisis:" we fail to manage our personal energy effectively and many of us wouldn't even know how to begin. Energy for Performance in Life teaches participants how to maximize their personal energy so they feel physically energized, emotionally connected and mentally focused.

One of the program's most important concepts is "full engagement." It occurs when you're able to invest your full *best* energy, *here and now*. It's an ability you can train yourself to achieve by becoming more cognizant of the four dimensions of full engagement:

- *Spiritual*—Are you purpose-driven, committed, passionate and principled?
- *Mental*—Are you present in the moment, focused and fully aware?
- *Emotional*—Are you effective in your interpersonal relationships? Have you embraced emotions such as hope, gratitude, compassion and "realistic optimism" that help you optimize performance, health and happiness?
- *Physical*—Are your nutrition, fitness, sleep and recovery patterns adequate to support you?

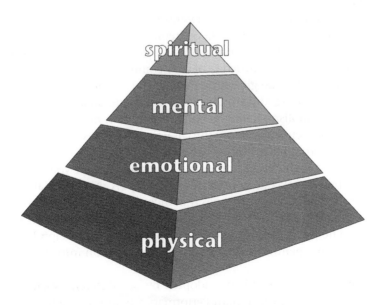

Figure 16.3 The four dimensions of full engagement

Energy for Performance in Life teaches that to become fully engaged, you must honestly assess your life and your choices from many different perspectives. One tool the program uses is journaling, which is also referred to as storytelling.

We each have a story. It's the story of what has happened (or not happened) in our lives—and why. It starts in the past (with rigorous self-honesty you describe where you have been). It looks forward to the future you want (you define where you genuinely want to be, what you truly want to achieve, what would make you happy, and what would make you feel fulfilled as human being). Then you define the actions—the course corrections—you must take in order to achieve your mission in life.

Achieving your mission will most likely not happen overnight, so the program encourages participants to develop "training missions" whose progress can be examined (even measured) after 90 days. Then a new training mission begins. Then another. Because most of us can't achieve the life we want instantly, the idea of training missions allows us to establish positive habits that become routines. Routines help us achieve our ultimate mission because they become second nature over time.

A particularly informative aspect of the program is a "360 Review." Participants' key health indicators are measured so they gain an accurate picture of their health. And because each of us has a different picture of ourselves than other people have of us, questionnaires are completed by participants' family members and co-workers; this is part of how program participants gauge the effectiveness of their relationships and evaluate whether their self-image is keeping them from being the person they wish to be.

Energy for Performance in Life also:

- Teaches participants to (a) assess who and what has been getting their energy and (b) address whether their energy expenditures are aligned with what they truly want or value.
- Encourages participants to limit multi-tasking. When you're fully engaged, you're laser focused.
- Teaches participants how to ensure that energy expenditures are balanced with periods of energy recovery and methods of energy replenishment. The lesson is to live life as a series of sprints, rather than a continuous wearisome race. The tools one needs for energy replenishment are knowledge of and commitment to "strategic eating" and getting adequate sleep. Strategic eating includes (a) not going for more than 4 hours in the day without eating and (b) choosing meals and snacks that stabilize glucose levels, improve metabolism, help you build or maintain muscle mass, and more.
- Provides tools so participants can put into practice what they've learned. For instance, there's a workbook that helps employees plan meals and snacks for sustained energy. The workbook also includes a sample plan for ensuring that your day has adequate recovery-time breaks, relaxation exercises and sleep. A meeting planner guide helps participants schedule and run meetings that include movement and stretching breaks and energy-enhancing snacks. And an e-mail information program builds on and reinforces the Energy for Performance in Life principles with helpful information on snacking, stretching, planning, incorporating more motion into the day, and more.

Energy for Performance in Life is being adopted by our different operating companies in different ways. In some cases, Human Performance Institute coaches are brought to a corporate site for partial-day to multi-day sessions. In other cases, employees are sent to the Human Performance Institute headquarters in Florida for intensive sessions. As you can imagine, this program entails a significant investment on the part of the operating company, so the next logical question is: Is it worth it? The answer is a resounding "yes." Executives and managers who have been through the Energy for Performance in Life program emerge with a greater appreciation for how happy, healthy, fulfilled employees add to the energy of the corporation—making it more competitive, more innovative and more creative.

This success has lead to a commitment on our part to bring Energy for Performance in Life to all of our employees around the world.

Better health and happier, more fulfilled employees are a possibility for every company and businesses of any size.

Readers whose companies are new to health and wellness programs, or readers whose companies are trying to improve the success of and expand support for their health and wellness programs may feel that the initiatives described here are too big—too unreachable—for them. But just as individuals must improve their health and well-being step by step, so too must companies take the steps they *can* take as the first step toward bigger achievements.

You may not, for instance, have corporate cafeterias with menus you can re-engineer. But you have vending machines with contents you can alter. And you can choose what to serve at meetings and company events.

You may not have corporate fitness centers, but you can partner with local gyms to make it easier and more affordable for employees to participate. And don't stop at gyms—you have local yoga instructors, dance studios, martial arts centers, and more that can become a healthful destination for your employees. Plus, the "energy and recovery spaces" described above are a way to turn empty space into visible support for employees who seek to work more activity into their work days.

You may not have a team of global health and wellness professionals, but you can test financial and non-financial incentives to see which employee behaviors you can impact. You can publicize and participate in global health observances such as Move For Health, World Diabetes Day, Breast Cancer Awareness, Alcohol Awareness Month, World AIDS day and more. You can disseminate health information to employees. And you can partner with organizations that manage health risk assessments.

You may not have thought-leaders sought by governments and publications, but you can provide leadership. You can be an unwavering proponent for establishing a culture of health—and you can support the other health-leaders in your organization. When an uninformed voice speaks of health and wellness programs as a cost you can do without, you can substantiate that health and wellness efforts are an *investment* you cannot do without.

Perhaps most important, every company can develop "health champions." These are individuals who lead by healthy example. They're especially effective at the top of the corporate ladder, but they're important at *every* level. They actively support your organization's efforts to be a healthier, safer and more energized workplace. They support co-workers in their effort to achieve work–life balance. They support co-workers in their effort to grow personally and professionally. They support co-workers who are seeking to make healthy changes in their lives. Their meetings include healthy food, and—

no matter the pressure or workload—they schedule breaks during which participants can refresh and revive.

These health champions have not only been taught about the correlation between the health of employees and the health of the company, they *believe* in the connection between healthy employees and successful companies. They fully embrace that when people feel fulfilled, success is the natural outcome.

Find your health champions. Nurture them. And give them the tools they need to succeed: they can be an enormous positive force as you pursue your corporate wellness objectives.

References

Towers Watson (2009/2010) Staying@Work Report/National Business Group on Health.

Towers Watson Survey Report (2010) Purchasing Value in Health Care. Selected Findings From the Annual National Business Group on Health.

Wellness & Prevention, Inc. Johnson & Johnson—Landmark Study (2009) A Pearson product-moment correlation coefficient was used to correlate aspects of job to "my satisfaction with job overall."

Index

For Product Safety Concerns and Information please contact our EU
representative GPSR@taylorandfrancis.com Taylor & Francis Verlag GmbH,
Kaufingerstraße 24, 80331 München, Germany

Printed and bound by CPI Group (UK) Ltd, Croydon, CR0 4YY
08/05/2025
01864497-0001